MW00604844

SECOND EDITION

Community Resources

A Guide for Human Service Workers

William Crimando
Southern Illinois University–Carbondale

T. F. Riggar
Southern Illinois University–Carbondale

WAVELAND

PRESS, INC.

Long Grove, Illinois

To my family

To S. W. R., without whom nothing is possible

For information about this book, contact:
Waveland Press, Inc.
4180 IL Route 83, Suite 101
Long Grove, IL 60047-9580
(847) 634-0081
info@waveland.com
www.waveland.com

Copyright © 2005 by William Crimando and T. F. Riggar
The first edition of this book was published as *Utilizing Community Resources*.

10-digit ISBN 1-57766-377-2
13-digit ISBN 978-1-57766-377-5

All rights reserved. No part of this book may be reproduced, stored in a retrieval system, or transmitted in any form or by any means without permission in writing from the publisher.

Printed in the United States of America

9 8

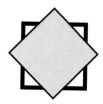

Contents

Section III: Rehabilitation and Vocational Services   95

Section IV: Legal and Social Services   185

Contents

Section V: Education and Human Services   267

Acknowledgments

Many voices have contributed to the diversified areas of knowledge and expertise and the comprehensive treatment and presentation of each community resource in this book. We would like to express our gratitude to our friends and colleagues who were willing to share their time and expertise by contributing a chapter. Their combined efforts have resulted in a truly informative and valuable compilation.

We also wish to thank Gayle Zawilla, our editor at Waveland Press. Her generous and timely feedback strengthened the readability and practicability of this book, and her willingness to solicit our input on format decisions was much appreciated.

Finally, we would like to acknowledge the many faculty, practitioners, friends, and colleagues over the years whose words of support encouraged us to work on this book.

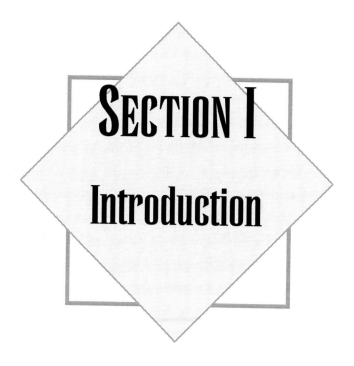

SECTION I

Introduction

Overview

T. F. Riggar

This book is intended to provide human service professionals with information to assist and guide their clients. To do this, the most prominent and beneficial human service agencies are examined. This book also looks to current trends and to the future by examining and detailing those organizations and programs that will play a significant part in the near future. In helping clients, it is often necessary for the professional social worker, rehabilitation counselor, substance abuse counselor, gerontology counselor or counselor of whatever type, to look outside her or his particular organization and enlist the expertise of professionals in other specialties.

When a client is accepted for service by a particular agency, and by a specific human service professional, the responsibility for the whole individual is also being accepted. Help for specific problems and enhancement of the client's interaction with the community and society at large is required. With an individual who is disabled in some way—be it physical, mental, or environmental—the services of one agency are usually too limited in structure and scope to remediate all of the client's handicaps. To intervene with such an individual, the specific counselor or case manager must enlist the aid of others to deal with problems outside the boundaries of the organization.

For a counselor to refer, transfer, or coordinate with one or more agencies, it is essential to be reasonably conversant with what the assisting agency can offer the client. For example, one may immediately note the variation among agencies, facilities and organizations in their reference to patients, clients, participants or consumers. A current trend, partially based on terminology used in some federal laws and regulations, is to denote all those individuals who receive human services as consumers of those services. For those human service professionals utilizing the contents herein, it is important to know how other agencies refer not only to themselves—counselor, social worker, human service worker, and so on—but also to know how they prefer clients to be recognized.

Our intent is to supply information that will assist human service counselors to help themselves and their clients. Despite the knowledge any counselor maintains, it is usually beyond the range of any one specialty area to fulfill all of the needs of an individual. For example, a social worker, a vocational rehabilitation counselor, or a mental health counselor may each be proficient in their respective areas, but one client may need the services of all three of these trained and educated professionals. Unless the initial contact professional is conversant with the range of professional activities of other counselors and their supporting agencies, it will be difficult for the client to obtain appropriate outside services.

Lack of knowledge of what can be obtained, and where it can be obtained, results in clients being rendered services that do not exactly fulfill their needs. It is incumbent upon service providers to know the "what, where, how, and why" of a broad range of community services. Only in this way may the helper confidently assist the client in gaining that which is needed. In essence, much of what is discussed in this book will allow an individual to be "plugged in" to existing human services within the community. Making a client aware of what exists in the area fosters a future independence. If the same or a similar problem arises, the client will know where to go, who to see, and what to get. This enlightenment of the population in general means that human service agencies, and their workers, may more effectively assist people. It also means that the population regularly frequents the organizations that provide necessary activities.

The principles of case management require that each counselor assist each client to the maximum. How much help the client receives will often depend on how much the assigned professional knows and accordingly is capable of assisting. Because the *total* individual is the target, each case must reflect efforts toward remediating *all* problems and disabilities. It does no good, for instance, to get a person a job (vocational rehabilitation) if he or she is confused, disoriented, and disturbed (mental health), and at the same time is hungry and without a place to stay (social services). Such a case is not unique. Too often the counselor initially interviewing a client will immediately note that the person needs functional help in many areas. Aside from their own specialties, how do counselors go about finding out who can help? What outside agencies will assist? Who in these agencies handles these specific matters? What will the other organizations and agencies really do? To what extent? How often? Other more generic questions also arise for human service professionals: What new helping organizations have been developed and programmed? What has new legislation funded? What new programs or program enhancements have resulted from societal or sociocultural trends?

The answers to these and other questions form the intent of this book. It is hoped that a human services professional following this guide will gain, over time, increased knowledge of the community and its resources. This information will be put to good use in helping individuals help themselves. Although this book contains detailed data about a variety of agencies and organizations, it does not, and cannot, provide information concerning the local addresses and individual referrals throughout the country. The responsibility for finding local community contacts rests with each professional. The location, development, and nurturance of community contacts are an important part of any counselor's job. Wide-ranging and versatile contacts expand the abilities and services a worker may bring to bear for a client.

The information provided herein addresses the responsibilities of the agencies in detail. When referring a client to another organization, it is far better to refer to a known fellow professional than to an entity. This means that although a counselor may know that certain services can be provided, actually making sure clients receive them is another matter. When transferring some of the responsibility for the total individual to another counselor, certain aspects must be considered. Among these are: (a) the ability of the client to carry through on the suggestion, and (b) the manner in which the referral is made.

The ability, desire, or necessity of a client to follow through on a suggested referral is usually determined by the initial counselor. Depending on the type of disability manifested, as well as the needs and capacities of the clients, a judgment may be made as to how well individuals can help themselves. Clearly, if they are unable to do what is actually required, the assigned counselor will have to make the necessary arrangements and expend extra effort to assist the clients.

From the counselor's perspective, perhaps the most important aspect of using community human services is possessing knowledge of services and personnel of other agencies. As noted, it is far better to refer to another professional than just to an "organization." A crucial ingredient in referring an individual to another agency is to clear the obstacles usually inherent in bureaucratic systems. Even though this book will enable any counselor to determine what is potentially available and where certain items and services are most easily obtainable, it does not put the counselor in touch with those who will, in fact, provide the outside assistance.

The resultant effectiveness of this outside assistance often depends on two factors: expectations and cooperation. The expectations of both counselor and client concerning ancillary services often vary with the level of knowledge the counselor has of the assisting agency. These expectations are imparted to the client in the form of advisements, suggestions, or comments about what the assisting agency may do for the individual. The second aspect, that of cooperation, relates to the interaction between the initial or sponsoring counselor and the cooperating counselor from the other agency. Cooperation is enhanced when both professionals are knowledgeable of the orientation and requirements of the other. When an unreasonable request for services is made, it is evident that the requesting individual is unfamiliar with the services of an agency.

With both factors—expectations and cooperation—the most important determinant of whether or not the client will receive appropriate services is the knowledge held by each counselor concerning other organizations. For all counselors, from all agencies, information about what exists by way of potential human services must be made available. The intent here is to make that much-needed information available in a form which can be easily assimilated and used in everyday practice. Basically, this is a reference book that can be used by the practicing human service professional on a daily basis. Although not always similar in format, most of the chapters attempt to give the reader an overview of the history and legislation, purpose and intent, and client services provided for each agency or organization.

The discussion on history and legislation examines the historical background of the agency, placing particular emphasis on the legislation that has influenced and is currently influencing the direction and goals of the organization. In addition, the authority under which the service operates, as well as funding sources (where appropriate) are examined. Readers will find information on agency personnel—particularly type and training—as well as any special organizational certifications, licensing, or accreditation.

The mission of any agency is described in discussion of its purpose and intent. In particular, the discussion explores the reasons for the agency's continued existence over the years, detailing what the organization strives to do for citizens and how it intends to do so. Another topic included in this discussion is utilization criteria. Particularly important for a counselor is the determination of how, potentially, a specific agency or organization may assist clients. Any pre-established special case management needs are examined in detail, with data concerning their utilization by counselors.

Client services are those particular ways in which the agency and its counselors attempt to aid clients. So that counselors from other organizations will have a clear picture of what the specific agency can offer, potential services are described and explained in some detail. Additionally, typical referral questions may be presented to assist counselors in proper presentation of client interests to a potential agency.

All three of these components—history/legislation, purpose/intent, and client services—are important. In the first instance, historical background provides knowledge about the organization's evolution over time. The evolution that takes place in any bureaucratic system is influenced by such things such as administrative changes, legislative mandates, and citizen demands. To understand what agencies do, it is sometimes necessary to know what and how they have performed in the past. A review of past activities provides a clear indicator as to how current and future activities will be conducted. Purpose and intent are indicators of the agency's mission and the path its administrators and counselors tread on the way toward reaching goals. Because of the ever-increasing diversification among agencies, it is necessary to know which particular segment of a population an agency represents. What the agency intends to do for this target group, including the precise services that it offers, describes its intended purpose.

As noted, there is considerable diversification and proliferation of human service agencies. As a result, an overlap often exists concerning both populations and possible services. However, for each service that may be provided, there is usually one agency whose history and intent focus directly toward that activity. All three of the above-mentioned components contain crucial information that will enable counselors to develop realistic expectations about each agency, and to facilitate efficient client cooperation with counselors.

The book itself can be used in a number of ways. As a handy reference, the counselor may investigate the agency and/or service(s) in which the client has either expressed an interest, or which the client is deemed to require. In this way, the book provides extensive information concerning service agencies that exist in every locale. If a particular service seems appropriate, the book may also be of use. When it is known that a client needs or requires assistance of a certain nature, the material can be used to indicate which is the appropriate agency offering that service as a primary responsibility or priority. As an overall source of information, the content is suitable for use in courses covering the types of human services that exist in every community, and as a follow-up or adjunct to case management courses. In this way, counselors who may have some in-depth knowledge about one or two establishments, programs, or specialty fields can learn and prepare to use similar information concerning dozens of other organizations. Such heightened knowledge not only increases professional expertise but also means that clients will be more effectively and efficiently served.

Case Management Implications

William Crimando

When a client is accepted for service in a human service agency, that agency may find that the person needs many other services outside of its scope, or outside the scope of the professional to whom the client is assigned. For example, a person seeking assistance in finding a job from a vocational rehabilitation agency may need medical restoration, mental health counseling, and financial assistance. In such situations, human service professionals frequently seek outside or "community" resources. A *community resource* is any service vendor available within a specific geographic area—public or private, fee-charging or not—that potentially can be used to aid our clients, ourselves, or our organizations. Community resources encompass a wide range of entities, such as comprehensive rehabilitation hospitals; social service agencies; neighborhood advocacy and service organizations; a variety of educational, legal, and employment agencies; and a host of small vendors such as physicians, counselors, pain management clinics, and churches. However broad, this definition is important. It implies the following critical aspects of community resources:

- they must be capable of providing a needed service or commodity;
- they must be willing to enter into a relationship in which those services and commodities can be purchased or otherwise secured;
- they must be located in a place that is geographically or electronically accessible; and
- they must have attainable (to us or our clients) eligibility requirements.

Thus, the terms *community* and *resource* are relative to the needs and abilities of our clients. A community could be as small as a city block or as large

8

as the entire nation, if the particular agency's services or commodities are readily available and accessible. Seider (1966) suggests that communities are not limited by geographic boundaries and are composed of interconnected social systems and institutions. One need only look to the wealth of resources available on the Internet as proof. Further, if we serve a caseload of indigent families, from our perspective a neighborhood grocer who is willing to give away day-old baked goods and produce is a resource, while a college placement office that only serves students may not be.

There are two types of community resources: single-service and multiple-service agencies. As their names imply, single-service agencies provide services of a single type, be it vocational, educational, social, or health; while multiple service agencies provide services from two or more types. Examples of single-service agencies include physicians, legal clinics, financial counselors, and transportation vendors (e.g., cab companies and bus lines). Single-service agencies have two potential advantages over multiple-service agencies: Because they can focus on a single mission, they are more likely to provide high-quality services, and they can hire specifically trained professional staff who are more likely to remain current in their skills.

IDENTIFYING AND SELECTING COMMUNITY RESOURCES

The importance of a systematic method of identifying and selecting community resources cannot be overstated. Sheafor, Horejsi, and Horejsi (1988) suggest that making effective referrals to community resources requires an understanding of existing resources. Case managers and other professionals must invest considerable time and energy in keeping up with changing community resources systems as well as with their clients' needs. The steps in systematically identifying and selecting community resources are (a) needs assessment, (b) potential resource identification, and (c) resource selection.

Needs Assessment

The first step is to conduct a thorough assessment of caseload needs. Three types of needs are at issue here: client needs, counselor personal-professional needs, and organizational needs. Often these overlap. Client needs, of course, are their requirements for survival, security, love and esteem, and growth. These translate to the basics—food, clothing, shelter, health, employment, and so on.

Often overlooked but just as important are professional counselor and organizational needs. While more than likely survival and security needs are being met, professionals frequently may have knowledge and skills deficits, may require emotional support to continue in a difficult situation, or may merely need another professional with whom to discuss new techniques or critical cases. Thus, counselors have needs revolving around a desire to be as effective as possible. Similarly, organizations have effectiveness needs, which naturally include funding, referrals, public relations, community support, and so on.[1] Frequently these needs are already being met through client, professional, or organizational assets, or through existing service agreements with other community agencies. The formal and informal relationships both within and outside the agency or clients' sphere of influence should be examined to determine met and unmet needs.

Needs assessment is the collection, analysis, and synthesis of data regarding the needs of a person or organizational entity (e.g., caseload, group, or agency) (McKillip, 1987).

Both unmet and met needs can be determined through a number of sources: (a) interviews with clients, other counselors in the agency, and collateral agencies; (b) caseload reviews; (c) reviews of existing interagency service agreements; and (d) self-examination of professional needs and assets.

Potential Resource Identification

Once needs have been identified, outside agencies, organizations, and programs should be identified which could potentially serve those needs. The objective at this step should be to identify as many potential vendors as possible for each service need, so that the most efficient, effective decisions can be made. This also lessens the possibility that a particular vendor will be chosen by "default," that is, because it is the only one identified.

Two sources of information about potential resources exist: formal and informal. Formal sources include all printed or published materials about community agencies, such as community assistance directories, information and referral network/databases, telephone books, procedures manuals, and the other public relations materials that individual agencies publish. An increasingly popular and commonplace formal source is the electronic clearinghouse on the Internet, developed through the collaboration of universities, service providers, businesses, and government offices. Informal sources are those other than published material. Primary among these are other counselors, supervisors, or professionals—within one's own agency or outside—that form one's professional network. While some professionals may be reluctant to share knowledge that could only be gained after years of experience (Vandergoot & Jacobsen, 1979), a well-cultivated network will provide a wealth of information. As an added incentive, this information will likely include contacts and tactics for working through bureaucracies.

File review from a variety of caseloads constitutes another informal source. Both referral sources and past vendors are potential resources. Personal visits to and from other agencies may be fruitful, both in gathering information and in expanding professional networks. Finally, clients and their friends, relatives, and acquaintances may be of assistance.

---

[1] While the emphasis in this book is on resources which serve clients' needs, these same resources could easily serve professional and organizational needs. Similarly, the techniques in this chapter are also applicable to professional and organizational needs.

Table 1 lists generic questions that may be considered when examining potential resources. Other questions may arise with regard to specific vendors. For example, in brain-injury rehabilitation, questions such as these may arise:

- Does the evaluation include a projected living status after discharge?
- Does the program employ a neuropsychology staff?
- Is the program setting consistent with the client's pre-injury lifestyle?

Table 1   Potential Selection Criteria for Community Resources

General
What is the purpose of the program/agency/organization?
Who is eligible to receive services?
What organizational patterns exist?
What is the nature of funding?
What constraints in service provision does the organization face?
Does the organization have appropriate accreditations?

Services
What services are provided?
Are services available to families?
Are case management services provided?
Are there emergency services?
What linkages or service agreements does the organization have with others to meet special needs?

Staff Composition
What is the size of the staff?
What is the average caseload size, or staff-to-client ratio?
What are the qualifications of the staff?
Do staff possess required/desired degrees, certifications, licenses, etc.?
What experience has staff had in working with your specific population?

Referral/Utilization
How should referrals be made?
How many people is the agency capable of serving at the same time?
Is there a waiting list? How long is it?
Are regular, meaningful reports issued for clients?

Program Planning
Is there a minimum/maximum length of program?
What post-discharge or follow-up services are provided or available?
Are programs tailored to meet individual consumer needs?
Is consumer or family input considered in program planning?

Cost
What is the cost per consumer day in the program?
What is the rate/pricing structure (e.g., uniform, cost reimbursement, cost plus fee)?
What discounts are available?

(continued)

Table I   *(continued)*

Outcomes
Does the organization have an acceptable number of successful outcomes (e.g., consumers placed, trainees graduated, clients detoxified)?
Is there a minimum of unsuccessful outcomes?
What attention is paid to the quality of successful outcomes?
Do outcomes match organizational goals and objectives?
Do outcomes match a reasonable professional standard?
Does the organization examine unsuccessful outcomes thoroughly?

Consumer/Public Relations
What is the reputation of the program in the community or among other professionals?
Are consumers satisfied with services?
Are consumer families satisfied with services?

Sources: Brain Injury Association, n.d.; Brolin, 1973; Hagebak, 1982; Hanley-Maxwell & Bordieri, 1989; Lewis & Lewis, 1983.

Resource Selection

Having identified needs and potential resources, the most appropriate resources are selected. Selecting the "best" resource requires problem-solving skills and a good decision-making strategy. Two decision strategies have been suggested: optimizing and satisficing.

Optimizing.   Optimizing is the examination of as many alternatives as possible to find the most beneficial. McCollum et al. (1979) and Vandergoot and Jacobsen (1979) discuss optimization as desirable in the selection of community resources, while Lewis, Lewis, Packard, and Soufleé (2001) describe the matrix that might be developed for optimizing. To optimize, one would first select a number of criteria (perhaps from table 1) that are most important in a resource for a specific client need, optionally weighting criteria by their relative importance. Next, a wide range of possible alternative resources are identified by "brainstorming" and are entered into an optimizing matrix. All identified alternatives are then rated or scored on their ability to meet those criteria, with different values assigned to "does not meet," "meets," "partially meets," and "unknown" states. An overall score is determined by summing across criterion scores. The resource receiving the highest score is chosen. Presumably, this would be done for each specific client need.

Satisficing.   While optimizing is ideal, the process is cumbersome for some decisions and "overkill" for others. A more likely strategy—satisficing—is suggested in the writing of Simon (1976) and represents a compromise between consideration of every conceivable alternative and the time and information constraints on such a strategy. In satisficing, a small number of "criteria of value" (p. 98) are established prior to identifying alternatives. Potential alternatives are then examined until one meeting all criteria of value is found, at which time the search stops. For example, in selecting training vendors for clients with brain injury, a counselor might use "experience with the population" and "multiple linkages for special needs," as well as a comprehensive list of services offered as criteria of value. Training alternatives are examined until one meeting these criteria is found.

USING COMMUNITY RESOURCES

Developing Service Delivery Systems

Once these steps have been accomplished, the counselor/organization can begin to implement specific plans for individual clients. In order to facilitate these plans, an effective and efficient service delivery system must be established. Three important parts of the service delivery system are discussed here: utilization of organizational and professional networks, types of fee mechanisms, and preparation of referral letters. The service delivery system must also develop policies and procedures for facilitating consumerism and informed choice, and more increasingly, the special use of computers in the system.

Networks. Human service professionals have long been advised to develop and use "networks" for both their own development and that of their clients. Carroll (1986) defines networking as the development of formal and informal linkages between service providers and agencies to promote resource sharing and information exchange. Three types of networks—often overlapping—can be delineated: personal, professional, and organizational. Personal networks are friends, relatives, and acquaintances who provide one with support, nurturance, information, and guidance. Professional networks provide information, guidance, and resources and usually consist of other service providers, professionals, mentors, teachers, and so on.

Organizational networks are usually established through formal linkages among the various service entities that exist in a local community. Hagebak (1982) discusses benefits of organizational networks, including:

- Local determination—Service integration is often mandated through legislation. By networking, local agencies can determine and control the implementation of that integration.

- Improved cost-effectiveness—By networking, agencies may be able to realize savings from reduced duplication of effort, equipment, staff, and physical facilities.

- Maximized professional relationships—Members working together may develop ideas—synergistically—that no single member could have produced alone.

- Elimination of service gaps—Joint needs assessment and planning ensures comprehensiveness in scope of services and target populations.

- Recruitment activities—Coordination of job listings and human resource planning may ensure that the *community* is able to recruit and retain the most qualified staff.

- Comprehensive data/evaluation systems—Shared data and data-collecting devices may lead to more efficient and effective program evaluation systems.

Even where organizational networks are not established, individual practitioners may realize benefits from professional networking with resource vendors: (a) a network member will better understand typical client needs and counselor expectations; (b) a network member may be more willing to discuss ways of cost containment that would not be harmful to the client's welfare; and (c) a member of a network can help cut through "red tape," thus ensuring timeliness of services.

Fee Mechanisms.   Thomas and Bordieri (1987) list four of the most common methods of arranging vendor services:

- Service contract—A service contract is a signed legal document specifying nature of services, method and rate of payment, time lines, and dollar amounts of particular services anticipated to be purchased during the contract period. The contract is legally binding.

- Written purchase of service agreement—Similar to a service contract, a written purchase of service agreement does not obligate purchase of services but only implies an option to purchase.

- Requests for proposal—RFPs specify services to be provided and special requirements for their provision. They are sent to a number of potential vendors, who bid on them by specifying how services will be provided and outlining projected costs. Chosen vendors are then sent service contracts or service agreements.

- Individual authorization without contract or agreement—As implied in the name, this mechanism authorizes specific services for specified fees. There is no obligation for number of persons served or expected outcomes, although there is usually an understanding of such. In a national survey among state directors of vocational rehabilitation agencies, Thomas and Bordieri (1987) found that the individual authorization without contract was the most favored mechanism, followed by purchase of service agreement, service contract, and RFP.

Referral Letters.   The most effective referral letter is one that follows a phone call to a fellow member of a professional or organizational network. In such a case, the letter reiterates the important points discussed on the phone, clarifies details of service provision, provides supplemental background information on the client, and establishes an often-necessary "paper trail." In discussing the establishment of local community resource systems, Hagebak (1982) lists key reasons for documentation such as referral letters: (a) a written document can be reviewed and modified; (b) it protects the resource relationship against "memory failure" and staff turnover; and (c) it "locks in" the commitment of parties involved, ethically if not legally. Further, where service contracts or purchase of service agreements are the fee mechanisms, the referral letter is the first document that specifies clients, services to be provided, outcomes expected, time lines, and so on.

Referral letters provide the following information:

1. An introduction of the client—It is important to include background information that is relevant to the presenting problem or is needed by the vendor in order to effectively serve the client. Clinical impressions and concerns are helpful. In presenting this type of information, care needs to be taken to uphold the policy on release of client information.

2. The specific services needed—If an evaluation of some type is being purchased, the specific questions in which the referring counselor is interested should be detailed.

3. The monitoring mechanism—Minimally, this includes clearly stated goals and objectives. Terms for renegotiation of service costs, mechanisms for joint case planning, and quality-assurance review procedures may be discussed.

4. Time lines—The date by which the services must be completed or renegotiated, should be specified.

5. Special considerations—A list of the ancillary services needed (e.g., transportation from home, lodging, and case management) should be detailed.

Monitoring. Finally, to remain truly efficient and effective, a service delivery system—whether that system includes a single referral relationship or a comprehensive community network—needs continuous monitoring. While table 1 can be used as a guide for monitoring, some points require particular attention:

• *Outcome*—Of primary significance in long-term service provision (e.g., training, physical rehabilitation, and psychological counseling) is whether the client is making satisfactory progress, and, if not, whether the vendor can provide a satisfactory explanation. If the vendor is providing a short-term service (e.g., vocational evaluation, housing assistance, and financial counseling), the concern is that these were completed satisfactorily. Finally, if the vendor is providing a commodity or equipment (e.g., prosthetic device, food, and modified transportation), the questions are: "Did the client receive the commodity?" and "Does it work as intended?"

• *Responsiveness to the client's primary and special needs*—The vendor's performance in responding to the needs (services, evaluations, special considerations) outlined in the referral letter is clearly important. The vendor's willingness to consider the input of the consumer and the family, as well as overall consumer/family satisfaction, also falls within this category.

- *Responsiveness to referring counselor's needs*—Similarly, referring counselors have needs, such as ensuring that the agency has adequate and appropriate staffing; having input on planning; receiving useful, timely, and accurate reports; and receiving cooperation in cost containment when appropriate.

- *Responsiveness to organization needs*—A final concern relates to whether the organization's needs—for timely billing, appropriate data for program evaluation and satisfying legal, funding, or accreditation authorities, and so on—are being satisfied.

Additionally, if both organizations are part of a community referral network, the rate at which the vendor is referring clients to the purchasing organization is important.

Raiff and Shore (1993) outline nine aspects of quality monitoring practice:

1. The case manager expends considerable effort, developing a relationship for free exchange of information, triangulating, and cross-checking data.

2. A regular monitoring schedule is planned and implemented.

3. Additional oversight is provided as needed.

4. The case manager uses and is comfortable with aggregate and computer-generated reports.

5. Clients and caregivers are encouraged to become knowledgeable consumers in regard to rights and standards of practice.

6. Clients and caregivers are assisted in developing simple systems with which they can do their own monitoring.

7. Measures of client satisfaction are routinely taken and used.

8. Considerable administrative support exists—in the form of time and resources—for program monitoring.

9. All services are monitored, regardless of their potential to directly influence change.

Careful monitoring is especially important in relationships with service providers that implement or experiment with service consolidation with other providers. An example of this is the congressionally mandated consolidation of Vocational Rehabilitation and Job Services. When these consolidations are not carefully planned, the various advantages of networked resources are not realized (Raiff & Shore, 1993), and client services may suffer.

Consumerism and Informed Choice. The role of the client in service planning has long been assumed in human services, and in some cases this role has become ever expanding. For example, in the state-federal rehabilitation system, clients are given "tickets" with which to purchase services from their choice of vendors. Moxley and Daeschlein (cited in Crimando, 2003) described the properties of a consumer-driven case management system. These properties are posed as questions: (a) Does the client possess an "active voice" that is respected and listened to in determining the purpose and direction of human services? (b) Does the client exercise control over outcomes and strategies used to achieve outcomes? (c) Is making meaningful choices from among substantive alternatives valued? (d) Can the client dissent safely, and does this dissent result in actions to rectify that with which the client is dissatisfied? (e) Does the system protect the reputation of the person it serves?

Implementing choice in community resources may take many forms. Minimally, a human service worker or agency should keep a catalog of community vendors (if one is not available on the Internet) and discuss the advantages and disadvantages of each with the client, who would then choose the vendor. Further steps may include joint development of the optimizing matrix, and visits to vendors. Finally, developmentally appropriate training on being an informed consumer can be provided.

Use of Computers. The expanding use of computers in human services since the 1980s has been adequately addressed in other sources. Such use ranges from functioning as simple repositories of forms and documents, billing and accounting tools, and preparing case notes; to intermediate use in identifying distant community resources, maintaining resource catalogs and information/referral services, and accessing peer self-help groups; to advanced use of comprehensive case management systems. While such use of computers can do much to improve the efficiency and effectiveness of human services, it raises new concerns about confidentiality and privacy. Federico and Bowley (1996) note that, despite efforts at control, hackers have been able to access online information. Human service professionals using computers to promote the service delivery system should take the following precautions: First, secure servers and encryption software should be routine if referrals are made online or sent by e-mail. Second, because of the immediacy and informality of e-mail, requests by vendors sent through e-mail should be scrutinized to make sure there is a current, signed release for the particular information being requested. Finally, client information stored at either agency or vendor sites must be protected by firewalls and other devices designed to keep information inaccessible to inappropriate users.

SUMMARY

This chapter has discussed case management implications of utilizing community resources. A broadened definition of community resource was given, as was a systematic process for identifying, selecting, and using resources. While the benefits for the process herein described are many, it may seem tedious and cumbersome to a few. These persons should bear in mind that a comprehensive needs assessment and resource identification need only be performed once, and that the entire organization can engage in the process. Periodic, cursory review of both client needs and available resources can then supplement. Finally, involvement in professional and organizational networks will make the latter activities easier.

References

Abramson, J. (1983). Six steps to effective referrals. In H. Weissman, I. Epstein, & A. Savage (Eds.), *Agency-based social work: Neglected aspects of clinical practice*. Philadelphia: Temple University.

Brain Injury Association. (n.d.). *A guide to selecting and monitoring brain injury rehabilitation services*. Retrieved September 1, 2004, from http://www.biausa.org

Brolin, D. (1973). The facility you choose. . . . *Journal of Rehabilitation, 39*(1), 24–26.

Carroll, R. A. (1986). Resource exchange: A catalyst for networking in rehabilitation. *American Rehabilitation, 12*(4), 3, 18–19.

Crimando, W. (2003). Addressing the employment needs of persons with physical disabilities: Implications for rehabilitation and mental health service workers. In D. P. Moxley & J. R. Finch (Eds.), *Sourcebook of rehabilitation and mental health practice* (pp. 379–399). New York: Kluwer Academic/Plenum.

Federico, R. F., & Bowley, J. M. (1996, January). The great e-mail debate. *HRMagazine on Human Resource Management, 41,* 67–72.

Hagebak, B. R. (1982). *Getting local agencies to cooperate*. Baltimore: University Park Press.

Hanley-Maxwell, C., & Bordieri, J. E. (1989). Purchasing supported employment: Evaluating the service. *Journal of Applied Rehabilitation Counseling, 20*(3), 4–11.

Lewis, J. A., Lewis, M. D., Packard, T., & Soufée, F., Jr. (2001). *Management of human service programs* (3rd ed.). Monterey, CA: Brooks/Cole.

McCollum, P. S., Swenson, E., & Hooge, N. C. (1979). Community resources revisited: Sources of support in the rehabilitation process. *Journal of Applied Rehabilitation Counseling, 10,* 72–77.

McKillip, J. (1987). *Need analysis: Tools for human services and education*. Newbury Park, CA: Sage.

Raiff, N. R., & Shore, B. K. (1993). *Advanced case management: New strategies for the nineties*. Newbury Park, CA: Sage.

Rossi, R. J. (1982). *Agencies working together*. Beverly Hills, CA: Sage.

Seider, V. M. (1966). *The rehabilitation agency and community work: A source book for professional training*. Washington, DC: U.S. Department of Health, Education and Welfare, Rehabilitation Services Administration.

Sheafor, B. W., Horejsi, C. R., & Horejsi, G. A. (1988). *Techniques and guidelines for social work practice*. Boston: Allyn & Bacon.

Simon, H. A. (1976). *Administrative behavior: A study of decision making processes in administrative organizations*. New York: Free Press.

Thomas, D. F., & Bordieri, J. E. (1987). Fees for services: Principles and practices among state vocational rehabilitation general agencies and facilities. *Journal of Rehabilitation Administration, 11,* 23–32.

Vandergoot, D., & Jacobsen, R. J. (1979). Identifying, developing and using community resources in rehabilitation counseling. *Journal of Applied Rehabilitation Counseling, 9,* 159–163.

Weissman, H., Epstein, I., & Savage, A. (Eds.). (1983). *Agency-based social work: Neglected aspects of clinical practice*. Philadelphia: Temple University.

SECTION II

Health and Diagnostic Services

Medical Providers

Thomas D. Upton

Human service workers have developed professional careers in response to problems people experience in life. More specifically, human service professionals have developed specialized expertise in identifying specific life needs (e.g., unemployment, homelessness, substance abuse) and linking consumers with community-based interventions (Beck, 1998; Upton & Beck, 2002). Locating and accessing medical providers is one social need that human service providers can help consumers to meet. As such, human service workers must understand the processes involved in order to aid consumers in meeting their medical needs and receiving appropriate interventions.

Purpose/Intent

At face value it is easy to underestimate the complexity of seeking medical services. It may appear that the linkage with medical service providers is simple to accomplish. However, consumers with multiple life needs may not have the initiative or knowledge necessary to find the appropriate specialist, obtain a referral, receive necessary interventions, and pay for these services. Human service workers should be prepared to assist consumers in obtaining the medical services they need.

Initially, human service providers must comprehensively understand each consumer by developing an assessment of the consumer and his/her potential needs by providing case management services. Moxley (1989) clearly showed that assessment, planning, intervention, evaluation, and monitoring are central features required to holistically provide case management. Presuming best practices, human service professionals use the initial interview as a means to begin understanding the comprehensive nature of a consumer's life needs by talking with the consumer, reviewing existing professional documentation, and collaborating with additional treating professionals. These different points of information will likely identify specific consumer needs to address. Many life needs may be identified. Identified problems may be related to unmet residential, economic, disability, or health-care needs. As a human service professional, one needs to know how to facilitate meeting identified life needs. This chapter provides an overview of accessing medical care for consumers.

Suppose after completing a comprehensive initial interview you become aware that a person with whom you are working has some potential medical problems for which he or she is not receiving treatment. Identified life needs may range from an alleged fracture of a bone to suspected diabetes. It is important to have a working knowledge of how to facilitate a consumer's search for necessary professional services.

Several benchmarks must be achieved in this process. These include locating the appropriate medical provider, acquiring a referral, arranging for payment, receiving medical interventions, and securing appropriate ongoing care. An elementary understanding of the consumer may provide hints as to what types of medical professional should be sought. The combination of professional training, experience, and professional consultation may facilitate the search for the appropriate medical professional. (Professional preparation is discussed later in the chapter.)

Consider the following example. By talking with a consumer to provide human services, you may become aware that the consumer hurt his right leg last week after falling down the stairs. The consumer manifests a noticeable limp and is experiencing a high level of pain. In such a straightforward case it isn't difficult to conclude that the services of an orthopedic physician would be advisable. However, with more complicated and subjective complaints (e.g., fibromyalgia), human service providers may need to rely on the collaborative efforts of their own training and professional experience, as well as consultation with other professionals. Inexperienced human service professionals with limited training must rely on mentors or databases within their agency as two means to successfully locate appropriate professionals.

Once the appropriate type of medical specialist is located, then the process of getting a referral for services and setting up an appointment may be undertaken. Referral procedures vary among providers and may be as simple as contacting the office, making an appointment, and assisting the consumer to attend the appointment at a free clinic. Conversely, referrals to specialists may require a relatively large amount of detailed information (e.g., medical records, specific diagnoses, comprehensive third-party insurance) in order for specialists to accept a referral and make an initial medical appointment for such a consumer.

Financial resources are intricately linked with medical treatment and overall access to medical providers (Franklin & Fraser, 1993; Institute of Medicine, 2001). As a general rule the more comprehensive a person's financial resources are, the broader and more specialized are the medical services available. Consumers seeking medical services can be divided into three major groups based on who is responsible for payment. First, consumers with private insurance/private pay represent the bulk of medical business. Health organizations (e.g., Blue Cross/Blue Shield, Unicare) work as medical care insurers for many large companies and organizations (universities, state and federal agencies). These organizations are responsible for managing services (i.e., keeping costs low) that are provided under a third-party insurance agreement. Also within this group are consumers who have substantial financial resources and no insurance resources. It is commonly known how some foreigners come to prestigious institutions (e.g., Mayo Clinic, Cleveland Clinic) and "buy" medical services as they would a precious commodity. Obviously, this group of people has no need for comprehensive private insurance.

Second, many consumers are enrolled in federal health-care insurance (e.g., Medicare, Medicaid) (Social Security Administration [SSA], 2003). The federal government provides medical insurance for these consumers. Both federal insurance and private insurance are huge organizations with many enrollees. Because of this large member base, specialized (reduced) medical cost rates are set for different services. In essence, when a consumer receives medical services, the medical provider is paid the negotiated rates for certain medical interventions. Two points are important to make here. First, federal insurance has lower rates of reimbursement for medical interventions. Second, the scope of services that federal insurance provides may be narrower than that of private insurance. Both of these factors can increase the difficulty of working with someone covered by one of these federal public insurance programs.

The last group of consumers has neither private insurance nor federal public insurance and has limited financial resources. Persons in this group may seek medical services at "free clinics" or seek medical services only on an emergency basis, following major illness or injury. These persons may be provided services as an indigent or may structure payment schedules to spread medical payments out over an extended period. Jackson, Derose, Chiesa, and Escarce (2002) suggest that providing medical service provision to consumers without resources increases overall costs of providing services for everyone.

Clearly, obtaining medical care for consumers can be complicated. However, the preceding paragraphs reviewed specific steps human service professionals must take. Following these guidelines can facilitate linkage to an appropriate medical provider for the consumer. Following are two examples of how human service professionals, specifically rehabilitation counselors, can gain the necessary background knowledge, abilities, and skills to assist consumers in accessing appropriate medical services.

Professional Preparation

Human service professionals enable consumer linkage with medical providers in at least two ways: specific pre-service training in a Council on Rehabilitation Education (CORE)-accredited program, and directed mentorship of novice counselors (Maki & Delworth, 1995) by more seasoned counselors. These two routes can provide counselors-in-training with requisite background information to successfully assist consumers in accessing needed medical services.

Specialized Curriculum.   One way to prepare human service professionals is through specialized training. Formal, comprehensive pre-service training facilitates a medical and psychosocial understanding of the body and of human service delivery. A nonspecific undergraduate degree in psychology may help foster students' abilities to read, write, and understand human functioning, but a more specialized approach to meeting unmet needs may be acquired throughout undergraduate preparation in rehabilitation (Southern Illinois University–Carbondale [SIUC], 2004a). An undergraduate course of study in human services can provide students with a breadth of relevant human service information, although such courses do not provide all the knowledge the human service professional will need.

However, graduate programs more comprehensively prepare students to identify and address rehabilitation needs. Graduate-level rehabilitation counselor education programs require coursework on medical and psychosocial aspects of disability, assessment, case management, counseling and consultation procedures, and service delivery systems (Council on Rehabilitation Education [CORE], 2004). Formal instruction in these areas can help students to identify potential human needs as well as how to access relevant human services to meet these identified needs. Clearly, preparation in required areas such as interpersonal skills, medical and psychosocial aspects of disability (Upton, 2004), vocational development and placement, case management, and clinical education can assist rehabilitation counselors-in-training to comprehensively understand human functioning and disability-specific needs. Ideally, once a student completes this specialized curriculum, he or she is prepared to holistically serve rehabilitation consumers.

Hands-On Mentorship Training.   Another alternative available to rehabilitation counselors is informal, on-the-job training. Many professionals in training have learned how to access medical providers with the assistance of more "senior" human service professionals who informally "teach" them how to do so. The new professional is taught how other agency professionals have done this in the past and learns the routine "ins and outs" of enabling consumer access to medical services. This technique is described in the literature by Maki and Delworth (1995), who suggest that rehabilitation counselor professional development progresses from a beginning level (level 1) to a mastery level (level 3) across the central constructs of self-awareness and other awareness, motivation, and autonomy. Ideally, this model posits that counselors will enhance other (consumer) awareness while decreasing self-awareness, will stabilize their motivation to help consumers, and will develop a high degree of professional autonomy.

The preceding model can be compared to an apprenticeship model prevalent in skilled construction trades (e.g., carpenter, pipe fitter, electrician). In these occupations a worker who wants to learn a trade goes through many years of observing, learning, and on-the-job training before he or she can enter the occupation as a skilled colleague. The Maki and Delworth (1995) model may work to train some professionals but has at least one weak spot: How does a novice counselor learn about a contemporary medical problem (e.g., managing fibromyalgia) to which the senior human service professional has limited or no previous exposure?

It appears that some combination of formal pre-service educational preparation and informal agency mentorship is the best solution overall. While pre-service education may be a prerequisite to human service employment, anecdotal evidence from human service providers suggests that specialized learning about a particular agency, its consumer population, and the community services available locally are achieved in the professional workplace. Armed with knowledge gained from both pre-service education and the mentoring process, the new human service professional will be best prepared to meet consumers' needs.

CLIENT SERVICES

Once a consumer is scheduled for an appointment with a medical provider, it is presumed that the consumer will receive necessary services. Emergency medical services are not likely to be sought through the collective efforts of a human service professional and a consumer. More likely, specific services may be sought for specific purposes, which may include an initial assessment/diagnosis, medical interventions, or treatment planning/referral to a specialist. Several distinct medical specialties exist, and a list of some common specialties are reviewed in table 1.

It is important to remember that learning about medical specialties can be a daunting task. While human service professionals are likely to observe symptoms of medical problems, they are not professionally qualified (in most cases) to make diagnoses about consumers. They are limited to citing observations, referring consumers to different medical specialists, and collaborating with treating professionals to ensure that consumers' identified needs are being met.

Even after a diagnosis has been made, human service professionals need to collaborate with the treating professionals. Collaboration requires that medical records are disseminated to all parties and that professionals clearly understand the technical information being discussed. Although human service professionals may have some pre-service formal training, they should also have access to relevant, user-friendly medical references (*Taber's Medical Dictionary* and the *Merck Manual* are readily available).

Many people in the United States are currently without medical insurance. These persons may not have many medical records to chart medical

Table I   Selected Medical Specialties

Specialty	Types of Illness/Injury
allergist	allergies and environmental pollutant problems
andrology	male reproductive system
cardiology	heart problems
gastroenterology	diseases of the gastrointestinal tract (e.g., ulcers, irritable bowel syndrome, gastroesophageal reflux disease)
gynecology	female reproductive system
nephrology	pathology of the kidney
neurology	neurological impairment (such as brain injury, spinal cord injury, epilepsy, etc.)
occupational and environmental medicine	prevention and management of illness, injury, and disability in the workplace
oncology	cancer
ophthalmology	visual problems
orthopedist	bone fractures, dislocations, and related problems
otolaryngology	ear, nose, throat specialist
pediatrics	childhood and adolescent problems
physiatry	physical injury and rehabilitation
pulmonology	respiratory problems
rheumatology	rheumatoid arthritis and other joint problems

changes over time. Consider the following case of a consumer who reports chest pain, shortness of breath, and fatigue but lacks medical records to document these symptoms. The consumer had recently lost his residence, his job, and his car (his sole means of transportation). Having no family in the rural area in which he lived, lack of transportation is a significant impediment to working, attending professional appointments, and completing the general activities of daily living. In this consumer's current situation, acquiring a medical diagnosis that notes his "medical need" for special public transportation may make him eligible for medically necessary county-based transportation services.

Once a consumer has been diagnosed, then specific medical interventions may be warranted as treatment. Ideally, consumer medical needs will be addressed by involved medical providers. For example, treatment interventions for the common disease of diabetes include ongoing medical monitoring by a physician, specialized medical equipment (e.g., lactometer), and ongoing use of medications (e.g., insulin). All of these medical interventions cost money and require the consumer to actively monitor the progression of this disease. In such cases where medical monitoring by a physician or the consumer is required, then it is probable that additional human and financial costs will be endured by this consumer and by society, respectively. The societal reality that the scope and frequency of treatment often are associated with one's relative financial resources (e.g., personal income, insurance) forces human service providers to be creative in seeking medical services for consumers.

Other medical services that human service professionals may assist their clients in obtaining are treatment planning and/or referral to a treating specialist. If a consumer has access to a medical provider but this provider cannot best treat this consumer, a referral to another facility or specialist is desirable. For example, a general practitioner treating a consumer learns that this consumer has many classic signs of Systemic Lupus Erythematosus (SLE). Furthermore, significant blood work supports this working diagnosis. It seems both prudent and reasonable that this medical provider refer this consumer to a SLE specialist in a nearby city.

This brief overview on medical providers should help human service professionals to facilitate consumer access to medical providers. It is clear there are many considerations and numerous steps involved to obtain the best level of medical care possible for consumers. The bottom line is that one must learn the how to locate medical specialists, gain a referral, and secure payment for required medical services. This process requires human service providers to collectively use their professional training, experiences, and collegial consultations to best serve the holistic needs of consumers.

Typical Referral Questions

1. What is reported to be medically wrong with the consumer?
2. What specific symptoms does the consumer have?
3. How long have these symptoms existed?
4. What medical interventions has the consumer received?
5. Have professional diagnoses been made for these symptoms?
6. What medical services are being sought for this consumer?
7. Does the consumer report any psychological symptoms?
8. Does the consumer's family have a history of medical or psychological problems?
9. Does the consumer have transportation?
10. Does the consumer have private insurance?
11. Does the consumer have private resources to pay for medical services?
12. Does the consumer receive any federal or state health benefits?

Specific answers to these questions may assist medical providers in more fully understanding a consumer's medical situation prior to the first appointment. Medical providers require certain referral information, and it is important that human service professionals provide copies of all professional records so consumers can be best served by medical providers.

References

Beck, R. (1998). Rehabilitation case management and managed care. In R. Roessler & S. Rubin (Eds.), *Case management and rehabilitation counseling: Procedures and techniques* (3rd ed., pp. 255–276). Austin, TX: PRO-ED.

Charles, B. (2000). Telemedicine can lower costs and improve access. *Healthcare Financial Management, 54*(3), 66–69.

Counsel on Rehabilitation Education (CORE). (2004, August). *Accreditation Manual.* Retrieved September 1, 2004, from http://www.corerehab.org/manual/manual.html#sectionCCurriculum

Franklin, D., & Fraser, L. (1993). Rich and poor: The health gap widens. *Health, 7*(6), 29–30.

Gatty, B. (1995). Patients and doctors need choices. *Ophthalmology Times, 20*(7), 4.

Institute of Medicine. (2001). *Coverage matters: Insurance and healthcare.* Washington, DC: National Academy Press.

Jackson, C., Derose, K., Chiesa, J., & Escarce, J. (2002). *Hospital car for the uninsured in Miami-Dade County.* Santa Monica, CA: Rand.

Maki, D., & Delworth, U. (1995). Clinical supervision: A definition and model for the rehabilitation counseling profession. *Rehabilitation Counseling Bulletin, 35*(4), 282–292.

Moxley, D. P. (1989). *The practice of case management.* Newbury Park, CA: Sage.

Roessler, R., & Rubin, S. (Eds.). 1998. *Case management and rehabilitation counseling: Procedures and techniques* (3rd ed.). Austin, TX: PRO-ED.

Social Security Administration (SSA). (2003, September 23). Retrieved September 1, 2004, from http://www.ssa.gov/work/ResourcesToolkit/redbook.pdf

Southern Illinois University–Carbondale (SIUC). (2004a, August 23). *Web site description of undergraduate curriculum required for B.S. in Rehabilitation Services.* Retrieved from http://www.siu.edu/~rehabbs/courses.htm

Southern Illinois University–Carbondale (SIUC). (2004b, August 23). *Web site description of graduate curriculum required for M.S./M.A. in Rehabilitation Counselor Training.* Retrieved September 1, 2004, from http://www.siu.edu/~rehabrct/

Upton, T. D. (2004, August 23). *Web site syllabus of Rehb 513 Medical and Psychosocial Aspects of Disability.* Retrieved September 1, 2004, from http://www.coehs.siu.edu/Rehb513/

Upton, T. D., & Beck, R. (2002). Case management: Rehabilitation applications and administrative implications. *Journal of Rehabilitation Administration, 26*, 39–46.

Home-Based Rehabilitation

H. L. Brostrand

Home-based rehabilitation (HBR) refers to rehabilitation services that are provided in the home, according to a treatment plan. The services may be short-term or long-term; they may be provided by certified, licensed practitioners or by paraprofessionals. Services commonly provided in the home setting include: skilled nursing, physical therapy, occupational therapy, speech therapy, social and educational services, hospice, and respite care.

Generally, the hospital discharge planner will arrange for in-home health services. A social worker, rehabilitation professional, or case manager may facilitate care in other settings. Hospitalization may be required prior to being eligible for home care, and the first visit may need to be made within a certain time following discharge.

There are advantages and disadvantages to providing rehabilitation services in a home setting. The speed and quality of recovery can be increased when an individual is more comfortable at home and following doctor's orders. Caplan and Moelter (2000) suggest that, following a stroke, patients who were transferred to rehabilitation units (as compared to returning to their homes) could experience "problematic emotional and cognitive responses" due to the institutional setting (p. 84). Geddes and Chamberlain (2003) found that the more comprehensive, home-based rehabilitation approach, with its greater emphasis on psychosocial functioning of the patient and family, was the preferred approach and was both financially and socially more effective. Improvement in quality of life and exercise levels in elderly cardiac rehab patients following home-based rehabilitation was found to be significantly greater than that of hospitalized patients (Warrington, Cholowski, & Peters, 2003). There are also situations where individuals

29

recovering from a hospital stay do not have family, friends, or neighbors available to provide support such as wound care, meal preparation, housekeeping, and personal care. Without HBR, a person may be forced either to recover or, depending on the duration of disability, even to reside in a nursing home. If there is a family member or other caretaker available, HBR can have the added benefit of involving and educating the family regarding the disability or illness and the individual's long-term needs.

However, one disadvantage of home-based rehabilitation is the lack of constant supervision and medical care that a hospital setting can provide. Though many people *feel* better recovering at home, some require more intensive supervision and medical care than HBR can provide.

HBR is often provided as a cost-saving mechanism. It is far less expensive to support someone's recovery at home than it is to support it in an institutional setting, such as a hospital or nursing home. For example, after surgery on a broken ankle, one week in the hospital can cost upwards of $5,000 in southern Illinois and $10,000 in San Francisco, whereas one week of in-home services could cost one-tenth that amount. According to the Visiting Nurse Association, a comparison made of average costs in 2000 revealed significant savings. A per-day hospital charge was approximately $2,700, a skilled nursing facility charge was approximately $400 per day, and the home-care charges per visit were $100 (Visiting Nurse Association [VNA], 2004). In New Zealand, Sweden, and Australia, similar cost savings and improved medical results were found with stroke rehabilitation (Anderson, Mhurchu, Brown, & Carter, 2002; Andersson, Levin, Oberg, & Mansson, 2002) and hip fracture recovery (Crotty, Whitehead, Gray, & Finucane, 2001). In addition, usage of home-based rehabilitation can free beds in hospital-based rehabilitation for those patients requiring closer monitoring or more intensive treatment (Shrier, 2003). As more health care falls under the control of managed care, such as health maintenance organizations (HMOs), home-based rehabilitation as an alternative to hospitalization and skilled nursing facilities will likely continue to be utilized.

Not all services provided in the home are necessarily rehabilitative. Though hospice is in-home medical care, to qualify for this service individuals with terminal illnesses must no longer be receiving active treatment for their conditions. However, an evaluation by a qualified nurse or therapist may allow for short-term in-home therapy to improve the quality of life for the terminal patient. Pediatric, postnatal in-home services would not generally be considered a standard part of home-based rehabilitation, but again, if medically necessary, short-term services may be provided in the home.

Respite care refers to services provided so that the primary caregiver(s) can have time away from responsibilities in the home. Child-care and transportation services may be offered as part of this service. Yet another nonrehabilitative home-based activity is preoperative physical therapy. Long-term outcomes following anterior cruciate ligament reconstruction were significantly improved in those individuals who undertook a regime of preoperative range-of-motion exercise (Bieze, 2004). People who are motivated to participate in home-based exercise and therapy seem to have better chances for improving their rehabilitation than do those who do not participate.

The Visiting Nurse Association is a well-known organization in the arena of home-based health services. Local branches, agencies, and mergers with VNA are found all over the country. The first visiting nurse associations in the United States were modeled after a movement that Florence Nightingale started in England. Nursing services were provided to infants, children, mothers, families, and sick adults who did not have financial resources in the late 1800s (VNA, 2004). Today there are many agencies, both private and not-for-profit, that provided home-based rehabilitation services.

WHAT SITUATIONS REQUIRE HBR?

There are any number of medical conditions and disabilities that may require home-based rehabilitation. Injury, illness, disability, and age-related conditions, depending on severity and duration, may require short-term or long-term in-home rehabilitation. Long-term care, which may include medical and custodial services over a long period of time, is often necessary for individuals with chronic illness or permanent disability. Psychoeducational services also may be appropriate for individuals with newly diagnosed chronic illness or long-term disability. The individual's quality of life, independence, and functional abilities are considered, and a treatment plan is developed. A doctor's prescription is required for most services. Some of the more common conditions that HBR is used for include:

- *Cardiac related.* Myocardial infarction and congestive heart failure might require medical services such as blood work; monitoring of vital signs; and physical, recreational, and occupational therapy. All these services can be done in a home setting.

- *Pulmonary.* Issues such as emphysema, lung transplant, or chronic obstructive pulmonary disease (COPD) may require skilled nursing; personal assistants and respiratory and occupational therapy may be provided.

- *Post-surgical wound care.* Education can be provided and in-home services may be short-term if the patient can care for him- or herself or if a caregiver is available. If assistance is not available, nursing and therapy staff can visit regularly and attend to a client's needs following hospitalization.

- *Diabetes.* Especially when newly diagnosed, diabetes may require education and skilled nursing care for complications.

- *Cancer.* Chemotherapy and other treatments can be performed in the home.

- *Cerebral vascular accident (CVA).* Someone who has experienced a stroke may have difficulty with speech production and language processing. He or she may also have difficulty swallowing, which can cause nutrition-related problems. A left-side CVA commonly effects expressive communication and swallowing. A right-side CVA may cause flat affect, visual perception difficulties, paralysis on one side (hemiplegia), and language-processing concerns.

- *Spinal cord injury (SCI).* Individuals with paraplegia, quadriplegia, or spina bifida may require more intensive services initially in adjusting to their disability. Those with higher-level injury may require more extensive and long-term nursing, therapy, and custodial care.

- *Mental illness.* Individuals with mental health issues may experience poor motivation. Patients that require treatment may have psychological stressors that keep them from participating in hospital-based activities. Skills that are learned in an institutional setting may also not generalize well to an individual's home setting. Sellwood et al. (1999) found that, in the United Kingdom, home-based rehabilitation was more effective than traditional outpatient rehabilitation for clients with chronic schizophrenia.

CASE STUDY

The following scenario is a conglomeration of possible issues that might be found in the treatment of an individual receiving cardiac rehabilitation.

José Jackson (we will call him "JJ") has suffered an acute myocardial infarction. His wife takes him to the emergency room, and he is admitted to the hospital. He is 50 pounds overweight, has a sedentary lifestyle, and is the father of two teenagers. His wife works full-time, and both kids are unavailable to provide care or transportation during the day. He is in the hospital for two days but must have bed rest and minimal activity for the following week. His doctor orders occupational therapy, recreational therapy, and rehabilitation. The day before he leaves the hospital, JJ meets with a discharge nurse. The nurse is an LCSW and recognizes the need for comprehensive home-based rehabilitation services. He arranges for JJ to meet with an occupational therapist three times per week to address his physical ability to conduct activities of daily living. He also schedules JJ to work with a recreation therapist, because JJ has no regular activities outside of work and watching sports on television. JJ expresses a desire to "get in shape," and a referral is also made to a nutritionist.

JJ is enthusiastic about his recovery, but his doctor wants him to "take it easy" for four weeks. He is restricted from driving and is not to return to work for at least six weeks. The doctor also wants JJ to get healthy at a reasonable pace and to maintain his healthy new lifestyle so as to reduce his chances of a second heart attack. She discusses the benefits of home-based rehabilitation with JJ and feels that he is a good candidate for this type of rehabilitation. By providing these therapy sessions in a home setting, there is a better chance the changes can be successfully integrated into JJ's lifestyle. By visiting with him at home, not only can rehabilitation providers accurately assess his environmental and medical needs, they also can more readily ensure that the treatment plan is being followed and that services are tailored to his individual needs. JJ's family can also be more involved in treatment if it is being provided at the home.

The occupational therapist, recreation therapist, and nutritionist all contact JJ by phone the following day to schedule intake appointments. If JJ had had additional needs, a case manager may have been assigned to meet with him and the therapists for the intake appointments. The case manager would also be able to coordinate services and assist JJ when he returned to the doctor for a follow-up appointment. Each therapist will conduct a one- to two-hour intake assessment with JJ and any family member that may be present and willing to participate. The therapists and therapy aides will generally complete paperwork for billing as well as questionnaires regarding JJ's medical condition. They will review medical records available from the hospital and will develop a treatment plan that is in accordance with JJ's needs and other services. Over the course of the next four to six weeks, they will schedule regular visits with JJ and his family to carry out the services in the treatment plan. Ades et al. (2000) found that home-based cardiac rehabilitation was ideal for the patient who needed monitoring of exercise and physical activities, had transportation issues, and had return-to-work needs.

WHO PAYS FOR HBR?

Funding for services provided in the home may come from a variety of sources. Public entities such as Medicare, Medicaid, Public Aid, and state medical programs generally provide for those services necessary to restore an individual to maximal health or to maintain independent living. The Veterans' Administration may provide benefits for active or retired military. All possible funding sources should be considered when trying to arrange for HBR.

According to the government Medicare Web site (2004), Medicare is a federally mandated health insurance program for adults 65 and older and those with particular disabling conditions. Those individuals receiving Supplemental Security Income (SSI) and Social Security Disability Insurance benefits (SSDI) usually qualify for Medicare. Almost 40 million Americans are covered by Medicare, which pays for skilled, intermittent, short-term home health care. This may include skilled nursing, speech pathology, physical therapy, occupational therapy, medical social, and home health aide services. Only those home health agencies that are Medicare certified may be utilized. Medicare type A does not generally cover long-term care. Medicare Part B is an additional benefit that may cover some types of long-term care.

Medicaid is a combination state and federal government program that will pay for some health services based on an individual's age, disability, and limited income. Someone requiring long-term care services at home who has limited assets is likely eligible for Medicaid; the benefits and eligibility requirements vary from state to state (Medicare, 2004). Medicaid is the largest funding source in the United States for medical and health-related services to individuals with limited assets (Center for Medicare, 2004).

Private health insurance is another avenue to pursue in the search for HBR funding. Hospitalization and HBR may be included in a policy, but there are deductibles and co-pays of which a patient will need to be aware. Prior to the situation requiring home health care, an individual may have purchased long-term care insurance. This type of health insurance specifically covers services that are not short-term. The policy may provide unlimited coverage, but it may also have exclusions, caps, and other limitations that affect funding.

Third-party payee refers to a situation where medical costs are the responsibility of another individual's or company's health insurance. For example, in a car accident where the other person is found to be at fault, his or her auto insurance may be responsible for medical costs related to the recovery of the injured party. The HBR provider usually has copious amounts of paperwork that will need to be completed so that the insurance company can be billed for services, supplies and equipment.

If an individual has been injured on the job and is receiving *workers' compensation* disability benefits, the workers' compensation insurance company (or the employer, if it is self-insured) is responsible for medical care related to the injury. A case manager from the insurance company or from a contracted agency generally coordinates and authorizes services. In the Workers' Compensation system, vocational rehabilitation is in considered to be an important part of clients' recovery. Perhaps more than in the other settings, workers' compensation and third-party payee cases often have attorneys involved. The attorney should ensure that his or her client receives the necessary and appropriate services.

Community service organizations, both local and national, may also provide assistance for funding home-based rehabilitation services. The Salvation Army, Easter Seals, Goodwill Industries, and religious institutions are excellent places to start when trying to locate and arrange for HBR. Most communities have independent living centers (or centers for independent living) that can provide referrals and resources to individuals with disabilities requiring in-home services. Community service organizations and centers for independent living are more thoroughly discussed in other chapters. The Internet must not be overlooked as a resource for locating home health agencies and funding sources. Keywords such as "home-based rehabilitation" and "home health services," along with your geographic area, can be typed into a search engine to reveal hundreds of related sites and services available.

In many states, the State Department of Rehabilitation (or Human Services) has established a program to provide in-home support for qualifying clients with disabilities. Orientation and mobility training for individuals with visual impairments is often provided through this avenue. Long-term medical and custodial care may be provided to assist individuals with chronic illness or disability to live more independently and at home instead of being compelled to live in a nursing home.

In the state of Illinois, for example, the Department of Human Services has a Home Services Program. This long-term home health service provides home-based rehabilitation to low-income, chronically ill, or disabled adults under the age of 62 who are in danger of being placed in a nursing home because of their medical or disability-related needs. For an individual to receive the services, HBR must cost less than an institutional setting and the recipient must not require around-the-clock care. This program is housed in the Department of Rehabilitation and most providers have a background in rehabilitation and/or nursing.

Some or all in-home services may be *privately paid* for "in cash" directly by the recipient or other interested party. Again, HBR may be the most economical route to consider when deciding on medical and long-term support.

Who Provides HBR?

Depending on the type of service being provided, a variety of rehabilitation professionals can provide HBR. Other services provided in the community can also be delivered in a home setting as part of a treatment plan. Chiropractors, massage therapists, acupuncturists, dietitians, spiritual advisers, dentists, and so on, may be called on to visit individuals in the home to facilitate rehabilitation. Many agencies such as pharmacies and medical supply companies provide home delivery. Some of the more common home-based rehabilitation service providers are discussed below.

Medical home care is generally provided through skilled *nursing*. According to the California Board of Registered Nursing, nurses provided direct and indirect patient services for safety, comfort, hygiene, disease prevention, and rehabilitation. They administer medications, perform tests, and withdraw blood as required by a treatment plan or doctor's orders (California Board of Registered Nursing [CBRN], 2003). There are many different types of nursing certifications, licenses, and specialties. The titles and education requirements vary from state to state. A registered nurse (RN) can generally provide IV therapy, wound care, injections, education, and other "noncustodial" services. RNs have completed a four-year Bachelor of Science degree (BSN) or a two- to three-year Associate of Science degree (ASN) in Nursing. Registered nurse practitioners (RNP) and clinical nurse specialists have the highest level of certification or specialization along with graduate education in nursing. Licensed vocational nurses (LVN) and licensed practical nurses (LPN) are usually not able to dispense medications or initiate IVs. They have completed a one-year nursing education program. Certified nursing assistants (CNA), nurses' aides, and home health aides provide medical services under the supervision of nursing or therapy staff (U.S. Dept. of Labor/OOH, 2004).

A practitioner licensed in *occupational therapy* (OT) will supervise and/or provide services to improve clients' ability to perform activities of daily living (U.S. Dept. of Labor/OOH, 2004). For example, following a stroke an individual may need to relearn to cook, bathe, and drive. Occupational therapist assistants and aides may provide services under the supervision of an OT.

Physical therapy is provided to help restore physical function, improve mobility, and relieve pain (U.S. Dept. of Labor/OOH, 2004). For example, following surgery, an individual will need to regain his or her strength and mobility. A licensed physical therapist (PT) will generally supervise, provide the services, or both. Physical therapy assistants may also visit clients in the home and provide services under the supervision of a PT.

Speech-language pathologists are able to assess, diagnose, and treat speech and language disorders. They also address cognitive, communication, and swallowing issues (U.S. Dept. of Labor/OOH, 2004). Speech therapists will often work with individuals who have had a stroke, brain injury, cerebral palsy, mental retardation, or hearing impairments.

According to the American Therapeutic Recreation Association's Web site, *therapeutic recreation* (TR) "utilizes various activities as a form of active treatment to promote independent physical, cognitive, emotional and social functioning" (ATRA, 2004, para. 2). For example, following a heart attack, an individual may require assistance to participate in activities both in the home and in the community. In addition, these various activities could be part of an exercise/recreation treatment plan. A certified therapeutic recreation specialist (CTRS) generally provides these services.

Social workers provide medical and psychosocial support to families and individuals receiving home-based rehabilitation. Education and emotional support may also be provided by human service assistants such as human service workers, case management aides, social work assistants, community support workers, mental health aides, community outreach workers, life skills counselors or gerontology aides (U.S. Dept. of Labor/OOH, 2004).

Case managers may have advanced education and specialization in any number of areas. Rehabilitation counselors, nurses, social workers, and other professionals are often case managers. National certification (CCM) is available for those who meet the education and experience requirements. These individuals may provide direct services in the home as well as plan and coordinate all services provided under a treatment plan. For example, a case manager is generally assigned to coordinate and follow up on services provided to someone receiving workers' compensation from a work-related injury. Insurance companies often use medical case managers to coordinate and approve services to the patient. Case managers may visit with a patient at home to determine his or her particular needs. The case manager may review records, contact other care providers, attend doctor or in-home appointments, negotiate equipment and services, refer for assessment, and make recommendations. Much of the communication is conducted by phone, and the Internet is increasingly utilized for case management activities.

Personal and home-care aides provide homemaking, personal care, and companion services. These individuals generally are not "skilled," but may assist other professionals in fulfilling the treatment plan. For example, an individual with paraplegia may require assistance with meal preparation, household chores, transportation, and personal care. These aides may be referred to as homemakers, personal assistants, attendants, or caregivers. They provide nonmedical, custodial care (U.S. Dept. of Labor/OOH, 2004). Consumer advocacy has led to increased "client choice"; the person with a disability or chronic illness usually makes the hiring and firing decisions regarding personal assistants.

Evaluations for needed services and equipment can be conducted in the home. Medical supply companies will send technicians to an individual's home to determine, according to a prescription, what specific supplies or equipment are appropriate. Some rehabilitation facilities have "mobile evaluation centers" that can provide services for individuals who cannot travel. A vocational evaluator may assess a client's skills, abilities, and functional limitations. An *assistive technology* practitioner will identify a consumer's needs and provide training in the use of assistive devices (Cook & Hussey, 2002).

ACCREDITATION, CERTIFICATION, AND LICENSURE

Agencies and practitioners may have local, state, and/or federal recognition of the services they provide. The Joint Commission on Accreditation of Hospitals (JCAH) is a national organization that accredits hospitals and home health services. There are other organizations that will evaluate agencies on their standards of practice. In every state, licensure may or may not be required for practitioners and agencies providing home health services. If licensure is required in your state, it is important that the services and providers be licensed. Again, the Internet is an excellent resource for determining what is required in your state and what agencies meet those requirements

Certification is available from both national and local agencies. For example, the Certified Rehabilitation Counselor Commission (CRCC) is a national body that certifies rehabilitation counselors. This is a voluntary process for professionals desiring recognition of their education, experience, and ethical conduct. Certification and accreditation may not be mandated, but it is often indicative of a company or practitioner's commitment to best practices. In order to find home-based rehabilitation, it may also be necessary for an organization or practitioner to have specific certifications. For example, Medicare does certify providers of home health services and only those agencies will be reimbursed. When evaluating home-based rehabilitation providers, questions about the agency's accreditation, certification, and licensure are relevant.

In summary, home-based rehabilitation is a viable and increasingly common alternative to institutional care. Services provided in the home can facilitate recovery and can allow an individual to feel more comfortable by remaining in his or her home and community. With chronic illness or long-term disability, institutionalization can be avoided and important relationships in the home and community can be maintained. There are many services available in the home, from physical therapy to psychosocial education. When an individual receives treatment in the home, there is a greater likelihood of family involvement. This can create natural, long-lasting supports for the person with a disability or illness. The competent rehabilitation professional must be aware of options available through home-based rehabilitation.

References

Ades, P. A., Pashkow, F. J., Fletcher, G., Pina, I. L., Zohman, L. R., & Nestor, J. R. (2000). A controlled trial of cardiac rehabilitation in the home setting using its electrocardiographic and voice transtelephonic monitoring. *American Heart Journal, 139*, 543–548.

American Therapeutic Recreation Association. (2004). *Recreational therapy: an integral aspect of comprehensive health care.* Retrieved June 24, 2004, from http://www.atra-tr.org

Anderson, C., Mhurchu, S. N., Brown, P. M., & Carter, K. (2002). Stroke rehabilitation services to accelerate hospital discharge and provide home-based care: An overview and cost analysis. *Pharmacoeconomics, 20*(8), 537–552.

Andersson, A., Levin, L-A., Oberg, B., & Mansson, L. (2002). Health care and social welfare costs in home-based and hospital-based rehabilitation after stroke. *Scandinavian Journal of Caring Sciences, 16*, 386–392.

Bieze, J. (2004, May). Reconstruction outcomes reveal complexity of ACL-meniscus link. *Biomechanics, 21*.

California Board of Registered Nursing (CBRN). (2003). *What is the RN scope of practice?* Retrieved June 24, 2004, from www.rn.ca.gov

Center for Medicare & Medicaid Services. (2004). *Medicaid homepage.* Retrieved July 1, 2004, from http://www.cms.hhs.gov

Caplan, B., & Moelter, S. (2000). Stroke. In R. G. Frank & T. R. Elliott (Eds.), *Handbook of rehabilitation psychology* (pp. 75–108). Washington, DC: American Psychological Association.

Cook, A. M., & Hussey, S. M. (2002). *Assistive technologies: Principles and practice* (2nd ed.). St. Louis: Mosby.

Crotty, M., Whitehead, C. H., Gray, S., Finucane, P. M. (2001). Early discharge and home rehabilitation after hip fracture achieves functional improvements: A randomized controlled trial. *Clinical Rehabilitation, 16*, 406–413.

Ehman, J. K. (2000). Home-based cardiac rehabilitation. *Clinical Exercise Physiology, 2*(3), 165–167.

Geddes, J., & Chamberlain, M. A. (2003). Stroke community rehabilitation: A classification of four different types of service. *International Journal of Therapy and Rehabilitation, 10*(7), 299–304.

Medicare. (2004). *The official U.S. government site for people with Medicare.* Retrieved July 1, 2004, from http://www.medicare.gov

Sellwood, W., Thomas, C. S., Tarrier, N., Jones, S., Clewes, J., James, A., et al. (1999). A randomized controlled trial of home-based rehabilitation versus outpatient-based rehabilitation for patients suffering from chronic schizophrenia. *Social Psychiatry Psychiatric Epidemiology, 34,* 250–253.

Shrier, I. (2003). Home-based rehab equal to hospital-based rehab for CABG patients. *Physician & Sports Medicine, 31,* 6.

U.S. Department of Labor, Bureau of Labor Statistics. (2004). *Occupational outlook handbook.* Retrieved June 28, 2004, from http://bls.gov

Visiting Nurse Association (VNA). (2004). *Cost-effectiveness.* Retrieved June 24, 2004, from http://www.vnahc.org

VNA of Porter County. (2004). *What is the VNA?* Retrieved July 25, 2004, from http://www.vnaportercounty.org

Warrington, D., Cholowski, K., & Peters, D. (2003). Effectiveness of home-based cardiac rehabilitation for special-needs patients. *Journal of Advanced Nursing, 41,* 121–130.

Mental and Behavioral Health Care

David P. Moxley & Michael D. Paul

Human service professionals in a variety of settings, such as rehabilitation, community support, employment services, or medical programs, likely work with individuals coping with mental health issues like depression, anxiety disorders, cognitive disorders, or behavioral challenges. Mental health, or behavioral health care, is increasingly an interdisciplinary field in which professionals from multiple disciplines, with different credentials, interact in programmatic and team structures in the provision of diverse services. Contemporary mental health care itself is quite diverse and, despite the dominance of medical perspectives and medication, this area of human service also incorporates rehabilitation and social, developmental, and educational services in addition to rights protection and community support of those individuals coping with serious mental health challenges.

The principal aims of this chapter are to apprise human service professionals of the transformation of mental and behavioral health care and to clarify for them the multiple models that characterize contemporary systems of mental health. Another aim is to help human service professionals serve as more effective referral agents in linking the people they serve to mental health care.

Transformation of Mental Health Care

In recent years it has become difficult to speak of a national mental health policy, since some experts mark the end of federal involvement in mental health care with the Reagan administration's rescission of the Mental Health Systems Act of 1980. Prior to this rescission, between 1963 and 1980 there was considerable involvement of the federal government in efforts to create universal mental health care, and in the development of locality-based comprehensive community mental health centers (Levine, 1981). The idea of comprehensive centers was revolutionary at the time, and federal start-up grants provided the impetus for the development of some 700 centers, but the number of centers never reached levels required by projected needs (Rochefort & Logan, 1989).

According to national policy those federal funds would decline over a period of time, while local funds would substitute for the loss of federal dollars, but many communities simply closed programs rather than devote the dollars required to support the operation of their local community mental health centers (Levine, 1981). Even the authorization of rescue funds by Congress in the mid-1970s did not alleviate this problem. Not only was community mental health underfunded, but the idea that local communities would find support for their centers through state and local taxes, private insurance, and third-party payers such as Medicare and Medicaid was not realistic (Levine, 1981). Congress was also disappointed with the lack of accountability of community health centers for the support of people with serious mental illness who had been administratively discharged or diverted from state institutions (Grob, 1991; Mechanic, 1987).

Within federal mental health policy, comprehensive community mental health centers were to provide preventive services to people at risk of mental health problems, as well as rehabilitative services to people coping with serious mental illness. The original Kennedy legislation assumed that resources would follow people leaving state institutions, and that these individuals would access appropriate and adequate services through their local community mental health centers (Rochefort & Logan, 1989). The federal program assumed that state mental health authorities would reallocate funds from institutions to community services. This strategy did not materialize across the country and, in response, Congress pressured the National Institute for Mental Health to create a reform program, resulting in the *community support model* (National Institute of Mental Health, 1980; Turner & TenHoor, 1978). From the perspective of Congress, the failure of community mental health centers to work effectively with people coping with severe and persistent mental illness required this reform.

The Mental Health Systems Act of 1980 provided for the development of additional community mental health centers (Levine, 1981). It also incorporated other provisions, including: (1) the coordination of the boundaries between mental health service areas and medical health service areas to strengthen state public health systems; (2) augmentation of the role of state mental health authorities, since historically federal programs bypassed these important entities that were responsible for public care of people with serious mental illness; (3) the development of state mental health service plans, including specialized service plans for children and adolescents, the elderly, and people with chronic mental illness; (4) projects to prevent mental illness;

(5) a mental health patients' Bill of Rights; and (6) services for victims and survivors of rape.

The Reagan presidency prioritized intergovernmental relations, seeking to transfer to the states specific functions the administration felt did not legitimately belong with the federal government (Rochefort & Logan, 1989). The rescission of the Mental Health Systems Act was an expression of the administration's policy commitment to state control, and through the Omnibus Budget Reconciliation Act of 1981 (OBRA, Public Law 97-35) the administration consolidated federal programs into block grant funding. Indeed, the administration quickly reorganized 57 federal aid programs into 9 block grants. One of these grants was for alcohol, drug abuse, and mental health services and formed the Alcohol, Drug Abuse, and Mental Health Administration within the federal government. The administration was responsible for the block grant program in which state governments received lump sums to support the delivery of substance abuse treatment and mental health services.

The impact on community mental health centers was significant, if not substantial. Many experienced tremendous cutbacks, and many needed to realign services from a more preventive and psychotherapeutic approach to a model that favored medical management of people with serious mental illness, a community support approach, and a business management model. The connection between the state mental health authority and the community mental health center formed an important new relationship, since this state authority now enjoyed more power and control in the design and direction of mental health services (Rochefort & Logan, 1989).

State authority and control over mental health services was part of the spirit and substance of the Mental Health Systems Act and a central requirement of the ADAMH block grant (Rochefort & Logan, 1989). The empowerment of state mental health authorities shifted the policy focus of community mental health from universal provision of prevention-oriented services to a focus on the rehabilitation and community support of people coping with severe and persistent mental illness. Thus, during the 1980s, the development of local community support services became a salient aspect of state mental health plans (Tessler & Goldman, 1982).

The movement of community mental health centers to a business model became more pronounced in the 1970s, in the face of reduced federal funding and as state and local dollars became increasingly limited, particularly by inflation. The restructuring of hospitals and health systems in the 1980s and their movement towards managed care was another important factor in the emergence of a managerial paradigm in mental health. The Tax Equity and Fiscal Responsibility Act of 1982 (TEFRA) introduced cost containment as an essential aim of health care delivery and created a whole new system of reimbursement through diagnostic related groups (Gottlieb & Shtasel, 2001). In addition, the economic crisis of the 1980s forced corporations and private business to carefully examine and redesign their models of financing employee health care. These events ushered in behavioral managed care, the paradigm now prevalent in contemporary mental health systems.

SCOPE OF CONTEMPORARY MENTAL HEALTH CARE

While what constitutes positive mental health is somewhat ambiguous across the core mental health disciplines, the issues and challenges that compromise mental health are seen more often from a negative perspective, as diseases or disorders of individuals, the causes of which reside in the interaction of organic, constitutional, developmental, and environmental factors.

The Purpose of Public Mental Health Systems

The goal of most contemporary public mental health systems is to facilitate the functioning of service recipients who face serious mental illness, a condition that can compromise how people fulfill their roles, the extent to which people can be productive, and their quality of life.

Most public mental health systems do not prioritize services to people who experience adjustment problems or even acute mental health concerns—people who mental health providers may characterize as the "walking wounded"—and, therefore, these systems are less likely to offer psychotherapeutic or counseling services and more likely to offer rehabilitative ones. These systems target their resources on helping people who experience serious mental health concerns to function better and on integrating, as a principal strategy of service, medical, social, and rehabilitative care on an individualized basis for those people coping with serious psychiatric issues. But even with this focus and emphasis on long-term community support, most state governments and local mental health systems still face considerable challenge in the provision of high quality and comprehensive support (Dixon, Ridgely, & Goldman, 2001).

Other Mental Health Services within Communities

In contrast to public mental health systems, employer-sponsored mental health programs and employee assistance programs provide a range of mental health services and care, including recovery services for substance abuse, psychotherapy and medical care for stress-related problems, and counseling or psychoeducational services for workers experiencing work-related adjustment problems. There is an increasing integration of rehabilitation and work-related services with mental health care (Moxley & Finch, 2003). Mental health services organized under the auspices of nonprofit organizations, including freestanding community counseling centers, family services, or pastoral care centers offer psychotherapy, group work, and marital and family counseling. These entities likely charge recipients for services through a fee-for-service arrangement or accept certain insurances.

Other mental health options may exist within comprehensive health systems, including treatment for urgent or crisis situations through emergency rooms, inpatient psychiatric facilities, day hospitals, and medication management programs. Mental health services may be available through a network of independent practitioners who deliver psychotherapeutic, counseling, or family services on a fee-for-service basis. These practitioners may affiliate with groups, form clinics, or deliver services through their own solo private practices. Depending on licensure, mental health professionals delivering private care and services may include psychiatrists, psychologists, counselors, social workers, nurses, and rehabilitation counselors.

Most communities possess other mental health providers. School-based professionals, including psychologists, counselors, social workers, and nurses, serve important roles in mental health systems and often are pivotal in the formal assessment of children's mental health needs and diagnoses, particularly of those impairments or disorders that influence student role performance and learning. These professionals also may serve important roles in the management of behavioral issues within school settings, work closely with parents in the management of hyperactivity and attention disorders, and consult regularly with teachers about mental health issues (Allen-Meares, Washington, & Welsh, 1999). All of these professionals may play important roles in formulating individualized education plans for those students who experience learning challenges.

The Important Role of Primary Care Physicians in Mental Health Care

Primary care physicians increasingly deliver mental health services through managed care networks and family health clinics (Browne, 2001). Primary care physicians may provide medication for anxiety disorders or depression, and they may help patients cope with the overall health consequences of mental health concerns such as sleep disorders, changes in weight and eating patterns, and addictive behavior. These practitioners often are the most likely to detect early signs of depression, anxiety, cognitive disorders, or substance use. They may manage mental health concerns as part of primary health care and they may provide case management when the plan of care calls for referral to more specialized medical services (Browne, 2001).

The demarcation between physical health and mental health is increasingly more ambiguous, particularly within primary health care, where physicians may use somatic procedures to manage mental health concerns and use mental health procedures to manage the consequences of physical illness. From a primary care perspective, health and mental health are closely related, and justifying their integration is a holistic orientation that guides total health-care delivery.

Informal Aspects of Mental Health Care

While these formal services form the core mental health service capacity of most communities, the scope of care also incorporates two critical elements: care and linkage services that informal caregivers provide to people in crisis or need, and groups or organizations that offer peer or mutual support and self-help resources. Informal care providers such as pastors or clergy, teachers, lawyers, and day-care providers can form the frontline response in detecting mental health concerns in children, adolescents, and adults, offering brief consultation and counseling, and referring people to appropriate services. Through early identification and linkage roles these individuals can help people with mental health concerns connect with formal mental health services. Thus, informal care is not of lower value. This form of care recognizes that although community-based professionals who interact daily with people in need may not be primary providers of mental health services, nonetheless they do pay close attention to the emotional, social, and interpersonal adjustment of the people they serve.

Peer and mutual support resources also serve as a frontline response for addressing mental health needs and concerns (Moxley & Mowbray, 1997). These resources may address both the causes and consequences of mental health issues, and they help people break through some of the serious secondary effects of psychiatric concerns such as isolation, stigma, and social marginalization (Mowbray, Moxley, & Van Tosh, 2001). In some ways, peer and mutual support may constitute core mental health service capacity. Through these resources, people access social and emotional support, community support (such as through a drop-in center), information and referral, and social action or community development opportunities (Mowbray & Moxley, 1997; Watkins & Callicutt, 1997).

Self-help may reveal the gaps and limitations of the formal mental health system. People coping with serious mental health concerns may create their own programs, support systems, and ideologies guiding their recovery and, as a consequence, augment the existing system of services. Self-help resources for substance-abuse recovery, phobias and anxiety disorders, manic-depressive illness, schizophrenia, and dementia provide communities with multiple options for mutual support and personal development. People labeled as seriously mentally ill, for example, may organize social action projects through which they meet the housing, educational, vocational development, employment, or socialization needs of their members. Affiliation, mutual support, and support for self-care may be some of the most important mental health options within particular communities, ones that formal mental health plans likely do not incorporate, given the medicalization of mental health care and the use of medical necessity as a criterion for controlling entry into service.

The Role of Law Enforcement Personnel in Mental Health Services

Law enforcement professionals are likely underappreciated for their mental health roles. Police personnel interact with people with mental health concerns on a daily basis. They often help people coping with domestic violence, and they can be the first responders in family emergencies. Deputy sheriffs or police officers sometimes escort people to psychiatric emergency units. Law enforcement officials often interact with homeless people and help them access services. Unfortunately, the criminalization of people with mental illness may result in their confinement to jails for minor offenses. In some situations, jails may now stand as a community's first line of response in meeting the mental health needs of people who may be least able to care for themselves. These persons may commit minor infractions simply because they possess limited self-direction. As a consequence, human service professionals may find themselves literally reaching out to people coping with serious mental health disorders who are in jail, or working directly with law enforcement personnel to facilitate a person's entry into services.

Disasters and Mental Health Services

One other critical but often unappreciated aspect of mental health care involves a community's coping with disasters. Natural disasters can produce serious mental health consequences. People can experience numerous and substantial losses involving the deaths of loved ones and neighbors, the destruction of housing and property, and displacement. Recent incidents of violence demonstrate the serious mental health consequences for victims and first responders alike. Mobilization of community responses to disasters and incidents of violence incorporate a mental health component, and mental health professionals often are frontline providers of grief and loss counseling, critical incident debriefing, crisis intervention, and brief therapy. The consequences of disaster and violence can induce delayed stress and trauma and can accelerate the need for mental health care long after the occurrence of the primary event. Increasingly, local mental health programs and services are key elements of emergency preparedness.

THE DOMINANT PARADIGM WITHIN CONTEMPORARY MENTAL HEALTH CARE

While there are multiple models of mental health care operating within any given community, there is one principal overarching paradigm that establishes the pattern for mental health care as a whole. A paradigm involves an acceptable pattern of care that finds legitimacy within the mental health field. Today, that pattern of care is most likely a managerial one (Talbot & Hales, 2001).

Now dominant within state and local mental health care as well as within the private sector, the *management paradigm* possesses several distinctive properties. Central to this paradigm is the economic assumption of the scarcity of resources, the ongoing and limitless needs of mental health care, and the necessity of rationalizing and prioritizing these needs by assigning the most (and perhaps only) priority to those consistent with medical necessity.

The management paradigm prevalent in contemporary approaches to behavioral managed care establishes a rational system of necessity, priority, accountability, and measurability for mental health services in which utilization, quality, cost control and management, and oversight constitute principal values (Yohanna & O'Mahoney, 2001). The management paradigm supersedes most other models or paradigms, since it focuses on the control and management of dollars and the financing of mental health care. A management paradigm places control of the system under a centralized authority, which then seeks to stimulate price competition among multiple providers through competitive bidding, contracting for services, and accountability for results. Unlike bureaucratic control, the management paradigm introduces economic considerations into the configuration of mental health services and seeks to lower costs, ration services, and substitute more costly services with less costly ones.

Human service professionals referring clients to mental health care will experience firsthand the consequences of the managerial paradigm. It is likely they will have to frame medical necessity at the point of intake and be mindful of the payment source for care. Potentially they will have to support the movement of recipients through triage and assessment systems that possess strong utilization controls. Some individuals will experience access barriers and considerable waits for service while others will receive medication and medical management solely to control symptoms. Other social, interpersonal, or emotional needs may fail to receive attention and priority within this paradigm.

Multiple Models of Mental Health Care

The managerial paradigm is so entrenched within the contemporary mental health care system that its pattern serves as a template for framing most models of mental health care, including the medical and neo-medical models, psychotherapy, rehabilitation, and community support. Most contemporary models are time limited, utilization focused, quality managed, and outcome driven. Human service professionals referring clients to mental health systems, either private or public, should be mindful of why they are referring recipients, and of the intended outcomes they seek to achieve through referral to this kind of care.

The Medical and Neo-Medical Models

The medical model views mental illness and mental health problems as disease states that require management like any other disease. Thus, within the medical model, people with mental health problems are sick and require diagnosis, treatment plans, active treatment, and vigilant monitoring under the guidance of a physician. Recovery within this model means that people will return to a level of functioning they enjoyed prior to the onset of their disease. This often is difficult or impossible when the situation constitutes a serious mental illness that induces substantial disability, such as in cases of cognitive or emotional disorders.

The neo-medical model incorporates an appreciation for multiple causes of mental health concerns, including metabolic, genetic, developmental, and environmental ones. This paradigm implicates a constitutional susceptibility to mental disease that environmental stress may trigger and exacerbate, particularly when individuals who possess such susceptibility experience serious and multiple life events. Of course, medication as a way of managing mental health concerns dominates this model, which also incorporates psychotherapeutic or rehabilitative options as secondary strategies to reduce stress or facilitate coping.

The Solution-Focused and Brief Treatment Model

The managerial paradigm has also influenced psychotherapy as a model within mental health service delivery. While relationship formation remains central to psychotherapy as a corrective interpersonal experience that can restructure emotions, attitudes, and behavior, long-term and insight-oriented treatment is no longer the treatment of choice, with more solution-focused and brief-treatment options now populating mental health care. Given the reality that managed care networks will only support a limited number of sessions, psychotherapy increasingly incorporates a short-term perspective in which brief treatment focuses on the achievement of specific aims.

Within solution-oriented and brief treatment, the therapist quickly forms a relationship with the patient and mobilizes his or her coping resources to immediately address a challenge that induces the need at hand. Therapists focus the attention of their patients on the search for solutions for the issues they find most pressing, mindful that the resolution of these issues will help their patients function better in their present situations and help them learn enough about themselves to address and resolve future issues with some competence (Fanger, 1995).

Thus, within this model, the therapist is actively managing the treatment situation, setting discrete and highly measurable goals, and using treatment procedures to stimulate the patient's coping, action, and problem-solving capacities. Ultimately, from the perspective of this model, the successful resolution of the challenge or issue at hand and also the patient's future coping ability are outcomes of the therapist's stimulation of coping, action, and problem solving.

Solution-focused brief treatment is a flexible model of psychotherapy. It facilitates reflection, action, and decision making and focuses on helping people change their behavior and their lifestyles. This model can incorporate crisis intervention with the aim of helping people achieve stable functioning during periods in which they experience considerable stress and, as a consequence, may manifest emotional and behavioral instability. By incorporating emotional catharsis and cognitive restoration, people experiencing crises can achieve a sense of stability and then focus on finding solutions to resolve the immediate difficulties they face (Slaiken, 1990).

The Rehabilitation and the Community Support Models

The rehabilitation model is likely reserved for people who experience psychiatric disability as a result of serious and persistent mental illness (Stroul, 1993). The determination of severity involves the fulfillment of several criteria, including a major psychiatric diagnosis typically involving a thought, affective, or personality disorder (as indicated by the Diagnostic Statistical Manual), duration of at least a year, and substantial deficits in personal or social functioning. People who are seriously or persistently mentally ill require considerable support and require an array of integrated services including medical, housing, vocational, and social support.

The psychiatric rehabilitation model focuses exclusively on meeting the needs of people coping with severe and persistent mental illness. Its mission is to help people to achieve success in daily life with continuous professional and peer support. By helping people who are coping with severe and persistent mental illness to achieve specific goals and acquire the skills and supports they need to achieve those goals (e.g., employment), psychiatric rehabilitation focuses on assisting people in overcoming personal and environmental barriers to success in environments in which they want to function, such as achieving a higher education or performing effectively in an employment setting.

A sound psychiatric rehabilitation program is supportive, matches support to the needs and preferences of participants, and integrates professional and peer support. In addition, a sound psychiatric rehabilitation program identifies and builds on the strengths of participants and helps them gain the knowledge and understanding of mental illness that they need in order to manage their own health and well-being. Psychiatric rehabilitation has a practical focus on helping people achieve those outcomes that enhance their quality of life. Thus, still another property of a sound psychiatric rehabilitation program is the support it offers participants in the achievement of practical outcomes of daily life such as housing success, vocational development, employment, and friendships and social interaction.

One of the core program elements of psychiatric rehabilitation is the clubhouse (Jackson, 2001). The clubhouse is a consumer-centered option in which people coping with severe and persistent mental illness have opportunities to participate in a work-ordered day, gain the support of their peers, and engage in vocational development through informal yet structured activities. Rather than being a patient or client, participants are members of the club, which requires the involvement of everyone so it can operate successfully, maintain a schedule of support and vocational development activities, and offer avocational opportunities such as recreation, cultural enrichment, and health-related education.

People who have histories of frequent inpatient care may benefit from assertive community treatment. Using assertive outreach and enhanced consumer-centered services, teams with integrated treatment plans can offer frequent and consistent support to individuals in their homes and in agency settings. Assertive community treatment teams maintain low caseloads, visit quite frequently with people they serve, offer enhanced monitoring, and help people manage their daily lives. The assertive community treatment team helps its clients remain outside of inpatient care, control or otherwise manage their symptoms, and enhance their quality of life.

Many professionals have held nihilistic perspectives about the rehabilitative potential of people coping with severe and persistent mental illness. Contemporary theory and practice in psychiatric rehabilitation eschews this nihilism and emphasizes the aim of recovery (Spaniol, Gagne, & Koehler, 2003). Breakthroughs in medication and its management, new forms of consumer-centered and consumer-driven support, disability management, and innovations in rehabilitation reframe the treatment of severe and persistent mental illness. However, rather than conceiving of recovery as a return to premorbid functioning, psychiatric rehabilitation recognizes the indelible changes the lived experience of mental illness makes in a person's self-concept, identity, and life direction (Deegan, 1997).

Movement through the experience of mental illness can create a new identity, foster new skills and perspectives, and influence how a person relates to the world and to other people. Recovery thus means the formation of a new sense of self—a self that possesses new goals and aspirations based on a sense of efficacy in the management of one's illness. Recovery services, therefore, may involve peer and mutual support, new forms of case management, and group and individual counseling, all of which help the person build a new identity, engage in self-care, and formulate a life purpose (Spaniol et al., 2003).

People recovering from severe and persistent mental illness not only must deal with the primary aspects of the mental illness but also must cope with its social consequences, including social reaction and stigma. Unemployment, barriers to involvement in higher education, and discrimination in daily life are just some of the serious issues people face. A sound program of psychiatric rehabilitation will help people address these issues in their daily lives. Advocacy and rights protection are central elements of any sound program of service.

Severe and persistent mental illness is one of the most complex mental health challenges. It can be even more complex when individuals are coping with concurrent substance use problems, homelessness, and other health concerns. A comprehensive assessment will help people coping with severe and persistent mental illness identify the full spectrum of their needs and facilitate the diversification of person-centered plans to incorporate the various services and supports they require.

Substance use services may include mutual and peer support in the form of a step program, harm reduction contingencies, enhanced education about the health consequences of substance use, and relapse prevention. People at risk of homelessness or who are homeless at time of entry into service may require enhanced supportive housing options and assertive outreach.

In many communities, a local mental health authority may integrate multiple psychiatric rehabilitation programs into a community support system (Moxley, 2002). The National Institute of Mental Health introduced the community support model in the late 1970s, when Congress was disappointed with the responsiveness of community mental health centers to people with serious mental illness. The model was introduced as a reform of community mental health centers as a result of deinstitutionalization, at a time when people with serious mental illness were becoming increasingly visible in local communities as they were going without the fulfillment of basic needs.

The suggested reform prioritized the system values of service access, adequacy, comprehensiveness, and coordination with the aim of creating locality-based community systems of support. These systems were to integrate medical, crisis, housing, advocacy, and social services for people coping with serious mental illness under the auspices of local mental health authorities. Today many local mental health systems maintain community-support systems; but the model itself has transformed from a medical and social-service entity to one incorporating a range of rehabilitation-focused opportunities, including vocational development, employment support, housing options, and recovery-based services (Moxley, 2002).

TYPICAL REFERRAL QUESTIONS AND ISSUES

It is likely human service personnel will be helping the people they serve to navigate mental health services, particularly if they serve in case-management roles. Indeed, human service personnel may serve as frontline advocates in helping people identify their mental health needs; assess their situations; and plan and implement referral, linkage, and follow-along activities to ensure the delivery of appropriate and timely care.

The Importance of Orientation and Relationship Building

Perhaps two of the most important activities human service personnel can undertake on an ongoing basis involve orienting themselves to what is available within their communities and maintaining relationships with important formal and informal providers of mental health care. Important questions for human service personnel related to orientation and relationship building include:

1. What is the scope of mental health services within the community? What services do public mental health authorities support? What pri-

vate resources exist within clinics, group practices, schools, and medical centers?

2. What is the scope of informal mental health resources within the community? In particular, what self-help, mutual-support, and peer-support resources exist, and for what mental health issues or needs? What voluntary groups or organizations advocate the fulfillment of mental health needs of particular groups, such as infants, children, adolescents, young adults, adults, and seniors?

3. To what extent do primary and specialized health programs incorporate mental health services? Do these programs sponsor specialized clinics for specific mental health concerns, such as anxiety disorders or depression?

4. Does a community support system exist within the community for people coping with severe and persistent psychiatric disabilities? If so, what are its key elements and programs? If not, where are people with serious mental illness getting the support they need, or are they going without such support?

5. Do major employers sponsor employee assistance programs, and what services do these entities offer?

6. With whom should the human service professional form relationships, such as police officers, sheriffs, teachers and physicians, day care operators, or attorneys?

The Importance of Assessment and Care Planning

Those questions that illuminate the scope of mental health services within a given community are particularly important as human service professionals assess the needs of the people they serve. Assessing the mental health needs of the people these professionals serve and identifying these needs within the action plans they formulate are important steps in ensuring that needs are recognized and fulfilled. Important assessment and care-planning questions are:

1. What are the principal needs that exist within the human service professional's caseload, and to what extent do recipients possess urgent unfulfilled needs? Do recipients have anxiety disorders or symptoms of depression? Are they experiencing phobias? Do they experience cognitive problems, memory lapses, or emotional concerns? If these problems are not severe but nonetheless interfere with daily tasks and activities, the professional may want to facilitate the referral of the people they serve to primary health-care services.

2. Are the issues recipients face serious ones, and does the human service professional sense that a major psychiatric problem of long duration compromises recipient functioning? If so, the professional may

want to consider referral to community psychiatric programs or community support systems.

3. In cases where people are dealing with the social consequences of a mental health concern, are there mutual-support, self-help, peer-support, or advocacy alternatives within the local community?

4. To what extent can the human service professional incorporate a mental health screen or assessment into a comprehensive case-management needs assessment and service-planning process?

The Importance of Service Advocacy

Human service professionals serve in frontline roles, where they often maintain strong relationships with the people they serve. They may be a recipient's principal advocate for service access and utilization. Important service advocacy questions include:

1. To what extent are there barriers to mental health service access within the particular community? Are there barriers to particular services such as long waiting lists, unjustified criteria for entry, and criteria that can disqualify recipients?

2. What resources, such as legal and advocacy services, can facilitate the removal of access and utilization barriers?

3. Do mental health professionals within the particular community have the skills and competencies to address the mental health needs of particular recipients? Are there specialized referral pathways the human service professional can identify to meet mental health needs that the local system cannot readily address in a competent manner?

4. Do major gaps within the mental health system limit how the system addresses the needs of particular groups of recipients? If so, to what extent should human service professionals take action to develop appropriate programs?

5. Do people who represent the most vulnerable in the community have access to appropriate mental health care? Are there accessible, appropriate, and adequate services for people who are homeless? Are there appropriate services for people who are coping with complex situations, such as homelessness compounded by serious mental illness?

6. Are there mental health professionals who are willing to reach out to particular individuals living on the streets, participating in other programs, or residing in shelters or homes?

7. Do assertive outreach and linkage activities exist within mobile teams?

The Importance of Service Monitoring and Vigilant Oversight

Once human service professionals have helped recipients gain entry into mental health care, they must remain vigilant in their oversight of the provision of services, particularly when the service system is managed for medical necessity. Following are important questions relevant to service monitoring and oversight:

1. Are the needs of recipients addressed in an adequate manner, and do recipients find the services beneficial, particularly in helping them function in settings or environments of choice?

2. Is the mental health program actively managing the treatment plan and ensuring that the recipient gets services of high quality?

3. Are other services substituting for what recipients want or need? Does medication substitute for other forms of more expensive but nonetheless more effective treatment?

4. Are recipients who face long-term mental health challenges forced into a short-term model of care? Is there a good match between the recipient, his or her needs, and the treatment?

5. Are recipients who face long-term mental health challenges receiving a consumer-centered or consumer-driven program of comprehensive services and supports designed to facilitate the achievement of a rehabilitative or recovery goal?

SUMMARY AND CONCLUSION

Mental health care within most communities has undergone considerable transformation as managed-care responses replace entitlement-oriented, comprehensive systems of geographically based mental health care. The community mental health center of old, in which a nonprofit entity received federal funding to start up an array of preventive and long-term care resources, no longer exists in many communities. Whether these centers were successful and whether their paradigm was effective is open to question. However, the mandate to provide universal mental health care was central to these centers.

This mandate has changed dramatically or it has simply evaporated. Behavioral health-care entities seek to integrate multiple models of care within a managerial paradigm. Universal access to mental health care is not the aim. Rather, the aim is to manage the provision of mental health care through highly structured procedures guided by a principle of medical necessity. Through this more selective approach, behavioral health-care entities ration services and contain costs. They seek to target services on those individuals who require them the most and to limit the temporal aspect of care as much as possible.

Human service professionals must interact with these systems, being mindful that getting mental health care for the people they serve may be an arduous task. As a consequence of the managerial paradigm, human service professionals may find themselves advocating more for the people they serve, finding alternative mental health resources, and relying more than ever on self-help, mutual-support, and peer-support options.

References

Allen-Meares, P., Washington, R. O., & Welsh, B. (1999). *Social work services in schools*. Englewood Cliffs, NJ: Prentice-Hall.

Browne, J. (2001). Changing roles of mental health professionals. In J. A. Talbot & R. E. Hales (Eds.), *Textbook of administrative psychiatry: New concepts for a changing behavioral health system* (2nd ed., pp. 181–192). Washington, DC: American Psychiatric Publishing.

Deegan, P. E. (1997). Recovery and empowerment for people with psychiatric disabilities. *Social Work in Health Care, 25*(3), 11–24.

Dixon, L., Ridgely, S., & Goldman, H. (2001). The evolving behavioral health system: The public sector: Past, present, and future. In J. A. Talbot & R. E. Hales (Eds.), *Textbook of administrative psychiatry: New concepts for a changing behavioral health system* (2nd ed., pp. 17–26). Washington, DC: American Psychiatric Publishing.

Fanger, M. (1995). Brief therapies. In R. Edwards & J. Hopps (Eds.), *Encyclopedia of social work* (pp. 245–267). Washington, DC: NASW Press.

Gottlieb, G. L., & Shtasel, D. L. (2001). The private sector: History, current status, and future implications. In J. A. Talbot & R. E. Hales (Eds.), *Textbook of administrative psychiatry: New concepts for a changing behavioral health system* (2nd ed., pp. 9–16). Washington, DC: American Psychiatric Publishing.

Grob, G. N. (1991). *From asylum to community: Mental health policy in modern America*. Princeton, NJ: Princeton University.

Jackson, R. L. (2001). *The clubhouse model*. Belmont, CA: Wadsworth/Thomson.

Levine, M. (1981). *The history and politics of community mental health*. New York: Oxford University.

Mechanic, D. (1987). Correcting misconceptions in mental health policy: Strategies for improved care of the mentally ill. *Milbank Quarterly, 65*(2), 203–230.

Mowbray, C. T., & Moxley, D. P. (1997). A framework for organizing consumer roles as providers of psychiatric rehabilitation. In C. T. Mowbray, D. P. Moxley, C. A. Jasper, & L. L. Howell (Eds.), *Consumers as providers in psychiatric rehabilitation* (pp. 35–44). Columbia, MD: IAPSRS.

Mowbray, C. T., Moxley, D. P., & Van Tosh, L. (2001). Changing roles for primary consumers in community psychiatry. In J. A. Talbot & R. E. Hales (Eds.), *Textbook of administrative psychiatry: New concepts for a changing behavioral health system* (2nd ed., pp. 201–210). Washington, DC: American Psychiatric Publishing.

Moxley, D. P. (2002). The emergence and attributes of second-generation community support systems for persons with serious mental illness: Implications for case management. *Journal of Social Work in Disability and Rehabilitation, 1*(2), 25–52.

Moxley, D. P., & Finch, J. R. (2003*). Sourcebook of rehabilitation and mental health practice*. New York: Kluwer Academic/Plenum.

Moxley, D. P., & Mowbray, C. T. (1997). Consumers as providers: Forces and factors legitimizing role innovation in psychiatric rehabilitation. In C. T. Mowbray, D. P. Moxley, C. A. Jasper, & L. L. Howell (Eds.), *Consumers as providers in psychiatric rehabilitation* (pp. 2–34). Columbia, MD: IAPSRS.

National Institute of Mental Health. (1980). *Guidelines for community support programs*. Washington, DC: Author.

Rochefort, D. A., & Logan, B. M. (1989). The alcohol, drug abuse, and mental health block grant: Origins, design, and impact. In D. Rochefort (Ed.), *Handbook on mental health policy in the United States* (pp. 143–171). New York: Greenwood Press.

Slaiken, K. (1990). *Crisis intervention: A handbook for practice and research* (2nd ed.). Boston: Allyn & Bacon.

Spaniol, L., Gagne, C., & Koehler, M. (2003). The recovery framework in rehabilitation and mental health. In D. Moxley & J. Finch (Eds.), *The sourcebook of rehabilitation and mental health practice* (pp. 37–50). New York: Kluwer Academic/Plenum.

Stroul, B. (1993). Rehabilitation in community support systems. In R. W. Flexer & P. Solomon (Eds.), *Psychiatric rehabilitation in practice* (pp. 45–61). Boston: Andover.

Talbot, J. A., & Hales, R. E. (Eds.). (2001). *Textbook of administrative psychiatry: New concepts for a changing behavioral health system* (2nd ed.). Washington, DC: American Psychiatric Publishing.

Tessler, R. C., & Goldman, H. H. (1982). *The chronically mentally ill: Assessing community support programs.* Cambridge, MA: Harper & Row.

Turner, J. C., & TenHoor, W. J. (1978). The NIMH Community Support Program: Pilot approach to a needed social reform. *Schizophrenia Bulletin, 4*(3), 319–348.

Watkins, T. R., & Callicutt, J. W. (1997). Self-help and advocacy groups in mental health. In T. R. Watkins & J. W. Callicutt (Eds.), *Mental health policy and practice today* (pp. 146–162). Thousand Oaks, CA: Sage.

Yohanna, D., & O'Mahoney, M. T. (2001). Behavioral health network establishment. In J. A. Talbot & R. E. Hales (Eds.), *Textbook of administrative psychiatry: New concepts for a changing behavioral health system* (2nd ed., pp. 97–105). Washington, DC: American Psychiatric Publishing.

HIV/AIDS Services

D. Shane Koch & Chris Wilkie

Coordinating services for persons with HIV/AIDS disabilities can be particularly challenging for rehabilitation professionals. There are several broad areas that must be addressed in order to assure that appropriate services are provided: first, testing, involving both risk reduction sessions and intervention, may be particularly daunting to rehabilitation professionals unfamiliar with the testing process and procedures, yet accurate diagnosis at the earliest stages of the disease is critical to ensuring enhanced rehabilitation and medical and vocational outcomes.

Next, when persons have been identified as being infected by the disease, they require substantial medical and psychosocial intervention over the course of the disability to stabilize the progression of the illness to the greatest degree possible, and to assist individuals in adjusting to the impact of the infection. These interventions are provided by a complex array of specialized service providers across all of the service sectors, and rehabilitation counselors may be unaware of where to find specific service providers.

After initial adjustment, individuals are increasingly able to live full and productive lives, including participation in competitive employment. Consequently, rehabilitation professionals working with this population must be able to access the necessary objective data and information about the infection and the disease process to anticipate the needs of the individuals as well as to combat the tremendous stigma and discrimination that have been present among the general public and employers in response to these disabilities. Finally, even when they do not have consumers diagnosed with HIV or AIDS, there is an obligation for rehabilitation professionals to be prepared to provide general prevention services to all clients who may be at risk for infection.

57

Rehabilitation researchers have increasingly recognized the need for vocational rehabilitation services for this population. As medical interventions designed to remediate the negative consequences of HIV/AIDS have improved and life expectancies have lengthened, rehabilitation counselors are ethically and professionally obligated to prepare themselves to provide vocational rehabilitation services for this population (Garcia, Froelich, Cartwright, Letiecq, Forrester, & Mueller, 1999; Glenn, Ford, Moore, & Hollar, 2003). Fesko (2001) supports this point by observing that the once prevalent myth of HIV diagnosis as an immediate death sentence has been forever overturned, and that rehabilitation counselors are being asked to recognize that most individuals who acquire HIV/AIDS are most often young and employable with many productive years ahead of them. Further, McReynolds (2001) reports that employment for persons with HIV/AIDS may be even more than life enhancing; it leads to better long-term health. Clearly, there is a substantial benefit to be accrued by ensuring that vocational rehabilitation counselors fulfill their roles and obligations to assist these consumers in achieving their employment goals.

However, there is a darker side to their obligations as well. It is the duty of the counselor to assist the consumer in weighing both the pros and cons of the employment goal. The counselor must be sensitive to the fact that while the job may satisfy the consumer's need for self-worth, independence, and financial success, it can also be detrimental for the individual concerning other aspects of life. The counselor has a duty to point out the fact that an increase of income could potentially affect current services and treatments that the consumer may be receiving for little or no out-of-pocket money. This is particularly important in sliding-scale models. The counselor's main role is to find a balance between the client's desires and the professional obligation to acknowledge and respond to the reality of each consumer's unique situation.

HIV/AIDS: BACKGROUND

The medical community first began to identify, and intervene in the lives of persons with, human immunodeficiency virus (HIV) in the early 1980s. In 1981, physicians began to notice that young, gay men were acquiring very rare disorders that would be wholly unexpected given their age and health status (Powell, 1996). Two conditions were particularly suspect. The first was caused in connection with an unusual parasitic infection of the lungs identified as *Pneumocystis carini* that resulted in pneumocystis carini pneumonia (PCP). The second was Kaposi's sarcoma, a rare and deadly form of cancer involving lesions that could potentially affect both external tissues and internal organs throughout the body (Falvo, 1999). Given the potential life-threatening consequences of these infections, medical professionals rushed to identify the factors that may have precipitated these disorders.

The threat produced by the infections themselves produced frightening public reactions, and the association with gay men produced a double layer of stigma that resulted in reluctance on the part of many public health authorities, public servants, and health-care professionals to investigate the problem and to provide resources for research and intervention. Legislators—U.S. Senator Jesse Helms was a prominent example—were extremely reluctant to provide public resources to assist those who were perceived as deviant or immoral, and this substantially hampered a coherent national response for some time (Powell, 1996). In 1981 *The New York Times* quoted Dr. Curran of the CDC as saying there was "no apparent danger to non-homosexuals from contagion. The best evidence against contagion," he said, "is that no cases have been reported to date outside the homosexual community or in women." At this point, all public health advisors involved in research involving the disease where convinced that the infection was limited to persons who were gay. This was illustrated best in the original name given to the virus in 1982, GRID (Gay Related Immune Deficiency). The outcome from these initial assumptions carried repercussions regarding the general public's beliefs and stereotypes that are still being felt today. It is critical for rehabilitation professionals to recognize that both consumers' negative feelings and emotions about the disease itself and the stereotypes held by the general public can become tremendous barriers to effective service coordination for this population (Glenn et al., 2003; McReynolds, 2001).

As resources for research became available, data indicated that both of the conditions that had been initially identified were present only among individuals whose immune system had been greatly compromised. At this point it was noted that *any* individual's immune system could be compromised by this virus and that it was not a gay-related disease. In 1983 the name of the virus was changed from GRID to AIDS (Acquired Immune Deficiency Syndrome). In addition, the infections began to be described as "opportunistic infections" because these conditions would not occur in individuals with fully functioning immune systems. The cause of the immune system breakdown that provided the "opportunity" was discovered to be a retroviral infection that specifically destroyed T4 lymphocytes, rendering infected individuals' immune systems much less capable of responding to bacterial and viral infection. While several researchers were involved in describing the virus, there is some debate about who "discovered" it. The virus itself came to be called HIV, and the array of subsequent opportunistic infections began to be described as AIDS (Falvo, 1999; Kalichman, 1997).

HIV/AIDS AS A DISABILITY

Formal recognition of HIV and AIDS as disabilities occurred with the passage of the Americans with Disabilities Act in 1990. Federal protections for this class of persons with disabilities are particularly important due to the extreme potential for discrimination throughout society, but particularly in the workplace. Glenn et al. (2003) and McReynolds (2001) insisted that one of the most significant barriers to achieving employment outcomes for this population was the lack of knowledge about their rights as persons with disabilities, coupled with employer resistance to hire based on fear. If effective services are to be provided, rehabilitation counselors must become familiar with the resources available to educate themselves and their consumers about specific accommodations that are appropriate and reasonable.

Fortunately, accommodations that are typically utilized with other long-term, chronic disabilities are also appropriate when persons with HIV/AIDS begin to experience the physical and psychological consequences of their disabilities (Hunt, 1996). Hunt indicated that accommodations for this population often included flexible hours, scheduling, sick leave, close access to restrooms, working at home, and part-time employment. Fesko (2001) stressed the importance of educating consumers about their employment rights, and this is a critical role for vocational rehabilitation counselors to serve within their communities. Some examples of the services that rehabilitation counselors may need to provide include information about employer obligations to provide leave, education about federal disability law, and accurate evaluation and documentation of functional limitations and ability.

Acquisition and Risk Factors

Rubin and Roessler (2001) have reviewed the importance of addressing perception of threat as a potential barrier to providing and accessing services for consumers with disabilities. Due to the anxiety associated with potentially contracting HIV/AIDS, rehabilitation counselors need to be aware of the actual risk associated with working with this population so as to alleviate their own fears, provide educational support to consumers, and address employer concerns. Fear of contagion can have a direct impact on counselor effectiveness by impeding counselor empathy as well as creating misperceptions regarding potential ethical obligations arising from the duty to warn (Garcia et al., 1999). Ensuring a safe work environment as well as protecting other service providers is easily accomplished when counselors have a basic understanding of transmission methods of the virus.

Transmission of HIV occurs when there is a point of exit from an infected individual, a potential to transport the virus to another person, and an entry point into a second body (Powell, 1996). Sexual intercourse is the most common mode of transmission, while injection drug use is the most efficient mode of transmission outside of a blood transfusion. In 1985 the United States started screening all donated blood for HIV. Today in the United States there is little to no threat of HIV infection through a blood transfusion.

Other potential modes of transmission can include accidental needle sticks, mucus membrane exposures, or any exposure to infected body fluids. Not all body fluids pose a threat to HIV transmission. The body fluids to be concerned with are blood, semen, vaginal secretions, and breast milk. The exception to this is any body fluid that becomes contaminated with one of the above fluids. Exposure to infected body fluids poses a variety of risks depending on how the individual was exposed. Consequently, casual contact with an infected individual will not pose a risk to professionals, employers or other consumers.

However, to fight the spread of all infectious diseases, professionals engaged in HIV prevention education have stressed the use of "universal precautions" to assure that everyone is treated as a potential risk and to minimize the opportunity for any exposure. Universal precautions generally include:

> wearing latex gloves when hands may come in contact with body substances, wearing masks or protective eye coverings when there is a chance for body substances to splash on the face, washing hands frequently, especially scrubbing under the fingernails, disposing of uncapped needles and syringes only in specially made, puncture-resistant containers, and discarding trash and linens in closed plastic bags. (Kalichman, 1997, p. 175)

Course of the Disability

According to Kalichman (1998), the most often used model for understanding the course of HIV/AIDS includes four stages. Stage one involves acute HIV infection and either aysmptomatic or acute viral infection reactions. In this stage it is likely that people do not know that they are infected or that they have a brief period of flu-like symptoms followed by perceived recovery. Stage two involves latent infection, when a person is infectious but typically experiences no symptoms or related physiological or psychological consequences. In stage three there is typically chronic lymphadenopathy; and in stage four consumers begin to experience significant negative consequences, including weight loss, fever, chronic diarrhea, HIV-induced neuropathology, peripheral neuropathy, opportunistic infections, and HIV-associated tumors.

Individuals in stage one or individuals who have engaged in risky behaviors (e.g., unprotected sex or multiple partners) are likely to benefit from screening, prevention education, and risk-reduction sessions where testing has been conducted. Those in stage two are also likely to benefit from services provided in stage one. If diagnosis of HIV has been confirmed, counselors will need to work on providing direct interventions regarding adjustment to the disability, and they will need to coordinate services directed toward assisting the consumer in educating family members and potential employers about the possible disability issues related to the diagnosis.

Finally, counselors need to ensure the mental health status of the newly diagnosed individual. A new diagnosis can create temporary periods of depression, isolation, and possibly suicide ideation. The counselor will need to assess clients' comfort and understanding of the diagnosis to ensure that consumers are not at any risk of hurting themselves or others. The counselor can expect that consumers in both stages one and two will begin to receive regular medical services, including blood screens to assess T-cell count and viral load as well as general physical exams to assist in detecting initial complications and potential movement into stages three and four.

During stage three consumers may begin to feel significant effects from HIV infection, including some fatigue and lymphadenopathy. Stage four is when critical medical complications begin, and rehabilitation counselors will necessarily become more involved in collaborating with their consumers and the consumer network of related services. This is to ensure that they have the necessary supports and resources to maintain the quality of life. Empowering the client to properly deal with employment issues and to adjust to the episodic, progressive nature of later-stage HIV infection is a critical role of the counselor during these later stages.

Common situations the consumer can expect to begin to experience include chronic low-grade fevers, persistent fatigue, diarrhea lasting at least two weeks, rashes or other skin conditions, unintentional weight loss, night sweats, and mild infections of the mouth or throat (Kalichman, 1998, p. 72). For consumers, these medical conditions typically will begin to directly interfere with job performance, and significant functional limitations may begin to impair the client's ability to perform physical tasks, endure long hours, and cope with stress (Hunt, 1996). Finally, at this time, counselors need to watch for signs of adjustment to the disability progression. Day-to-day life will become much more challenging for the consumer, perhaps requiring intervention from licensed mental health or family counselors to prevent possible depression or other negative psychological consequences.

There are many clinical conditions caused by HIV that arise during the late stages of infection, including, in almost all cases, an AIDS diagnosis. Kalichman (1997, 1998) lists the following classes of conditions most typically experienced by persons with HIV/AIDS as HIV-related wasting syndrome and HIV-related neurological disease. AIDS-related malignancies that are considered to be AIDS-defining conditions include Kaposi's sarcoma, invasive cervical cancer, pneumocystis carini pneumonia, candidiasis, coccidiodomycosis, crytococcoses, and histoplasmosis. Other AIDS-defining conditions include viral infections such as cytomegalo virus, herpes simplex infections lasting for more than one month, Epstein-Barr virus, and progressive multifocal leukoencephalopathy. Finally, individuals may contract opportunistic infections involving protozoa and bacteria such as toxoplasmosis, cryptosporidiosis, isoporiasis, mycobacterium diseases, recurrent bacterial pneumonia, and nonpneumonia-causing bacterial infections. During this final stage it will become extremely difficult for individuals to maintain employment, and rehabilitation counselors' roles will increasingly become centered on providing assisted living supports, assuring transportation, securing familial support, and assisting consumers in coping with an ever-increasing regimen of medical interventions that will become more and more intrusive as the infections progress and the immune system weakens.

SERVICES

HIV/AIDS-related services are grouped into several components (including educational, prevention, intervention, case management, and medical services). These services may be delivered concurrently according to individual needs and interests, and consumers typically will require a variety of services at any given point during the course of their disability. For example, although the consumer is "asymptomatic" during stage one, rehabilitation counselors may provide referrals for educational counseling or other educational services, medical testing, and mental health counseling to deal with adjustment issues concurrently during this stage.

Educational Services

Educational services may be necessary for consumers and their families, as well as for professionals. Fortunately, there are a plethora of excellent resources that are easily accessible and may provide accurate and comprehensive data regarding HIV/AIDS. Given the wide availability of the Internet to most professionals and consumers, the most accessible "community resource" available for educational materials is most definitely the World Wide Web. Perhaps the most valuable resource available to consumers is the Web site for the Centers for Disease Control. Counselors would direct consumers to access the links specific to HIV/AIDS at http://www.cdc.gov/hiv/dhap.htm. Resources available on this site include general information on HIV/AIDS, HIV/AIDS FAQ, and a variety of downloadable educational brochures that are among the most useful tools available on the site. There are three series of brochures available: the opportunistic infection series, general information (risk factors, prevention, caring for someone with AIDS at home, and HIV and its treatment), and special populations (health-care workers and multicultural issues).

Another extremely valuable resource for consumers is the site administered by AVERT. Counselors can refer consumers to http://www.avert.org/ or visit the site to download a variety of resources, including specific information about infection, transmission, and testing; information for young people; common questions and answers about sex; and HIV/AIDS treatment and care. Particularly useful to consumers are printable resources, including brochures on sexually transmitted diseases—symptoms, treatments, and facts; HIV/AIDS treatment; and an HIV/AIDS treatment glossary.

Finally, as with professional education, the most comprehensive Web-based site providing a wide range of consumer educational materials is the site for the HIV/AIDS Education and Training Center (AIDS-ETC). Consumers may be directed to a link containing a plethora of detailed "patient information" at http://www.aids-etc.org/aidsetc?page=et-05-00 under the heading "clinical information and resources." However, this site also contains a wide range of information for consumers who follow the "clinical top-ics" link found on the home page for AIDS-ETC.

Community-Based Education Services. For local referrals concerning client education, there are many public and not-for-profit resources available, but they vary to such a great degree geographically that most rehabilitation counselors could benefit from contacting either their state department of health (DOH) or the state provider of alcohol and other drug abuse (AODA) services. Examples of typical community-based organization services can be reviewed at the following links: Health Education Resource Organization (HERO) of Balti-more Maryland (at http://www.critpath.org/aric/pwarg/local/hero.htm), or AIDS Services of North Texas (at http://www.aidsntx.org/). While it can be more challenging to find direct-service education providers in rural areas, counselors may be surprised to find that local substance abuse providers or the local department of health will often provide basic educational services, includ-ing testing and counseling.

Professional Education Services. For professionals seeking education about HIV/AIDS, one of the best Web-based resources is the AIDS-ETC Web site (http://www.aids-etc.org/). The site provides comprehensive train-ing materials, including training curricula that can be used to prepare rehabil-itation counselors to gain sufficient knowledge and skills regarding HIV/AIDS to effectively coordinate necessary services for consumers affected by these disabilities. It is the best "one-stop shop" for educational materials available via the World Wide Web. Certainly, professionals may find consid-erable valuable information at the AVERT and CDC sites as well.

As with consumer education, there are typically local providers, both pub-lic and nonprofit, who will provide on-site training or educational programs at no cost or low cost to professionals. The AIDS-ETC site is particularly useful in that it contains a wide variety of links to continuing education providers.

Prevention Services

Prevention is the key component encompassed in all interventions regardless of the individual's current stage of infection. Prevention is always aimed towards preventing the spread of the HIV virus, including initial infec-tion, infecting others, and individual re-infection. Risk-reduction sessions might include outreach to high-risk populations, risk-reduction education and facilitation, and HIV testing.

Both paraprofessionals and professionals use risk-reduction sessions to assist individuals who are at risk of acquiring the virus, infecting others, or re-infecting themselves. These professionals and paraprofessionals, often referred to as risk reduction specialists (RRSs), are not typically licensed, but they may be certified through state health departments or the Centers for Dis-ease Control and Prevention.

Risk-reduction sessions and prevention education may be delivered through a variety of service models. They may include, but are not limited to, individualized counseling, health fairs organized by community organizations, and "street outreach" with risk-reduction specialists going directly to high-risk consumers in their home, social, or business environments. These services are provided through a number of different venues, including schools, community based non-profit organizations, local and state health departments, churches, and other community organizations.

Intervention Services

From the perspective of vocational rehabilitation counselors, intervention with individuals who have tested reactive for the HIV virus consists primarily of three components: explanation of the testing, risk-reduction sessions, and medical services. For the purposes of this text each component will be reviewed in a general way, but professionals may obtain further helpful information on each of these topics by visiting the educational Web sites listed in the previous sections.

HIV Testing. When rehabilitation counselors encounter consumers who are concerned about possible infection, or when professionals become aware that consumers may be engaging in high-risk behaviors, referral for HIV testing may become necessary. Testing can be a traumatic experience for consumers and counselors alike and can precipitate client crises if handled incorrectly. Consequently, rehabilitation counselors who make referrals for testing are under an ethical obligation to ensure that they understand the commonly used testing procedures as well as the limitations of those procedures.

Most importantly, the counselor should be able to assess whether an HIV test is appropriate at the current time. The counselor must express the testing limitations and the inability of the HIV tests to immediately detect exposure to the HIV virus. Consumers may engage in risky behaviors and have a "morning after" reaction that precipitates a desire to be tested for HIV. Unfortunately, HIV screenings rely on the presence of antibodies and will not reveal exposure until the body has had sufficient time to produce antibodies in detectable quantities (approximately three months). The counselor will need clients to disclose their most recent potential exposure to the virus. It is the counselor's responsibility to explain the three-month "window period" in regard to HIV testing. While some individuals produce detectable quantities of antibodies in two weeks, professionals most often recommend that two tests be administered three months apart, during which time the consumer refrains from any risky behavior (Kalichman, 1997, 1998).

Testing and Risk Reduction. Prior to the administration of HIV tests, rehabilitation counselors are strongly advised to refer their clients to trained professionals who can provide adequate risk reduction during the administration of the test and when the results are given. Typically, agencies that administer the tests will also provide these resources as a component of the testing services. There are two screening processes used for detecting the presence of HIV antibodies that are utilized private and public medical providers. If an individual has an HIV test performed, the first screening a laboratory will typically run is the enzyme-linked immunosorbant assay or ELISA. The ELISA is a very effective screening instrument because it has a very low rate of false negatives. A false negative occurs when a lab result reads that the person is not infected when in reality the individual is infected with the HIV virus. As a consequence, when an individual obtains a nonreactive result on the ELISA, no further screenings are administered in typical situations. Unfortunately, the ELISA is vulnerable to false positive results (Powell, 1997), so in preparing consumers for HIV testing it is critical to explain the obvious limitations of the ELISA prior to having the HIV test performed. This can assist in preparing consumers to accurately interpret the meaning of the results when they arrive as well as to assist them in understanding why further screening may be necessary.

In cases where the ELISA produces a reactive result, it is always repeated (Kalichman, 1997); if a further reactive result is obtained, a confirmation screening is recommended. The confirmation screening is more sensitive and known as the Western Blot. The Western Blot screens for specific components of the HIV antibodies (Powell, 1996), and a reactive Western Blot confirms the diagnosis of HIV. The Western Blot confirmation allows the provider to produce a Letter of Diagnosis (LOD). The LOD does several things for the consumer, including provision of proof of the HIV diagnosis with the Western Blot confirmation, ability to access treatment for the diagnosis, and access into social service assistance programs. Without the LOD the client is not able to access any services related to HIV.

Falvo (1999) and Kalichman (1997, 1998) warn that HIV testing necessarily places consumers at risk for experiencing significant anxiety. Testing should only occur when the counselor has assessed that the individual who is to be tested is emotionally stable and has adequate resources in place to cope with potential results. Many extremely negative consequences can arise when individuals are not fully prepared to receive an HIV diagnosis. Likewise, if testing limitations are not fully explained, there can be serious complications due to an inaccurate test result.

In addition to determining infection status, there are other reasons for providing risk reduction prior to and following an HIV test. Trained risk-reduction specialists will use the testing event to provide risk reduction by seeking to engage the client in behavioral change (i.e., modifying risk-taking behavior). This will help ensure that they are less likely to infect themselves or others in the future. Most risk-reduction protocols throughout the nation are built upon Prochaska and DiClimente's behavioral "stages of change" (1986). Additionally, the risk-reduction specialist will seek to address possible avoidance behaviors that may be triggered by raised anxiety levels, potentially resulting in failure of consumers to return for results.

Medical Intervention Services. Consumers who are HIV positive will require constant medical involvement from the time of diagnosis through the advanced stages of the disease. However, this involvement varies significantly and unpredictably for each individual; the course of the disease across a group of consumers can be incredibly diverse. For most individuals in the initial stages of infection, medical intervention may be quite limited. Since they are not experiencing significant negative physiological effects, highly intrusive procedures may not be necessary.

Despite the fact that life-threatening opportunistic infections will not be present, medical interventions are necessary in the earlier stages of infection. Several approaches may be utilized, including immunity-bolstering therapies, antiviral therapies, and protease inhibitors. While these approaches have dramatically lengthened the life expectancy of consumers with HIV, they are quite expensive and individuals must often make dramatic dietary changes in conjunction with careful administration of numerous medications (Kalichman, 1997, 1998). The availability of these therapeutic interventions should in no way serve to lessen the perception of the serious nature of HIV infection. Consumers may be less likely to take appropriate precautions to protect themselves through a false sense of security, given that many individuals now falsely believe that there are mediations that can "cure" or "treat" HIV infection. However, at best today the HIV treatment allows the consumer to manage the disease, which can dramatically improve their quality of life over the disease spectrum.

As the disease progresses and opportunistic infections begin to manifest, medical interventions will become much more intrusive and will demand considerably greater resources from both the rehabilitation counselor and the consumer. Medical management of the opportunistic infections may require extended hospitalization, hospice services, or home nursing to support family members or partners who may not be able to fully cope with the highly intrusive medical interventions necessary to stabilize the health of their loved ones.

Rehabilitation counselors may be referred to medical specialists serving persons with HIV/AIDS through community nonprofit providers such as those described above, as well as through the local offices of their state department of health, or often through public substance-abuse treatment providers. Additionally, there are several useful text references to help rehabilitation counselors understand how they may provide appropriate support to consumers who are receiving pharmacological interventions. They include *The HIV Drug Book* (1998), written by the staff of Project Inform; the *Manual of HIV Therapeutics*, edited by W. G. Powderly, M.D. (2000); and the *Current Clinical Strategies Manual of HIV Therapy* (Princeton, 2003). Finally, the above-mentioned AIDS-ETC Web site, the CDC Web site, and the AVERT Web site all contain the most accurate, up-to-date information regarding both preventative and medical interventions currently being utilized.

LEGAL AND ETHICAL ISSUES

Confidentiality

HIV/AIDS presents significant ethical challenges when professionals seek to assure consumers' rights to confidentiality. Powell (1996) suggests that any individuals involved in HIV testing have a clear duty to inform consumers of the limits of confidentiality for HIV test results that are applicable within their state jurisdiction. Given that states' laws regarding confidentiality of test results vary considerably, rehabilitation counselors have an ethical obligation to become adequately informed about the availability of "anonymous" testing services or the potential for disclosure that may occur when an individual is referred to a testing site.

Additionally, Garcia et al. (1999) state that many professionals are caught in an ethical dilemma when they are obligated to a "duty to warn" by their counselor code, while at the same time they are obligated to protect their consumers' confidentiality. Rehabilitation professionals should consult with their supervisors well in advance of making referrals for testing services to assure that they will be in compliance with the policies of their agency and within applicable state and local statutes.

Scope of Practice

Rehabilitation counselors have an obligation to obtain adequate knowledge and skills to perform appropriate case coordination with this population, but unless they receive specialized training through accredited providers that leads to appropriate certification or licensure, they may not have adequate preparation to provide mental health services supporting adjustment of their clients to HIV/AIDS, as well as providing risk-reduction sessions or consultation services for their clients. Consequently, counselors should take particular care to recognize that HIV/AIDS disabilities represent an extremely complex challenge requiring specialized preparation for achieving professional competence.

Finally, the counselor must recognize that this is a unique disease impacting *all* areas of the consumer's life. In addition to all the services described above, rehabilitation counselors should be prepared to reflect empathy and concern regarding the consumer's sexuality and sexual desires/experiences. In the case of HIV/AIDS, the most intimate aspects of an individual's life are dramatically impacted and changed throughout the spectrum of this disease.

References

Fesko, S. L. (2001). Workplace experiences of individuals who are HIV positive. *Rehabilitation Counseling Bulletin, 45,* 2–11.

Falvo, D. (1999). *Medical and psychosocial aspects of chronic illness and disability.* Gaithersburg, MD: Aspen.

Garcia, J. G., Froelich, R. J., Cartwright, B., Letiecq, D., Forrester, L. E., & Mueller, R. O. (1999). Ethical dilemmas related to counseling clients living with HIV/AIDS. *Rehabilitation Counseling Bulletin, 43,* 41–50.

Glenn, M. K., Ford, J., Moore, D., & Hollar, D. (2003). Employment issues as related by individuals living with HIV/AIDS. *Journal of Rehabilitation, 69*(1), 30–36.

Hunt, B. (1996). Rehabilitation counseling for people with HIV. *Rehabilitation Education, 62,* 68–74.

Kalichman, S. C. (1997). *Answering your questions about AIDS.* Washington, DC: American Psychological Association.

Kalichman, S. C. (1998). *Understanding AIDS: Advances in research and treatment* (2nd ed.). Washington, DC: American Psychological Association.

McReynolds, C. (2001). The meaning of work in the lives of people living with HIV disease and AIDS. *Rehabilitation Counseling Bulletin, 44,* 104–115.

Powderly, W. G. (Ed.). (2000). *Manual of HIV therapeutics* (2nd ed.). Philadelphia: Lippincott Williams & Wilkins.

Powell, J. (1996). *AIDS and HIV-related diseases: An educational guide for professionals and the public.* New York: Plenum.

Princeton, D. C. (2003). Current clinical strategies of HIV therapy. Laguna, CA: Current Clinical Strategies Publishing.

Prochaska, J. O., & DiClemente, C. C. (1986). Toward a comprehensive model of change. In W. R. Miller & N. Heather (Eds.), *Treating addictive behaviors: Process of change.* New York: Plenum.

Project Inform. (1998). *The HIV drug book* (rev., 2nd ed.). New York: Pocket Books.

Rubin, S. E., & Roessler, R. T. (2001). *Foundations of the vocational rehabilitation process* (5th ed.). Austin: Pro-Ed.

Work-Hardening Programs

V. Robert May III

Work hardening has evolved from the early 1980s into a dominant, highly structured work evaluation and treatment protocol originally tailored for the private vocational and industrial rehabilitation sectors (Matheson, 1988; May, 1988a). State rehabilitation agencies quickly noticed how effective work hardening was in resolving disability issues presented by injured workers who were managed by private-sector case managers. The subsequent state agency response was to modify and adapt work-hardening program models in state vocational evaluation centers, thus allowing the work-hardening movement to have a pronounced influence in both rehabilitation sectors.

The acceptance of work hardening evolved as a result of the frustration of workers' compensation administrators over the lack of traditional rehabilitation-program response to their injured claimants. Program outcomes resulted in excessive medical reserves that led to high costs of case management from the insurance benefit provider's perspective. With the insurance industry searching for change in therapeutic rehabilitation approaches, the rehabilitation community responded by implementing a more aggressive treatment plan—one that was more proactive, such as those rehabilitation programs provided to injured high school, college, and professional athletes (Darphin, 1995). For example, when an athlete reports with injury, treatment is immediate and rehabilitation follows that requires the full participation of the athlete through assigned exercises, modalities, and resistive modalities. Why wouldn't a similar approach work for the injured worker?

The primary goal of the insurance industry is cost-containment of medical expenditures, such that medical case reserves are held to within reasonable and acceptable levels (May, 1986). This perception evolved in the early

1980s as a result of the private health-insurance sector's attempt to curtail medical insurance costs and expenses through the development of innovative but controversial payment systems (i.e., the Diagnostic Related Group's [DRG] Medicare freeze of physician fees). Under the current DRG system, funding is predicated on the type of illness rather than on actual patient need (May & Reifsteck, 1986). Thus, patient exposure to medical and rehabilitation treatments is greatly reduced, and with Medicare payments providing approximately 40% of an average hospital's income, public and private hospitals' revenue bases have experienced significant cuts. To counter decreased revenues, hospitals, private physician groups, and independent health-care centers have had to focus on attracting markets with guarantee payment systems that are protected by state law (i.e., workers' compensation insurance payment systems). By the nature of its program design and funding appeal, work-hardening program development "exploded"; its position of prominence has become unparalleled, and work hardening has become a "buzzword" in rehabilitation, industrial medicine, labor law, and the nation's media (Matheson, 1988).

Bear in mind that work-hardening programs are not intended for "walk-in," self-referral patients who may have sustained a debilitating injury from a non-work-related event. Work-hardening programs are expensive and are underwritten by a multitude of insurance benefit programs that may include state workers' compensation programs; the Federal Employee Liability Act (FELA) for railroad workers; the Jones Act for seamen; the Federal Employees' Compensation Program administered by the Office of Workers' Compensation Programs for all federal employees excluding railroad workers, seamen, and longshore and harbor workers; and the Longshore and Harbor Workers' Compensation Act for workers adjacent to the navigational waters of the United States (Randolph, Demeter, & McLellan, 2003). However, there are instances where "walk-ins" do receive work-hardening therapy, such as for sports-related injuries, yard-work injuries, or auto injuries when their private health-care insurance will cover the costs.

DEFINITION

Work hardening is a combined evaluative and treatment process originally designed to resolve disability or dysfunctional issues confronting industrially injured workers. The early, developmental stages of work hardening limited the scope of this definition to suggest that it is a work-oriented treatment program that has as an outcome measured in terms of improvement in the client's productivity (Matheson, Ogden, Violette, & Schultz, 1985). However, as work-hardening development progressed, its seemingly simplistic definition became more diversified and complex. Matheson (1988) upgraded his definition such that this process is now defined as a prescriptive, individually structured productivity development program that uses conditioning tasks and simulated work activities graded to present to the disabled worker increased work demands to improve work tolerances and facilitate a return-to-work status. Darphin (1995) further upgraded the definition when she surmised that work hardening is a highly structured, goal oriented, individualized treatment program designed to return a person to work. It uses real and simulated work activities designed to restore physical, behavioral and vocational function. She added that it addresses the issues of productivity, safety, physical tolerance and work behaviors. To summarize, a more practical interpretation suggests that work hardening combines job simulation (physical and emotional conditioning) with physical work-capacity evaluation to achieve a return-to-work outcome (May, 1988a).

HISTORY/LEGISLATION

Work hardening has many different forms depending on the specific influence of the discipline managing the outpatient, industrial rehabilitation program. For example, an industrial rehabilitation program with work-hardening components managed by physical therapists will have a strong physical therapy influence in its program goals/objectives as well as in its delivery of services. Similarly, programs managed by occupational therapists will have that discipline's influence in service delivery and program goals/objectives, and the state agency vocational evaluation centers which offer work-hardening services will demonstrate a strong vocational evaluation/case management influence. However, regardless of what discipline manages the work-hardening program, the present form of work hardening, as practiced across the United States, Canada, and Australia, was developed at Rancho Los Amigos Hospital in Downey, California, by Dr. L. Matheson (Matheson et al., 1985). Programs modeling Matheson's concepts have been described by practitioners, including Bettencourt, Carlstrom, Brown, Lindau, and Long (1986); Matheson (1984); Matheson and Ogden (1983); Matheson et al. (1985); May (1985, 1986, 1988a, 1988b); May and Reifsteck (1986); May, Stewart, and Barnes (1986); Stewart, Peacock, Parsons, and Johnson (1985); and White (1986).

Matheson et al. (1985) and May (1988a) traced work-hardening program evolution to the early professional developmental efforts of occupational therapy leaders, beginning with the *work cure* movement for World War I veterans by *reconstruction workers* (as the first occupational therapists were called), and culminating with the profession's focus on industrial work-therapeutic programming in the 1980s (May, 1988a). Matheson et al. (1985) traced the occupational therapy influence to its development of industrial therapy programs in mental hospitals. These programs, well developed by the late 1930s, were defined as the prescribed use of activities inherent to the hospital operation and were planned for the mutual benefit of the patient and the institution. Occupational therapy programs originally adopted craft activities that provided bedside occupations for patients, and they assisted in the selection of appropriate types of vocational training for the patients (May, 1988a). However, as the industrial programs evolved within the hospitals, various jobs were analyzed within the institution and assigned to patients according to skill level, physical demands, and mental demands (Matheson et al., 1985). The occupational therapists coordinated work assignments ensuring that proper patient/job matches were achieved (i.e., patients' worker-trait profile fit their aptitudes, interests, experiences, and therapeutic goals).

The craft approach to simulated work (as cited in May, 1988a) fell into discord with the medical profession in the early 1950s due to the medical community's increasingly scientific approach to disease and treatment, thus claiming that craft therapy lacked scientific rationale. Therefore, the medical profession proved to be the influential body that compelled the occupational therapy profession to accept and apply *work* therapy as it is regarded in private-sector industry (i.e., specific work-skill development, remuneration for work performed, work conditioning).

Certain legislation, combined with the medical profession's endorsement, facilitated the occupational therapy profession's prominence in work-hardening program development. The passage of the Vocational Rehabilitation Act of 1920 provided funding for states to develop vocational rehabilitation programs for disabled persons (May, 1988a). This act provided occupational therapy administrators the justification to include the development of vocational evaluation components in their program goals, with the focus being to return the patient to gainful employment (May, 1988a). Hospital program expansion for occupational therapists was perpetuated by subsequent amendments to the 1920 Act in 1943 and 1954 (Barden-LaFolette Act, P. L. 113; Vocational Rehabilitation Amendments of 1954, P. L. 565). This legislative activity expanded the populations eligible for vocational rehabilitation services to include patients with psychogenic illnesses and those in need of physical restoration (May, 1988a). Occupational therapy programs based in hospital settings were ideally structured to service these new eligible populations.

As opportunities for occupational therapists in vocational rehabilitation program development became abundant in the late 1940s and early 1950s, curative workshops evolved (Matheson et al., 1985). The primary function of these workshops was to restore the impaired body part to as normal a level of function as possible, with return to work as the eventual goal. These workshops used graded activities to improve function and were often planned in accordance with the patient's physical demands of his or her job (May, 1988a). Thus, the first *work-hardening* programs were put into practice, paving the way for the more sophisticated models practiced today.

The vocational evaluation component of the work-hardening process evolved during this period with the aid of the occupational therapy professional movement. Prior to this period, occupational therapists used work samples they had developed from their earlier days in the work-cure movement. The early 1950s period lacked appropriate evaluation tools or had tools which lacked validation criteria and normative data (May, 1988a). This void was filled by the efforts of the Institute for the Crippled and Disabled Rehabilitation and Research Center in New York City (May, 1988a). This research facility developed the *Tower* work-sample system, which was the first effort toward establishing normative data for individual performances for specific work tasks (May, 1988a), As a result, occupational therapists employed in the curative workshops and other work-hardening industrial rehabilitation settings were sent for training in the *Tower* system.

The occupational therapy movement underwent a change in its therapeutic focus beginning in the late 1950s and early 1960s. During this period, occupational therapists returned to medical/physical rehabilitation centers in an attempt to develop a stronger professional identity (Matheson et al., 1985). However, by the late 1960s, occupational therapists had made the transition back into vocational rehabilitation centers, but with an emphasis on prevocational and work adjustment programs. It would not be until the 1980s that the occupational therapeutic movement reached the status in industrial rehabilitation settings that it enjoys today. The emphasis in work hardening is on task analysis (simulated work activity with repeated measurement of the participant's progress) that evolved from the occupational therapy curative workshop movement and the work-sample developmental efforts of this professional body.

Work-hardening program staff typically include a physical therapist and/ or an occupational therapist. More recent program development literature has incorporated the expertise of the vocational evaluator (May, 1987). Other staff members may include psychologists, in addition to the respective attending physician, program medical director, rehabilitation nurse, social worker, or vocational rehabilitation case manager (Darphin, 1995). The exact team-member composite is contingent on the organizational structure of the facility (i.e., freestanding physical therapy/occupational therapy clinic, hospital, independent medical clinic, public rehabilitation facility).

What determines the constitution and complexity of the program, as well as the comprehensiveness of the team, is not so much what the facility administration prefers, but rather what funding in terms of insurance reimbursements are required to maintain solvency. It is well known that psychological services and vocational services have difficulty with reimbursement from third-party insurance benefit providers. Workers' compensation benefit providers will not authorize payment for such services if preauthorization is not obtained. Thus, program administrators have a tendency to utilize the professionals whom third-party benefit providers recognize and accept for such funding (i.e., physical therapists, occupational therapists).

As noted earlier, program solvency supersedes staff composition considerations. More often than not, solvency is determined by the ability of the organization to secure patient-referral sources, either through various financial arrangements/incentives with physicians or through securing contracts with local industry. Such contracts specify to the respective referral source which work-hardening programs will be financially accepted and supported. Thus, staff composition, expertise, or service-delivery quality may have little bearing on whether an injured worker is referred to a particular program.

Purpose/Intent

The goal of industrial rehabilitation is to return injured workers to work (May et al., 1986). Thus, the primary work-hardening goal is to assist the injured worker in achieving a level of productivity (within the confines of a clinically controlled setting) that is acceptable in the competitive labor market (May, 1986). This process incorporates graded work activities as conditioning tools, and assists the injured worker in reaching selected critical demands (i.e., those demands that are more likely to produce symptoms that limit work tolerances) and developing worker traits (Holmes, 1985; Matheson & Ogden, 1983). Work hardening assists a person with developing a sufficient amount of physical stamina such that an eight-hour workday can be achieved with minimal discomfort.

Although appearing simplistic in scope, the work-hardening process is rather complex and conceptually involved. The *true* work-hardening program is based on the *Stage Model of Industrial Rehabilitation* developed by Matheson (1984). This model is presented in table 1.

Pathology (stage 1) is defined as an injury or disease process (Matheson, 1988). This stage is where the injured worker's pathological findings are explored. The physician is the key team member at this stage, but other members may play a significant role in determining the decree of pathology.

Impairment (stage 2) is defined as the measurable consequence of pathology taken as a disruption of physical or mental integrity (Matheson, 1988). Again, physicians are responsible for this rating procedure.

Functional limitations (stage 3) are measured in terms of general tasks that are not specifically tied to any one role, but are found in many of the roles associated with each respective injured worker during the course of his or her daily activities. The injured worker's reports of symptoms and limitations are corroborated through behavioral observations of function.

Disability (stage 4) reflects the effects of functional limitations on one's daily roles, and is defined as the social consequence of the injured worker's functional limitations. The degree of disability is noted in the manner in which these functional limitations affect the injured worker's customary roles. The team member most associated with this assessment is the occupational therapist.

Feasibility (stage 5) for competitive employment (vocational feasibility is defined as the acceptability of the injured worker as an employee to the employer). This stage is where the "patient" or "client" is first regarded as an "employee" in the industrial rehabilitation process, and specific work behaviors are assessed. The occupational therapist and the vocational evaluator are

Table 1   Stage Model of Industrial Evaluation

Stage	Area Assessed	Measured by or in Terms of
one	pathology	physicians, psychiatrists, psychologists
two	impairment	physicians, psychiatrists, psychologists, physical therapists, exercise physiologists, occupational therapists
three	functional limitations	physicians, psychiatrists, psychologists, physical therapists, exercise physiologists, occupational therapists
four	disability	occupational therapists, vocational evaluators, physical therapists, psychologists
five	feasibility	occupational therapists, vocational evaluators, rehabilitation counselors, case managers
six	employability	occupational therapists, vocational evaluators, rehabilitation counselors, case managers
seven	vocational handicap	occupational therapists, vocational evaluators, rehabilitation counselors, case managers
eight	earning capacity	economists, vocational experts

Adapted from Matheson, 1984.

best suited for this stage, and work characteristics involving safety, productivity, and interpersonal behavior are assessed.

Employability (stage 6), or the individual's ability to become employed within a certain labor market, is best reviewed by the occupational therapist, the vocational evaluator, and the rehabilitation case manager as a team. This stage is unique from feasibility in that while feasibility addresses the general acceptability of a person as an employee, employability addresses the ability for an individual to become employed within a particular labor market.

Vocational handicap (stage 7) concerns the individual's ability to become employed within a particular occupation. How the individual functions within the demands of a specific occupation is assessed, and the occupational therapist, vocational evaluator, and the rehabilitation engineer are the key team members to make this assessment.

Earning capacity (stage 8) is best determined by the economist and labor market analyst, with support provided by the vocational evaluator and vocational expert. Earning capacity is measure in terms of work-generated income over the worker's life.

Applying the stage model to a typical work-hardening program, the consumer will find that *pathology* and *impairment* have (or should have) been identified prior to the injured worker's admission to the program. The final stage, *earning capacity*, is a service typically reserved for litigation purposes, since a change in earning capacity should have no bearing on an individual's functional potential to work. Attorneys will request this information to build a plaintiff's case for damages or, from a defense counsel's perspective, attempt to minimize damages if earning capacity can be shown to have been minimally influenced by the injured worker's post-work-hardening disability status.

CLIENT SERVICES

The true work-hardening program involves the injured worker in a simulated work environment, complete with similar work time schedules that include breaks and lunch periods. The injured worker is expected to spend between four and eight hours in the daily program, which may involve a consecutive-day period totaling between one and six weeks. The program is designed to simulate the individual's customary work in terms of environment and tasks. The hourly workday, as well as task complexities, may be graduated with the goal of achieving the worker's current job's physical exertion demands, environmental demands, and productivity criteria.

The admissions procedure to a work-hardening program is as complex as the actual treatment program. Before any individual is admitted to work hardening, it must be determined that the individual can benefit from the prescribed therapeutic regimen. This is best determined through one of several evaluation procedures.

Work-Tolerance Screening

This screening procedure is designed to address the physical capacity forms often submitted to physicians by case managers or insurance adjustors when questioning the physician about a worker's specific work-functioning parameters. Early development of this procedure was documented by Reuss, Rawe, and Sunquist (1958); and modification of their evaluation techniques was researched by Harrand (1986), who redesigned the procedure to fit in today's work-hardening models.

Work-tolerance screening is a three- to six-hour intensive evaluation procedure measuring the physical work-performance factors that are basic to work output (Matheson & Ogden, 1983). More specifically, it assesses the worker's total functional work tolerances involving trunk and extremity strength and flexibility, maximum lifting capacity, general mobility, and tolerance for repetitive work capacity (May & Reifsteck, 1986). It also measures the worker's critical work demands, which are simulated in the controlled, clinical setting.

In work hardening, work-tolerance screening has two basic applications: First, it can be used as a diagnostic tool with which to determine the need for further medical intervention versus proceeding with work-hardening treatment. Secondly, it can be used as a "benchmark" for determining the worker's progress during the therapeutic treatment program; it allows the rehabilitation team to pace the worker's program based on the physical limitations identified in the initial tolerance screening (Crewe, 1986; Reuss et al., 1958).

Work-Capacity Evaluation

Work-capacity evaluation (WCE) is defined as a comprehensive vocational evaluation process that usually takes place over three to five consecutive days. It assesses the person's vocational work tolerances, aptitudes, temperament, and attitudes, as well as work feasibility (i.e., safety, productivity, interpersonal work behaviors) (May, 1988a,b). It also measures a person's ability to sustain work performance dependably in response to broadly defined work demands.

WCE is a multi-component evaluation process, consisting of the work-tolerance screening procedure, vocational evaluation work samples and pencil/paper tests, and simulated work activities. This process may also utilize actual work equipment required of the employee to perform his or her job. It is this procedure that determines the injured worker's potential to benefit from work hardening, an essential criterion by which one is either accepted or rejected from the therapeutic program.

Today's programs may offer both work-tolerance screening and work-capacity evaluation, but the WCE is the most popular of the two procedures, because of its evaluative comprehensiveness and the wealth of information that can be assimilated and processed before admitting the injured worker to the program. Work-tolerance screening is best applied in situations where time is a factor, or where the referral source desires to have a WCE form completed and no work-hardening program has been authorized or scheduled.

Standardization Criteria

When an injured worker first enters a work-hardening program, that person should see an apparent industrial complex with many different types of industrial tools, standardized work samples, building supplies, treatment rooms, and staff offices. Programs offering physical therapy services in conjunction with the hardening procedures will include the treatment rooms, either separated by curtains or enclosed by walls. The square footage of the hardening floor may range between 500 to 10,000 square feet. The injured worker should begin the program with a clinical intake interview, followed by a work-capacity evaluation that includes musculoskeletal screening and physical therapy assessment, and then a functional analysis provided by either the occupational therapist or the vocational evaluator. If a vocational evaluator is involved, then an occupational therapist will also be utilized for the functional study, but the inverse is not necessarily applied.

There is no guarantee that such a scenario will occur when an injured worker enters any work-hardening program, and there is no guarantee that services offered will be beneficial to the injured worker. However, efforts have been made to standardize work-hardening program policy, protocol, and organizational structure through the development of program standards. The California Vocational Evaluation and Work Adjustment Association attempted to establish guidelines for all programs in California in 1984, supported by the State Division of Industrial Accidents and by workers' compensation benefit providers (Edgcomb, 1987). The Commission on Accreditation of Rehabilitation Facilities (CARF) soon followed suit and assembled a professionally representative steering committee in 1988 to establish specific clinical standards of practice in work hardening. These standards were disseminated to clinical and therapeutic personnel for comment and revision. The first year for facility accreditation under the CARF guidelines was 1989. Since this first accrediting year, Florida and Ohio have established that only facilities meeting CARF accrediting standards for work hardening will be reimbursed for services rendered to injured workers. While it was anticipated that several more states would adopt similar policy over the next five-year period (by 1995), this simply did not happen. Additionally, the anticipation was that only CARF-accredited programs would be eligible for state workers' compensation reimbursement by the year 2000, but this policy has been adopted only by a limited number of states outside of Florida and Ohio.

Accreditation does not guarantee quality. It only assures the consumer that the program has met a set of standards determined to be necessary to minimize risk or harm to the injured worker and to maximize his or her therapeutic benefit. Accreditation applies only to the facility and not to the individual clinicians administering the services. However, there are several clinical standards worth noting that the reader may consider when selecting a work-hardening program in the client's local community. These CARF standards are summarized as follows:

- Program goals should be identified and documented during the admission stage of the program. This is best accomplished at the onset with the submission of specific referral questions. Once the team understands what the referral source desires from the program, then specific goals and objectives can be delineated.

- Program time frames should be documented at the admission stage of the program. The exact length of the program should be documented in writing by the evaluating team at the conclusion of the work-capacity evaluation. The referral source is encouraged not to accept an indefinite time period. Often, evaluation teams will conclude that more time is needed before a definite discharge date can be determined. This is not acceptable, as the discharge date is easily determined by a well-experienced industrial rehabilitation team.

- The evaluation process should take place within the context of the demands of competitive employment. The process should document a benchmark from which to establish the initial plan or the person's functional/vocational disposition and should include, but not be limited to, one or more of the following functional capacity evaluations: baseline evaluation, job-capacity evaluation, occupational-capacity evaluation, and work-capacity evaluation.

- Assessment, coordinated program planning, and direct services should be provided on a regular and continuing basis by the interdisciplinary team, which should be made up of the following professionals: occupational therapist, physical therapist, psychologist, and vocational specialist.

- The exit/discharge criteria should include, but not be limited to, the following issues concerning the person served:

  Returning to work—Will the client return to work at the time of discharge from the program?

  Meeting program goals—Were all goals met, and if not, which ones were not, and why?

  Declining further services—Why were services declined by the injured worker? Referral source?

  Noncompliance with organizational policies—Which policies were violated and why?

  Limited potential to benefit—Has the injured worker peaked in his or her performance? Has this person reached maximum medical improvement (MMI)?

  Requiring further health care interventions—Did other problems surface which suggest additional medical interpretation and diagnostics are warranted?

- The exit/discharge summary should delineate the following:

  The person's present functioning status and potential, and

  The functional status related to the targeted job, alternative occupations, or the competitive labor market.

- The exit/discharge summary should be prepared and disseminated within seven working days of the exit/discharge date. The consumer should expect to receive a full and detailed report of the injured worker's experience in the work-hardening program within a seven-day period postdischarge (Commission on Accreditation of Rehabilitation Facilities [CARF], 1991).

Problematic Accreditation Issues and Resulting Development

Problems remain with CARF accreditation in spite of its national influence in health-care facilities. Many practitioners were not prepared to meet the demands of the CARF criteria. Darphin (1995) identified the following issues as primary deterrents for achieving CARF accreditation among physical and occupational therapy-based programs:

1. Many practitioners providing work-hardening and work-conditioning services found the CARF non-work-hardening standards cumbersome, expensive, and not necessarily related to the quality of care provided.

2. Physical therapy frequently provided successful return-to-work services as a single-discipline program and did not comply with the multidiscipline definition of CARF.

3. CARF accreditation standards apply to institutional multidisciplinary models of care, thus excluding most private physical therapy practices from achieving CARF accreditation.

As a result, the American Physical Therapy Association (APTA) established the Industrial Rehabilitation Advisory Committee (IRAC) to (1) accurately reflect contemporary practice, and (2) standardize terminology, in order to address the needs of the clients, providers, regulators, and payors (Darphin, 1995; Isernhagen, 2003). Thus, the IRAC performed two functions which resulted in the introduction of the concept of work conditioning in conjunction with work hardening:

1. Development of guidelines for work-conditioning programs for injured workers with only physical disabilities.

2. Development of guidelines for work-hardening programs as a viable alternative to CARF standards.

IRAC defined work conditioning as a work-related, intensive, goal-oriented treatment program specifically designed to restore an individual's systemic, neuromusculoskeletal (strength, endurance, movement, flexibility, and motor control), and cardiopulmonary functions (Darphin, 1995, Isernhagen, 2003). Thus, the objective of work conditioning is to restore the client's physical capacity and function so the client can return to work.

Isernhagen (2003) labeled this work-oriented rehabilitation focus "work rehabilitation." She defined work rehabilitation as a

> . . . work-oriented, structured treatment program that utilizes the restorative philosophy of rehabilitation for the goal of a safe and functional return to work. A work rehabilitation program utilizes a [whole person] approach to improve the functional ability of a potential worker to match the physical demands of gainful employment. (p. 771)

Regarding the differences between work conditioning and work hardening, Isernhagen drew the distinction that while work-conditioning programs address the physical issues of the disability in question, work-hardening programs require interdisciplinary intervention to address issues beyond the physical attributes of the disability that may include functional, behavioral, and vocational needs of the injured worker.

Referral Considerations

Work-hardening programs have evolved into sophisticated evaluation and treatment programs designed specifically to assist injured workers with their reentry into the competitive labor market. Programs have experienced a phenomenal growth over the last 11 years, though their roots can be traced back to the early occupational therapy movement in the 1930s. Today's programs reflect a comprehensive structured program with multidisciplined evaluation and treatment staff. The more sophisticated programs may consist of physical therapists, occupational therapists, vocational evaluators, vocational rehabilitation counselors/case managers, social workers, psychologists, rehabilitation nurses, and physicians. Those with lesser budgets may include only a physical therapist and one or more team members.

When choosing a work-hardening program, the consumer may benefit from considering the following questions:

- *Goal structuring:* Are specific program goals structured at the onset of the program and monitored to ensure that specified time frames for goal attainment are met? Are time frames for predicting goal attainment established at the onset of the program?

- *Accessibility:* How accessible are the therapists, program manager, and medical director (if there is one) for questions regarding client progress? Are phone calls immediately returned? Does the facility allow the rehabilitation specialist onsite access to the client and staff for periodic follow-up conferences? Are weekly staffings open to family members and/or case managers?

- *Report dissemination:* Is the final report of the client's performance disseminated within a seven-day period? Does it address the specific referral questions submitted at the time of referral? If program goals are not met and the client fails, are recommendations provided in writing to address the next rehabilitation step in the individual's health care?

The referral source should be aware that work-hardening programs neither guarantee that injured workers will return to work nor guarantee that program goals will be met within the specified time frames. The injured worker may demonstrate an ability to benefit from the program but may not achieve the program goals necessary to qualify for placement in the competitive labor market. If program goals are not met but the program has demonstrated good goal structuring, planning, and delivery of service, the referral source should at least know which is the best direction to pursue for the injured worker in terms of continuing rehabilitation efforts, if at all appropriate.

Work hardening is still in its developmental stages, and research on such programs is still in its infancy. The consumer plays a significant role in the development and maintenance of quality standards for work-hardening programs through his or her choice of programs. With such influence potential, the consumer can provide the necessary input and influence to ensure that established standards of practice are met, and that modifications to existing standards, as well as new standard development, remain ongoing.

References

Bettencourt, C., Carlstrom, P., Brown, S., Lindau, K., & Long, C. (1986). Using job simulation to treat adults with back injuries. The *American Journal of Occupational Therapy, 40,* 12–20.

Commission on Accreditation of Rehabilitation Facilities (CARF). (1991). *Standards manual for organizations serving people with disabilities.* Commission on Accreditation of Rehabilitation Facilities, 101 North Wilmot Road, Suite 500, Tucson, AZ 85711.

Crewe, N. (1986). Assessment of physical functioning. In B. Bolton (Ed.), *Handbook of measurement and evaluation in rehabilitation* (pp. 235–247). Baltimore: Paul H. Brookes.

Darphin, L. (1995). Work hardening and work-conditioning perspectives. In S. Isernhagen (Ed.), *The comprehensive guide to work injury management.* Gaithersburg, MD: Aspen Publishers, Inc.

Edgcomb, J. (1987). Work hardening guidelines 1984: As proposed by California V.E.W.A.A. *Vocational Evaluation and Work Adjustment Bulletin, 20,* 133–134.

Harrand, G. (1986). *The Harrand guide for developing physical capacity evaluation.* The Career Development Center, 1515 Ball Street, Box 600, Eau Claire, WI 54702.

Holmes, D. (1985). The role of the occupational therapist-work evaluator. *The American Journal of Occupational Therapy, 39,* 308–313.

Isernhagen, S. (2003). Work hardening. In S. L. Demeter and G. B. J. Anderson (Eds.), *Disability evaluation* (2nd ed.). St. Louis: Mosby.

Matheson, L. (1984). *Work capacity evaluation: An interdisciplinary approach to industrial rehabilitation.* Anaheim: Employment and Rehabilitation Institute of California.

Matheson, L. (1988). Integrated work hardening in vocational rehabilitation: An emerging model. *Vocational Evaluation and Work Adjustment Bulletin, 21,* 71–76.

Matheson, L., & Ogden, L. (1983). *Work tolerance screening.* Anaheim: Employment and Rehabilitation Institute of California.

Matheson, L., Ogden, L., Violette, K., & Schultz, K. (1985). Work hardening: Occupational therapy in industrial rehabilitation. *American Journal of Occupational Therapy, 39,* 314–321.

May, V. R. (1985). Physical capacity evaluation and work hardening programming: The Carle Clinic association model. In C. Smith & R. Fry (Eds.), *The national forum issues in vocational assessment: Issues papers* (pp. 233–239). Materials Development Center, Stout Vocational Rehabilitation Institute, School of Education and Human Services, University of Wisconsin–Stout, Menomonie, WI.

May, V. R. (1986). Integrating vocational rehabilitation in medical settings. *American Archives of Rehabilitation Therapy, 34,* 1–8.

May, V. R. (1987). Work hardening: A multidisciplinary team approach. *West Work Newsletter, 4*(1), 1.

May, V. R. (1988a). Work hardening and work capacity evaluation: Definition and process. *Vocational Evaluation and Work Adjustment Bulletin, 21,* 61–66.

May, V. R. (1988b). Work capacity evaluation and work hardening: Process and applications in private sector rehabilitation. In P. Deutsch & H. Sawyer (Eds.), *A guide to rehabilitation* (pp. 6A-1–6A-46). New York: Matthew Bender.

May, V. R., & Reifsteck, S. (1986). Surviving the crunch: Developing and marketing an industrial rehabilitation program. *Journal of the Medical Management Association, 33*(5), 50–56.

May, V. R., Stewart, R., & Barnes, L. (1986). Industrial rehabilitation: A physical capacity evaluation and work hardening model. *Carle Selected Papers, 38*(2), 39–43.

Randolph, D., Demeter, S., & McLellan, J. (2003). The historical development of disability programs in the United States. In S. L. Demeter and G. B. J. Anderson (Eds.), *Disability evaluation* (2nd ed.). St. Louis: Mosby.

Reuss, E., Rawe, D., & Sunquist, A. (1958). Development of a physical capacities evaluation. *American Journal of Occupational Therapy, 12*(1), 1–8, 14.

Stewart, W., Peacock, C., Parsons, D., & Johnson, P. (1985). A triadic approach to the vocational assessment of the industrially injured. In C. Smith & R. Fry (Eds.), The issue papers: *National forum on issues in vocational assessment* (pp. 185–189). Materials Development Center, Stout Vocational Rehabilitation Institute, University of Wisconsin–Stout, Menomonie, WI.

White, G. (1986). Work hardening. *The Claimsman, 10*(1), 17.

Speech Pathology and Audiology

Kenneth O. Simpson & Jill Anderson

Audiologists and speech-language pathologists provide services to persons with communication impairments. Impairments involving hearing, speech, language, and swallowing can create substantial disability. Hearing loss occurs in one-third of people older than 60 and half of those older than 85 (National Institute on Deafness and Other Communication Disorders, n.d.). Younger persons can also experience hearing impairment, for approximately 5% of children and adults through age 44 have hearing loss (Dept. of Health and Human Services, 1991). Severity of hearing impairment can range from minimal to complete, with the resulting degree of disability varying as well. Some individuals with minimal hearing impairment do not seek any intervention and experience only occasional, slightly annoying loss of the acoustic signal; individuals with significant impairments are likely to experience a major impact on their lives. For example, young children are at risk for speech and language delays if they do not hear the speech and language of others. Hearing loss can even be life-threatening if one cannot hear sounds of impending danger; it can also be a sign of a serious medical condition such as a stroke or brain tumor.

Speech-language pathologists (SLPs) provide services to persons with impairments involving speech, language and swallowing, which are quite common types of impairment. For example, the National Institute on Deafness and Other Communication Disorders (n.d.) estimates that 80,000 people in the U.S. acquire aphasia (language impairment due to brain injury) each year, and that there are over one million Americans now living with aphasia. Three to nine percent of the total population of the United States have voice disorders (Ramig & Verdolini, 1998). About 1% of the general population (approximately 3 million Americans) stutter, and between 6 and 8 million individuals in the United States have some form of language impairment (National Institute on Deafness and Other Communication Disorders, n.d.). Comprehension and use of oral and written speech and language is vital for social interaction, for educational and vocational involvement, and for meeting health and safety needs of individuals.

HISTORY/LEGISLATION

The fields of speech-language pathology and audiology did not develop from a single source. Rather, each developed separately, due to the efforts of an eclectic mix of individuals. Audiology as a distinct profession developed from the disciplines of medical science, psychology, speech-language pathology, and special education, with the initial emphasis on pathology of the ear (O'Neill, 1987). During the 1800s, physicians and scientists focused on the development of basic hearing testing, which expanded from using tuning forks to using electric audiometers capable of varying intensity as well as frequency of sound (O'Neill). Intervention for hearing impairment may have begun during prehistoric times, with the use of hearing tubes developed from hollowed-out cow horns. This intervention method did not change dramatically until the introduction of the electric hearing aid (an outgrowth of the telephone) in 1899 (O'Neill). Since then there have been continual advances in behavioral and medical intervention, as well as in the variety of devices that can improve hearing.

The discipline of speech-language pathology developed slowly from the works of individual physicians, educators, and scientists in Europe and the United States during the 1800s and early 1900s. Early areas of interest included stuttering and speech articulation, investigated by Samuel Potter and Edward Scripture (Duchan, n.d.); aphasia, investigated by Paul Broca and Carl Wernicke (Damasio, 2001); and voice, investigated by J. Muller and M. Garcia (O'Neill, 1987). Speech and language intervention suggestions during this time were very diverse and included tongue surgery, tongue levers and retractors (O'Neill), behavioral management, electrotherapy, hypnotism, psychotherapy, massage, and "medications" such as arsenic, quinine, and strychnine (Duchan, n.d.).

The first U.S. university programs for speech-language pathology began in the 1930s, emphasizing intervention methods that focused on modeling target behaviors and controlling the stimuli (McLean, 1983). During the 1960s, two very divergent models competed for precedence in explaining speech and language behavior. Noam Chomsky advocated the generative grammar model, which held that humans have an innate capacity for speech and language (McLean). B. F. Skinner, on the other hand, advocated a radical behavioral model, which held that speech and language behavior is learned through contingent reinforcement of those same behaviors (McLean). The discipline has neither wholly accepted nor rejected either model; instead it has absorbed elements of both. The 1970s saw an expansion of the definition of language to include syntax, and receptive and expressive skills, as well as cognitive aspects affecting language such as attention and memory (Bricker, 1993). The most recent major change in the discipline occurred in the 1980s with a shift toward the social use of language (Bricker). This shift meant that SLPs became increasingly interested in the functional nature of speech and language in a social context. No longer was it viewed as appropriate for a client to spend clinical sessions learning names of objects in a non-contextual setting; the measure of success began to emphasize changes that modified performance in natural situations and environments.

Several legislative mandates have resulted in significant enhancement of services for persons with communication impairments. Two examples of critical federal legislation are The Individuals with Disabilities Education Act (IDEA), and The Assistive Technology Act of 1998 (Tech Act). IDEA (P.L. 105-17) is the single most important law in the country intended to provide for the education of students with disabilities. The law is significant because it provides an individual education program, civil rights, and due process protections for children with disabilities up to age 21. Speech, language, and hearing impairments are considered to be types of disorders covered by IDEA. The Tech Act supports access to assistive technology (for example, communication devices, environmental control units, adapted computers and other equipment, specialized software) and services to limit the effects of impairments.

States also legislate services to persons with communication impairments, or to the professionals who provide these services. Nearly all states have licensure laws that regulate professional preparation and continuing education requirements for audiologists and speech-language pathologists. States can also regulate audiologists in their services related to hearing-aid dispensing ("State Requirements," n.d.). Other laws address services related to hearing impairment, although they may not specifically address the service provider. For example, laws mandating newborn hearing screening became common in the late 1990s, passed by state legislatures interested in reducing the detrimental effects of hearing impairment that can occur as early as the first few months of life. Because these laws were developed by individual states, there is some variation in the regulations. As of 2003, 39 states had passed some form of this legislation ("Status of State," n.d.) One example of this legislation is in the state of Illinois, which passed the Hearing Screening for Newborns Act, 410 ILCS 213/1, P.A. 91-67, which requires hearing screenings of newborn children, and follow-up evaluation and intervention for those with hearing impairments. Seven states (Connecticut, Kentucky, Louisiana, Maryland, Minnesota, Missouri, and Oklahoma) even require that health insurance plans cover provision of hearing aids for children ("State Insurance," n.d.).

OPERATING AUTHORITY, ACCREDITATION, AND PROFESSIONAL CREDENTIALING

The American Speech-Language-Hearing Association (ASHA) is the credentialing association for more than 110,000 audiologists and speech-language pathologists ("About ASHA," n.d.). ASHA has developed a scope of practice, preferred practice patterns, position statements, and practice guidelines for each of these professions that describes in detail the specific nature of the roles of practitioners in each discipline. The audiology scope of practice indicates that "audiologists provide audiological (aural) rehabilitation to children and adults," they "select, fit, and dispense . . . hearing aids and related devices," and they "prevent hearing loss through the provision and fitting of hearing protective devices, consultation on the effects of noise on hearing, and consumer education" (American Speech-Language-Hearing Association [ASHA], 1996, p. 13). The speech-language pathology scope of practice states that SLPs provide "prevention, diagnosis, habilitation, and rehabilitation of communication, swallowing, or other upper aerodigestive disorders, elective modification of communication behaviors, and enhancement of communication" (ASHA, 2001, p. 4).

ASHA considers audiologists and SLPs to be autonomous professionals, by which is meant that these professions are self-governing and that the practitioners have "the qualifications, responsibility and authority for the provision of services which fall within its scope of practice" (ASHA, 1986). Therefore, "their services need not be prescribed or supervised by individuals in other professions" (ASHA, 2001, p. 4). This does not mean that one never needs a referral to an audiologist or SLP; referral may be required by agencies employing audiologists and SLPs, or by a third-party payer. However, professional certification regulations do not limit the provision of audiological or speech-language services only on referral or only under the supervision of another profession.

Professional preparation is also regulated. The Council on Academic Accreditation (CAA) of ASHA grants accreditation of entry-level professional preparation programs with a major emphasis in audiology or speech-language pathology. The CAA is recognized by the U.S. Department of Education and the Council for Higher Education Accreditation as the only agency allowed to accredit graduate education programs in these two disciplines ("Council," n.d.).

Having completed a professional preparation course of study, audiologists and speech-language pathologists may obtain professional credentials. Certification requires completion of a graduate degree from an accredited professional preparation program, passing of the national board examination, and completion of an extended clinical fellowship under the supervision of a professional who is certified in the same discipline. This professional certificate, the Certificate of Clinical Competence (CCC-A for audiologists, or CCC-SLP for speech-language pathologists), is granted by ASHA and allows the holder to engage in clinical service provision.

Although the CCC is considered to be the primary certificate necessary in order to provide clinical services to clients (ASHA, 2003), audiologists and SLPs may also hold other required credentials (e.g., state licensure, registration, or teaching certification) (ASHA, 1996, 2001). Licensure is a mechanism that is used by states to regulate professionals and commonly relies on state licensure boards. Audiologists are regulated in 48 states (all except Idaho and Michigan); SLPs are regulated in 46 states (all except Colorado, Idaho, Michigan, and South Dakota) ("States Regulating," n.d.). A final mechanism of regulation involves the K–12 public education system, which is overseen in most states by a state department of education. States typically require a master's degree for employment in the public school; however, several allow employment of speech-language personnel who have a bachelor's degree. Because of the variety of professional credentials, individuals making referrals to an audiologist or speech-language pathologist may appropriately inquire whether the service provider holds an audiology or speech-language pathology Certificate of Clinical Competence, or other professional credentials.

Both disciplines function in a wide variety of professional settings providing services to infants, children, and adults of all ages. Audiologists typically practice in schools, hospitals, and physicians' offices; rehabilitation centers; home health, sub-acute rehabilitation, long-term care, and intermediate care facilities; industry, government health facilities, and research laboratories; private practice; managed-care systems; and the military (ASHA, 1996). SLPs practice in schools, health-care settings (e.g., hospitals, medical rehabilitation facilities, long-term care facilities, home health agencies, community clinics, behavioral and mental health facilities), private practice, group homes and sheltered workshops, correctional institutions, and government agencies (ASHA, 2001). Audiologists and SLPs are usually paid for their services directly by the agency for which they work; however, the professional services may be reimbursed by third-party payers such as insurance companies, Medicaid, and Medicare.

PURPOSE/INTENT

Audiologists and speech-language pathologists are professionals who evaluate, treat, and conduct research into human communication and its disorders. Audiologists engage in identification, assessment, prevention, and management of hearing, balance, and related disorders. They do this by (a) assessing and diagnosing hearing, balance, and related disorders in infants, children, and adults of all ages; (b) prescribing and dispensing hearing aids and assistive listening devices, as well as instructing people in their use; (c) striving to prevent hearing impairments through hearing conservation programs; and (d) providing intervention with children and adults in need of audiologic rehabilitation services (ASHA, 1996).

Audiologists provide particular types of assessment and intervention for persons with hearing impairment; they assess the degree, type, and configuration of hearing impairment. Degree of hearing impairment refers to the severity of impairment and ranges from slight to profound. Impairments also vary by type, so audiologists seek to determine the location of the auditory pathology along the auditory pathways. When assessing the configuration of impairment, audiologists seek to determine whether the impairment affects one or both ears, the differences in the sound frequencies that are involved, and whether the impairment came on suddenly or gradually (ASHA, 1996). They can also measure the status of the ear, detecting the presence of fluid in the middle ear, a perforated eardrum, or excessive accumulation of wax in the ear canal (ASHA).

Speech-language pathologists help people to develop and maximize their speech, language, and swallowing abilities. Their services include prevention, screening and diagnostic assessment, diagnosis, intervention, counseling, consultation, and follow-up services. The primary types of impairments for which SLPs provide services include speech sound articulation, language, voice, fluency, and swallowing (ASHA, 2001).

Speech sound articulation impairments involve problems in saying speech sounds correctly. Language impairments can include five distinct areas: (a) phonology, knowing the correct patterns in which speech sounds occur in a language; (b) morphology, the smallest meaningful units of language such as suffixes (e.g., -ing, -ed) and prefixes; (c) syntax, the organization of words within sentences; (d) semantics, the meaning of word; and (e) pragmatics, the functional use of language within a social context. Voice is produced by the larynx ("voice box") on certain speech sounds, but not others. For example, by placing one's hand on the neck, one can feel vibration that indicates voicing when producing "zzzz," but not when producing "ssss." Impairments of voicing can occur due to trauma, diseases such as cancer, emotional disorders, and misuse of the larynx as can occur when there is too much tension when speaking.

Fluency refers to the rhythmic flow of speech. A well-known fluency disorder is stuttering, in which the speaker repeats words or sounds in words, or has difficulty in the smooth production of speech. Swallowing disorders occur when an individual cannot properly ingest food or liquid. This can result in social problems because much social interaction occurs around eating, as well as health problems if an individual is unable to eat enough food or if food or drink is aspirated into the lungs while swallowing. An SLP can even provide services to a client who produces no speech by, for example, teaching the client to use assistive technology such as a talking computer.

SLPs can also provide services to persons who do not exhibit a disorder but who still wish to maximize their communication abilities. For example, SLPs can provide services to modify or enhance communication performance, such as accent modification, improvement of the professional voice, and personal or professional communication effectiveness (ASHA, 2001). Table 1 provides a list of questions helpful to SLPs when considering a client referral.

Table I   Evaluation Questions

Referral Questions—Audiology		
Regarding hearing, does the client . . .	Yes	No
have difficulty hearing a doorbell or telephone ring?		
play the radio or television too loudly?		
report that some sounds seem abnormally loud?		
have difficulty locating the source of sounds?		
report being able to hear, but unable to understand the speech of others?		
report that looking at the face of a conversational partner makes that partner easier to understand, especially when in a noisy places?		
often ask conversational partners to repeat themselves, or believe that most conversational partners frequently mumble when they talk?		
report hearing better in one ear than the other when using the telephone?		
often hear a ringing, buzzing, roaring, or hissing sound in one or both ears?		
experience unexplained dizziness?		
experience pain in the one or both ears, or have recurring ear infections, or drainage of fluid or blood from one or both ears?		
Referral Questions—Speech, Language, and Swallowing		
Regarding speech, does the client . . .	Yes	No
produce speech that is difficult to understand?		
experience difficulty in saying or imitating speech sounds, either consistently or inconsistently?		
appear to be groping for sounds when speaking?		
have difficulty imitating non-speech movements, such as sticking out the tongue or moving the tongue from one corner of the mouth to the other?		
speak either too slowly or excessively fast?		
use abnormal intonation when speaking?		
Regarding language, does the client . . .	Yes	No
have difficulty understanding questions?		
have limited ability to understand extended speech?		
have problems following spoken directions, especially those involving multiple steps?		
display limited ability to follow social rules of communication (e.g., knowing how to interpret jokes, sarcasm, or common expressions such as "it's raining cats and dogs")?		
experience problems understanding or using vocabulary or grammar?		
have difficulty producing complete sentences?		
have problems when relating steps needed to complete a task?		
have difficulty initiating conversation, or changing topics during conversation?		
lack the ability to self-correct or clarify when the conversational partner does not understand?		

(continued)

Table I   *(continued)*

	Yes	No
struggle in telling an extended story or narrative, either spoken or written?		
experience problems in reading and writing letters, words, phrases, sentences, and paragraphs?		
get criticized by others for unusual communication characteristics?		
Regarding fluency, does the client . . .	Yes	No
repeat sounds (e.g., p-p-p-pie), syllables or parts of words (e.g., pan-pan-pan-pantry), whole words (e.g., How are—are—are you?), or phrases (e.g., I am—I am—I am glad to meet you)?		
prolong (stretch out) sounds or syllables (e.g., fffffffish)?		
pause or hesitate between words of a sentence, when such pauses are not expected?		
feel that speaking causes embarrassment, shame, or loss of control?		
Regarding swallowing, does the client . . .	Yes	No
drool saliva, or seem unable to keep food or liquid from leaking out of the mouth?		
often have food become stuck in the mouth?		
often cough during or right after eating or drinking?		
produce a wet or gurgly sounding voice during or after eating or drinking?		
require extra effort or extra time for chewing or swallowing?		
feel congestion in the chest after eating?		
display limited food intake, resulting in weight loss or dehydration?		
experience embarrassment or isolation in social situations involving eating?		
Regarding voice, does the client . . .	Yes	No
use a pitch that sounds too high or too low for the client's age and gender?		
often speak with an intensity that is too loud or too soft?		
often speak with a hoarse, breathy, or nasal quality?		
experience pain or discomfort when speaking or singing?		

Treatment for Communication Impairments

Just as there are a variety of causes of hearing impairment, there also are various interventions. Some interventions are medical in orientation. For example, if the impairment is due to infection, then oral antibiotics or eardrops may be the treatment of choice. Other medical interventions can include removal of earwax in the ear canal, surgery to modify physical structure, and surgery to implant prosthetic hearing devices into the inner ear. Non-medical interventions can include (a) hearing aids, which are small devices that increase the loudness of sound projected to the ear; (b) personal listening systems (a.k.a. auditory training systems) that limit the effects of environmental noise; (c) direct audio input hearing aids, which are hearing aids that improve the sound quality from televisions or audio equipment, auditory trainers, or personal FM systems; (d) telephone amplifying devices, developed to work with certain hearing aids that have a "T" switch thereby providing better amplification of sound over the phone than do typical hearing aids; (e) auditorium-type assistive listening systems, available in public places equipped with special sound systems that send sound signals directly to the ears of persons with hearing impairment; and (f) lip reading, in which the person with hearing impairment carefully watches the mouth and the body movements of a communication partner to obtain visual cues about the message that is being spoken ("Hearing Loss," n.d.).

There is no one single method of intervention with persons who have communication impairments. Intervention methods, intensity, and duration vary greatly due to factors such as the course and type of disease or disorder, type and severity of impairment, client's motor and cognitive abilities, and client's level of awareness and motivation. When speech-language pathologists provide intervention for speech and language impairments they often do so through behavioral means, identifying behaviors that the client needs to learn in order to reach target goals. While the emphasis of intervention is often directly with the client, significant others may also be directly involved. In addition, the environment in which intervention occurs may vary greatly. At times intervention will occur in a therapy room with only the client and the speech-language pathologist and involve drill and practice; at another extreme it could occur in a functional location such as a restaurant and could involve the client interacting with the staff and patrons.

Both disciplines can be either primarily responsible, or involved on the team that provides services to persons with speech, language, or hearing impairments. When functioning as a part of a team, they engage collaboratively with other educational, rehabilitation and medical professionals (e.g., doctors, nurses, neuropsychologists, occupational therapists, physical therapists, social workers, and teachers) and families to provide comprehensive assessment and intervention for the person with communication impairments.

References

About ASHA. (n.d.). Retrieved September 30, 2003, from http://www.asha.org/about/

American Speech-Language Hearing Association (ASHA). (1986). Autonomy of speech-language pathology and audiology. *ASHA, 28,* 53–57.

American Speech-Language-Hearing Association (ASHA). (1996). Scope of practice in audiology. *ASHA, 38* (Suppl. 16), 12–15.

American Speech-Language-Hearing Association (ASHA). (2001). *Scope of practice in speech-language pathology.* Rockville, MD: Author.

American Speech-Language-Hearing Association (ASHA). (2003). Code of ethics (revised). *Asha Supplement, 23*, 13–15.

Bricker, D. (1993).Then, now, and the path between: A brief history of language intervention. In A. P. Kaiser & D. B. Gray (Eds.), *Enhancing children's communication: Research foundations for intervention* (Vol. 2, pp. 11–13). Baltimore, MD: Brookes.

Council on Academic Accreditation in Audiology and Speech-Language Pathology. (n.d.). Retrieved September 30, 2003, from http://www.asha.org/about/academia/accreditation/CAA overview.htm

Damasio, H. (2001). Neural basis of language disorders. In R. Chapey (Ed.), *Language intervention strategies in aphasia and related neurogenic communication disorders* (4th ed.). Philadelphia, PA: Lippincott Williams & Wilkins.

Department of Health and Human Services. (1991). Healthy people 2000: National health promotion and disease prevention objectives. (DHHS Publication No. 91-50121). Washington, DC: US Government Printing Office, Superintendent of Documents.

Duchan, J. F. (n.d.). *Getting here: the first hundred years of speech-language therapy in America.* Retrieved August 25, 2003, from http://www.acsu.buffalo.edu/-duchan/history.html

Hearing loss and older adults. (n.d.). Retrieved September 30, 2003, from http://www.nidcd.nih.gov/health/hearing/older.asp#4

McLean, J. E. (1983). Historical perspectives on the content of child language programs. In J. Miller, D. E. Yoder, & R. Schiefelbusch (Eds.), *Contemporary Issues in Language Intervention.* Rockville, MD: American Speech-Language-Hearing Association.

National Institute on Deafness and Other Communication Disorders. (n.d.). *Hearing loss and older adults.* Retrieved September 30, 2003, from http://www.nidcd.nih.govlhealthlhearinglolder.asp

National Institute on Deafness and Other Communication Disorders. (n.d.). *What is voice? What is speech? What is language?* Retrieved June 18, 2004, from http://www.nidcd.nih.gov/health/voice/whatis_vsl.asp

O'Neill, J. J. (1987). The development of speech-language pathology and audiology in the United States. In H. J. Oyer (Ed.), *Administration of programs in speech-language pathology and audiology.* Englewood Cliffs, NJ: Prentice-Hall.

Ramig, L. O., & Verdolini, K. (1998). Treatment efficacy: Voice disorders. *Journal of Speech, Language, and Hearing Research, 41,* S 101–S 116.

State insurance mandates for hearing aids. (n.d.). Retrieved September 30, 2003, from http://www.asha.org/aboutJlegislation-advocacy/state/issues/ha reimbursement.htm

State requirements for audiologists to dispense hearing aids. (n.d.). Retrieved September 30, 2003, from http://www.asha.org/about/legislationadvocacy/state/state_licensure. htm#requirements

States regulating audiology and speech-language pathology. (n.d.). Retrieved April 16, 2004, from http://www.asha.org/about/legislation-advocacy/state/state_licensure. htm#regs

Status of state universal newborn and infant hearing screening legislation and laws. (Aug. 13, 2004). Retrieved September 30, 2003, from http://www.asha.org/about/legislation-advocacy/state/bill_status.htm

SECTION III

Rehabilitation and Vocational Services

Vocational Rehabilitation

Carl R. Flowers

THE SOLDIERS REHABILITATION ACT TO THE WORKFORCE INVESTMENT ACT AND ONE-STOPS

Early efforts to address the influx of unskilled workers to urban areas included the passage of the Soldiers Rehabilitation Act of 1918. The 1920 Rehabilitation Act served as the beginning of federal involvement in employment assistance. Later programs were enacted, focusing on education and training of economically disadvantaged workers in expanding labor markets, including the Manpower Development Act (1962), Economic Employment Act (1964), and the Comprehensive Employment and Training Act (1973). Amid these legislative actions, several rehabilitation and disability-specific measures with linkages to employee assistance and workforce development, including the Randolph-Sheppard Act (1936) and the Barden-LaFollette Act (1943), were also enacted.

This chapter reviews the early rehabilitation-related legislation, as well as the legislation of rehabilitation's more recent "Golden Era," and explains their shared importance as major breakthroughs for individuals with disabilities and their vocational rehabilitation. The chapter concludes with an overview of the Workforce Investment Act (WIA) (1998), the most recent program focusing on access, employment, and workforce development. With its wide-ranging reforms, WIA targets all groups and encompasses two primary goals: (1) improving training and (2) improving employment options and opportunities for individuals, including persons with disabilities, through universal access to information and career-oriented services. The enactment of the WIA addresses many of the barriers and disincentives faced by individuals with disabilities in their efforts to obtain employment.

HISTORY/LEGISLATION

More than 80 years have passed since the establishment of vocational rehabilitation as a public program. The passage of the Soldiers' Rehabilitation Act (1918) became the thrust for the establishment of a civilian program serving individuals with physical disabilities. While the early programs were designed to serve injured veterans facing employment handicaps, the Soldiers Rehabilitation Act led to the enactment of the Smith-Fess Act (1920), which established a similar national program for civilians with physical disabilities. Two provisions of the early programs are noteworthy: First, program participation by states was optional, with agreements available to partially fund services for those states choosing to participate; and second, funding for the federal program was not guaranteed but rather was based on annual/biannual funding appropriations, as opposed to permanent authorizations. These funding provisions remained until the early 1930s when major reductions were proposed. President Roosevelt's signing of the Social Security Act (SSA) (1935) removed the provisional and fragile funding for vocational rehabilitation and made funding permanent. Under regulations of the SSA, funding was assured, and discontinuance would be allowed based on lack of program need and then only by Congressional action. As importantly, the legislation created a unique solution to the problem of old-age pensions and provided funds to assist children, the blind, and the unemployed; to institute vocational training programs; and to provide family health programs.

While early rehabilitation legislation focused on services to individuals with physical or orthopedic disabilities, the enactment of the Randolph-Sheppard Act (1936) resulted in the first major enhancement of services for persons with disabilities. Provisions of the Randolph-Sheppard Act (1936), and later the Javits-Wagner-O'Day Act (1938), targeted programs and services for persons with blindness and visual impairments. The legislation mandated expansion of programs and services for the blind, as well as federal support for goods produced by blind individuals (Benshoff & Janikowski, 2000). Rehabilitation legislation of the next decade included the Barden-LaFollette Act (Vocational Rehabilitation Act Amendments, 1943), the next significant legislative action impacting persons with disabilities. This legislation extended services to a new group of individuals—persons with mental illness or mental retardation. This inclusion marked a significant shift in the philosophy, from rehabilitation of persons with proven work histories to habilitation of persons with nonexistent or sporadic work histories (Inge, Barcus, Brooke, & Everson, 1995). However, it was not until the enactment of the National Mental Health Act (1946) that extensive services for this group were realized.

The passage of the Vocational Rehabilitation Amendment Act (1954) (P. L. 565) ushered in the beginning of the rehabilitation's golden era, which continued through the early 1970s with the enactment of the 1973 Rehabilitation Act (Rusalem & Malikin, 1976). The period was characterized as "golden," based on the major changes aimed at funding increases for programs and service enhancements, as well as increasing professionalism in the field. With respect to major funding appropriations for development of rehabilitation programs and services, appropriations surpassing $150 million highlighted this period and included expansion of services (legislated some ten years earlier) for individuals with mental illness (Rubin & Roessler, 2001). Significant funding increases were also appropriated to develop graduate counselor training programs aimed at preparing professional rehabilitation practitioners for both public and private sectors. A number of significant developments, including the establishment of professional associations with codes of ethics and regulation of practices, also occurred during this period (Emener & Cottone, 1989; Leahy, 2002). Several VR Act amendments were passed within the 20-year period. One of the major highlights of the 1965 Vocational Rehabilitation Act Amendments was the change in federal-state funding match, which increased federal share to 75/100 and 25/100 for the state share.

Rehabilitation's golden era (1954–1973) occurred during a period when the country was experiencing civil unrest: those protesting the Vietnam War made the nation's streets virtual battlefields, while protests of the nation's social and racial injustices were more visible and demonstrative. This greater social consciousness was important because it has been suggested that enactment of rehabilitation legislation during and subsequent to this period depicted the first attempts by the federal government to bring a collective social consciousness to the forefront regarding persons with disabilities (Shapiro, 1993; Wolfe, 1996). The initial focus on independent living of persons with disabilities served as a catalyst and integral component in reshaping the way these individuals were viewed during this period and forever thereafter (Flowers, Edwards & Pusch, 1996). The 1964 Civil Rights Act (P.L. 88-352), focusing on inclusion and prohibition of discrimination of minority groups, was also a major highlight of this period and tremendously influenced the rehabilitation legislation—the 1973 Rehabilitation Act—that followed.

The 1973 Rehabilitation Act (P.L. 93-112) was regarded as the civil rights act for persons with disabilities, as many of the congressional commitments of the civil rights legislation were also found in this legislation (Rubin & Roessler, 2001). Four sections of the Rehabilitation Act were very direct in their focus on eliminating discrimination against persons with disabilities. Section 501 mandated nondiscrimination by federal agencies in their hiring practices and also established affirmative action plans. Section 502 targeted elimination of physical and transportation barriers and included establishment of the Architecture and Transportation Barriers Compliance Board to enforce accessibility standards. Section 503 prohibited discrimination against persons with mental and physical disabilities and mandated affirmative action plans for all federal contract recipients and subcontractors receiving annual contracts in excess of $2,500. Finally, Section 504 targeted elimination of discrimination against individuals with disabilities in programs and activities. The enactment of this legislation also included a revised definition of a person with a disability and brought new attention and focus to three closely related areas: (a) services for the severely disabled, (b) greater client involvement in decision-making processes regarding services received, and (c) additional support for research related to persons with disabilities. The Individual Written Rehabilitation Plan (IWRP) was introduced and made a requirement in planning rehabilitation programming for individuals served by the state-federal program as a component of the Act. The influence of the earlier referenced independent living movement (Shapiro, 1993) was further enhanced with the 1978 Amendments to the Rehabilitation Act (P.L. 95-602), as independent living centers were established as a part of the state-federal rehabilitation program, thereby creating increased independence, integration, and employment opportunities for individuals with disabilities.

Technological advances, and their importance in increasing the ability of individuals with disabilities to participate in society, were key highlights of the 1986 Amendments to the Rehabilitation Act (P. L. 99-506). The availability and utilization of rehabilitation engineering services by state vocational rehabilitation agencies as mechanisms for increasing services, along with the emphasized options for increasing employability, were other key components of the amendments (Rubin & Roessler, 2001). Supported employment as a rehabilitation outcome was also included, with federal funds available to states for their *exclusive* use in serving individuals in supported employment programs. It is quite apparent that these changes were important for individuals with severe disabilities, as new, previously unavailable options for employment were created.

Additional legislation, including the Civil Rights of Institutionalized Persons Act (1980), Carl D. Perkins Vocational Education Act (1963), and Fair Housing Act (1968), were designed over the next few years to increase accessibility, programs, and services for persons with disabilities. The next major legislative actions were the Americans with Disabilities Act (ADA) (P.L. 101-336), the reauthorization of the Individuals with Disabilities Education Act (1991), and the Rehabilitation Act Amendments of 1992. Increased services (such as transition, on-the-job, and other personal assistance services for persons with disabilities), coupled with strengthened and clearly articulated anti-discrimination measures, were emphasized in these legislative actions (Whitney-Thomas & Thomas, 1996). Brooke (1999), noting the societal move away from professional dominance and toward increased consumer choice and integration, provides a snapshot of rehabilitation's recent history and associated societal trends, beginning with the 1950s and culminating with the 1998 Act amendments.

Table 1 Historical Overview of the Vocational Rehabilitation Act

Time Period Public Law and Policy	Societal Trends
Middle of the 20th Century Federal/state rehabilitation programs received large increases in funding. Participation limited to acquired disabilities with a clear demonstration of employment potential. <div align=center>PL 113 of 1943; PL 82-565 of 1954; and PL 89-333 of 1965</div>	**Medical model** with veterans and those who acquire disabilities representing the majority of persons being served. The majority of people with developmental disabilities are unemployed, live with families or in institutions where they are cared for by the state.
Early 1970s Increased awareness of employment services to all eligible persons regardless of their disability and its severity. <div align=center>PL 93-112 of 1973</div>	**Deinstitutionalization movement** begins primarily for persons with psychiatric disabilities. Beginning of "equal opportunity" with IL Centers receiving funding. The civil rights of people with disabilities are advanced.
Later 1970s Provided a clear delineation of employment rights with affirmative action provisions and funding for Independent Living Services. <div align=center>PL 95-602 of 1978</div>	**Readiness model** is very strong concept with people with disabilities earning their way to the next level of least restrictive alternative on the continuum. Services are constructed around security, consistency, and safety.
1980s National examination of values and approach to rehabilitation. Expanded the Act to include a definition and funding for supported employment. <div align=center>PL 99-506 of 1986</div>	**Functional supports** for all persons regardless of the level or type of disability is the new emphasis and becomes the model for rehabilitation. The old readiness model is judged to be an out-of-date concept.
Early 1990s Amendments guided by a statement of presumption of employability for most individuals with disabilities, provides for choice of services and service providers, defines integration, and emphasizes careers, not just entry jobs. <div align=center>PL 102-569 of 1992</div>	**Personal dignity and natural supports** represent the predominant thinking of this period with a clear rejection of professional dominance.
Late 1990s Streamlined administrative procedures and expanded assurances for informed choice with individuals developing their own Individualized Plan for Employment (IPE). <div align=center>PL 105-220 of 1998</div>	**People with disabilities are speaking out, asserting choice, and taking control** of their career paths and ultimately their lives. National recognition among policy leaders that systems change needs to occur across federal organizations to remove the barriers to employment for people with disabilities.

Reprinted from Brooke, V. (1999), It's up to us: Practice and attitudes cannot be legislated, *Journal of Vocational Rehabilitation, 12*, 1–5, with permission from IOS Press.

Americans with Disabilities Act

President George H. W. Bush signed the Americans with Disabilities Act (P. L. 101-336) into law on July 26, 1990, following passage of the bill by Senate (91-6) and House (377-28) votes. The ADA is considered *landmark* legislation in that it provided additional federal civil rights protections for people with disabilities, as evidenced in the purpose statement: the ADA provides

> a clear and comprehensive national mandate for the elimination of discrimination against individuals with disabilities and guarantees disabled people access to employment, public accommodations, transportation, public services and telecommunications. (Americans with Disabilities Act, 1990, p. 32)

The prototypes for the ADA included the earlier referenced 1964 Civil Rights Act, which prohibited discrimination based on race, color, sex, religion, and national origin in employment, public accommodations, and the provision of state and local government services; and Section 504 of the Rehabilitation Act (1973), which prohibited discrimination against individuals with disabilities by recipients of federal funds. The ADA focuses on two basic mandates to employees, public facilities, and providers of goods and services: First, individuals with disabilities must be given an equal opportunity to gain access to available employment and public accommodations; and second, public accommodations and employers must attempt to make reasonable accommodations to the physical and mental limitations of individuals with disabilities. Passage of the ADA has generally been viewed as a historically significant event, given the Act's emphasis on competitive employment for all persons with disabilities, regardless of severity.

1992 Rehabilitation Act Amendments

The Rehabilitation Act Amendments of 1992 (P. L. 102-569) became law on October 29, 1992, and formalized several rudimentary needed changes to the 1973 Rehabilitation Act, including the manner in which rehabilitation services were offered and provided to Americans with disabilities through the public rehabilitation program. Additionally, the amendments explicitly recognized individual competence and choice, and they afforded individuals with disabilities access to the services and supports they need to live, work, and meaningfully participate in community life. The legislation, with total funding appropriations exceeding $2 billion annually for programs, was built on the foundation of the ADA.

1998 Rehabilitation Act Amendments

The 1998 Rehabilitation Act Amendments, the last major rehabilitation legislation of the twentieth century, will likely be remembered as much for their content as for their placement within other legislation. Historically, with the Vocational Rehabilitation Act of 1954 and continuing through the original Rehabilitation Act of 1973 and its subsequent amendments as examples, legislation has been continuous in its aim to assist individuals with disabilities in achieving full integration into society via access to employment opportunities and ultimately obtaining employment. While those efforts were *stand-alone* legislative actions—that is, not directly tied to other legislation— the inclusion of the 1998 Rehabilitation Act Amendments as part of the Workforce Investment Act (WIA) (Workforce Investment Act of 1998, 2000) marked the first time that vocational rehabilitation initiatives were embodied in another workforce development program. While retaining and strengthening its language on the rights of persons with disabilities to make choices and enjoy full inclusion and integration in the economic, political, social, cultural, and educational mainstream of American society, amendment findings cited data and statistics related to disabilities faced by ethnic and racial minorities, and corresponding service delivery irregularities in the public rehabilitation system. Specifically, the findings restated concerns initially included in the 1992 amendments:

> Patterns of inequitable treatment of minorities have been documented in all major junctures of the vocational rehabilitation process. As compared to white Americans, a larger percentage of African-American applicants to the vocational rehabilitation system are denied acceptance. Of applicants accepted for service, a larger percentage of African-American cases are closed without being rehabilitated. Minorities are provided less training than their white counter parts. Consistently, less money is spent on minorities than their white counter parts. (Rehabilitation Act Amendments of 1992–2000, p. 4364)

At the same time, the amendments strengthened the public rehabilitation program with streamlined administrative procedures. It also placed additional emphasis on *choice* for individuals with disabilities, giving them the opportunity to make decisions affecting their own career direction (Shroeder, 1998). As part of the 1998 amendments, choice and quality outcomes (i.e., Individual Plan for Employment) were two of the major focal areas. It was toward that end that the Rehabilitation Act Amendments were included in the Workforce Investment Act (1998).

WORKFORCE INVESTMENT ACT AND ONE-STOP CENTERS

The Workforce Investment Act of 1998, which became effective in July 2000, was the culmination of a nearly decade-long negotiation process aimed at streamlining and unifying the nation's workforce development system. The legislation involved several employment and training programs, including the Job Training Partnership Act (JTPA) (1982), Omnibus Budget Reconciliation Act (1981), Family Support Act (1988), Personal Responsibility and Work Opportunity Reconciliation Act (PRWOA) (1996), and the Temporary Assistance to Needy Families (TANF) Act of the late 1980s and early 1990s. The JTPA served as the nation's largest federal employment training program from the early 1980s until 2000 and served dislocated workers, homeless individuals, and economically disadvantaged adults, youths and older workers. While the WIA legislation incorporated those same groups and added persons with disabilities as another target group, the funding for WIA and JTPA came from different sources. With enactment of the WIA legislation, the accompanying rules provided the clear expression of legislator's intent:

> WIA reforms Federal job training programs and creates a new, comprehensive workforce investment system. The reformed system is intended to be customer-focused, to help Americans access the tools they need to manage their careers through information and high quality services, and to help U.S. companies find skilled workers. . . . The underlying notion of One-Stop is the coordination of programs, services and governance structures so that the customer has access to a seamless system of workforce investment services. We envision that a variety of programs could use common intake, case management and job development systems in order to take full advantage of the One-Stops' potential for efficiency and effectiveness. A wide range of services from a variety of training and employment programs will be available to meet the needs of employers and job seekers. The challenge in making One-Stop live up to its potential is to make sure that the State and Local Boards can effectively coordinate and collaborate with the network of other service agencies, including TANF agencies, transportation agencies and providers, metropolitan planning organizations, child care agencies, nonprofit and community partners, and the broad range of partners who work with youth. (Rules and Regulations for Workforce Investment Act, 2000, p. 49294)

Two major differences, however, exist between the JTPA and the WIA with regard to the funding processes. In the JTPA, separate funding streams and authorizing legislation for this act, as well as the Wagner-Peyser Act, vocational education, adult education, and vocational rehabilitation, were maintained. Additionally, with JTPA, the funding streams were separated even further with specific funds established for disadvantaged adults, dislocated workers, disadvantaged youth, and summer youth. WIA, on the other hand, was organized into five titles: Title I, Job Training; Title II, Adult Education; Title III, amendments to Wagner-Peyser and related Acts; Title IV, amendments to the Vocational Rehabilitation Act; and Title V, miscellaneous linking and transitioning from the JTPA. While the Rehabilitation Act Amendments were incorporated into WIA, the state federal system was to be maintained as an autonomous system (Shroeder, 1998).

Purpose/Structure

As noted above, WIA combined more than 50 federal job training resources and programs of the Departments of Labor, Education, and Health and Human Services, and focused on two primary purposes: addressing the needs of employers seeking skilled workers, and providing programs and services to all job seekers seeking employment and career advancement. Prior to the WIA, efforts at combining and integrating the various workforce employment and training programs, including Youth, Adult, and Dislocated Worker Activities; Job Corps; Native American Programs; Migrant and Seasonal Farmworker Programs; Veterans' Workforce Investment Programs; Youth Opportunity Grants; and rehabilitation, were voluntary. This voluntary arrangement has been viewed as a significant barrier to full access for all desiring to use one or more of the programs. Initial WIA program administration involved several organizations and partnerships thorough collaborative efforts. While WIA regulations mandated local, state created, business-led Workforce Investment Boards to ensure local participation, few other restrictions were placed on the program, with the exception of establishment of fund distribution allocation formulas as methods of evaluating program performance and accessible one-stop career centers.

One-Stop Centers

The one-stop centers, a key component of the WIA workforce development program, began in the 1990s as demonstration projects designed to address federal reports highlighting a fragmented national employment and training system (Imel, 1999). The initial focus of the centers was consolidation of programs, resources, and services—for example, state job services, unemployment insurance, public assistance, and career services—operated through a nationwide network (Perry-Varner, 1998). Under WIA, the one-stop center approach was expanded, combining several federal jobs-related programs to offer prospective employees more options and better opportunities. For employers, the one-stop centers provided a central clearinghouse where workforce needs could be reported and job seekers could access relevant information on the openings. While most states in the WIA program have multiple or networked centers, all states are required to maintain a minimum number of accessible, comprehensive centers in each local service delivery area. In 2000, more than 900 one-stop centers were in operation, with the number of service delivery areas and number of centers within an area based on several factors, including population, local labor market areas, and the identified need for services within a *reasonable* travel distance.

The goals of the WIA were encapsulated in several principles, including state and local flexibility, individual empowerment, and youth programming. In addition, WIA facilitated universal access, promoted streamlined services, and required accountability of programs and services. Based on those principles, the WIA offers multiple benefits for persons with disabilities. The principles of universal access, streamlined services, and accountability are discussed below.

Universal Access. Under this principle, one-stop centers must be available and accessible to all individuals seeking employment, as well as to employers. WIA's universal access allowed and supported the notion that individuals with disabilities were to be viewed as full partners—that is, able to access the same services in the same locations as everyone else—in the new workforce development program. Another key element enabled persons with disabilities to utilize the services without having to *request* accommodations. Alternately, the universal access principle made explicit the idea that individuals with disabilities also have the right to reasonable accommodations in accessing WIA services.

Streamlined Services.   A key component of this principle is that all job seekers should be brought together and philosophically served in the same one-stop centers, where a variety of employment and training programs are available. This represented a literal as well as logistical change for individuals with disabilities, who, prior to this legislation, received services from dedicated staff in rehabilitation agencies. For these individuals—and more specifically, those with severe disabilities—WIA's aforementioned universal access principle has the potential to increase opportunities for employment, training and self-sufficiency through the availability of three groups of services: core, intensive, and training.

Core services.   Services in this phase include those which are generally referred to as self-service and informational, and which are available to everyone using the centers. The initial assessment, as well as job search and placement assistance, are two minimal services that might be included in this service area. The initial assessment determines the individual's skill levels, aptitudes, and supportive services needs. The job search and placement assistance helps the individual determine whether he or she is unable to obtain employment and therefore requires additional, more intensive services to obtain employment.

Under WIA, one-stop program participants are under no set time lines for receiving core services prior to moving to the intensive service phase; and decisions on which core services to provide and the timing of their delivery are made on a case-by-case basis at the local level, depending on participant needs. Other potential one-stop center core services include counseling, individual job development, job clubs, and screened referrals (when requested by the employer).

Intensive services.   The second service grouping is designed for unemployment program participants unable to obtain a job subsequent to utilizing the core services. Individuals who require these services to obtain or retain employment may also participate in more comprehensive assessments of skill levels and receive additional assistance and services. Other services in this phase include individual employment-plan development, group counseling, individual counseling, case management, and short-term pre-vocational services.

Training services.   The third service grouping available for WIA program participants involves activities for individuals who remain unemployed or are unable to retain employment but are still eligible for services. Services in this grouping can take many forms but usually involve training specifically to workforce needs of the local area (or another area in which the program participant is willing to relocate). Occupational skills training, on-the-job training, adult education, and literacy training are examples of services that could be customized to meet the needs of a specific employer (or group of employers) who commits to hiring individuals upon successful completion of training.

When training funds are limited within local service delivery areas, regulations mandate priority for three groups: persons with low income, persons receiving public assistance, and individuals with disabilities. Small-business or entrepreneurial training to assist individuals in starting and growing a business, job-readiness training, and on-the-job training are other examples of services that could, under some circumstances, be provided. Additionally, employment-related informational training for both individuals and employers may be available. Training on workplace accommodations, recruitment law, labor law, and the ADA are examples of other ancillary services that can increase the opportunities of unemployed workers.

Accountability. This principle addresses the concern that programs and services become responsible for outcomes. It was based on previous workforce development programs, including JTPA, Dislocated Worker, and Welfare-to-Work, which lacked oversight and performance measures (Pantazis, 1999). For example, under WIA reporting and evaluation mechanisms, a number of criteria, including the number of individuals acquiring and retaining jobs as well as the satisfaction of customers with the process (i.e., those seeking jobs and those employers looking to hire), were established.

CONCLUSION

While the WIA program and the cornerstone one-stop centers are not trouble free, it is essential that individuals with disabilities recognize the numerous options available as a result of the legislation. These options include services and programs that are disability and non-disability specific, including service access and full inclusion. Regarding access to services, individuals who are eligible for vocational rehabilitation services have the choice of accessing all one-stop services, including core, intensive, and training components, from the one-stop centers or the VR agency, whichever is more convenient. In the area of full inclusion, it is not a secret that individuals with disabilities have typically not benefited from the standard services available in workforce development programs. However, the inclusion of the Rehabilitation Act Amendments as part of WIA and its accompanying regulations makes it apparent that individuals with disabilities are a population that must be served to the same extent as other targeted groups.

References

Americans with Disabilities Act (P.L. 101-336) (n.d.). Retrieved September 10, 2004, from www.usdoj.gov/crt/ada/pubs/ada.txt

Benshoff, J. J., & Janikowski, T. P. (2000). *The rehabilitation model of substance abuse counseling.* Belmont, CA: Wadsworth.

Brooke, V. (1999). It's up to us: Practice and attitudes cannot be legislated. *Journal of Vocational Rehabilitation, 12,* 1–5.

Carl D. Perkins Vocational Education Act of 1963, 20 U.S.C.A. § 1241 *et seq.* (West 2000).

Civil Rights of Institutionalized Persons Act of 1980, 42 U.S.C.A. § 1997 (West 2000).

Comprehensive Employment and Training Act of 1973, 18 U.S.C.A. § 655 *et seq.* (West 2000).

Economic Employment Act of 1964, 42 U.S.C.A. § 2701 *et seq.* (West 2000).

Ellis, N. S. (2001). Individual training accounts under the workforce investment act: Is choice a good thing? *Georgetown Journal on Poverty Law & Policy, 8*(1), 235–247.

Emener, W. E., & Cottone, R. R. (1989). Professionalism, deprofessionalism and reprofessionalism of rehabilitation counseling according to criteria of professions. *Journal of Counseling and Development, 67*(10), 576–581.

Fair Housing Act of 1968, 42 U.S.C.A. § 3601 *et seq.* (West 2000).

Flowers, C., Edwards, D., & Pusch, B. (1996). Rehabilitation cultural diversity initiative: A regional survey of cultural diversity with CILs. *Journal of Rehabilitation, 62*(3), 22–28.

Hershensen, D. B. (2001). Promoting work adjustment in workforce investment act customers: a role for employment counselors. *Journal of Employment Counseling, 38,* 28–37.

Individuals with Disabilities Education Act of 1990, 20 U.S.C.A. § 871 *et seq.* (West 2000).

Imel, S. (1999). One-stop career centers (Report No. EDO-CE-99-208). Columbus, OH: Clearinghouse on Adult, Career, and Vocational Education. (ERIC Document Reproduction Service No. ED434244.)

Inge, K. J., Barcus, J. M., Brooke, V., & Everson, J. (1995). *Supported employment staff training manual* (2nd ed.). Richmond: Virginia Commonwealth University, Rehabilitation Research and Training Center on Supported Employment.

Javits-Wagner-O'Day Act of 1938, 41 U.S.C.A. § 41 *et seq.* (West 2000).

Leahy, M. J. (2002). Professionalism in rehabilitation counseling: A retrospective review. *Journal of Rehabilitation Administration, 26*(2), 99–109.

National Mental Health Act of 1946, 42 U.S.C.A. § 201 *et seq.* (West 2000).

Pantazis, C. (1999). The new workforce investment act. *Training and Development, 53*(8), 48–50.

Perry-Varner, E. (1998). One-stop career centers: An emerging concept for delivering employment services. *Journal of Vocational Rehabilitation, 10*(1), 39–50.

Randolph-Sheppard Act of 1936, 20 U.S.C.A. § 107 *et seq.* (West 2000).

Rehabilitation Act Amendments of 1992, 15 U.S.C.A. § 1431; 29 U.S.C.A. § 701 *et seq.* (West 2000).

Rubin, S. E., & Roessler, R. T. (2001). *Foundations of the vocational rehabilitation process* (5th ed.). Austin, TX: Pro-Ed.

Rules and Regulations for Workforce Investment Act, 20 CFR Part 652 and Parts 660 through 671 (West 2000).

Rusalem, H., & Malikin, D. (1976) *Contemporary vocational rehabilitation.* New York: New York University Press.

Shapiro, J. P. (1993). *No pity: People with disabilities forging a new civil rights movement*. New York: Times Books.

Shroeder, F. K. (1998) A summary of the rehabilitation act amendments of 1998. *American Rehabilitation, 24(*4), 1–2.

Smith-Hughes Vocational Education Act of 1917, 20 U.S.C.A. § 11 *et seq.* (West 2000).

Social Security Act of 1935, 42 U.S.C.A. § 301 *et seq.* (West 2000).

Vocational Rehabilitation Act of 1918, Pub. L. No. 178, § 107 Stat. 617 (West 2000).

Vocational Rehabilitation Act Amendments of 1943, 29 U.S.C.A. § 31 *et seq.* (West 2000).

Vocational Rehabilitation of Persons Injured in Industry Act of 1920, 29 U.S.C.A. § 31 *et seq.* (West 2000).

Whitney-Thomas, J., & Thomas, D. M. (1996). Multiple perspectives on implementing the Rehabilitation Act Amendments of 1992. (Report No. EC 305 755). Boston: Institute on Community Inclusion, Children's Hospital. (ERIC Document Reproduction Service No. ED410705.)

Wolfe, K. E. (1997). *Career counseling for people with disabilities*. Austin, TX: Pro-Ed.

Workforce Investment Act of 1998, 20 U.S.C.A. § 9201 (West 2000).

Community Rehabilitation Programs/Supported Employment

Karen Barrett & Jewell Jones

History/Legislation

Community rehabilitation programs cannot escape the impact of the historical and legislative context in which they provide their services. Early rehabilitation history reflected services motivated by feelings of pity, one of the first themes seen in service delivery to people with disabilities. Church groups, motivated by morality, operated almshouses and charities to which people with disabilities could come for help and support. The first sheltered workshops for the blind were developed by Valentin Hauy in Paris in 1784 (Rubin & Roessler, 1995).

Though many people with disabilities were either institutionalized or employed in workshops, a second theme—indebtedness—began to emerge as soldiers returned from various wars. These soldiers, having survived injuries due to advances in medical technology were re-entering civilian life with significant disabilities. Motivated by a sense of debt to these soldiers returning from the war, vocational education services were legislated in part by the Soldiers Rehabilitation Act of 1918 (Rubin & Roessler).

Income tax laws and the Social Security Administration helped to provide funds for public services and reflect the third historical theme, that of social investment. Once people began availing themselves of necessary governmental support, the government saw a need to help people re-enter the workforce as a way to save money, thereby making taxpayers out of tax users.

110

Legislation in the 1950s saw expansion of the range of consumer services, from people with physical disability to people with mental re and mental illness, and the civil rights movement began to champion the consumer perspective. The landmark case, *Brown v. Board of Education,* set the stage with the ethic that "separate is not equal," a value that continues to guide rehabilitation services today. The growth of social activism for women and minority groups and the passage of the Civil Rights Act of 1964 (Rubin & Roessler, 1995) laid the groundwork for the Rehabilitation Act of 1973. The Rehabilitation Act, though motivated in part by the idea of turning tax users into taxpayers, also incorporated the first legislation of affirmative action for people with disabilities, charging that work was not charity but was a right of people with disabilities.

Federal legislation continued to expand with the Rehabilitation Act Amendments of 1986. These amendments provided federal funds for demonstration projects specifically for supported employment programs and expanded federal support for community rehabilitation providers (Brooke, Inge, Armstrong, & Wehman, 1997). The idea that a person had to be employable or "work ready" prior to starting a job also began to be challenged on a national level (Brooke et al.). Though many services to people with disabilities continued to be facility based and nonwork related at this time, community rehabilitation programs began to convert these services to supported and competitive or integrated placements (Brooke et al.).

In 1988, the Technology-related Assistance for Individuals with Disabilities Act was signed into law. The central purpose of the act was to expand the availability of assistive technology services and devices to people with disabilities, by providing federal support and financial assistance to states (Technology-related Assistance for Individuals with Disabilities Act of 1988).

The Americans with Disabilities Act of 1990 confirmed the nation's commitment to equal access for people with disabilities to employment, transportation, and public services, and it paved the way for further employment options and protections for people with disabilities. The 1992 Amendments to the Rehabilitation Act strengthened the ideas of consumer involvement and competitive employment in integrated settings. Additionally, sheltered work was no longer considered an appropriate long-term vocational goal by many rehabilitation professionals. This legislation championed the theme of equal rights and choice for people with disabilities, and the ethic that people with disabilities should work in integrated settings continued to gain strength.

In order to strengthen civil rights laws and in effect level the playing field for persons with disabilities, the Civil Rights Act of 1964 was amended. The passage of the Civil Rights Act of 1991 allowed for monetary compensation and punitive damages for intentional discrimination and unlawful harassment for religious, sex, and disability discrimination in the workplace (Civil Rights Act of 1991).

In 1995, the Social Security Administration initiated the alternative provider program. Studies had shown that although 15%–30% of recipients of Supplemental Security Income (SSI) and Social Security Disability Insurance

(SSDI) indicate an interest in returning to work, only .25% were being returned to work through state vocational rehabilitation programs (Marini & Stebnicki, 1999). Though state vocational rehabilitation programs have the first opportunity to work with recipients, qualifying community rehabilitation programs can gain access after four months to the names of SSI and SSDI recipients in order to recruit the recipients as clients in their return-to-work programs (Marini & Stebnicki).

Yet despite legislative change efforts, vocational rehabilitation programs were not making significant headway towards reducing unemployment of people with disabilities. The unemployment rate of people with disabilities in 2000 was still more than 80% (Louis Harris & Associates, 2000). Part of the unemployment picture was the significant disincentives for people with disabilities to return to work, including loss of medical benefits. In an attempt to address these issues, Congress passed the Ticket to Work—Work Incentives Improvement Act of 1999 (TW-WIIA). The primary purpose of this act was to increase the employment rates of Social Security recipients (Roessler, 2002). Included in the legislation is a "ticket to work," which individuals can use to purchase vocational rehabilitation services from a provider who is part of an employment network (Roessler). Qualified and approved community rehabilitation programs are equal partners in these networks, which include state vocational rehabilitation agencies, schools, employers, and career centers (Roessler). Although legislation has traditionally supported the employment of people with disabilities, unemployment and underemployment are still significant issues to be addressed by providers of rehabilitation.

PURPOSE/INTENT

Supported employment endures because of the continued commitment to employment of people with significant disabilities. It can take many forms, and it has grown from its initial use, with people with developmental disabilities, to an employment strategy utilized for many populations.

Supported employment is defined by the Rehabilitation Amendments of 1986 (P.L. 99-506) and 1992 (P.L. 102-569) as "competitive employment in an integrated setting with ongoing support services for individuals with the most severe disabilities" (Substance Abuse and Mental Health Services Administration [SAMHSA], 2003, p. 20). Founders of the supported employment model challenged the prevailing attitude in rehabilitation of getting individuals with disabilities job ready, instead advocating for a "place-then-train" approach (West, 1995). Instead of learning skills in order to become employed, people who use supported employment services are first placed on the job, and then provided with supports necessary to maintain the job (West).

The Rehabilitation Research and Training Center on Supported Employment housed at Virginia Commonwealth University has outlined nine core values for supported employment (Brooke et al., 1997; Wehman & Targett, 2002):

1. the belief that all people can work and have a right to work;
2. the idea that this work should occur within regular local businesses;
3. the value that people should choose the supports they want;
4. the right to equal wages and benefits;
5. a focus on abilities rather than on disabilities;
6. the importance of community relationships;
7. personal determination of goals and supports;
8. challenging traditional service systems which do not emphasize a consumer-driven perspective; and
9. the importance of both formal and informal community connections.

In January of 2001, the Rehabilitation Services Administration helped to define what supported employment is *not*, by redefining the term "employment outcome" to mean "an individual with a disability working in an integrated setting" (*Federal Register*, 2001). Because of this policy change, individuals who had employment outcomes in non-integrated or sheltered employment settings could no longer receive funding for supported employment through state vocational rehabilitation services. Services have reflected these policy changes by slowly, but steadily, converting facility-based employment services to more competitive, supported employment models (West, Revell, & Wehman, 1998).

There are a number of incentives for employers to participate in hiring people with disabilities in the supported employment process. According to the U.S. Department of Labor, Office of Disability Policy (2003), there are several funding opportunities for businesses, including: the Small Business Tax Credit (Internal Revenue Service IRS Code Section 44), Disabled Access Credit, Architectural/Transportation Tax Deduction (IRS Code Section 190), and the Barrier Removal and the Work Opportunity Tax Credit (WOTC). The Small Business Tax Credit allows for small business to take a tax credit for improving accessibility for individuals with disabilities. The Architectural/Transportation Tax Deduction allows employers to offset the cost of accommodations for people with disabilities with a tax deduction for the business. Similarly, the WOTC provides a tax credit to employers who hire certain groups who have low incomes, including recipients of vocational rehabilitation services and Supplemental Security Income (SSI).

CLIENT SERVICES

Supported employment has challenged the widely-held perception that people with significant disabilities cannot work in competitive settings (Brooke et al., 1997). A number of supported employment models contribute to the success of the approach. Generally, supported employment models come in two types: group placement and individual placement. Perhaps because the individual model of competitive employment is "considered by many to be the least restrictive and most normalizing" of the service models (Brooke et al., p. 5), the vast majority of people (77.4%) in supported employment participate in individual placements (Wehman & Bricout, 1997).

Group models are known as "enclaves," "mobile work crews," "clusters," and "entrepreneurial models" (Wehman & Bricout, 1997), and at one time there may have been some agreement among professionals as to what these terms mean. As models have evolved over time and been modified, professionals may have differing understandings of the terms above.

Group models differ in a number of ways. One way groups differ is in how the group is supervised. For example, in a mobile work crew the supervisor may be responsible for traveling with the group to various sites and may be responsible for contract acquisition. The supervisor may be employed by the agency providing the supported employment or may be employed by the business who is hiring the group. Job training may be provided by the employer or by the supported employment agency. The group may work together in a community-based business, be dispersed throughout the business, or work together and travel to different businesses and sites. The group may be paid on a production or piecework basis or may be paid individually, commensurate with nonsupported employees at the same business (Wehman & Bricout, 1997).

Supported self-employment is a type of individual placement that is gaining continued support in rehabilitation (Rizzo, 2002). This service model has a number of advantages. It can provide employment in an interest area where no current job opportunities exist. It can provide the client–business owner a great degree of autonomy and flexibility (e.g., scheduling work hours), and she or he does not have to be concerned about accommodation and discrimination (Hagner & Davies, 2002; Rizzo, 2002). Some of the challenges of self-employment include the amount of work it takes to make a business successful, accurate record keeping, and social isolation of the business owner (Hagner & Davies, 2002). An additional challenge is that most businesses take a significant length of time before they generate income (Hagner & Davies).

Individual placement is characterized by one person with a disability, working in a competitive setting of his or her choice, supported by an employment specialist (Brooke et al., 1997). Employment specialists, also known as job coaches, play a number of roles in the supported employment process. They help job seekers identify and develop interest and skill profiles; identify jobs and careers that match their individual interests, skills, and choices; provide on-the-job training and supports; and identify and set up long-term supports (Brooke et al.).

A growing initiative in individual placement is the use of existing supports at the workplace. One such example would be enlisting the support of the company's Employee Assistance Program in restructuring a job or work environment (Unger, 1999). Other examples of workplace supports are schedule, task, and job changes; social supports; training; and assistive technology, all provided by the employer (Wehman & Bricout, 1997).

Assistive technology is defined as "any item, piece of equipment, or product system—whether acquired off the shelf, modified, or customized—that is used to increase, maintain, or improve functional capabilities of individuals with disabilities" (Assistive Technology Act of 1998). Assistive technology need not be high-tech or expensive. For example, if an individual worker needs a job aid to remember the steps in meal preparation, an employer might purchase a $20 disposable camera, have the employment specialist take pictures of the job steps, print them, and post the steps on the wall to help guide the employee through the meal preparation process.

Two individual models traditionally affiliated with services for people with mental illness are the Choose-Get-Keep model (Danley, Sciarappa, & MacDonald-Wilson, 1992), and the individual placement and support model (Becker & Drake, 1994). Each model emphasizes consumer choice; exploration and identification of skills, interests, and resources; and provision of whatever support is necessary for job acquisition and long-term retention (Pratt, Gill, Barrett, & Roberts, 1999). An employment specialist may also engage in a process known as "job carving" in supported employment. This is a process by which an employment specialist creates a job that matches a particular client's job skills, where a job does not currently exist (Pratt et al.).

Unger (1999) identified the supports that are most commonly needed by supported-employment consumers as the areas of training, advancement, benefits, and organizational culture. Learning how to do the job, remembering how to do the job, and completing job duties were some of the most frequently reported employee training needs. Workplace culture, though cited less often as a support need, included problem behaviors, arranging work schedules, taking breaks, and getting along with co-workers. The areas of career advancement (e.g., asking for promotion) and employee benefits were cited least often by employers as supports needed by their supported employees (Unger).

Whatever the model used in designing services, the dictates of best practice include customer direction and control, career development, full participation in the community, supports for long-term job retention, use of existing and natural supports at the employer site, evaluation and improvement of services, use of assistive technology, and person-centered planning (Brooke et al., 1997). Best practice is also defined by national accrediting bodies. For example, the Commission on Accreditation of Rehabilitation Facilities (CARF) sets national minimum standards for employment-services programs, and these standards include specific requirements centered around individualized service planning, design, and delivery (Commission on Accreditation of Rehabilitation Facilities [CARF], 2003). Additionally, CARF has identified employment-services standards to which organizations must comply in order to obtain or maintain its accreditation.

COSTS AND FUNDING

The costs of supported employment vary widely from state to state. Fiscal year 1997 data indicate that $2,733 is expended on average for each person receiving supported employment (Kregel, Wehman, Revell, Hill, & Cimera, 2000). Typically, state vocational rehabilitation agencies fund the initial costs of placement in supported employment, and other agencies (state mental health and developmental disability agencies) then pick up the costs of long-term supports (Kregel et al.). Supported employment services also tend to be a less expensive alternative to sheltered work programs by 40 to 60% (Kregel et al.). When extended service funds are in short supply, vocational rehabilitation programs may see an increase in their portion of the cost of service delivery. Without financial support for extended services, there may be delays in getting the extended service plans written and implemented, and the individual may lose the job due to lack of extended service supports (Kregel et al.).

Community rehabilitation programs that contract with state vocational rehabilitation agencies are often required to meet minimum standards of quality. CARF reports that more than 40 states either require or recognize its standards for organizations in order for them to be on the state vendors list (CARF, 2003). As of 2003, CARF accredits 10,000 services in over 3,500 different organizations in the United States and Canada (CARF). Community rehabilitation programs (CRPs) in most states must meet minimum and national standards of quality in order to be reimbursed by the state vocational rehabilitation agencies for services, including job development, placement, job coaching, and supported employment. Yet, often the state reimbursement rate authorized to pay for the CRP services barely covers the cost of providing those services. This can be a disincentive for CRPs to serve clients from state vocational rehabilitation programs.

Despite the demonstrated success and cost effectiveness of supported employment services when compared to day programs and facility-based or sheltered employment (Revell, Kregel, Wehman, & Bond, 2000) often the state reimbursement rate for those services does not cover the cost of those services. Additionally, there are other continued challenges to supported employment (West, Revell, & Wehman, 1998). For example, if CRPs become part of the employment network outlined with the Ticket to Work—Work Incentives Improvement Act (TW-WIIA) there are significant challenges for CRPs due to the complex reimbursement process (Roessler, 2002).

Another funding stream that is being utilized to provide supported employment services in the long term is the Home and Community-Based Services Medicaid Waiver Program (Kregel et al., 2000). In 1981, President Reagan signed legislation that provided states a way to use Medicaid funds for services not traditionally covered by Medicaid—specifically, services offered at home and in the community (Centers for Medicare and Medicaid

Services [CMS], 2003). In 1997, the Balanced Budget Act removed the requirement of prior institutional placement of individuals in order to be eligible for supported employment services provided under a waiver program (Richardson, 1998).

The last way in which supported employment services are funded is through extended-services monies provided by state mental health and developmental disabilities (MH/DD) agencies. Traditionally, state vocational rehabilitation programs have provided the financial support for the initial and time-limited placement in supported employment, and state MH/DD have paid for the long-term supports (Kregel et al., 2000). Efficiency and effectiveness of management practices in these areas impact the quality of services delivered. For example, if funding streams are fiscally mismanaged, services will cease, ultimately impacting both staff and consumers. Management practices that affect staffing are also crucial to effective delivery of supported employment services.

Though certainly competence in management of a supported employment agency is crucial to effective service delivery, perhaps the most important position in the process is the job coach or employment specialist. "Over half (60%) of supported employment costs are attributed to direct services personnel (employment specialists)" (Kregel et al., 2000, p. 156). The role of this staff person is often seen as that of a paraprofessional, which implies lack of professional preparation and results in low salary and benefits when compared to those of other rehabilitation professionals (Wehman & Targett, 2002). This may lead to role confusion, lack of opportunity for career advancement (Wehman & Targett), and other issues (e.g., lack of recognition), which in turn may contribute to staff turnover. Though the costs of turnover have been delineated (Barrett, Flowers, Crimando, Riggar, & Bailey, 1997), the most immediate effect of staff turnover is the consumer's loss of a job coach, which can result in loss of information (Wehman & Target) that is crucial to the continued success of that individual on that job. Additionally, this negative experience may preclude the placement of any individuals with that employer in the future. The federal government has allotted monies for training for supported employment agencies in order for providers to have a better understanding of their job duties, including working with individuals with disabilities.

The Rehabilitation Services Administration operates training centers across the United States to serve the current staff development needs of state VR agency staff, and for staff of public and private nonprofit rehabilitation agencies. The Community Rehabilitation Program–Rehabilitation Continuing Education Programs (CRP–RCEPs) are specifically charged with the human resource development of staff employed by community rehabilitation programs (Dept. of Education, n.d.). This is evidence of continued federal support for human resource development within CRPs. CRPs, with the help of federal support, provide training so that staff can do their jobs more efficiently and effectively, and they also inform and educate staff about the organization's mission, values, and services. When done well, this training prepares staff at the organization to be able to articulate this vision and describe the services of the agency when there are inquiries from potential customers and other stakeholders.

REFERRAL QUESTIONS

The Rehabilitation Research and Training Center (RRTC) on Supported Employment at Virginia Commonwealth University (VCU) has outlined a number of questions customers can use to evaluate and choose employment support agencies (Brooke, Wehman, Inge, & Parent, 1995; Brooke et al., 1997). The RRTC at VCU suggests that customers ask about the organization's vision, the types of services provided, and how they see the role of the customer in the process. The customer should ask about the degree of experience the organization has in working with people with different types of disabilities, and whether the agency has ever excluded anyone with a disability from participating in its services. If so, the reason for that exclusion should be determined. In determining how the agency markets itself, the customer should ask for copies of its marketing materials and determine how the agency approaches potential employers. The customer needs to ask specific questions in regard to staffing and turnover levels, especially the average length of employment of key frontline staff. Types and quality of job placements, as well as average earnings, are additional items for customers to explore before choosing a supported employment agency. The customer will want to ask how much leeway he or she will have in the choice of an employment specialist. Customers needing help with Social Security issues or extended services should ask if the agency provides these services. Lastly, the RRTC at VCU suggests that customers ask to see customer satisfaction data and be provided references from other customers, employers, and family members (Brooke et al., 1995; Brooke et al., 1997). Answers to these questions will greatly aid in an informed decision in choosing a provider of supported employment services.

CONCLUSION

Community rehabilitation programs and services reflect these same historical themes of pity, debt, social investment, and civil rights in their service delivery. Some continue to be affiliated with religious organizations (e.g., Catholic Charities, Jewish Vocational Services); others are tied to funding through federal government's vocational rehabilitation program, while still others operate under a civil rights and advocacy mission. Over time, the treatment of individuals with disabilities has continued to improve. Legislation such as the Americans with Disabilities Act has played a strong role in improving the basic civil liberties for persons with disabilities. However, disparities still exist in the employment rates for persons with disabilities. The Rehabilitation Act Amendments of 1986 played a significant role in increasing the employment for persons with significant disabilities by providing appropriate supports, including job coaches and increasing access to assistive technology. Various types of supported employment models exist, each serving the needs of different populations of persons with disabilities (e.g., persons with mental illness or persons with developmental disabilities); nonetheless, the crux of supported employment includes serving persons with disabilities in the least restrictive environment where they can have the most normalizing experience as possible.

Despite recent legislation aimed toward improving employment outcomes for individuals with significant disabilities, hurdles still exist, such as funding problems and staff training. Even with new legislation such as the TW-WIIA and tax incentives, challenges often exist because the reimbursement process can be complex or the disincentives are too great. Other funding sources that may be utilized include state or private funding such as vocational rehabilitation agencies, mental health agencies, and developmental disabilities agencies.

Many of these agencies have undergone rigorous credentialing standards under CARF. Regardless, some agencies have a high turnover rate among job coaches due to inadequate training and management, increasing the importance of supported employment consumers to act as their own advocate when choosing or evaluating employment support agencies. Research has demonstrated that supported employment programs that possess "a higher opinion of the abilities, talents, and spirit of their consumers" outperformed those who did not have that opinion in the areas of interest in work and getting and maintaining employment (Gowdy, Carlson, & Rapp, 2003, p. 238). Supported employment in its many forms has been an effective employment strategy for persons with significant disabilities.

References

Assistive Technology Act of 1998, 29 U.S.C. § 3001 et seq. (1998).

Barrett, K., Flowers, C., Crimando, W., Riggar, T. F., & Bailey, T. (1997). The turnover dilemma: A disease with solutions. *Journal of Rehabilitation, 63*(2), 36–42.

Becker, D. R., & Drake, R. E. (1994). Individual placement and support: A community mental health center approach to vocational rehabilitation. *Community Mental Health Journal, 30*(2), 193–206.

Brooke, V., Inge, K. J., Armstrong, A. J., & Wehman, P. (Eds.). (1997). *Supported employment handbook: A customer-driven approach for persons with significant disabilities.* Richmond: Virginia Commonwealth University Rehabilitation Research and Training Center on Supported Employment.

Brooke, V., Wehman, P., Inge., K., & Parent, W. (1995). Toward a customer-driven approach of supported employment. *Education and Training in Mental Retardation and Developmental Disabilities, 30*, 308–320.

Centers for Medicare and Medicaid Services (CMS). (2003). *Home and community-based services waiver program.* Retrieved November 16, 2003, from http://cms.hhs.gov/medicaid/1915c/history.asp

Civil Rights Act of 1991, Pub. L. No. 102-166, 105 Stat. 1071 (1991) (codified as amended in scattered sections of 42 U.S.C.).

Commission on Accreditation of Rehabilitation Facilities (CARF). (2003). *Employment and community services standards manual: July 2003–June 2004.* Tucson, AZ: Author.

Danley, K., Sciarappa, K., & MacDonald-Wilson, K. (1992). Choose-get-keep: A psychiatric rehabilitation approach to supported employment. In R. P. Liberman (Ed.), *Effective psychiatric rehabilitation: New directions for mental health services* (pp. 87–96). San Francisco: Jossey-Bass/Pfeiffer.

Department of Education. (n.d.). Programs & projects in RSA: Formula grants, rehabilitation continuing education programs: Rehabilitation continuing education programs. Retrieved November 1, 2003, from http://www.ed.gov/students/college/aid/rehab/catrcep.html

Federal Register. (2001, January 22). *66*(14), 7249–7258. 34 CFR 361.

Gowdy, E. L., Carlson. L. S., & Rapp, C. A. (2003). Practices differentiating high-performing from low-performing supported employment programs. *Psychiatric Rehabilitation Journal, 26*(3), 232–239.

Hagner, D., & Davies, T. (2002). "Doing my own thing": Supported self-employment for individuals with cognitive disabilities. *Journal of Vocational Rehabilitation, 17,* 65–74.

Kregel, J., Wehman, P., Revell, G., Hill, J., & Cimera, R. (2000). Supported employment benefit-cost analysis: Preliminary findings. *Journal of Vocational Rehabilitation, 14,* 153–161.

Louis Harris & Associates. (2000). 2000 N.O.D. Harris survey of Americans with disabilities. Washington, DC: Author.

Marini, I., & Stebnicki, M. (1999). Social Security Administration's alternative provider program: What can rehabilitation administrators expect? *Journal of Rehabilitation Administration, 23*(1), 31–41.

Pratt, C. W., Gill, K. J., Barrett, N. M., & Roberts, M. M. (1999). *Psychiatric rehabilitation.* Boston: Academic Press.

Revell, G., Kregel, J., Wehman, P., & Bond, G. R. (2000). Cost effectiveness of supported employment programs: What we need to do to improve outcomes. *Journal of Vocational Rehabilitation, 14,* 173–178.

Richardson, S. K. (1998). Letter to state Medicaid directors from the director of the Center for Medicaid and State Operations (February 20). Retrieved November 16, 2003, from http://www.cms.hhs.gov/states/letters/bba2208h.asp

Rizzo, D. C. (2002). With a little help from my friends: Supported self-employment for people with severe disabilities. *Journal of Vocational Rehabilitation, 17,* 97–105.

Roessler, R. T. (2002). TW-WIIA initiatives and work incentives: Return-to-work implications. *Journal of Rehabilitation, 68*(3), 11–15.

Rubin, S. E., & Roessler, R. T. (1995). *Foundations of the vocational rehabilitation process* (4th ed.). Austin, TX: Pro-ed.

Substance Abuse and Mental Health Services Administration (SAMHSA). (2003). *Work as a priority: A resource for employing people who have serious mental illnesses and who are homeless.* Washington, DC: U.S. Department of Health and Human Services.

Technology-related Assistance for Individuals with Disabilities Act of 1988. Pub. L. No. 100-407.

Unger, D. D. (1999). Workplace supports: A view from employers who have hired supported employees. *Focus on Autism and Other Developmental Disabilities, 14*(3), 167–179.

United States Department of Labor, Office of Disability Policy. (2003). *Tax incentives for businesses.* Retrieved October 16, 2003, from http://www.dol.gov/odep/pubs/ek97/tax.htm

Wehman, P., & Bricout, J. (1997). Supported employment: Critical issues and new directions. In G. Revell, K. J. Inge, D. Mank, & P. Wehman (Eds.), *The impact of supported employment for people with significant disabilities: Preliminary findings from the National Supported Employment Consortium.* Richmond: Virginia Commonwealth University Rehabilitation Research and Training Center on Supported Employment.

Wehman, P., & Targett, P. (2002). Supported employment: The challenges of new staff recruitment, selection, and retention. *Education and Training in Mental Retardation and Developmental Disabilities, 37*(4), 434–446.

West, M. D. (1995). Supported employment. In A. E. Dell Orto & R. P. Marinelli (Eds.), *Encyclopedia of disability and rehabilitation* (pp. 708–715). New York: Simon & Schuster Macmillan.

West, M., Revell, G., & Wehman, P. (1998). Conversion from segregated services to supported employment: A continuing challenge to the VR service system. *Education and Training in Mental Retardation and Developmental Disabilities, 33,* 239–247.

Forensic Rehabilitation

Rodney Isom

Many people do not see the forensic rehabilitation consultant as a community resource, but in actuality the value of the rehabilitation counselor is woven into the very fabric that covers the needs of the disabled. When someone suffers a catastrophic disability or illness, often a rehabilitation consultant is asked to prepare a report that evaluates the individual's need for rehabilitation services, including vocational rehabilitation if he or she suffered a loss to their ability to earn a living (better known as *earning capacity*). A rehabilitation consultant will often also determine the individual's future medical and rehabilitation needs (better known as a "life care plan").

These evaluations frequently take place within the framework of a legal system, where a third party may be responsible for paying for the above-mentioned services. The value of the third party paying for requisite medical services cannot be undervalued when considering the much higher mortality rate of some groups with disabilities that rely on Medicaid and Medicare. Third-party payers have the funds not just for *necessary* medical care but for *optimum* medical care (Blackwell, Krause, Winkler, & Stiens, 2002). The professional rehabilitation consultant is often, by definition, the area expert on disability. To understand this, one must first look at how an expert is defined and what systems provide the opportunity for professional growth.

LEGAL DEFINITIONS

Black's Law Dictionary (1990) defines forensic rehabilitation as the practice that takes place in a legal setting. A series of court cases have largely, and at least legally, defined what an expert is and who is qualified as an expert. In 1923, *Frye v. United States* set the standard. *Frye* provided that a person needed a history of understanding in a particular field with a high level of knowledge, skill, or experience in the discipline (Isom, 2001). In 1976, this basic definition was clarified to some degree with *Kim Manufacturing v. Superior Metal.* An expert was defined as having specialized knowledge/education that allows the use of *accurate conclusions* and/or *valid opinions* that people with the knowledge and/or experience would otherwise not offer (Weed & Field, 1994).

In 1991 the rules changed, and the standard of who is an expert was reset with *Daubert v. Merrill Dow Pharmaceuticals,* S. Ct. (1993). "*Daubert* addressed the admissibility of scientific testimony on the basis of being relevant and reliable, making the *Frye* standard if not obsolete at least no longer the standard" (Isom, 2001, p. 83). The idea was that before *Daubert* experts could testify solely on their beliefs and based on their personal experience; now the experts not only need experience to support the opinions but also need "scientific evidence" to support the opinions that are consistent with their experiences.

Field (2000) identified five areas or tests to assist the court in determining the admissibility of scientific knowledge:

1. A key question to be answered is, ordinarily, whether the theory or technique can be and has been tested;

2. A pertinent consideration is whether the theory or technique has been subjected to peer review and publication, although the fact of publication or lack thereof in a peer review journal is not a dispositive consideration;

3. The court should ordinarily consider the known or potential rate of error of a particular scientific technique;

4. The assessment of reliability permits, but does not require, explicit identification of relevant scientific community and an express determination of a particular degree of acceptance of the theory or technique with that community, as (a) a widespread acceptance can be an important factor in ruling particular evidence admissible, and (b) a known technique that has been able to attract only minimal support within the scientific community may properly be viewed with skepticism; and

5. The inquiry is a flexible one, and the focus must be solely on principles and methodology, not on the conclusions that such principles and methodology generate. (pp. 7–8)

The issue of whether the rehabilitation consultant was a "scientist" or a "technician" perplexed many of us after the *Daubert* decision (Isom, 2001), but the question was clarified for us and others in similar disciplines or professions with *Kumho Tire Co. v. Carmichael* (1999). *Kumho* placed the judge as the "gatekeeper" in the determination of who qualifies as an "expert," but the testimony still needs to be relevant and reliable regardless of the expert's status as a scientist or technician (Isom, 2001).

In summation, the rehabilitation counselor (RC) needs the credentials, the experience, and an understanding of the research methodology associated with the development of the expert's opinion. The RC must understand validity and reliability of the models used for evaluation, assessment, and plan development. The standard is now very different than what it was in the past.

History/Legislation

Most rehabilitation counseling experts start in either of two different venues: The first is in public sector rehabilitation, working for the state/federal vocational rehabilitation program where they develop a broad and in-depth understanding of an individual disability or, for that matter, multiple disabilities. The rehabilitation counselor would understand not only the etiology of the disease or disability type, but also the prognosis, the required or recommended accommodations, the appropriate work environments, useful assistive devices/aides, and the costs associated with the maximization of the individual's ability to live independently and work. The state vocational rehabilitation counselor has traditionally provided comprehensive service and planning to their clients for over a half-century (Isom & Marini, 2002; Wright, 1980).

The other venue deals with the private-for-profit sector, which grew out of the liberalization of the worker's compensation laws of the 1970s (Holt, 1993). In 1975 California passed the first workers' compensation law that provided for vocational rehabilitation of injured workers, AB 760. Willie Brown, a black assemblyman who originally grew up in east Texas and later became the Speaker of the Assembly in California, wrote AB 760. He believed that medical treatment was not sufficient and that mandatory vocational rehabilitation should be offered to completely heal the injured worker.

AB 760 became Labor Code 139.5. The code originally called for an injured worker to be returned to a job consistent with the worker's abilities, aptitudes, and personality and at an equivalent level of pay that he or she enjoyed at time of injury or at least show why the injured worker was unable to return to the same level of pay. The last test proved to be a major hurdle, given that many California workers at that time were union workers receiving high wages and often with little education to support those wages. The inability to achieve this goal would often bring an attorney to the case to represent the injured worker and to insure that the worker was offered an appropriate amount of vocational rehabilitation to achieve the above-stated goal. This no-fault system for all practical matters ceased being no-fault and became highly litigious. The injured worker would often have representation, which created three outcomes: (a) the employer/insurance carrier had to provide for sufficient rehabilitation services to get the injured worker back to work at comparable pay—that is, there must be sufficient funds to pay for significant rehabilitation services; (b) vocation rehabilitation counselors (VRCs) were forced to learn to defend their vocational recommendations in a legal environment; and (c) if the VRCs were not good at putting people back to work, they stopped getting referrals!

This system was particular to California but soon after enactment of LC 139.5 other states followed with similar legislation. The growth in the private sector continued until the mid-1980s, when many state legislatures started changing their laws to lessen the employer's responsibility. This was driven by the perceived "high cost" to rehabilitate injured workers. However, by that time other systems were in place to provide this type of comprehensive rehabilitation work: auto no-fault legislation, long-term disability insurance, and disability management are but a few examples.

One last point on the history of private-for-profit rehabilitation: these services were based on what has become known as the *strengths model*. Services were based on what clients brought with them in terms of strengths, not what they left behind in terms of functional limitations. Focus was on what a person could do rather than what they could not do. Out of this concept, disability management grew as a method to control costs, offering workplace accommodations to people with disabilities rather than simply retiring them with disability. This aspect alone was a major contribution to the field of rehabilitation and to people with disabilities in general. The concept was first noted by Arne Fougner (Holt, 1993), a pioneer in the integration of rehabilitation in liability coverage. He is credited with saying in early 1962 that rehabilitation was designed not to settle an argument but rather to fix a problem (Holt, 1993). The idea that rehabilitation could be used to "mitigate damages" was born, and the experts evolved thereafter.

PURPOSE/INTENT

Earning Capacity Evaluations

The rehabilitation counselor is concerned with evaluating the value of damages in personal injury cases. These damages—the real costs associated with disability—are known as "special" and often are referred to as "compensatory" (Isom, 2001). They do not cover pain and suffering. Costs such as wage loss, earning capacity loss, and future medical costs required would all be considered *special* or *compensatory* damages. Damages known as pain and suffering are *hedonic* damages (Isom, 2001). Pain, suffering, and punitive damages are now regularly being capped to reduce the size of the awards juries are finding against defendants. The need to accurately and fully document the value of special damages is increasing as we see more tort reform, and there is no move to limit the value of these compensatory damages. The rehabilitation counselor needs to understand how to calculate the following aspects of compensatory damages: wage loss, the cost of an appropriate rehabilitation plan, and the effects of the injury or illness on future earning capacity.

Wage loss represents that period between when an accident or illness occurs and a person can no longer work his or her customary occupation, until the time that person can go back to work or the treating physician knows and/or reports that the individual can no longer return to his or her normal and usual occupation (Isom, 2001). The ending point may be when the carpenter who falls and suffers a spinal cord injury is diagnosed as tetraplegic (the day of the accident or very soon thereafter). Or it can be months later when the treating physician is sure the carpenter can no longer return to work in his or her normal and usual occupation. The latter situation may occur when the injury or accident tends to resolve over a long period of time (such as when a person suffers a head injury) and the extent of recovery cannot be accurately predicted. The most basic example is a mechanic who is injured and is off work for three months. If he earns $2,000 per month in wages, he would suffer a total of $6,000 in wage loss.

If the individual is unable to return to his or her normal or usual occupation, then the rehabilitation counselor must look at how to get the person back to work to at least a comparable level, if not a maximal level. The RC must identify the vocational objective, how the person with the disability is going to achieve the objective, and all the costs associated with implementing the rehabilitation plan (tuition, fees, per diem, uniforms, tools, tutors, books, and so on). The rehabilitation plan is designed to mitigate the effects of the injury or illness. Standard practice or commonly used models of evaluation should be employed. Ideally, in their daily activities in an effort to put people with disabilities to work, practicing rehabilitation counselors would commonly use a model. Weed's RAPEL model (Weed & Field, 1994), Isom's IDEA model (2001), and Field's transferable skills analysis (1985) all are good examples of how such an evaluation may take place.

After the rehabilitation plan is developed, the rehabilitation counselor can examine the person's earnings capacity. There are three aspects in the evaluation of an individual's earning capacity: determination of pre-morbid earning capacity, determination of future earning capacity, and the disabled individual's residual work life expectancy.

Pre-morbid earning capacity is simply those occupations that the injured party could have pursued, if he or she had not been injured or become ill, but now can no longer pursue. Imagine that a 22-year-old male college senior, 6'2" tall and 215 pounds, was working as an usher for minimum wage and was injured after work in a motor vehicle accident. For that period of time when the student cannot return to work, he would be entitled to wage loss, which is the minimum wage he was earning at time of injury. The treating physician says that he can no longer work as an usher or in other occupations that call for walking. Assuming this man was relatively healthy, he could have chosen to work as a carpenter, truck driver, or firefighter and made a much higher wage than he would have as an usher. The salaries of those occupations would represent the pre-morbid earning capacity.

The residual earning capacity is that salary the person can hope to make after vocational rehabilitation is considered. Given our example stated above, if the young man had a back injury with no paralysis, he might not be able to work in occupations that require standing and/or heavy work, but he is about to graduate from college and could earn more than he would have given his pre-morbid earnings. On the other hand, if he suffered a severe head injury, he might not be able to earn as much as he would have prior to his injury, and he therefore experiences an *earning capacity loss*.

If the injury is permanent, then his loss would be permanent and would have to be projected for the remainder of his working life, better known as his work-life expectancy. Typically, an economist can address the work-life expectancy. The federal government at one time published work-life tables (Isom, 2001) but no longer does so. However, these data are available elsewhere (see Ciecka, Donley, & Goldman, 1995). Gamboa (1998) attempts to join the effects of disability with the work-life expectancy of workers, but his model seems to overestimate the work-life expectancy of the severely disabled and underestimate the work-life expectancy of the less severely disabled worker (Isom, 2001).

Life Care Planning

The International Academy of Life Care Planners defined life care planning in 1998 as:

> a dynamic document based upon published standards of practice, comprehensive assessment, data analysis and research, which provides an organized concise plan for current and future needs with associated costs, for individuals who have experienced catastrophic injury or have chronic health care needs." (Weed, 1999, p.1)

Philosophically, the life care plan is designed to optimize a person's future health by outlining specific health needs of the individual, and ideally to prevent future potential health complications. "The life care plan is intended to be a *living*, lifelong document that outlines the unique aspects of an individual's needs to ensure his or her future mental and physical well-being needs" (Marini, Isom, & Reid, 2003, p. 248).

Life care planning was originally termed *comprehensive rehabilitation planning* and was mandated and defined in 1943 by the enactment of Public Law 78-113, the Barden-LaFollette Act (Wright, 1980). Life care planning as we know it today was introduced in Deutsch and Raffa's book, *Damages in Tort Actions* (1981).

Presently, there are many different certifications that are appropriate for a life care planner: Certified Life Care Planner, Certified Case Manager, Certified Rehabilitation Counselor, Certified Nurse Life Care Planner, Certified Disability Management Specialist, and Certified Rehabilitation Nurse are only a few (Isom & Marini, 2002; Marini et al., 2003). Rehabilitation professionals from many different rehabilitation backgrounds, including rehabilitation counselors, social workers, physical therapists, occupational therapists, nurses, and physicians (Marini et al.), are developing life care plans.

The life care planner functions somewhat as a case manager. However, once the plan is completed the life care planner usually offers no follow-up (Marini et al., 2003). The plan itself is developed after reviewing all medical documents and depositions. The regular evaluation process consists of meeting with the disabled individual and his or her caregivers, and interviewing those responsible for treatment, such as the physician, therapists, and so on (Isom & Marini, 2002; Marini et al.). Other data may be appropriate to review, such as psychological reports, educational records, work and earning histories, and W2s. Once these data are collected the life care planner may request further evaluations to determine functional abilities/limitations, future medical needs, cognitive abilities, and so on.

When all the data are collected, they are organized into a set of tables that now have become fairly standardized (Deutsch & Sawyer, 1985; Isom & Marini, 2002; Marini et al., 2003; Reavis, 2002). These tables provide for the services, prescriptions, devices, and other adaptations that are recommended for the individual (Marini et al.). Typically the tables provide for the date or age at which the service or goods would be provided, the costs associated with procuring the goods or services, replacement and maintenance schedules of any recommended goods or equipment, and the frequencies of medications, or appointments with treators and evaluators.

Marini et al. (2003) outlined the tables' contents as follows:

- *Allied health assessments*
  Allied health evaluations *not* performed by a physician (e.g., speech, occupational, or physical therapy evaluations)
- *Therapeutic modalities*
  Treatments by allied health professionals (e.g., speech, physical and/or occupational therapy, psychotherapy)
- *Diagnostic evaluations and educational assessments*
  Vocational evaluations, psychological and/or neuropsychological evaluations, and other patient testing
- *Wheelchair needs*
  Wheelchair type and configuration, replacement schedule as required by client (e.g., manual, electric, commode, sports)
- *Wheelchair accessories and maintenance*
  Funds required to maintain wheelchair(s) and associated components (e.g., new tires, batteries, spokes, headrest extensions, thoracic supports, and lapboards)
- *Aids for independent function*
  Items allowing for increased independence (e.g., environmental control units, reachers, cup holders, sliding boards, talking kitchen utensils, braille printers)

- *Prosthetics and orthotics*
  Braces and body part (prosthesis) replacements, fitting, maintenance, and replacement schedules and costs
- *Home furnishings and accessories*
  Hoyer lifts, air mattress beds, ramps, electric door openers, standing recliners, and other home accessories needed for home living
- *Drug and medical supply needs*
  Required medications, prescribed dose, frequency, and unit costs (Supplies may include ostomy supplies such as catheters, leg bags, diapers, G tube, and ointments.)
- *Home care vs. facility care*
  Specific needs of the client regarding assistance in activities of daily living and/or supervision (in-home care needs include PCA, LPN, RN, or live-in caregiver, homemaking assistance, yard care, etc.). Also includes option for facility placement (e.g., residential brain-injury program, assisted living facility, nursing home)
- *Routine future medical care*
  Future evaluation and treatments that the client will definitely require (Often the medical evaluations are broken out into a separate table due to cost differences in evaluations versus office visits.)
- *Transportation*
  Specialized driver's training or adapted vehicles, including wheelchair lifts, hand controls, bumper mounts, tie downs, etc., and replacement/maintenance schedules associated with the disability
- *Health and strength maintenance*
  Recreation and physical training needs (e.g., recumbent bicycle for clients who are blind, hand-cycle for wheelchair users, balance balls for clients with cerebral palsy, summer camps for children with disabilities, therapeutic horseback riding)
- *Housing and architectural renovations*
  Specific requirements to make the home more accessible, either by building a new home because the existing one cannot be retrofitted, or retrofitting (e.g., enlarging the bathroom for wheelchair use, wheel-under sinks, ramps, ceiling tract lifts)
- *Future medical care: Aggressive treatment or surgery*
  Surgeries or other medical treatments that the client has a medical probability of undergoing (e.g., casting for severe contractures, subsequent cosmetic surgery for burns, cochlear implants, botox injections)
- *Orthopedic equipment needs*
  Walkers, canes, crutches, standing frames, ankle-foot orthoses
- *Vocational and/or educational plans*
  Itemized parts of the vocational rehabilitation plan, including voca-

tional evaluation, counseling, and guidance; training workstations (includes start and end dates and associated costs)

• *Potential complications*
Complications individuals may experience as a result of the disability, illness, or injury that are not typically included in other costs

After completion of the life care plan, it is normally offered to all appropriate parties. Once each party has had the opportunity to review the plan there is often a deposition where the opposing counsel is afforded the opportunity to question the life care planner regarding specific elements of the plan, how the plan was prepared, and what information was taken into consideration and why. Additionally, questions may address the life care planner's credentials and qualifications, reviewing academic background, work history, post-academic training, certifications, and/or licenses relating to life care planning.

Once the deposition is over, the life care planner might have to testify before a jury and explain how the life care plan was developed, what models of evaluation were used, what the costs of services are for the individual, and so on. Certainly, the opposing counsel again gets to question the life care planner regarding the plan and how it was prepared.

SUMMARY

The court system occasionally requires the rehabilitation counselor to evaluate and make recommendations regarding the earning capacity and future needs of people who have suffered catastrophic injury or illness. The person providing this testimony needs to have the appropriate education, training, and work experience to be qualified as an expert in the field. Certainly, holding the correct certifications, as well as maintaining one's credentials and expertise through appropriate post-graduate continuing education, is important. Publication is not required, although it is an excellent way to establish one's expertise. Experts need to understand the court system and be prepared to defend their opinions. The expert must be able to express those opinions both verbally as well as in written format. The rehabilitation counselor who has done all this and can perform in the above-outlined manner has the ability to offer a significant contribution to the community.

References

Black, H. (1990). *Black's law dictionary* (6th ed.). St. Paul, MN: West Group.

Blackwell, T. L., Krause, J. S., Winkler, T., & Stiens, S. A. (2002). *Spinal cord injury desk reference: Guidelines for life care planning and case management.* New York: Demos Medical Publishing.

Ciecka, J., Donley, T., & Goldman, J. (1995). A Markov model of work-life expectancies based on labor market activity in 1992–1993. *Journal of Legal Economics, 5* (3).

Daubert v. Merrill Dow Pharmaceuticals, 951 F2d 1128 9th Cir. (1991).

Deutsch. P., & Raffa, F. (1981). *Damages in tort actions.* (8 & 9). New York: Matthew Bender.

Deutsch, P. M., & Sawyer, H. W. (1995). *A guide to rehabilitation.* White Plains, NY: Ahab.

Field, T. (1985). *Transferable work skills.* Athens, GA: E & F.

Field, T. F. (2000). *A resource for the rehabilitation consultant on the Daubert and Kumho rulings.* Athens, GA: E & F.

Field, T., Grimes, J., Havranek, J., & Isom, R. (2001). *Transferable skills analysis: An overview of the process integrating the O*NET database.* Athens, GA: E & F.

Frye v. United States, 293 F. 1013 (1923).

Holt, L. M. (1993). The history of private sector rehabilitation. In L. G. Perlman & C. E. Hansen (Eds.), *Private sector rehabilitation: Insurance, trends & issues for the 21st century. A Report on the 17th Mary E. Switzer Memorial Seminar* (pp. 63–65). Alexandria, VA: National Rehabilitation Association.

Isom, R. (2001). The vocational expert: Qualifying and methodological approaches to earning capacity evaluation. *Direction in Rehabilitation Counseling, 12,* 81–90.

Isom, R., & Marini, I. (2002). An educational curriculum for teaching life care planning. *Journal of Life Care Planning, 1,* 239–264.

Kumho Tire Co. v. Carmichael, 97-1709, S. Ct. (1999).

Marini, I., Isom, R., & Reid, C. (2003) Integrating life care planning and expert testimony into rehabilitation education. *Rehabilitation Education, 17*(4), 248–255.

Reavis, S. L. (2002). Standards of practice. *Journal of Life Care Planning, 1*(1), 49–57.

Weed, R. O. (1997). Life care planning: An overview. *Directions in Rehabilitation Counseling, 9*(11), 135–146.

Weed, R. O. (1999) Life care planning: Past, present, and future. In R. Weed (Ed.), *Life care planning and case management handbook* (pp.1–11). Boca Raton, FL: CRC Press.

Weed, R. O., & Field, T. F. (1994). *Rehabilitation consultant's handbook* (p. 209). Athens, GA: E & F.

Wright, G. N. (1980). *Total rehabilitation.* Boston: Little, Brown, and Company.

Assistive Technology Services

Frank D. Puckett

Assistive technologies (AT) are devices or strategies used by individuals to accommodate functional limitations because of a physical, sensory, or cognitive disability. If something is out of reach, use a ladder. If using a standard computer keyboard proves difficult due to a physical impairment affecting the upper extremities, use voice-input computer control software. Accommodating for functional limitations has always been a factor in what it means to have a disability. In early human experience, a person might have used a cane or crutch fabricated from a tree branch to compensate for a physical impairment. A series of poles and a rope might have been used to mark the travel path for a person with a severe visual impairment. Early efforts to establish graphical representations for language were primarily to communicate with others across time. However, this became assistive technology, allowing individuals who did not have functional hearing to see graphical representations of the verbal language. Solving problems by adapting to physical or functional limitations is a common human experience, whether or not one has a disability. The development of technologies in the last 20–25 years has significantly changed the lives of people who have a disability. The provision of AT services should be viewed as one of the key elements for addressing the needs of individuals with physical, sensory, or cognitive impairment. Additional discussion and description of AT can be found through various Web sites, such as the Rehabilitation Engineering and Assistive Technology Society of North America (RESNA, 2003a) and Genasys (2002).

Whether one is working in the medically related field of sensory aids and artificial limbs, or working with individuals to remove architectural/physical barriers, the goal of AT is to address the problems confronting persons with disabilities. Often the problems are simple, and occasionally they ¿ plex, but the focus of AT is to assist individuals in their pursuit of basic life goals such as employment and independent living. It has been suggested that the ultimate outcome measure for assistive technology should be whether or not it enhances the quality of life for individuals with disabilities (Cook & Hussey, 2002; Scherer, 2002).

History/Legislation

The Rehabilitation Act of 1973 (P.L. 93-112) introduced sweeping changes into the federal–state vocational rehabilitation program, which included an early reference to assistive technology devices identified as "telecommunications, sensory, and other technological aids and devices" (Rehab. Act of 1973, 87 Stat. 369). These aids and devices were listed under Sec. 103, "Scope of Vocational Rehabilitation Services" (Rehab. Act of 1973, 87 Stat. 368). The Rehabilitation Act Amendments of 1986 defined rehabilitation engineering (another early term used to describe the applications of assistive technologies) as:

> The systematic application of technologies, engineering methodologies, or scientific principles to meet the needs of and address the barriers confronted by individuals with handicaps in areas which include education, rehabilitation, employment, transportation, independent living, and recreation. (Rehab. Act Amend. of 1986, 100 Stat. 1810)

The 1986 Amendments required state vocational rehabilitation agencies to document that individual rehabilitation plans include, "where appropriate, the provision of rehabilitation engineering services to any individual with a handicap to assess and develop the individual's capacities to perform adequately in a work environment" (Rehab. Act Amend. of 1986, 100 Stat. 1809). The intent of this legislation was to ensure that assistive technology services were seen as an important element of vocational rehabilitation services.

The Technology-Related Assistance for Individuals with Disabilities Act of 1988 (P.L. 100-407) provided additional clarification regarding the importance of assistive technology services and was the first federal legislation to define assistive technology devices and services. These definitions would appear in subsequent legislation, such as the Americans with Disabilities Act of 1990 and the 1994 Amendments to the Individuals with Disabilities Education Act. Under the 1988 Tech Act, grants are awarded to "provide financial assistance to the States to help each state to develop and implement a consumer-responsive statewide program of technology-related assistance for individuals of all ages with disabilities . . ." (Tech. Act of 1988, 102 Stat. 1045). In the 1988 Tech Act, an assistive technology device is defined as "any item, piece of equipment, or product system, whether acquired commercially off the shelf, modified, or customized, that is used to increase, maintain, or improve functional capabilities of individuals with disabilities" (Tech. Act of 1988, 102 Stat. 1046). Assistive technology services are described as "any service that directly assists an individual with a disability in the selection, acquisition, or use of an assistive technology device" (Tech. Act of 1988, 102 Stat. 1046). Through these legislative initiatives, it seems clear that Congress intended that persons with disabilities have full access to the benefits of assistive technologies in various settings to include work, school, and leisure activities.

Personnel

Within the professional practice of assistive technology services in the last 25 years, a consensus has been reached regarding definitions for assistive devices and assistive technology services. Additional clarification has also emerged regarding individuals who are qualified to render these services, and who should carry the title of *Assistive Technology Specialist* or *Rehabilitation Engineer*. One distinction for these job classifications is that the classification of rehabilitation engineer would be reserved for an individual who holds a degree in engineering (Scheck, 1990). Other professionals in this field might identify themselves as a rehabilitation technologist, adaptive equipment specialist, or assistive technology practitioner. More important than a title is the training and professional competence an individual has in assistive technology.

PURPOSE/INTENT

The Rehabilitation Engineering and Assistive Technology Society of North America (RESNA), a national association for the advancement of rehabilitation and assistive technologies, classified AT services in the following manner:

- personal vehicles and driving aids,
- prosthetics and orthotics,
- home modifications,
- worksite and vocational equipment modifications,
- communications and controls,
- computer applications, and
- quantification and diagnosis of human performance (OSERS Task Force, 1988).

Another method for classifying assistive technology services describes the types of client services typically provided by counselors or human services caseworkers:

- adaptive devices for independent living and activities of daily living,
- sensory aids for individuals with hearing or visual impairments,

- adaptive driving controls and modified vehicles for transportation,
- wheelchairs and other mobility devices,
- custom seating and corrective postural positioning,
- augmentative communication devices,
- adapted worksites and tool modification, and
- adapted computer systems and controls.

AT specialists often describe AT interventions as high-tech or low-tech and commercial or custom (Cook & Hussey, 2002). The counselor or case-worker should obtain a clear understanding from the AT provider regarding the possible options and alternatives for any person's needs. An AT specialist or vendor who suggests there is only one option is likely not being candid or else should admit that only one option was considered. Costs, complexity, and availability of maintenance services are the factors routinely evaluated for most AT interventions.

Adaptive Devices for Independent Living and Activities of Daily Living

Activities of daily living (ADL) are those tasks performed routinely to meet one's basic daily needs (e.g., dressing, eating, and bathing). Specifically, ADL tasks are separated from work-related activities such as employment and education. Most individuals prefer to do these tasks as independently as possible. Through the appropriate use of assistive devices, a person with a physical or sensory impairment can often regain lost capability or independence for one or more of these ADL tasks. Occupational therapists (OT) are specifically trained to perform this type of assessment. Most therapists will attempt to recommend devices that will restore independence for the task or assist the individual in performing the task in a more timely fashion, or with a greater degree of safety. The types of devices prescribed for ADL include simple eating utensils, bath sponges, commode chairs, and electronic environmental control units that control lights, appliances, television, telephone, and heating/cooling systems.

Sensory Aids for Individuals with Hearing and Visual Impairments

For individuals with a significant hearing loss, communication and signaling often rely on visual input and to a lesser degree on tactile sensation (vibrations). Simple solutions, such as flashing lights for a doorbell ring or alarm clock, are quite easily accomplished.

Electronic communication devices allow deaf and hearing-impaired persons to use the telephone. Speech recognition software is currently available for word-processing and computer commands and may have application for hearing-impaired persons in the future as a real-time translator system. In the area of medical research, cochlear implants continue to improve their ability to provide functional hearing for formerly deaf persons.

For persons with a severe visual loss, the opposite approach is taken: signals and messages are converted to auditory or tactile signals. Talking books and speech output from computers are typical adaptations to meet this need. Text-to-speech software programs are available and have created direct access to electronically formatted information for persons with vision or reading disorders. Sonic or sonar aids to assist individuals with mobility have been developed and tested in various locations but, as yet, are not widely used by persons with visual impairments.

Adaptive Driving Controls and Modified Vehicles for Transportation

The application of technology to allow persons with disabilities to access private and public transportation (e.g., bus, plane and train) has significantly increased the personal mobility and ease with which persons with disabilities can travel. Although not always convenient, these services are becoming more accessible. Additional attention was given to transportation issues with the passage of the Americans with Disabilities Act of 1990. Wheelchair lifts for buses and vans as well as loading ramps for trains and airplanes have reduced, though not eliminated, many transportation barriers for individuals with mobility impairments.

New technologies, such as reduced-effort acceleration/braking and steering systems, allow persons with limited strength to operate a personal vehicle (typically a van). A recent technology in adaptive driving controls is a joystick-controlled system for individuals who have adequate functional use of their upper extremity. Except for traditional automotive hand controls, most adaptive control systems are quite costly and require that careful assessments be conducted in order to assure safety in vehicle operation. Personal wheelchair restraint systems are often an overlooked issue. Whether the individual is driving or riding as a passenger, separate restraints for the individual and the wheelchair are critical for ensuring safety. A number of wheelchair restraint systems have been crash tested and should be the systems of choice for personal transportation applications. Given the new technologies, more individuals with severe disabilities can achieve the goal of driving a personal vehicle. The question remains, "Are they able to accomplish this in a safe manner?" Current information on adaptive technology for personal vehicles can be obtained through Web resources published by the National Highway Traffic Safety Administration, at http://www.nhtsa.dot.gov/cars/rules/adaptive/brochure/brochure.html. Procedures for evaluating a person for adaptive driving equipment can be found through the Association of Driver Rehabilitation Specialists at http://www.driver-ed.org.

Wheelchairs and Other Mobility Devices

New designs and materials have radically changed the appearance of wheelchairs and other equipment for individuals with mobility impairments. The choice for mobility aids ranges from manual wheelchairs, to versatile motorized scooters for individuals who can ambulate for short distances, to full-size, power-base wheelchairs that can accept a number of specialized seating units. Various control systems exist for individuals to operate powered wheelchairs, including joystick, chin control, head control, foot control, and sip-n-puff (breath control). Physically gaining control over a powered wheelchair is secondary to determining that the individual has the reasoning, visual perception, and judgment to operate the wheelchair. With proper training and support, children as young as five years old have successfully used powered mobility. Many options and features exist, and the assessment to determine the optimal mobility system for an individual should include exploring as many of these features as possible.

Custom Seating and Corrective Postural Positioning

It is often the case that the standard seating system in a wheelchair or motorized scooter is not adequate or optimal for the person. Improper positioning in a wheelchair or other seating unit can adversely affect one's health and comfort. The individual's physical needs for postural positioning and comfort and the potential problem with decubitus ulcers require that special attention be given to the wheelchair seating system. In these circumstances, a specialized seating system is required, offering both corrective postural positioning to address problems of scoliosis or other spinal deformity and some degree of protection against the development of pressure sores or decubitus ulcers.

Materials utilized in these systems take several forms: plywood, foam and vinyl, custom-formed plastics, and mold-injection foam products. Often commercial products, such as Roho® or Jay® cushions, will meet the individual's needs. This area of custom seating and positioning is highly specialized, requiring the services of trained and experienced clinicians. A typical clinical team for specialized seating would include physical therapy, occupational therapy, and assistive technology. Satisfying the client's needs for proper wheelchair seating and positioning can result in improved comfort, work tolerance, and functional capability for the upper extremities.

Augmentative Communication Devices

When individuals cannot utilize speech to fully meet their needs for communication, they are potential candidates for some type of augmentative or assistive communication aid. Conditions such as cerebral palsy, stroke, brain injury, and various types of neuromuscular diseases often result in diminished communication ability. Despite the severity of the disability, almost anyone who has a desire to communicate can realize some benefit from properly prescribed augmentative communication assistance. The devices used for augmentative communication can be as simple as letter boards or as high-tech as electronic communication systems. The assessment protocol in augmentative communication focuses on cognitive ability; level of language development; and physical ability to access a keyboard, electronic switch, or other control device. A speech pathologist is usually the key clinician for this type of evaluation.

Adaptive Worksites and Tool Modification

The goal of worksite modification is to maximize the individual's functional capability and independence, in the safest and most cost-efficient manner possible. Simply gaining entrance into buildings can present obstacles. Accessibility to restrooms and food service areas are also frequent problems in work environments. An assistive technology specialist and an occupational therapist would make an excellent team to address workplace modifications, along with building or maintenance engineers, if the company or industry employs them. Worksite and tool modification projects typically follow a systematic protocol. If the individual cannot adequately perform the task, then an assistive technology specialist could examine it and suggest changes, either to the task, to the way it is done, or to the person performing it. Solutions might include the use of assistive devices and adapted tools, changing the process by which the task is performed (choosing a more ergonomically efficient approach for the individual), or exploring a job-sharing option whereby the target individual shares/swaps some of the tasks with another co-worker.

Adapted Computer Systems

The development of the personal computer and the Internet has revolutionized employment and educational opportunities for persons with disabilities. If one has the cognitive ability to work with computers, there is virtually no one so physically disabled that he or she cannot gain access to a personal computer. Input to a computer can be accomplished by voice command or by any voluntary physical movement, including simple eye movements. Computer output can be converted to speech, print, visual/graphical images, or Braille. Systems are being developed to convert computer output into animatronic sign language (DePaul University CTI, 2002). Accessing a computer is a matter of gaining control over input of data and commands to the system and converting output into a form which is readily accessible to the user. Simple guidelines for choosing a computer system are: identify the task to be performed, choose the software programs which will best handle the task, then select the computer and adaptive peripherals required to meet the client's needs. Choosing the computer before attempting to make it fit the client's needs can often lead to frustration and less than optimal results.

CLIENT SERVICES

Usually, one of the first questions asked by counselors and caseworkers is: "How can I determine if my client will benefit from assistive devices or specialized equipment?" When planning assistive technology services, it is important to obtain assistance from personnel skilled in assistive technology. Use of technological devices should be guided by the following considerations:

- the ability of the individual to comprehend and benefit from the technology,
- the financial resources needed to purchase and maintain the devices or equipment, and
- availability of a sufficient support system for training and continuing maintenance of the technology (Corthell & Thayer, 1986).

With careful consideration of these issues, one can minimize the number of improper prescriptions for assistive technology. The approach least likely to succeed is to simply purchase devices and let the client and family determine how best to use them. Phillips and Zhao (1993) reported that approximately 30% of individuals discontinue their use of assistive devices. Occasionally a person's needs change and the device no longer meets their needs. Often, however, the device is not used because the individual's input and preferences were not adequately explored during the assessment for the device. Scherer (2002) and Cook and Hussey (2002) describe a systematic approach to assessment and prescription of assistive technologies which documents the individual's personal preferences and tolerance for technology and the environments in which the device(s) will be used. It seems that an individual's "personality" is a significant factor in predicting successful use of AT and is just as important as the "fit" of the AT for the person's physical or sensory needs. Good rehabilitation practice applies to applications of assistive technology, as it would for more traditional services, where careful planning and competent assessment services are more likely to lead to a successful outcome.

To assess an individual's potential benefit from assistive devices, one could begin by evaluating the person's level of independence for various activities of daily living. The potential benefit of assistive devices in ADL generalizes rather well to other areas such as work, education, and leisure. The rating procedure illustrated below (adapted from Appendix C in Puckett, 1984) provides some indication of the level of need for technological assistance.

Rating Scale

A. Independent, no assistance needed; no other concerns noted

B. Independent, but uses an assistive device; necessary effort and level of safety are acceptable

C. Partially dependent on another person, or task is difficult and too time consuming, or task is not performed in a safe manner

D. Totally dependent on other person(s)

While not exhaustive, this scale represents a sufficient sample of tasks to obtain a baseline for determining level of need for assistive technology. For all items rated "A" or "B," the individual appears to be meeting his or her needs in a reasonable fashion. However, for those items classified as "C" or "D," an evaluation should be conducted to determine the client's potential benefit from adaptive and assistive devices. A key consideration is how easily or safely individuals are able to meet basic daily needs. Assistive devices are often appropriate in situations where an individual can perform a task independently, but the task requires an unusually long time, the required effort is exhausting, or the task is performed in a way that places the person at risk of injury.

This rating scale focuses primarily on daily living tasks and not specific work activities. Work-related tasks are highly variable. It can be argued that if one is sufficiently independent in most or all daily living tasks, it is reasonable to expect those skills and compensatory strategies to be applicable in an employment or educational setting.

Use the following scale to assess a person's level of independence for self-care and other daily living activities:

Eating, food preparation	Bathing
Dressing, undressing	Grooming
Transferring to/from a wheelchair	Toileting
Propelling a wheelchair	Ambulation
Use of public/private transportation	Use of phone
Handling crisis/emergency situations	

Obtaining Competent Evaluation for Assistive Devices

A comprehensive rehabilitation center which has assistive technology specialists, occupational therapists, speech pathologists, and rehabilitation engineers on staff would likely be able to address this need. Other potential sources of help include these:

- Assistive technology service center in a university
- Rehabilitation technology specialists working in state vocational rehabilitation programs
- Durable medical equipment (DME) dealers
- Private rehabilitation technology companies
- National disability organizations
- Information/referral centers on disability issues
- State programs funded under the Technology Assistance Act

RESNA (2003b) maintains a nationwide list of specialists in assistive technology and provides certification for AT specialist in the following categories:

- *Assistive Technology Practitioner* (ATP), for individuals who evaluate a person's need for AT and may provide training on the use of AT devices.
- *Assistive Technology Supplier* (ATS), for individuals who are involved in the sale and maintenance of commercial AT devices.

- *Rehabilitation Engineering Technologists* (RET), for providers who apply engineering principles to the design, modification, or fabrication of AT devices.

Each state rehabilitation agency has information on facilities that provide these types of services. State and local disability advocacy organization will usually have information on AT providers. If the same person or facility was recommended by more than one of these resources, it would suggest that the individual or facility has attained a certain reputation for this area of technology. Resource manuals and textbooks on rehabilitation technology are also helpful in this regard (Cook & Hussey, 2002; Corthell & Thayer, 1986; Scherer, 2002).

There are no foolproof methods for selecting a competent consultant in assistive devices. Some indicators of an individual's knowledge and experience are

- holds one of the national RESNA certifications: ATP, ATS, or RET
- is a member of the National Special Education Alliance
- routinely attends assistive technology conferences
- is recognized as having appropriate expertise in a specific area of assistive technology.

Contacting a national organization, such as United Cerebral Palsy, can provide an objective resource to determine the level of expertise a potential consultant should have for a specific area of assistive technology. These resources should be able to provide guidance with regard to what questions should be asked of a potential AT vendor or assistive technology service consultant. For example, questions that could be asked of a potential consultant for assistive technology include:

- Do you have the ATP credential from the RESNA organization?
- Have you completed any AT credentialing or certification programs?
- Which assistive technology conferences have you attended in the last two years?

A person who cannot answer these questions satisfactorily is not well informed in the area of assistive technology and, therefore, his or her chances of prescribing an appropriate solution are somewhat diminished. Obviously, a person could be well informed on specific AT equipment and still not arrive at the optimal solution for a specific individual.

When Several Options Exist, Who Decides Which Device Is Best?

Input can be obtained from various sources; however, the decision must be made jointly by the individual, his or her family, and the funding source. If any one of these individuals is opposed to the choice, then the chances of success are compromised. An improper decision on AT which leads to device abandonment wastes time, effort, and resources for all parties involved

(Riemer-Reiss & Wacker, 2000). Clinical input can be obtained from occupational therapists, physical therapists, speech pathologists, physicians, and rehabilitation technologists. These clinicians may make recommendations and provide options, but the decision rests with the individual, his or her family, and the funding source representative (e.g., counselor, caseworker).

Other Issues to Consider When Purchasing Assistive Devices

The following key issues should be addressed with regard to the performance characteristics of the device, and the ease and availability of repairs and maintenance:

- The performance characteristics of the device should be carefully evaluated. How well does the device meet the requirements of the individual? Does the device have extra functions or capabilities that are of no value in this situation? For the same performance characteristics, is the device substantially more expensive than other units?

- The durability and reliability of the unit are important considerations. How does it perform in various environmental settings, such as excessive heat or cold? What data exist to describe the reliability of this unit versus others of the same type?

- With respect to repairs and maintenance, it is important that these be obtained locally. A potential problem will exist for the client and the counselor when arrangements for repairs and maintenance are not clarified before the device is delivered.

Some caseworkers/counselors consider waiting until a client has completed a certain phase of rehabilitation or training before considering a complete assessment for assistive technology. A point to consider, however, is that the individual's progress in the rehabilitation or training program may be compromised if he or she does not have the proper equipment to perform optimally. An experienced clinician/technologist can guide the individual and his or her caseworker as to what equipment should be considered at various points in the client's rehabilitation program. Also, constantly changing technology makes periodic reassessment of the need for, and potential benefit of, assistive technology a necessary component of rehabilitation.

Assistive technology is a relatively new discipline in rehabilitation practice; policy, procedures, and expected outcome are still evolving. Also, for some counselors and caseworkers, there is limited knowledge and confidence when prescribing assistive devices. Certainly, there are examples where this effort went awry and the device/equipment failed to meet expectations, or perhaps proved useless. However, in most situations, competent assessment and careful delivery of assistive technology services resulted in a person accomplishing a task that was felt to be impossible. When applied in a cautious and careful manner, assistive technologies can have tremendous impact on the quality of life and rehabilitation potential of persons with disabilities.

References

Cook, A. M., & Hussey, S. M. (2002). *Assistive technologies.* St. Louis, MO: Mosby, Inc.

Corthell, D. W., & Thayer, T. (1986). *Rehabilitation technologies.* Thirteenth Institute on Rehabilitation Issues. Menomonie, WI: Stout Vocational Rehabilitation Institute.

DePaul University CTI. (2002). *The DePaul University Sign Language Project.* Retrieved September 12, 2003, from http://asl.cs.depaul.edu/ project_info.html

Genasys. (2002). *Assistive Technology.* Retrieved October 4, 2002, from http://www.genasys.usm.maine.edu/assist.htm

OSERS Task Force. (1988, May). *Rehabilitation engineering services in the state-federal vocational rehabilitation system.* Report from OSERS Task Force on Rehabilitation Engineering. Washington, DC: Office of Special Education and Rehabilitative Services.

Phillips, B., & Zhao, H. (1993). Predictors of assistive technology abandonment. *Assistive Technology, 5,* 36–45.

Puckett, F. (1984). Assessing the reliability and validity of a rehabilitation engineering services scale. (Doctoral dissertation, Southern Illinois University–Carbondale, 1984). *Dissertation Abstracts International (A), 46* (03), 687.

Rehabilitation Act Amendments of 1986, Pub. L. No. 99-506.

Rehabilitation Act of 1973, Pub. L. No. 93-112.

Rehabilitation Engineering and Assistive Technology Society of North America (RESNA). (2003a, July 03). *AT connections: Assistive technology information.* Retrieved September 13, 2003, from http://128.104.192.129/taproject/at/atinformation.html

Rehabilitation Engineering and Assistive Technology Society of North America (RESNA). (2003b, n.d.). *RESNA policy on the qualifications of service providers in assistive technology.* Retrieved August 3, 2003, from http://www.resna.org/PracInAT/CertifiedPractice/Qualifications.html

Riemer-Reiss, M., & Wacker, R. (2000). Factors associated with assistive technology discontinuance among individuals with disabilities. *Journal of Rehabilitation, 66*(3), 44–51.

Scheck, A. (1990). Rehab engineers vote for two certification levels. *Team Rehab, 1*(2), 30–31 (publication discontinued).

Scherer, M. J. (Ed.). (2002). *Assistive technology: Matching device and consumer for successful rehabilitation.* Washington, DC: American Psychology Association.

Technology-Related Assistance for Individuals with Disabilities Act of 1988, Pub. L. No. 100-407.

Alcohol-Drug Treatment Programs

Susan Harrington Godley, Mark D. Godley, & Russell J. Hagen

Treatment services for individuals with substance-use disorders (alcohol and other drugs) are now widely available, although sometimes difficult to access due to the demand and limitations of public funding. It is estimated that 8% of Americans aged 12 or older can be classified with a substance-abuse or dependence disorder. More than half of these abuse or depend on alcohol, and about one in seven are classified with dependence on or abuse of both alcohol and illicit drugs (Substance Abuse and Mental Health Services Administration [SAMHSA], 2003). The general economic impact of substance use, abuse, and dependence in the general population of the United States was estimated to be $143.4 billion in 1998. This estimate attempts to quantify the effects of these problems on general health costs, lost productivity, and other costs to society such as those in the criminal justice system (White House Office of National Drug Control Policy, 2001). Thus, substance-use problems are of epidemic proportion in America today, and many different people suffer the effects, whether directly (as in the case of family and friends) or indirectly (through social costs).

Persons with alcohol and drug problems *will* be encountered by helping professionals, and most counselors will have occasion to refer an individual to an alcohol or drug treatment program. The purpose of this chapter is to provide a practical, working knowledge of how the treatment system works for those who have substance-use disorders, what to expect from it, and how to help an individual access services when the need arises. Substance-use problems are common for both adults and adolescents, but because different age groups have different problems and needs, treatment approaches should also differ.

History

American approaches to treatment for alcohol and drug problems have varied in accordance with changing moral attitudes and the development of scientific knowledge. Alcohol use was prevalent in colonial America, and its excessive use led to laws that attempted to control public drunkenness. Benjamin Rush, who is considered a significant historical figure in the evolution of thinking about alcoholism, suggested in a 1784 treatise that chronic drunkenness was a progressive medical condition that could be arrested by abstinence. Other common views of addictive behavior through the years characterized it as a moral problem and judged addicted individuals to be evil, morally weak, or possessed by evil spirits. Between 1790 and 1830, Americans' average alcohol consumption tripled and the resulting public drunkenness and related problems raised new concerns among many about the country's drinking practices, which eventually led to different efforts to control it. Cultural views of alcoholism, addiction, and, more recently, scientific research have all influenced treatment throughout the decades.

Four Pivotal Historical Events

In his history of addiction treatment and recovery in America, William White (1998) noted that there were four pivotal events prior to 1940. The initial event was the emergence of the first addiction treatment centers, known as inebriate homes and asylums, during the latter part of the nineteenth century. The second event was the drug prohibition movement in the United States, led by Carrie Nation and the Women's Christian Temperance Union, which sought a "legal cure" to alcoholism by initiating prohibition. The Harrison Tax Act of 1914 was passed to regulate and tax the production, importation, distribution, and use of opiates. In 1919 the Eighteenth Constitutional Amendment prohibited the manufacture, sale, or transportation of intoxicating liquors. The third event was the founding of Alcoholics Anonymous (AA) in 1935. The fourth milestone was the opening of two narcotic treatment "farms" in the mid-1930s by the federal government, marking the beginning of its direct involvement in addiction treatment.

Changing Perceptions of Alcoholism and the Alcoholic

During the 1930s and 1940s, multiple movements came together to change the perception of alcoholism and the alcoholic (White, 1998). As mentioned above, Alcoholics Anonymous was founded in 1935, when two alcoholics began to help one another. Meeting in small groups, AA's members strive to attain abstinence from alcohol as they work through the twelve-step program. The small beginning of AA has since led to the establishment of local groups all over the world, composed of addicts who offer each other mutual aid and support. Another movement was led by Marty Mann, who established the National Council on Alcoholism in 1944 after undergoing her own recovery from alcoholism. She published *Primer on Alcoholism* (Mann, 1950) and later, *New Primer on Alcoholism* (Mann, 1958), which included many concepts still in use today. In *Primer*, terms such as "loss of control drinking," "compulsive drinking," "denial," and "rationalization" were used to describe the alcoholic. Haggard and Jellinek of the Yale School of Alcohol Studies were also influential in the development of modern treatment through their advocacy for the education of addiction professionals.

Evolution of a Drug Treatment Approach

Another recovering individual founded a treatment approach in the late 1950s that came to be known as Synanon. This approach had a large impact on drug treatment. Originally, the Synanon community included both alcoholics and drug addicts, but later primarily targeted drug addicts. Its founding marked the birth of ex-addict-directed therapies. One outgrowth was a type of residential program called therapeutic communities (TC), many of which are still in existence today. TCs have evolved over the years, but their underlying approach includes a fairly distinctive milieu with the goal of having community members attain abstinence and re-enter society as productive members. Traditionally, these programs have fairly lengthy periods of stay (greater than one year), and many of the staff members are recovering addicts.

Medical Influences on Treatment

Medicine has also played a significant role in addiction treatment. In 1957, the American Medical Association (AMA) endorsed the concept of alcoholism as a disease. Soon afterward, Jellinek (1960) published an influential book, *The Disease Concept of Alcoholism*. He noted that alcoholism follows a similar course in many individuals, and he suggested that it was useful to *conceptualize* alcoholism as a disease. Within addiction treatment, medical detoxification is one of the most widely used applications of medical services. This is the process in which an alcoholic or other drug addict withdraws from foreign substances under medical supervision, occasionally with the brief use of tranquilizers.

Several other pharmacotherapy interventions for alcohol and drug abuse have been used. For example, some professionals believe that alcoholics drink to relieve stress. To counteract this, doctors have prescribed tranquilizers or antidepressants as alternatives to alcohol. Another medical intervention is to prescribe disulfiram (Antabuse®), which acts as a deterrent to drinking by making the patient violently ill if he or she drinks alcohol. In 1995, the pharmacologic agent naltrexone (ReVia®) was approved as a safe and effective adjunct to psychosocial treatments for alcoholism. Research has suggested that this medication helps reduce alcohol cravings and prevents early return to heavy drinking for some alcoholics (Volpicelli, Alterman, Hayashida, & O'Brien, 1992). Although approved by the Federal Food and Drug Administration (FDA), naltrexone is still more likely to be found in clinical trial research studies than in general practice.

Methadone maintenance is a treatment that began to be used in the 1960s for heroin addiction. These programs greatly increased during the Nixon years in an attempt to reduce burgeoning street crime thought to be the result of drug-seeking behaviors. Methadone is typically taken by mouth once a day, and its purpose is to suppress narcotic withdrawal and hunger, allowing an individual to function at an acceptable level in vocational and social activities. Other drugs approved for use in treatment of opiate addiction are LAAM and naltrexone. As of this writing, there are no medications approved by the FDA for treating addiction to cocaine, LSD, PCP, marijuana, methamphetamine and other stimulants, inhalants, or anabolic steroids. However, the National Institute of Drug Abuse (National Institute of Drug Abuse [NIDA], 2004) has placed a high priority on the development of a medication for treating cocaine addiction.

Treatment Placement Criteria and the Continuum of Care

Two of the major influences on modern treatment are the patient placement criteria established by the American Society of Addiction Medicine (American Society of Addiction Medicine [ASAM], 2001) and the concept of a continuum of care. The ASAM placement criteria can be used to help determine the severity of an individual's substance-use problems and the appropriate level of intervention. The continuum-of-care concept is in response to a realization by researchers and clinicians that alcohol and drug disorders are not acute illnesses and will rarely be "cured" with one brief treatment. Individuals require a variety of treatment options, from least restrictive outpatient interventions at one end of the continuum to residential/inpatient treatment at the other end, as well as the opportunity to move from one level of treatment to another (in any direction) as their symptoms dictate.

Specifically, ASAM placement criteria outline descriptions across six assessment dimensions that are crosswalked across service levels, from Early Intervention (Level 0.5) to Medically Managed Intensive Inpatient Treatment (Level IV). These criteria evolved from those initially developed in Ohio, dubbed the "Cleveland Criteria," to a compilation in *Patient Placement Criteria for the Treatment of Psychoactive Substance Use Disorders*, published by ASAM in 1991. The criteria have since been revised and are expected to continue to evolve in response to research findings and clinical practice. Many states include the use of these criteria as part of program licensing requirements, which has led to an emphasis on assessment procedures.

Research and Practice

Another major influence on the evolution of treatment has been clinical research, but concerns have been raised about the gap between science and practice. Criticism of the poor scientific foundation for treatment approaches has been long standing (White, 1998). Recent reviews of substance-abuse treatment research have often concluded that the most successful interventions are not part of mainstream substance-abuse clinical practice, and that mainstream approaches lack scientific support (Lamb, Greenlick, & McCarty, 1998; Miller & Hester, 1986). Influenced by developments in psychotherapy research, alcohol and drug treatment researchers have advocated for and adopted methods (including evidence-based treatment manuals) to improve alcohol- and drug-treatment research and practice (Carroll, 1997; Carroll & Nuro, 1996). A number of treatment models have been evaluated in clinical trial research, including cognitive-behavioral coping-skills therapy (Longabaugh & Morgenstern, 1999), the community reinforcement approach (Azrin, Sisson, Meyers, & Godley, 1982; Meyers & Smith, 1995), motivational interviewing (Miller & Rollnick, 1991; Project Match Research Group, 1997), contingency management (Bickel, Arnass, Higgins, Badger, & Esch, 1997; Higgins et al., 1994), and family therapy approaches (Liddle et al., 2001).

LEGISLATION/AUTHORITY

The Hughes Act of 1970 recognized alcohol abuse and alcoholism as public health problems and created the National Institute on Alcoholism and Alcohol Abuse (NIAAA), the primary funding source for research related to the causes and treatment of alcoholism. The National Institute on Drug Abuse was established in 1974 as the federal focal point for research, treatment, prevention, and training services. Its mission changed in 1981, when legislation created the Block Grant Programs, which gave states more control over treatment and prevention services. A series of federal laws, including the Comprehensive Crime Control Act of 1984 and the Anti-Drug Abuse Acts of 1986 and 1988, increased sanctions for drug offenses and trafficking.

Legislation targeting demand reduction has not been as prevalent as that targeting supply reduction. A U.S. Supreme Court decision in 1962 held that it was cruel and unusual punishment to imprison persons under California law who had the "illness" of narcotic addiction. This decision led to an increase in federal support for treatment efforts. The 1968 Amendments to the Community Mental Health Centers Act of 1963 identified "narcotic addiction" as a mental illness, which allowed federal support for local efforts. Under Public Law 102-321, the Substance Abuse and Mental Health Services Administration (SAMHSA) was established. SAMHSA has three centers, two of which are dedicated to substance abuse. Of these two, one promotes better prevention efforts (Center for Substance Abuse Prevention), and the other one promotes better treatment efforts (Center for Substance Abuse Treatment). Both centers have funded capacity-expansion and demonstration projects that have helped expand prevention and treatment services in the United States.

The confidentiality of the person who seeks treatment for alcohol and substance-use problems was protected by federal legislation in the early 1970s (42

U.S.C. §§ 290dd-3 and §§ 290ee-3), and the Department of Health and Human Services issued regulations in 1975 (42 C.F.R. Part 2 modified in 1987) that governed the release of identifying information in a substance abuser's records. Essentially, these regulations protect the alcohol- and drug-treatment participant's privacy by prohibiting treatment providers from disclosing patient identifying information except under extraordinary circumstances.

Funding

Funding for alcohol- and drug-treatment programs varies dramatically from state to state. Treatment can be an expensive proposition, so it is necessary for a referring counselor to understand the funding mechanisms that will be relevant for any individuals he or she might refer to treatment. It is important to determine if a given treatment provider receives state funds that can help defray the costs to the individual, the individual's insurance benefits (both private and public), and whether a treatment provider is "certified" to receive compensation from the individual's insurance plan.

Each state typically commits a portion of its general revenue to services for alcohol and other drug treatment. States also receive funding from the federal Alcohol, Drug and Mental Health Block Grant, a significant portion of which is allocated to subsidizing alcohol and drug treatment services. Federal and state funds are targeted for treatment services in order to make such services available to chemically dependent individuals who do not have the ability to pay for services. States use either grant-in-aid or a purchase of care mechanism to help finance treatment. The organizations that receive state tax dollars to provide substance-abuse treatment services are usually private, not-for-profit agencies, or local or state government agencies.

Many private health-care insurance plans include benefits for a range of chemical dependency treatment services, including detoxification, outpatient, intensive outpatient, and residential/inpatient services; it is important to help an individual understand these benefits, if he or she has them. Chemical dependency outpatient services are frequently treated similarly to outpatient mental health and psychiatric services and require a 50% co-payment (the amount for which the participant is responsible). Detoxification and inpatient rehabilitation are frequently treated the same as inpatient medical treatment in terms of patient co-payment (generally ranging from 10 to 30%).

Almost all private insurance benefits for chemical-dependency treatment include some type of case management. Insurance case management typically takes the form of treatment pre-authorization and continued treatment authorization at predetermined intervals during the course of treatment. Failure to acquire the required authorizations frequently results in the reduction of insurance coverage or the denial of coverage altogether. While most insurance policies include benefits for inpatient rehabilitation, access to those benefits is not automatic. These high-cost benefits are frequently subject to review by insurance case managers to determine "medical necessity." If the information reviewed by the case manager fails to meet the medical necessity criteria of the insurance plan, reimbursement for this level of care can be denied. Even in the same locale, insurance plans may not apply equally to all treatment facilities. Some plans restrict reimbursement to providers that have been screened and included in the insurance plan's network of providers. Other insurance plans restrict reimbursement to only those providers that hold certain licenses, certifications, or accreditations.

In recent years, the number of hospital-based and freestanding proprietary chemical-dependency treatment facilities has been significantly reduced, largely due to the restrictions placed on access to residential/inpatient treatment by managed care. While these treatment facilities still exist, typically they are not subsidized by state or federal government funds. As a result, they are difficult to access *unless* individuals are covered by private insurance or otherwise have the ability to pay for treatment.

Each state has its own process for determining the eligibility of treatment providers and to what extent they may provide services included in the state plan. Organizations eligible to provide services under the state plan are generally considered "Medicaid-certified providers." Medicaid-eligible individuals referred to Medicaid-certified providers can receive treatment services included in the state plan without incurring personal charges, as the provider is reimbursed by the state Medicaid program. As with private insurance, not all treatment organizations are certified to provide treatment services included in the state Medicaid plan, and the counselor is advised to be aware of the status of a particular provider in this regard before making a referral of a Medicaid-eligible individual.

Medicaid reimbursement for individuals under the age of 21 is subject to a special provision in the federal Medicaid statute referred to as early and periodic screening, diagnosis, and treatment (EPSDT). Medicaid statutes mandate that states participating in the Medicaid program provide medical screening for adolescents to determine the need for medical services. When a need for any medical service is identified, including chemical-dependency treatment services, the state is obligated to insure that the young person receives the required treatment and is reimbursed for it through the state's Medicaid program. If seeking treatment for adolescents, a counselor would want to understand the degree to which a particular state is in compliance with the provisions of EPSDT. Unfortunately, the potentially rich benefits of EPSDT are not available in all states due to the failure of some states to fully comply with this Medicaid provision.

Personnel

Alcohol- and drug-treatment professionals come from a variety of disciplines and backgrounds. Increasingly, states require counselors to meet state licensing or certification guidelines in order to license programs and reimburse treatment services provided by staff members. In general, personnel can be classified as counseling staff or medical staff. Within each of these classifications, staff can have backgrounds in social work, rehabilitation, psychology, psychiatry, nursing, or can have life experience with substance abuse.

While playing a critical role in the management of medical and psychiatric problems that arise out of substance abuse, physicians play a small role in substance-abuse treatment itself. However, physicians are likely to play a role in medical detoxification, approve treatment plans, and may provide medical consultation to other treatment staff members. Beyond this, the nonmedical staff of the substance-abuse treatment center generally has responsibility for participants' daily treatment regimens. The treatment team usually includes a primary counselor, who is responsible for treatment planning, ensuring that the participant receives appropriate services, and communicating with referral sources. Other members of the treatment team could include nurses, recreation therapists, shift counselors who monitor patients on residential/inpatient units, and educators, especially for adolescents.

Training. Alcohol and drug treatment professionals may be either degreed or nondegreed, but as certification standards become more widespread and stringent, professional degrees are becoming more common. Degreed staff have been trained in a human service field (e.g., social work, rehabilitation, psychology, and nursing) and have chosen substance-abuse treatment as their area of expertise. There are still relatively few post-secondary training programs that specialize in substance abuse; most degreed individuals obtain general education in human services and gain expertise in the substance-abuse field later. The second type of alcohol and drug treatment professional is the nondegreed staff member. Most of these individuals are themselves recovering from alcohol problems, drug problems, or both, and they acquire their skills through life experience, their own recovery, and training after being hired by a treatment center.

Certification, Licensing, and Accreditation. In 1990, the National Association of Alcoholism and Drug Abuse Counselors (NAADAC) Certification Commission instituted three levels of credentials specifically for alcoholism and drug-abuse counselors. Many states also have voluntary counselor certification boards operated by private, not-for-profit corporations to assure professional competence. These certification requirements and credentials may vary by state.

The quality of substance-abuse programs is monitored by outside agencies in two separate ways: licensure and accreditation. The *licensure* standards of each state provide the consumer the assurance that the treatment center meets the minimum acceptable standards for life safety, confidentiality, and treatment. Each individual treatment component of the substance-abuse center is usually licensed separately (e.g., inpatient, outpatient, intensive outpatient, detoxification). *Accreditation* of organizations is voluntary and recognizes compliance with state-of the-art standards for treatment, facilities, and staff. Accreditation comes from two primary sources: the Joint Commission on Accreditation of Health Organizations (JCAHO) and the Commission on Accreditation of Rehabilitation Facilities (CARF), both of which are private organizations.

PURPOSE/INTENT

Goals of treatment. Organizations that provide services for those with drug and alcohol disorders strive to return the individual to a normal level of functioning. Counselors working for licensed or accredited agencies will work with the individual to develop an individualized treatment plan, which outlines treatment goals, objectives related to each goal, and activities that will help the individual achieve his or her goals. Treatment goals will definitely address substance use but will also often target other life areas, including vocational, educational, psychiatric, emotional, family, legal, and spiritual needs.

Special case management needs. Most individuals who are referred to treatment for alcohol and drug problems have other important issues that need addressing besides their substance use. For this reason, counselors often need to help people access additional needed services through ongoing assessment and referrals to relevant practitioners. Examples of additional services that might be needed include family counseling, relationship and marriage counseling, treatment for sexually transmitted diseases, parenting classes, and educational services for adolescents.

CLIENT SERVICES

Drug and alcohol abuse treatment centers provide a variety of services. Most centers provide assessment services and one or more of the following: outpatient, residential/inpatient, and continuing care. Many centers offer additional services, such as detoxification, intensive outpatient, and educational programs. The major treatment modalities are described below.

Assessment. Typically, an individual will begin his or her treatment episode with an assessment to determine the severity of his or her alcohol or drug problems and problems in other life areas. This assessment helps staff members decide the best treatment recommendation and provides the counselor with information about the most critical issues in the individual's life for treatment planning. More and more frequently, addiction professionals are using a standardized assessment measure like the Addiction Severity Index (ASI; McLellan et al., 1992) or the Global Appraisal of Individual Needs (GAIN; Dennis, 1999) during a semi-structured interview to ensure that the staff members who conduct assessments are consistent in how they assess each individual. Following the assessment, a treatment recommendation is made and an evaluation report is developed to guide treatment planning and to document the results of the assessment. If an individual has signed an authorization that allows it, evaluation reports can be shared with the referral source.

Detoxification. Frequently, the first referral needed by an individual with alcohol or other drug problems is to attend a detoxification center. All general medical hospitals are capable of providing this service; however, their willingness to do so will depend on the availability of physician expertise. Hospitals with substance-abuse specialties or other freestanding substance abuse treatment units should be consulted as to the availability of detoxification services and cost information. Some community-based organizations are licensed to provide lower-cost, nonmedical detoxification. In these programs, individuals are supervised by trained staff members for a three- to five-day period and referred to a hospital if necessary, or to additional treatment after detoxification.

During detoxification, the individual will receive supportive nursing care and pharmacotherapy for withdrawal, if necessary. During the detoxification process, patients are often remorseful and more likely to accept additional assistance (e.g., outpatient or inpatient substance-abuse therapy). It is important to stress with addicted individuals that detoxification is *not* the treatment. It only helps the individual attain a physical and mental readiness for beginning treatment. Ideally, the individual will enter a treatment program immediately after discharge from the detoxification unit.

Outpatient Services

Outpatient treatment is a less costly alternative to residential/inpatient treatment, allowing an individual to continue working or attending school and conducting his or her daily responsibilities. Like all alcohol and drug-treatment modalities, outpatient treatment seeks to focus the individual's initial efforts on maintaining abstinence. There are usually two levels of outpatient treatment: outpatient and intensive outpatient. Intensive outpatient programs will typically meet more frequently and for a greater length of time each week so that they provide more structure and a higher dosage of treatment. Most treatment programs provide multiple components to promote abstinence that may include: (a) motivational interviewing; (b) 12-step work; (c) attendance at AA; (d) medication for co-occurring mental health disorders; (e) coping skills training; and (f) relapse prevention training. Most individuals require ongoing support from some combination of a therapist, other recovering persons, family, or friends to stay drug free. However, once an individual has demonstrated some ability to do so, outpatient therapy may begin to assist him or her and significant others in healing damaged relationships and facilitating adjustment to a lifestyle free of alcohol and other drugs.

Outpatient treatment is not recommended for individuals whose substance-use frequency and problems have progressed to the point where there is almost no stability in life functioning or social support in their environment. This level of intervention is often the first treatment experience because of low cost and unobtrusive effect on the individual's life. It is most appropriate for those individuals whose drinking or other drug use is beginning to or periodically interferes with one or more aspects of their life (e.g., relationships, employment, health, legal). Should the individual's alcohol or other drug use not show significant improvement while in outpatient treatment *and* deterioration in one or more life/health areas continues, then referral to a detoxification or residential/inpatient treatment unit is indicated.

Residential/Inpatient Services

Although inpatient substance-abuse treatment programs formerly could be found in many hospitals, they are less common now. Many large cities, however, have freestanding proprietary and not-for-profit residential treatment centers. Lengths of stay will vary widely depending on funding, but for the year 2000 in the state of Illinois, the average length of stay for adults in a residential rehabilitation program was 28 days, and for adolescents it was 62 days (Illinois Division of Alcohol and Substance Abuse [I-DASA], 2002). Residential/inpatient treatment provides a controlled, safe environment, which removes the individual from the substance-using environment and permits the initial stages of recovery to begin. During treatment, individuals will receive medical monitoring and intervention when indicated, a psychological assessment, a nutritional assessment, and a healthy diet.

Most residential/inpatient programs are highly structured and provide intensive alcohol and drug education, individual and group therapy, and self-help group meetings. Individuals are typically oriented to the 12-step approach to recovery and their individual therapist monitors, advises, and supports their progress in "working the steps" toward recovery. Family or significant-other involvement in the individual's treatment is usually required during the course of the residential stay. Nearly all residential/inpatient programs offer some form of post-discharge follow-up counseling or continuing care, which might be referred to as aftercare or continuing care. Because addictive disorders are similar to other chronic illnesses (i.e., compliance to lifestyle modifications is critical and difficult), continuing-care monitoring and counseling is essential.

Continuing Care Services

Continuing care following residential/inpatient treatment is considered an important, if not essential, follow-up service to help an individual maintain progress made while in residential/inpatient treatment. The main purposes of continuing care are to monitor, support, and reinforce the use of new skills and behaviors learned in treatment, and to help the individual correct any problems or relapses that may occur. Continuing care usually includes a combination of referrals to outpatient services and mutual aid groups such as AA, Narcotics Anonymous, or Cocaine Anonymous. During continuing care in an outpatient setting, the individual will be asked to participate in either group counseling, individual counseling, or a combination of both for an extended period of time. Continuing care can last for an extended period of time, but typically individuals are involved for a three- to six-month period following discharge from residential treatment. Following outpatient treatment, individuals usually are not referred to a "formal" continuing care program but are encouraged to participate in mutual aid groups.

Typical Referral Questions

After a referral to a treatment center, best practice guidelines suggest an assessment by a qualified alcohol and drug professional to help determine if the individual being referred has a problem and if so, what level of care is appropriate. Certain pieces of information will facilitate this process.

What agency do you work for and how can you be contacted?

The staff member who assesses the individual may want to contact you for further information or to provide you with the outcome of the referral. To permit you to receive such information, the individual whom you referred will need to sign an authorization allowing the treatment agency to release the information.

What is the reason for referral?

The reason for referral is often important for understanding the extent of consequences an individual has had from his or her alcohol or drug use. The most common reason adolescents and adults are referred to the public treatment system is because of legal consequences and, if so, they may be in a diversion program or a judge may have mandated treatment. Individuals also may be referred because of school or work problems, family problems, or health-related problems.

What is the person's age and gender?

A growing number of agencies have entirely different assessment procedures and treatment programs based on age and gender, so this information is as important as deciding where an individual would begin his or her assessment process. Providing assessment and treatment services based on age and gender is considered best practice because of the differing needs of these groups. For example, adolescents and adults have developmental differences that should be taken into account by treatment programs (Drug Strategies, 2003) and it has been well documented that many females enter alcohol and drug treatment with histories of victimization and often have other unique issues due to their role as mothers (Ladwig & Andersen, 1989; Wechsberg, Craddock, & Hubbard, 1998).

What is the extent of family involvement?

Because alcohol and drug problems impact an individual's family relationships, many treatment programs have a family component. Family involvement may also enhance an individual's treatment success. Program personnel will want to know what family members are available to assist the

assessment and treatment process with the client. It is very helpful for referring agencies to prepare families for their role in collaborating in the recovery
process with the identified client.

Are there any other physical or behavioral health problems that you know about?
If you are aware of any other physical health problems that the individual
has, the treatment agency would like to know about them. Most, but not all,
hospital-based treatment facilities have limited resources available to manage
acute medical problems. Typical concerns, some of which may be associated
with alcohol or drug use, could include pancreatitis, diabetes, hepatitis, HIV
infection, prescribed medications, and pregnancy. Assessment staff will also
want to know if you judge the individual to be currently in crisis or suicidal, or
if you have evidence that he or she has a co-occurring mental health disorder.

References

American Society of Addiction Medicine (ASAM). (2001). *Patient placement criteria for
the treatment for substance-related disorders* (2nd ed.). Chevy Chase, MD: Author.

Azrin, N. H., Sisson, R. W., Meyers, R., & Godley, M. D. (1982). Alcoholism treatment
by disulfiram and community reinforcement therapy. *Behavioral Therapy and Experimental Psychiatry, 13,* 105–122.

Bickel, W. K., Amass, L., Higgins, S. T., Badger, G. J., & Esch, R. (1997). Behavioral
treatment improves outcomes during opioid detoxification with buprenorphine.
Journal of Consulting and Clinical Psychology, 65, 803–810.

Carroll, K. M. (1997). New methods of treatment efficacy research: Bridging clinical
research and clinical practice. *Alcohol Health and Research World, 21,* 352–359.

Carroll, K. M., & Nuro, K. F. (Eds.). (1996). *The technology model: An introduction to psychotherapy research in substance abuse* (Yale University Psychotherapy Development
Center Training Series 1). New Haven, CT: Yale University Psychotherapy Development Center.

Dennis, M. L. (1999). *Global Appraisal of Individual Needs (GAIN): Administration guide
for the GAIN and related measures (Version 1299).* Bloomington, IL: Chestnut Health
Systems.

Drug Strategies. (2003). *Treating teens: A guide to adolescent drug programs.* Washington,
DC: Author.

Higgins, S. T., Budney, A. J., Bickel, W. K., Foerg, F. E., Donham, R., & Badger, G. J.
(1994). Incentives improve outcome in outpatient behavioral treatment of cocaine
dependence. *Archives of General Psychiatry, 51,* 568–576.

Illinois Division of Alcohol and Substance Abuse (I-DASA). (2002). DARTS record
system for state fiscal year 2000 [Computer file]. Prepared by Chestnut Health Systems, Bloomington, IL [producer and distributor].

Jellinek, E. M. (1960). *The disease concept of alcoholism.* New Haven: Hill House.

Ladwig, G. B., & Andersen, M. D. (1989). Substance abuse in women: Relationship
between chemical dependency of women and past reports of physical and/or sexual abuse. *The International Journal of the Addictions, 24,* 739–754.

Lamb, S., Greenlick, M. R., & McCarty, D. (Eds.). (1998). *Bridging the gap between practice and research: Forging partnerships with community-based drug and alcohol treatment.*
Washington, DC: National Academy Press.

Liddle, H. A., Dakof, G. A., Parker, K., Diamond, G. S., Barrett. K., & Tejeda, M. (2001). Multidimensional family therapy for adolescent substance abuse: Results of a randomized clinical trial. *American Journal of Drug and Alcohol Abuse, 27*, 651–688.

Longabaugh, R., & Morgenstern, J. (1999). Cognitive-behavioral coping-skills therapy for alcohol dependence: Current status and future directions. *Alcohol Research and Health, 23*, 78–85.

Mann, M. (1950). *Primer on alcoholism.* New York: Holt, Rinehart and Winston.

Mann, M. (1958). *New primer on alcoholism.* New York: Holt, Rinehart and Winston.

McLellan, A. T., Kushner, H., Metzger, D., Peters, R., Smith, I., Grissom, G., et al. (1992). The fifth edition of the Addiction Severity Index. *Journal of Substance Abuse Treatment, 9*, 199–213.

Meyers, R. J., & Smith, J. E. (1995). *Clinical guide to alcohol treatment: The community reinforcement approach.* New York: Guilford.

Miller, W. R., & Hester, R. K. (1986). The effectiveness of alcoholism treatment: What research reveals. In W. R. Miller & N. Heather (Eds.), *Treating addictive behaviors: Processes of change, applied clinical psychology* (pp. 121–174). New York: Plenum.

Miller, W. R., & Rollnick, S. (1991). *Motivational interviewing: Preparing people to change addictive behavior.* New York: Guilford.

National Institute on Drug Abuse (NIDA). (2004). Drug addiction treatment medications. Retrieved from: http://www.nida.nih.gov/infofax/treatmed.html.

Project MATCH Research Group. (1997). Matching alcoholism treatments to client heterogeneity: Project MATCH posttreatment drinking outcomes. *Journal of Studies on Alcohol, 58*, 7–29.

Substance Abuse and Mental Health Services Administration (SAMHSA). (2003). *Results from the 2002 National Survey on Drug Use and Health: National findings.* Rockville, MD: Office of Applied Studies (NHSDA Series H-22, DHHS Publication No. SMA 03-3836).

Volpicelli, J. R., Alterman, A. I., Hayashida, M., & O'Brien, C. P. (1992). Naltrexone in the treatment of alcohol dependence. *Archives of General Psychiatry, 49*(11), 876–880.

Wechsberg, W. M., Craddock, S. G., & Hubbard, R. L. (1998). How are women who enter substance abuse treatment different than men? A gender comparison from the Drug Abuse Treatment Outcome Study (DATOS). *Drugs & Society, 13*, 97–115.

White, W. L. (1998). *Slaying the dragon: The history of addiction treatment and recovery in America.* Bloomington, IL: Chestnut Health Systems.

White House Office of National Drug Control Policy. (2001). *The economic costs of drug abuse in the United States, 1992–1998.* Washington, DC: Executive Office of the President (Publication No. NCJ-190636).

Peer Self-Help Groups

John J. Benshoff

Peer self-help groups have come to occupy a prominent place in the retinue of available community services. Generally modeled on the successful Alcoholics Anonymous, these groups offer guidance, support, and solace to individuals suffering from a variety of societal, behavioral, or medical conditions. They are typified by their absence of formal, professional leadership, acceptance of all comers who indicate an interest in change, and their emphasis on change occurring through participation within the structure of the program.

ALCOHOLICS ANONYMOUS

The best-known and oldest peer self-help group is Alcoholics Anonymous (AA). The founding of Alcoholics Anonymous can be traced to the chance encounter in 1935 of two recovering alcoholics, Dr. Bob Smith and Bill Wilson. Smith and Wilson had tried many avenues seeking their own recovery and were determined in that fateful meeting in the kitchen of the Smith home in Akron, Ohio, to divine a successful method for recovery from alcoholism. From that humble beginning, AA has grown to include 1.5 million members in 115 countries around the world.

The sole criteria for AA membership, as articulated in AA Tradition 3, ". . . is a desire to quit drinking." There are no dues except for the dollar bills dropped in the basket when it is passed to help pay for the ubiquitous coffee and snacks, and literature for new members. The local meeting or group is the keystone of AA. Members may choose to affiliate with a *home* group or may choose to attend a variety of groups. In general, most individuals select a group in which they feel comfortable.

In urban areas, there are special meetings for alcoholics of all persuasions: professional groups, old-timer groups, gay groups, Hispanic groups, physician groups, women's groups, and so on. Most AA meetings, and there are thousands of them occurring daily, are *open meetings*—as the name implies, open to all comers, both alcoholic and nonalcoholic. In more populated areas, *newcomer's meetings* cater to AA beginners; Big Book meetings center on discussion from *Alcoholics Anonymous* (Alcoholics Anonymous World Services, 1976), the aptly named AA bible; Step and Tradition meetings focus on the Twelve Steps and Twelve Traditions of AA; and *closed* meetings are limited to members of local groups or visiting members from other groups to provide a forum for those unique and common problems faced by all recovering alcoholics. Meeting times and places are often advertised in the daily paper and, generally, a local phone number will be listed to provide information about meetings. Meetings are generally held in church basements, community centers, group halls, or other public locations. Meetings are also held in hospitals and chemical dependency treatment centers for the convenience of individuals in treatment. These meetings, while hosted by the institution, are conducted according to the tenets of Alcoholics Anonymous and are viewed as a service for the host institution.

A member's participation in AA is grounded in the Twelve Steps:

1. We admitted we were powerless over alcohol—that our lives had become unmanageable.

2. Came to believe that a Power greater than ourselves could restore us to sanity.

3. Made a decision to turn our will and our lives over to the care of God *as we understood him.*

4. Made a searching and fearless moral inventory of ourselves.

5. Admitted to God, to ourselves, and to another human being the exact nature of our wrongs.

6. Were entirely ready to have God remove all these defects of character.

7. Humbly asked Him to remove our shortcomings.

8. Made a list of all persons we had harmed and became willing to make amends to them all.

9. Made direct amends to such people wherever possible, except when to do so would injure them or others.

10. Continued to take personal inventory and when we were wrong promptly admitted it.

11. Sought through prayer and meditation to improve our conscious contact with God as *we understood Him,* praying only for the knowledge of His will for us, and the power to carry that out.

12. Having had a spiritual awakening as the result of these steps, we tried to carry this message to alcoholics, and to practice these principles in all our affairs.

From a clinical perspective, the Twelve Steps of AA neatly encapsulate the treatment issues of problem recognition, insight, help seeking, restitution, stress reduction, and assumption of a healthy, non-egocentric lifestyle. Perhaps, however, the Twelve Steps are best understood in the words of Nan Robertson (1988), Pulitzer Prize-winning journalist and longtime AA member:

> We admit we are licked and cannot get well on our own. We get honest with ourselves. We talk it out with somebody else. We try to make amends to people we have harmed. We pray to whatever greater power we think there is. We try to give of ourselves for our own sake and without stint to other alcoholics, with no thought of reward. (p. 26)

Fundamental to the belief system espoused by AA is the concept that alcoholism is a lifelong illness, for which there is treatment resulting in remission of the disease through abstinence, but not a cure. Consequently, AA members refer to themselves as *recovering* alcoholics, not recovered alcoholics.

Just as individual participation centers on the Twelve Steps, the Twelve Traditions of AA guide the functioning of the organization:

1. Our common welfare should come first; personal recovery depends upon AA unity.
2. From our group purpose there is but one ultimate authority—a loving God as He may express himself in our group conscience. Our leaders are but trusted servants; they do not govern.
3. The only requirement for AA membership is a desire to stop drinking.
4. Each group should be autonomous except in matters affecting other groups or AA as a whole.
5. Each group has but one primary purpose—to carry its message to the alcoholic who still suffers.
6. An AA group ought never endorse, finance, or lend the AA name to any related facility or outside enterprise, lest problems of money, property, and prestige divert us from our primary purpose.
7. Every AA group ought to be fully self-supporting, declining outside contributions.
8. Alcoholics Anonymous should remain forever nonprofessional, but our service centers may employ special workers.
9. AA, as such, ought never be organized; but we may create service boards or committees directly responsible to those they serve.
10. Alcoholics Anonymous has no opinion on outside issues; hence the AA name ought never be drawn into public controversy.

11. Our public relations policy is based on attraction rather than promotion; we need always maintain personal anonymity at the level of press, radio, and films.

12. Anonymity is the spiritual foundation of all our traditions, ever reminding us to place principles before personalities.

As the Traditions suggest, the local group is the basic functional unit of AA. It is independent and autonomous from other groups, often fiercely so. There are no membership applications, requirements for a quorum, conformity to rules and regulation of meeting decorum, subservience to an overseeing body, or obeisance to professional groups. Indeed, the long form of the Traditions suggests that where two or three members are gathered for sobriety, a meeting may occur. Obviously, a group as wide-ranging as AA cannot exist in a totally unstructured state. At the group level, officers may be elected for short terms as chairperson, secretary, or treasurer, or to various committees with responsibility for carrying on the logistics of the meetings.

In larger communities, Regional Service Boards exist to coordinate group meeting times and places and to deal with issues that concern the welfare of groups within the region. Often, for example, Regional Service Boards will sponsor quarterly or annual breakfast or dinner meetings, bringing together all of the members of all of the groups in a region.

Overall responsibility for the service standards of Alcoholics Anonymous rests with the General Service Board, based in New York City. This 21-member board is composed of both AA members and nonalcoholic members, with the unique feature that only nonalcoholic members can assume positions of financial responsibility within the board. This longstanding tenet is based upon Bill Wilson's recognition that even the most firmly committed AA member can experience a slip, a temporary relapse from sobriety. Wilson's fear was that a slipped alcoholic with fiscal responsibilities could do great financial and moral damage to the Fellowship. The Board oversees the operation of the General Service Board, the publishing and supporting arm of AA, and serves as a central clearinghouse for information. In recent years, the General Service Board has assumed responsibility for devising strategies to underserved minority groups, both within the United States and around the world. AA's only paid staffers work for the General Service Office.

Anonymity—The Essence of AA

The late Bill Wilson wrote in *AA Comes of Age* (Alcoholics Anonymous World Services, Inc., 1957),

> Moved by the spirit of anonymity, we try to give up our natural desires for personal distinctions as AA members both among our fellow alcoholics and before the general public. As we lay aside these very human aspirations . . . each of us takes part in the weaving of a protective mantle that covers our whole society and under which we may grow and work in unity.

The anonymity principle serves to keep the new AA member focused on the newly recovering self, and for controlling urges for power and prestige, urges that are seen as contrary to the notion of a sober life.

Secondly, anonymity allows the newly recovering person safe haven from the stigma of alcoholism. Despite the recent gains which have been made in society's understanding and perception of alcoholism problems, negative social, economic, and familial consequences from the former alcoholic lifestyle exert pressures which can be damaging to sobriety. Anonymity does not, however, provide an excuse or alibi for past irresponsible or harmful behaviors. Indeed, throughout the Twelve Steps AA members are called to assume individual, personal responsibility for their behavior, past and present.

Finally, the anonymity principle promotes participation by individuals from all walks of life, with anonymity the great leveler. Members are asked to give only their first names in meetings and all are viewed as fellow travelers on the road to sobriety. No member, by virtue of experience, rank, or expertise, is placed above any other member, and the Fellowship has been quick to separate itself from those who flaunt their recovery for personal aggrandizement or gain. Indeed, anonymity is seen as a method for members to develop a new, humble sense of self, devoid of the ego demands which are felt to lead to a return to drinking behavior.

The only role that members can assume which distinguishes individuals from one another is the role of sponsor. New members are commonly encouraged to find a sponsor, in effect a mentor, who can provide guidance, support, and understanding, both in normal and trying times. Typically, sponsors should have several years of quality sobriety and an interest in providing empathetic guidance and assistance. The organization establishes no formal guidelines for sponsorship, nor does it provide any training except that which occurs serendipitously through attending meetings and observing other individuals in action.

Consistent with the anonymity principle, Alcoholics Anonymous has steadfastly refused to have its name associated with *any* other organization, nor does it accept donations, believing to do either could divert the organization from its primary purpose. Many alcoholism treatment programs will advertise themselves as AA model programs, an appellation which is self-ascribed, and which should not be construed as AA endorsement. Similarly, AA has refused to allow bumper stickers, jewelry, trinkets, and the like to be imprinted with the AA logo or other identifying marks. Recently a series of bumper stickers, T-shirts, and other paraphernalia have appeared with AA slogans on them (e.g., Easy Does It, I'm a Friend of Bill's, One Day at a Time), however, the feeling of the membership and the General Service Board was that these sayings were sufficiently unknown to the general public and, hence, not a danger to any member's anonymity. Alcoholics Anonymous supports itself primarily through the sale of books and pamphlets about AA, all of which are inscribed "AA General Conference-approved literature."

Who Joins AA?

The sole criteria for AA membership is a desire to quit drinking. In its early days, Alcoholics Anonymous meetings were apt to be filled with middle-aged, white, male alcoholics. As drug use has grown more prevalent, the composition of the membership has expanded to include younger individuals and people from a variety of ethnic backgrounds. Similarly, more women are now seen in AA meetings. In the past the lead speaker might have started his address with the statement, "Hello, my name is Joe, and I'm an alcoholic." Today, it is increasingly probable that the lead speaker will say, "Hello, my name is Joanne, and I'm an addict and an alcoholic."

This changing composition has not always been greeted enthusiastically by individual members. Many "old deacons," long-time recovering alcoholics, regard this new breed of member with a history of multiple addictions to multiple substances with some disdain. Fortunately, these individuals nearly always are in the minority, and there is growing, explicit recognition that, just as society has changed, so too have addictive diseases, and consequently the membership of AA.

Ogborne and Glaser (1981), in a review of the literature on affiliation with AA, suggested that members tended to be white males, middle-aged, and from upper- or middle-class backgrounds. In addition, they tended to be binge drinkers, with a physical dependence on alcohol and a history of loss-of-control drinking. Membership has also been associated with external locus of control, strong affiliation needs, and the loss or threatened loss of a lifestyle because of drinking.

Emrick (1987) suggested that successful participation (i.e., development and maintenance of sobriety) among AA members is related to leading meetings, having a sponsor and acting as a sponsor, and working Steps 6 through 12 following residential treatment. Frequency of attendance was also correlated with sobriety status and duration. Hoffman, Harrison, and Belille (1983) reported the efficacy of AA as an aftercare strategy, correlating weekly AA attendance with preservation of sobriety. As one might expect, "AA members who are more active in the organization, both with frequency of attendance and participation in the organization's therapeutic mechanisms, have an outcome status that is as good as and probably better than those members who attend or participate less actively" (Emrick, 1987, p. 420).

From an empirical perspective, aside from the studies previously mentioned and a handful of others, relatively little is known about the treatment efficacy of AA. The anonymity principle, while fostering membership growth and participation, also effectively hinders an in-depth research understanding of who attends meetings, for how long, and how often. Little is known, for example, about the recovery success of individuals who attend a few meetings for a short time and then drop out, or about individuals who attend meetings sporadically over a number of years. Moreover, meager knowledge exists about persons who attend one AA meeting, and never go back. AA freely admits that the program is not for all people. It concedes that AA is not for the individual who is unwilling to frankly admit to being an alcoholic, or who cleaves to the notion of a return to social drinking.

PEER SELF-HELP PROGRAMS FOR CODEPENDENTS

Alcoholism has been generally conceptualized as affecting not only the identified alcoholic but also the family, with recurrent problems evident. Individuals affected by and enmeshed in the problems of an alcoholic are broadly considered to be *codependents*. They include spouses, children, teenagers, and most recently adult children of alcoholics. The best-known peer self-help group for codependents is Al-Anon.

Begun in the early 1950s in response to the need to provide support and guidance for spouses in alcoholic marriages, the program has grown to include 25,000 groups worldwide. Just as a basic premise of AA is that the alcoholic is powerless over alcohol, Al-Anon members learn that they are powerless over alcohol and the alcoholic. The Al-Anon recovery program emphasizes independence, abandonment of previously held control notions, and detachment, a willingness to allow the world to run itself (Young, 1987). Just as in AA, the membership of Al-Anon has grown increasingly diverse. No longer are meetings attended only by white females in their middle age. Males, minorities, and younger people make up a significant proportion of the membership today.

Although not formally affiliated with Alcoholics Anonymous, Al-Anon uses a 12-step model, and meetings are frequently scheduled concurrently with AA meetings. There are no dues, no membership lists, and no requirements for participation. Some Al-Anon members join because a loved one has joined AA. For others, Al-Anon provides support and guidance about living with a family member who is continuing to drink. Teenagers from alcoholic homes can receive support and guidance from Alateen. Again, there are no dues and no rules and regulations governing membership. However, adult leadership is provided, often from a recovering individual or spouse.

In the late 1970s, clinicians identified a complex set of characteristics found in adults who had been raised in alcoholic homes, and the Adult Children of Alcoholics (ACOA) movement was born. Children who grow up in alcoholic homes have to learn a complex set of survival skills to cope with the exigencies of living with an alcoholic parent. They learn to live and adjust to shifting, and generally dysfunctional, patterns of communication, intimacy, behavior, and relationships. Unfortunately, these survival skills, which served them well as children, may result in problems in adult life. Frequently, adult children of alcoholics experience difficulties with interpersonal relationships, intimacy, trust, and an inability to develop a healthy sense of self-esteem and personal identity. Because they have been raised in homes full of turmoil, their lives may be characterized by disorder, thrill seeking, and risk taking.

Finally, there is a high incidence of alcoholism among this group. Adult Children of Alcoholics groups are found in most areas of the country, and a considerable popular press has emerged concerning the problems of ACOAs.

NARCOTICS ANONYMOUS, COCAINE ANONYMOUS, AND OTHER PEER SELF-HELP GROUPS

The history of Narcotics Anonymous (NA) can be traced to the late 1940s and early 1950s when concerned recovering drug addicts, recognizing the success of AA, realized that a similar program could be beneficial to drug addicts. Just as in AA, NA is a fellowship of sufferers; hence, leadership and authority within NA flows from the bottom up, not the top down. NA maintains its own World Service Board and has evolved its own Twelve Steps and Twelve Traditions. In part, NA originated in response to the implicit, and occasionally explicit, rejection by AA of addicts and their problems. Today, however, NA members often attend AA meetings and vice versa, and just as in the AA community, relatively few *pure* addicts are seen.

The core belief of NA is that members suffer from the disease of drug addition, without specific recognition of any particular drug. This addiction is thought to be a lifelong addiction for which the only treatment is abstinence from *all* potentially addicting substances including alcohol. As the group name implies, the focus tends to be on the universality of potential problems caused by addicting drugs—narcotics—rather than on the unique problems of individual members. From an ideological viewpoint, NA is intolerant of any drug consumption other than that which is medically necessary, although slips (relapses) are recognized as intrinsic elements of the addictive process. Addicts who slip are allowed to remain in the fellowship, provided, of course, that they cease using drugs.

NA meetings include testimonial meetings in which lead speakers deliver speeches about their addiction and subsequent recovery, step-study and tradition-study meetings, and discussion meetings often focusing on questions and answers about NA and addiction (Peyrot, 1985). NA holds both open and closed meetings that are advertised in local newspapers and directories of human services.

The expanding cocaine epidemic of the 1980s resulted in the establishment of a number of treatment alternatives for cocaine and crack addiction, including the formation of Cocaine Anonymous. Modeled on traditional 12-step, peer self-help principles, this fellowship provides assistance, guidance, and support specifically for those addicted to cocaine and its derivatives. Cocaine Anonymous groups tend to be found in large urban areas, but as cocaine addiction continues to expand, groups are forming in less populated areas.

Women for Sobriety (WFS) is a peer self-help program begun by Dr. Jean Kirkpatrick in 1976 to meet the needs of women with alcoholism problems. The focal-point of WFS is the "New Life Program" that promotes behavioral change through positive reinforcement, positive thinking strategies, and wellness activities such as meditation, nutrition, diet, and exercise. The Thirteen Statements of WFS seek to empower women to develop richer, fuller lives.

The peer self-help model has proven popular for treating a variety of other social ills. Gamblers Anonymous serves individuals with compulsive gambling disorders; Overeaters Anonymous provides support for individuals with eating disorders. These and other groups are widely available throughout the country.

PEER SELF-HELP GROUPS AND THE PROFESSIONAL COUNSELOR

For the counselor seeking help for a client with an alcoholism or addiction problem, peer self-help groups present a number of advantages. They are easy to refer to, and there is never a waiting list. Indeed, often regional service boards or individual groups will arrange for newcomers to be accompanied to meetings by veteran fellowship members. Peer self-help groups present the additional advantage of being free, also an important consideration in these times of escalating health-care costs.

This cost-free benefit may have a multiple impact. Not only is the identified client spared the direct cost of services, but also the dollars saved can be used to purchase other services or to provide services to other clients. Finally, both popular literature and the nonempirically based professional literature strongly suggest the efficacy of peer self-help groups. Part of their success may rest with a preconceived notion that clients and counselors may have that the treatment will work.

Despite these advantages, counselors need to guard against the assumption that peer self-help groups will work for every patient, every time. Peer self-help groups are not a panacea for all ailments. Indeed, in most cases they should serve as an adjunct to the already established therapeutic relationship.

Peer self-help groups are not for all clients. Addicts or alcoholics who are unwilling or uninterested in stopping all alcohol or drug-consuming behavior—those individuals who wish to drink or use drugs socially—are not good candidates for peer self-help groups. Individuals whose recovery will require close monitoring generally will not make good peer self-help group members, initially. The leaderless, anonymous characteristics of these groups make close scrutiny and accountability difficult in many instances. Groups will provide feedback about individual attendance if asked, usually through the mechanism of a signed note from the group secretary. Counselors requiring feedback information should establish a procedure for getting this information from the local group or meeting and should not place this logistical burden on the client. At best, it may raise the anxiety level of the first-time group participant and serve as a deterrent to group participation. At worst, clients in denial of their addictive disease may take advantage of the situation and not attend meetings, but return notes signed by friends or family.

Peer self-help assistance is based on a unitary premise: abstinence from chemicals. Clients presenting multidimensional problems (e.g., dual addictive disease, psychiatric diagnoses) will require more intervention than a peer self-help group may be capable of giving. While group participation may be a useful adjunct for therapy, peer self-therapy cannot substitute for the intensive therapy often needed in these situations, or for required psychotropic medications.

Counselors need to carefully monitor clients who are taking psychotropic or other therapeutic medications and who are attending AA or NA meetings. While these groups recognize and support the consumption of medication for valid medical or psychiatric purposes, individual group members may espouse a totally different philosophy to the detriment of clients who require medication to function in society.

Both the Twelve Steps and the Twelve Traditions of Alcoholics Anonymous refer to spirituality as the foundation for recovery, and the third step explicitly calls for members to turn their will and lives over to the care of God. References to God and spirituality lead many clients and counselors to believe that AA is a religious organization, a belief bolstered by the reality that many AA groups (and other peer self-help groups) meet in church basements or church fellowship halls. While it is impossible to ignore the religious undertones in the steps and traditions, AA views itself as a spiritually-based organization and not an agent or arm of organized religion. Spirituality is viewed as more of an individual, self-guided experience as opposed to the collective, dogma-guided nature of religion. Many clients have issues with religion, and counselors should discuss these issues openly and honestly.

Finally, counselors who choose to refer clients to peer self-help groups should become aware of the value structures, mores, and cultural traditions of local groups. Almost by definition, peer self-help groups represent a microcosm of society, reflecting both that which is positive and that which is negative. Groups, while espousing openness to all, may have taboos about race, gender, gender preference, or other issues that may alienate certain individuals.

Despite these cautions and disadvantages, peer self-help groups represent a vital, growing, and effective way for many individuals to cope with the problems of life. They serve as a useful adjunct to therapy and, for some clients, may be the critical element in achieving recovery from addiction or alcoholism.

Useful Addresses

Al-Anon Family Group Headquarters, Inc.
Box 182 Madison Square Station
New York, NY 10159-0182
(212) 683-1771
www.al-anon.alateen.org/

Alcoholics Anonymous World Services
Box 459 Grand Central Station
New York, NY 10163
(212) 686-1100
http://www.alcoholics-anonymous.org

Cocaine Anonymous World Services
3740 Overland Ave., Suite C
Los Angeles, CA 90034
(310) 559-5833
www.ca.org

Narcotics Anonymous World Services Office
P.O. Box 9999
Van Nuys, CA 91409
(818) 773-9999
www.na.org/

National Association for Children of Alcoholics
Box 421961
San Francisco, CA 94142
(415) 431-1366
www.nacoa.org/

Women for Sobriety, Inc.
P.O. Box 618
Quakertown, PA 18951-0618
(215) 536-8026
www.Womenforsobriety.org/

References

Alcoholics Anonymous World Services, Inc. (1957). *Alcoholics Anonymous comes of age: A brief history of AA.* New York: Author.

Alcoholics Anonymous World Services, Inc. (1976). *Alcoholics Anonymous* (3rd ed.). New York: Author.

Emrick, C. D. (1987). Alcoholics Anonymous: Affiliation processes and effectiveness as treatment. *Alcoholism Clinical and Experimental Research, 11,* 416–423.

Hoffman, N. G., Harrison, P. A., & Belille, C. A. (1983). Alcoholics Anonymous after treatment: Attendance and abstinence. *The International Journal of Addictions, 18*(3), 311–318.

Ogborne, A. C., & Glaser, F. B. (1981). Characteristics of affiliates of Alcoholics Anonymous: A review of the literature. *Journal of Studies on Alcohol, 42*(7), 661–675.

Peyrot, M. (1985). Narcotics Anonymous: Its history, structure, and approach. *The International Journal of Addictions, 20*(10), 1509–1522.

Robertson, N. (1988, Feb. 21). The changing world of Alcoholics Anonymous. *New York Times Magazine,* pp. 24–26, 47, 57, 92.

Young, E. (1987). Co-alcoholism as a disease: Implications for psychotherapy. *Journal of Psychoactive Drugs, 19,* 257–268.

Social Security Disability Insurance/ Supplemental Security Income

Blanca B. Robles & Irmo Marini

History/Legislation

The fallout of the Great Depression of 1929–1933 in the United States led then-President Franklin D. Roosevelt to announce to Congress on June 8, 1934, his intention to make available a program for Social Security. The president created the Committee on Economic Security, which was charged with studying the national problem of economic insecurity and making recommendations ultimately designed to minimize the devastating economic impact the Depression had wrought. The term Social Security was first used in the United States by Abraham Epstein in connection with his group, the American Association for Social Security. Originally, the Social Security Act of 1935 was named the Economic Security Act but was later changed during Congressional consideration of the bill. By early January 1935, the Committee gave its final report recommendations to the president. After introducing the report to Congress on January 17 and both Houses subsequently passing their own versions, President Roosevelt signed the Social Security Act into law on August 14, 1935. Besides several provisions for general welfare, the new Act created a social insurance program that would pay retired workers aged 65 or older a continuing income after retirement.

Another provision of the Act established a bipartisan Social Security Board (SSB). One of the main responsibilities faced by the SSB was to provide information on how to report earnings and benefits available to employers, employees, and the public in general. The SSB needed to register employers and workers by January 1, 1937, when workers would begin acquiring credits toward old-age insurance benefits. Being unable to accomplish this task due to limited resources, the SSB contracted with the U.S. Postal Service to distribute the applications beginning in November 1936. The post offices collected the completed forms, typed the Social Security Number (SSN) cards, and returned the cards to applicants. Applications were sent to the SSB's processing center in Baltimore, where the SSB registered the numbers and established employment records. During 1936–1937, over 35 million SSN cards were issued.

Under the 1935 law, monthly benefits were to begin in 1942. From 1937 until 1942, Social Security was to pay benefits to retirees in the form of a single, lump-sum refund payment. The average lump-sum payment during this period was $58.06. The smallest payment ever made was for 5 cents. In 1950, major amendments were enacted that raised benefits for the first time. The Social Security Amendments of 1954 initiated a disability insurance program that provided the public with additional coverage. There were no cash benefits offered at the time; however, it did prevent any periods of disability individuals might sustain from reducing their retirement or survivor benefits in the future. On August 1, 1956, the Social Security Act was amended to provide benefits to workers with disabilities aged 50–65 and disabled adult children. Over the next two years, the scope of the program expanded, permitting workers with disabilities under age 50 and their dependents to qualify for benefits, and eventually workers with disabilities at any age were able to qualify.

In the original 1935 Social Security Act, programs were introduced for disadvantaged, aged, and individuals who were blind, and, in 1950, disadvantaged individuals with disabilities were added. These three programs were known as the "adult categories." State and local governments with partial federal funding administered them. In 1969, President Nixon identified a need to reform these and related welfare programs due to some overlapping aspects of the programs. In the Social Security Amendments of 1972, Congress federalized the adult categories by creating the Supplemental Security Income (SSI) program and assigned responsibility for it to the Social Security Administration (SSA). The disability program experienced many changes in the Social Security Amendments of 1980. Most of these changes focused on various work incentive provisions for both Social Security and SSI disability benefits. The 1980 amendments required SSA to conduct periodic reviews of current disability beneficiaries to certify their continuing eligibility. In 1984, Congress passed the Disability Benefits Reform Act modifying how disability reviews were conducted. Also in the early 1980s, the Social Security program was facing a serious financial crisis. Consequently, a bill was passed in 1983, which made numerous changes in the Social Security and Medicare programs, including the taxation of Social Security benefits, the first coverage for federal employees, raising the retirement age beginning in the year 2000, and increasing the reserves in the Social Security Trust Funds.

In April 1996, legislation changed certain rules for qualifying for disability benefits. New applicants for Social Security or SSI disability benefits could no longer be eligible for benefits if drug addiction or alcoholism was a material factor in their disability or if it was considered the primary disabling cause. Also in 1996, President Clinton signed welfare reform legislation, which terminated SSI eligibility for most non-citizens. Finally, the eligibility rules for awarding SSI disability benefits to children were tightened in diagnosed cases of behavioral or emotional disturbance.

The most recent significant change in Social Security legislation occurred on December 17, 1999, when President Clinton signed the Ticket to Work—Work Incentives Improvement Act. This law provides disability beneficiaries with a voucher they may use to purchase vocational rehabilitation services, employment services, and other support services from an employment network of their choice. In addition to allowing beneficiaries to purchase vocational services, the law provides incentive payments to providers of vocational rehabilitation services for successfully returning beneficiaries to work. The Ticket to Work initiative seeks to shift the emphasis of the disability program away from mere maintenance of benefits and more toward rehabilitating beneficiaries with disabilities in an attempt to return them to productive work.

On April 7, 2000, President Clinton signed into law H.R. 5, The Senior Citizens' Freedom to Work Act of 2000, eliminating the Retirement Earnings Test (RET) for beneficiaries at or above normal retirement age (NRA). (The RET still applies to beneficiaries below NRA.) This prohibited approximately 900,000 people who were collecting benefits and also working from being penalized with a reduction of benefits because of work.

The Social Security Administration, established in 1946, is a federal agency that administers two benefit programs for people with disabilities known as Supplemental Security Income and Social Security Disability Insurance (SSDI). The Social Security Administration's mandate is to provide benefits to those entitled to the provisions of the Social Security Act and to protect the Social Security Trust Fund.

The Office of Employment Support Programs (OESP), headed by an associate commissioner, was established in 1999. OESP contains two divisions with a staff of 77 people. The mission of OESP is to: (a) plan, implement, and evaluate SSA programs and policies related to SSDI and SSI beneficiaries with disabilities; (b) promote innovation in the design of programs and policies that increase employment opportunities for Social Security beneficiaries; (c) educate the public about the SSA and other public programs that support employment and provide employment-related services; and (d) join with other public and private entities to remove employment barriers for people with disabilities.

Another related SSA department is the Division of Employment Policy, which is comprised of three teams: the Employment Policy Team (leads operational policy development and implementation), the Employment Support

Service Delivery Team (conducts pilot tests to try out new services, evaluates new field positions), and the Program Innovations Team (manages research and demonstration projects).

Finally, the Division of Employment Support and Programs Acquisitions is comprised of four teams: Communications and Training, Legislative Implementation, Program Acquisitions, and Provider Operations. Tasks include but are not limited to coordinating, implementing, and supporting the Ticket to Work Program. Furthermore, part of this team is responsible for administering the Vocational Rehabilitation (VR) Reimbursement Program.

Social Security Disability Insurance (SSDI)

The Social Security Disability Insurance Program is part of the Old Age, Survivors, and Disability Insurance (OASDI) Program that was enacted in 1954. The program insures workers against loss of income due to a physical or mental disability.

Benefits

SSDI benefits are paid to individuals and their dependents who have been employed and have paid Social Security taxes for a certain time. When individuals work, employees and their employers contribute to Social Security taxes that are reflected on their paychecks as Federal Insurance Contributions Act (FICA). Any revenues not needed to finance current benefit levels are invested in interest-bearing U.S. treasury securities. The interest on these securities is accrued to the trust funds. Social Security tax contributions for 2004 were 7.65% of an individual's wages. These annual contributions are then matched by employers and submitted to the Internal Revenue Service (IRS). For individuals who own their own businesses the contribution is not shared, and they are solely responsible for submitting both shares to the IRS (15.3% of their earned wages). The 7.65% tax rate is a combined rate for Social Security and Medicare (6.20% for OASDI and 1.45% for the Medicare portion).

As contributors, SSDI beneficiaries and their dependents/family members may receive benefits when they retire, become disabled, or die. Specifically, Social Security will provide SSDI benefits to qualifying individuals who are retired and 62 years of age or older who are deemed disabled by SSA when satisfying the Administration's eligibility criteria (see definition of disability on pp. 175–176), and cannot perform substantial gainful activity/employment. Benefits are also paid to spouses and children of deceased, disabled, or retired workers.

Disability insurance benefits are disbursed in the form of cash payments and "provisions." Benefit payments are distributed monthly by check or direct deposit. According to SSA policy, every legally competent beneficiary or recipient has the right to manage his or her own cash benefits. If there is evidence that an individual is not able to manage or direct the management of benefit payments, a representative payee is selected.

Benefits in the form of protections provide for hospital and supplementary medical insurance, as well as vocational rehabilitation services. Medicare provides medical insurance coverage to SSDI beneficiaries. Medicare has two parts: hospital insurance (Part A) and medical insurance (Part B). Individuals must complete a five-month waiting period from the month of disability onset before benefits begin, and an additional 24-month waiting period (Medicare Qualifying Period) after disability cash benefits begin is required before individuals are entitled to receive Medicare coverage. Since the 24 months do not need to be accumulated consecutively, an individual may accumulate 12 months of the 24-month waiting period before losing cash benefits due to earnings over Substantial Gainful Activity (SGA). If individuals re-establish entitlement for Social Security at a later date, they would only need to complete the final 12 months of the 24-month waiting period before Medicare coverage begins. Furthermore, if SSDI beneficiaries complete the two-year waiting period prior to losing Social Security and become entitled again for Social Security within five years (seven years for childhood disability beneficiaries), a new 24-month period would not be required. If entitlement for disability benefits is re-established after five years based on the same or directly related disabling impairment, a new 24-month Medicare waiting period would also not be required.

Eligibility for Benefits

SSDI is not a program based on financial need; consequently there are no restrictions on unearned income. The monthly dollar amount awarded to individuals varies depending on the level of contributions they have paid into the program. There are also no gradual reductions in cash benefits as one's earnings increase. As such, beneficiaries either receive the full amount of their SSDI or no income support at all.

The number of credits required for disability benefits depends on age and onset of disability. If disabled before age 24, a person generally needs six credits during the three-year period, ending when the disability begins. If disabled at age 24 through 30, a person generally needs credits for half of the period between age 21 and the onset of disability. If disabled at age 31 or older, a person needs the number of credits shown in the following table. In addition, he or she must have earned at least 20 of the credits in the 10 years immediately before becoming disabled.

Age at Disability	Credits Needed
31 through 42	20
44	22
46	24
48	26
50	28

52	30
54	32
56	34
58	36
60	38
62 or older	40

In some cases, people 18 and over can qualify for disability insurance even though they may not have contributed through payroll taxes. Individuals would be eligible if they were totally and permanently disabled before age 22, and if they had been dependent on an insured worker who is currently disabled, retired, or deceased. Persons who are eligible for disability benefits are:

1. An insured worker with a disability who is under age 65.

2. A spouse of a disabled worker who is entitled to benefits, who is age 62 or older, has in his or her care a child under the age of 16, or someone over 16 who is disabled.

3. A divorced spouse of a disabled worker who is entitled to benefits, if age 62 or older and married to a worker for at least 10 years.

4. A divorced spouse of a fully insured worker who has not yet filed a claim for benefits, if both are age 62 or older, were married for at least 10 years, and have been finally divorced for at least 2 continuous years.

5. A dependent, unmarried child of a retired disabled worker entitled to benefits, or if a deceased insured worker of the child is: (a) under age 18; (b) under age 19 and a full-time elementary or secondary school student; or (c) age 18 or over, but having a disability that began before age 22.

6. A disabled, surviving spouse (including a surviving divorced spouse in some cases) of a deceased insured worker, if the widow(er) is age 50–59 and becomes disabled within the specified period.

Vocational Rehabilitation Benefits

Law requires the Social Security Administration to provide information about a claimant who applies for benefits to the State Vocational Rehabilitation (VR) Agency. The state VR would assist the individual with services that may help recover the ability to work. While the claimant receives services, disability benefits would continue until the impairment improves and the individual returns to work. Interestingly, the Government Accounting Office has indicated that less than 1% of all persons on the SSI/SSDI beneficiary roles have ever returned to gainful employment, which ultimately led to the Ticket to Work legislation opening the way for alternative providers to offer vocational rehabilitation services.

Definitions of Adult and Child Disability

The criteria and process used to establish an individual's disability status for initial eligibility is the same for SSI and SSDI. However, for the SSI program, the disability eligibility requirement and process for determining eligibility for individuals under the age of 18 versus those age 18 or older differ slightly. Therefore, it is important to know that section 223(d) of the Social Security Act defines the adult disability requirements as follows:

> The inability to engage in any substantial gainful activity by reason of any medically determinable physical or mental impairment which can be expected to result in death or which has lasted or can be expected to last for a continuous period of not less than 12 months. An individual shall be determined to be under a disability only if physical or mental impairment or impairments are of such severity that he is not only unable to engage in his previous work, but cannot, considering his age, education, and work experience, engage in any other substantial gainful work which exists in the national economy, regardless of whether such work exists in the immediate area in which he lives, or whether a specific job vacancy exists for him, or whether he would be hired if he applied for work.

Conditions for the disability requirement are as follows:

- Individuals must have a disability that can be documented by a qualified medical examiner. Individuals must also meet or equal a certain SSA listing level of disability;
- The disability must be expected to last 12 or more months or be expected to result in death;
- Individuals cannot be working at the time of application or, if working, cannot be earning more than the Substantial Gainful Activity (SGA) level of $810 (2004) for individuals with a disability other than blindness or $1,350 (2004) if they are blind.

Blindness is defined by SSA as either a central visual acuity of 20/200 or less in the better eye with use of a corrective lens, or a limitation in the field of vision so that the widest diameter in the visual field subtends an angle of 20 degrees or less. Since blindness is a separate statutory definition, individuals who are blind and applying for SSI do not need to meet SGA but rather satisfy a test to ascertain level of blindness.

The Social Security Act defines the child disability requirement as follows:

> An individual under the age of 18 shall be considered disabled for the purposes of the SSI program if that individual has a medically determinable physical or mental impairment which results in marked and severe functional limitations, and which can be expected to result in death or which has lasted or expected to last for a continuous period of not less than 12 months.

SSA has clearly stated that they will no longer discuss disability in terms of child's ability to function independently, appropriately, and effectively in an age-appropriate manner. The new definition of disability has four main parts, which guide the sequential evaluation process. The disability must have a medically determinable impairment meet the duration requirement, have no current SGA, and have an impairment resulting in "marked and severe" functional limitations.

Evaluation Process

A five-step sequential evaluation process is applied by the Disability Determination Service (DDS) in making a disability decision. Social Security regulations pertaining to the sequential evaluation process require these steps to be followed in specific order, and to stop if at some point a determination of "disabled" or "not disabled" can be made. The five questions of this step-by-step process are:

1. *Is the person working at a substantial level?*
   If the individual's earnings exceed $810 (for 2004) a month, he or she would generally not be considered disabled. If the individual is not working, DDS would proceed to the next step.

2. *Is the individual's medically determinable impairment(s) "severe"?*
   Social Security policy requires that for an impairment to be severe, it must significantly limit the individual's physical or mental ability to perform one or more basic work activities, such as walking, standing, seeing, hearing, following simple instructions, and the use of judgment. If it does, DDS proceeds to the third step.

3. *Is the individual's condition found in the SSA's listing of impairments?*
   A list of impairments that are considered severe is maintained for each of the major body systems. If all requirements are met, it would automatically mean the individual is disabled. If the medical condition does not meet a listing, but the medical evidence supports the fact that the individual has an impairment that is equal in severity to those described in the listings that can be or is expected to last for 12 months and/or will result in death, then step four of the sequential process is next.

4. *Does the individual retain the capacity to do his or her past work, considering his or her residual functional capacity?*
   At this point, if the individual's condition is severe but not at the same or equal severity level as impairments on the list, then it must determined if the impairment interferes with the ability to engage in the work previously performed. If it does, DDS proceeds to the next step. If the impairment does not prohibit performing past relevant work, the claim is denied.

5. *Does the individual retain the capacity to do any other kind of work (which exists in significant numbers in the national economy), considering the individual's residual functional capacity and the vocational factors of age, education, and work experience?*

The claim would be approved if the individual could not adjust to any other type of work. However, if it is determined he or she could adjust to other jobs that exist in significant numbers, the claim would be denied.

Disability Determination Service

Disability Determination Services (DDS) are state agencies that are fully funded by the federal government to develop and review the medical and nonmedical evidence and render a determination on whether an individual is disabled under the law (SSA, 2004). The state DDS branch makes the disability decision for the SSA. Once an application for the SSI program is completed at the SSA office, it is forwarded to the state DDS office. If DDS is still unable to make a decision regarding disability status, it will pay for any other specific medical examination(s) needed.

Continuing Disability Reviews

Continuing disability reviews (CDR) are a requirement of the Social Security Act, where SSA periodically updates records and reviews the disability status of SSI/SSDI beneficiaries and recipients to evaluate whether they continue to be disabled and eligible for benefits. Review frequency depends on the typical severity and prognosis of the impairment(s) pertaining to potential for medical improvement. The range in frequency of disability reviews for beneficiaries can be from six months to seven years. Reviews are initially conducted between six to 18 months following an award and when medical improvement can be determined (e.g., surgery to repair a herniated lumbar disk). If medical improvement is difficult but possible to predict, a three-year CDR may occur; however, in cases where little or no improvement is expected (e.g., complete spinal cord injury), five to seven years is the standard review period. A review may also occur when a beneficiary's earnings are substantial.

Procedurally, a CDR occurs either in person or by phone. An SSA representative explains the process and procedures for the review and will be interested in any changes in the beneficiary's medical condition as well as whether he/she has engaged in any work. This information is added to the beneficiary's file and forwarded on to the state DDS branch where an evaluative decision is made by a disability examiner (and a physician if needed) regarding the beneficiary's continued eligibility for benefits. Beneficiaries receive a written notice about their review and whether or not they either: must report for further medical exams; are no longer deemed disabled; or can continue to receive benefits. In cases where a beneficiary is not satisfied with the findings of review, he or she has 60 days to appeal the decision in writing. Appeals are reviewed by an independent SSA panel not related to the cessation of benefits. If benefits are terminated, beneficiaries generally receive two more months of benefits after the last determined month of disability.

Work Incentives

In an attempt to encourage beneficiaries to join the workforce, the federal government and SSA have made legislative and regulatory changes in the SSI and SSDI programs during the last two decades. These changes comprise work incentives intended to reduce the risks and costs associated with the loss of benefit support and medical services as a result of employment. As part of those work incentives, individuals receiving SSDI are entitled to a nine-month trial work period (TWP). This allows individuals willing to join or rejoin the workforce to test their work ability while receiving full benefits, regardless of their income. For SSDI beneficiaries, SSA counts the gross monthly income earned in the calendar month. Individuals are entitled to a TWP for each period of disability. Annual increases to the amount of earnings are linked to the national average wage index.

Effective January 2004, only the months during which an individual earns over $580 or works over 80 hours in self-employment count as TWP months. The nine-month trial period does not need to be consecutive. The TWP ends only if an individual has performed nine months of trial work within a rolling period of 60 consecutive months. A 36-month extended period of eligibility (EPE) begins immediately after the nine-month TWP ends. The first month of substantial gainful activity during the EPE is called a "cessation month." The individual will be eligible for SSDI benefits for that month and the following two months. These three months are referred to as a "grace period." Thereafter, the individual will not be paid for any month in which he or she performs at SGA level (the individual will be paid for any month he or she does not earn SGA). When the individual stops performing SGA during the 36 months, benefits will be reinstated without a lengthy reapplication process.

Expedited reinstatement (EXR) allows SSDI benefits to be re-established without filing a new application as long as the individual

- is eligible for SSDI;
- lost SSDI due to performing SGA;
- requests reinstatement within 60 months of the last month of entitlement, or the request is filed after 60 months and he or she establishes good cause for missing the deadline;
- has a disability that is the same as (or related to) the physical or mental disability that was the basis for the original claim; and
- has a disability which renders him or her incapable of SGA based on application of the medical improvement standard.

If the beneficiary satisfies the EXR criteria, his or her benefits and the benefits of dependents can be reinstated. While the EXR request is pending, a person is eligible for up to six consecutive months of temporary benefits that begin when the EXR is requested.

Most disabled individuals who work will continue to receive at least 93 consecutive months of hospital and medical insurance under Medicare. The

93 months start the month after the last month of the individual's TWP. In order to qualify, an individual must work and perform SGA, but not have medically improved. After Medicare coverage ends due to work, some individuals may buy Medicare coverage in participating states, as long as they remain disabled and are not yet age 65.

SUPPLEMENTAL SECURITY INCOME

The Supplemental Security Income (SSI) Program authorized by title XVI was established in 1974 to provide benefit assistance to individuals who demonstrate economic need and who are over 65 or have a disability as defined by the SSA. The primary objectives of Congress in establishing the SSI Program are to: provide a uniform, minimum income level that is at or above the poverty line; to establish uniform, national eligibility criteria and rules; to provide fiscal relief to the states; and to provide efficient and effective administration.

Before SSI, states provided public assistance to individuals with disabilities according to varying degrees depending on the state. When SSI went into effect in January of 1974, individuals who were eligible for benefits under the prior federal/state matching grant program in December 1973 were "grandfathered." Congress established this provision to facilitate the conversion to SSI. There are two types of supplementary payments: mandatory and optional. Mandatory payments are for individuals converted to SSI from state assistance programs. Optional supplementary payments are currently provided by 26 states that have chosen to administer their own supplements. These supplements vary from state to state depending on the cost of living of each region.

Funding and Eligibility

In order to be eligible for SSI, individuals must be deemed disabled (as defined by the Social Security Disability Insurance Program), blind (as defined by SSA), 65 years of age or older, or any combination there of. SSI benefits are not based on an individual's work history but rather are determined by financial need. The program is financed by general funds of the U.S. Treasury—personal income taxes, corporation taxes, and other taxes. Social Security taxes withheld under the Federal Insurance Contributions Act (FICA) do not fund the SSI program. The program operates in the 50 states, and although it is administered by the SSA, states have the option to supplement the basic SSI benefit as well as decide to administer the program themselves.

As part of the eligibility criteria, individuals applying must be a resident of one of the 50 states, the District of Columbia, or the Northern Mariana Islands; be a citizen of the United States or an authorized alien; and not be a resident of a public institution (with some exceptions). Individuals must also not be absent from the United States for more than a calendar month and must accept appropriate available treatment such as vocational rehabilitation services. The SSI program should be considered as a last resort for assistance; therefore, individuals must also file for any other benefits for which they may be potentially eligible.

Since the SSI Program is a program determined by financial need, the amount of an individual's income and resources is used to determine both eligibility and the potential cash benefit payment he or she receives. Income includes both earned income (monthly gross earnings) and unearned income, such as Social Security or other benefits, pensions, annuities, and inheritances, as well as in-kind support such as vehicles and a home. Available work incentives such as impairment-related work expense (IRWE), blind work expense (BWE), and plan for achieving self-support (PASS) further impact the amount of benefit payments.

The dollar amount received varies from person to person. The federal benefit rate (FBR) is the maximum dollar amount individuals or couples can receive and is subject to annual increases as dictated by cost-of-living adjustments (COLA). In 2004, SSI beneficiaries received a 2.1% COLA and the FBR for individuals was $564, while the amount for married couples was $846. SSA considers as resources any liquid assets or personal property that can be converted to cash for the purpose of self-support or maintenance. As of 2004, SSI resource limits were $2,000 for an individual and $3,000 for a couple.

Benefits

When filing an application for SSI with the local SSA office, the individual, parent, or guardian must provide a Social Security card or record of the social security number; a birth certificate or other proof of age; information about the home where the claimant resides, such as a mortgage or lease; payroll slips, bank books, insurance policies, car registration, burial fund records, and other information about income and resources; and names and addresses of doctors, hospitals, and clinics that have treated the claimant.

The SSA is responsible for notifying individuals in writing of potential eligibility for other benefits. Individuals have 30 days from the date shown on the letter to file for potential benefits. If a benefit determination is unfavorable and the individual disagrees, he or she can appeal for an administrative review of the decision. If the appealed decision is still unfavorable for the claimant, he or she may initiate court action.

The SSI benefit payment comes in the form of a check or direct deposit and is paid either to the claimant or to his or her representative payee (if the beneficiary is unable to manage finances). Medicaid provides health insurance coverage to SSI recipients and is funded through a federal-state health insurance program for persons of low income. The Centers for Medicare and Medicaid Services (CMS) oversee states' administration of Medicaid, and if the participating state does not require the individual to file a separate application for Medicaid, these health benefits will begin on the same day the individual is awarded SSI.

Work Incentives

The SSI Program incorporates work incentives that enable persons who are blind or have other defined disabilities to join or rejoin the workforce while receiving SSI. SSI employment supports include:

- impairment-related work expense,
- student earned income exclusions,
- subsidy and special conditions,
- unincurred business expenses (self-employed only),
- unsuccessful work attempt,
- earned income exclusion,
- blind work expense,
- plan for achieving self-support,
- property essential to self-support (e.g., tools or equipment),
- special SSI payments for people who work [section 1619 (a)],
- reinstating eligibility without a new application, and
- continued payment under a vocational rehabilitation program (section 301).

Following is a brief explanation of some of the work incentives. Other explanations may be found on the SSA's Web site at http://www.ssa.gov.

An impairment-related work expense pertains to certain impairment-related items and services that an individual may need in order to work, and which are paid for from his or her gross earnings. SSA deducts an IRWE from SGA earnings when:

1. the item or service enables the individual to work (e.g., child care, bus money, assistive devices);

2. the individual needs the item or service because of his or her disabling impairment;

3. the individual pays fully for the expense and is not reimbursed by any other source such as Medicare, Medicaid, or private insurance;

4. the cost is "reasonable"—that is, it represents the standard charge for the item or service in the community; and

5. the individual pays the expense in a month that he or she is working.

6. Another available work incentive is student earned income exclusions, which assist individuals who are under age 22, single, are not head of a household, and are attending school. As of January 2004, when figuring SSI payments, SSA will not count up to $1,370 of monthly

earned income and a maximum of $5,520 annually for students with disabilities in this category.

Subsidy and special conditions are supports that the individual receives at work, resulting in payments greater than the actual value of the services or work the individual performs. Subsidies and special conditions are applicable to both SSI and SSDI beneficiaries. The dollar amount of these is subtracted from gross monthly earnings during the initial eligibility process, potentially reducing gross earnings below the SGA level.

Earned income exclusions pertain to the first $65 of an individual's earnings in a month plus one-half of the remainder that SSA does not count when calculating SSI payments. In addition, there is a $20 general income exclusion applied to any unearned income (e.g., pension, VA, alimony).

Blind work expense replaces impairment-related work expenses for individuals whose disability is blindness. According to SSA, the expense does not have to be related to blindness, and may include: (a) helper animal expenses; (b) transportation to and from work; (c) federal, state, and local income taxes; (d) Social Security taxes; (e) attendant care services; (f) visual and sensory aids; (g) translation of materials into Braille; (h) professional association fees; and (i) union dues. If the individual meets the medical definition for blindness, SGA is not a factor for SSI eligibility. SSI eligibility will continue until, or if, the individual medically recovers.

A plan for achieving self-support is considered when the individual would like to set money aside which would eventually be used toward a feasible occupational goal. This plan must be expected to increase a person's prospects for self-support.

Public law has established two special provision status positions: Section 1619(a) and 1619(b). An individual receiving SSI and Medicaid could continue to receive medical benefits under Section 1619(a)—extended Medicaid coverage—after losing SSI due to earnings exceeding SGA but remaining lower than the break-even point. The break-even point is the exact amount of monthly gross earnings that will reduce cash payments to zero. Other factors that will affect the break-even point calculation could include a spouse's income. Section 1619(b) of the 1987 legislation provides for continued Medicaid eligibility for individuals whose income is too high to qualify for an SSI payment, but not high enough to offset the loss of Medicaid or publicly funded attendant care. A second criterion for 1619(b) status requires that individuals' gross earnings fall below certain limits called threshold amounts. These amounts vary from state to state due to variations in the cost of medical services.

Ticket to Work

President Clinton signed the Ticket to Work—Work Incentives Improvement Act (TW-WIIA) on December 17, 1999. Final regulations on what became the Ticket to Work and Self-Sufficiency Program of the Social Security Administration were completed in December 2001.This program provides health-care incentives and employment service choices to promote work and independence among individuals with disabilities receiving SSI and SSDI. The main purpose of the Ticket program is to empower people with disabilities and give them more control over where, how, and from whom they would like to obtain employment and support services. The ticket holder is not obligated to work, and participation is voluntary. Ticket to Work is administered by the SSA and managed by a company called MAXIMUS, which has more than 245 offices and 5,600 employees nationwide. MAXIMUS provides overall program management and recruits, trains, and supports employment networks as well as links beneficiaries to employment networks (EN) and verifies ticket assignment status.

Social Security's role concerning the Ticket to Work continues to be that of determining benefit eligibility as defined earlier. As part of the individual's choices for employment services besides their local state rehabilitation agencies, ticket holders can now choose from new service providers (employment networks). The Administration will award EN contracts to qualifying organizations or sole proprietors interested in becoming part of the new employment service options available to beneficiaries. Entities that can potentially qualify as an EN include: rehabilitation providers, WIA-one stop centers, state vocational rehabilitation agencies, employers, disability councils/boards, and independent living centers. The EN may offer some or all of the following services: employment, job placement, case management, vocational assessment, career counseling, transportation assistance, service coordination and referrals, mentoring programs or internships, job accommodations, and training and retention services.

Program Implementation

The implementation of the Ticket to Work Program was divided into three phases. Phase I was completed in November of 2002 and included 13 states: Arizona, Colorado, Delaware, Florida, Illinois, Iowa, Massachusetts, New York, Oklahoma, Oregon, South Carolina, Vermont, and Wisconsin. All the tickets for Phase II were released in September 2003 to 20 additional states: Alaska, Arkansas, Connecticut, Georgia, Indiana, Kansas, Kentucky, Louisiana, Michigan, Mississippi, Missouri, Montana, Nevada, New Hampshire, New Jersey, New Mexico, North Dakota, South Dakota, Tennessee, and Virginia, as well as District of Columbia. Finally, release of Phase III tickets began in November 2003 and included approximately 3.5 million tickets and the rest of the states: Alabama, California, Hawaii, Idaho, Maine, Maryland, Minnesota, Nebraska, North Carolina, Ohio, Pennsylvania, Rhode Island, Texas, Utah, Washington, West Virginia, and Wyoming, as well as American Samoa, Guam, Northern Mariana Islands, Puerto Rico, and Virgin Islands. As of July 2003, SSA had released over 4.7 million tickets, with 20,501 of these tickets being assigned.

With more and more people applying for SSI/SSDI benefits each year and the estimated 76 million baby boomers nearing retirement (Marini & Reid, 2001), the Administration continues to explore ways to streamline applications as well as assure the solvency of the Trust Fund. The Ticket program may also give those beneficiaries who wish to return to work a greater opportunity to do so.

References

Fast Facts & Figures about Social Security, 2002—All Beneficiaries. (2002, December) Retrieved July 25, 2003, from http://www.ssa.gov/policy/docs/chartbooks/fastfacts/2001/slide27-0html

Golden, T. P., O'Mara, S., Ferrel, C., & Sheldon, J. (2002) Benefits supporting career development and employment of individuals with disabilities. *Planning, Assistance and Outreach: (BPA&O) and Protection and Advocacy for Beneficiaries of Social Security* (PABSS), Edition SSA, Pub. No. 63-003. Retrieved August 4, 2004, from http://www.ssa.gov/understanding.htm

Marini, I., & Reid, C. R. (2001). A survey of rehabilitation professionals as alternative provider contractors with social security: Problems and solutions. *Journal of Rehabilitation, 67*(2), 36–41.

Social Security Administration. (2000, August). *Reports & studies: Brief history of Social Security.* SSA Publication No. 21-059, ICN 440000. Retrieved July 29, 2003, from http://www.ssa.gov/history/reports/briefhistory.html

Social Security Administration. (2003, February). *Disability benefits.* SSA Publication No. 05-10029, ICN 456000. Retrieved August 1, 2003, from http://www.ssa.gov/pubs/10029.html

Social Security Administration. (2004). *2004 Red Book. A summary guide to employment support for individuals with disabilities under the Social Security Disability Insurance and Supplemental Security Income programs.* Retrieved September 30, 2004, from http://www.ssa.gov/work/ResourcesToolkit/redbook.pdf

SECTION IV
Legal and Social Services

Civil Rights and Equal Employment/ Americans with Disabilities Act

Cheryl L. Anderson

History/Legislation

In 1990, the United States Congress passed what is arguably the most monumental piece of civil rights legislation enacted since the Civil Rights Act of 1964. That legislation, the Americans with Disabilities Act (ADA), prohibits discrimination by both private and public entities in such varied aspects of daily life as employment, access to goods and services, access to government services, mass transportation, and telecommunications.

The ADA has its origins in the vocational rehabilitation system. Although early versions of the legislation centered on providing retraining opportunities for soldiers returning from World War II, in 1973 Congress repealed that legislation and enacted the Rehabilitation Act, a precursor to the ADA. The Rehabilitation Act not only removed "vocational" from the title; it also included a new provision, section 504, which provides that

> . . . [n]o otherwise qualified handicapped individual in the United States . . . shall, solely by reason of his handicap, be excluded from or denied the benefits of, or be subjected to discrimination under any program or activity receiving Federal financial assistance.[1]

With the passage of section 504, the disability movement permanently changed from one centered almost exclusively on rehabilitating individuals with disabilities to one focused on guaranteeing those individuals the same civil rights enjoyed by other people in society.

Section 504 applies only to entities that receive federal funding. When Congress passed the ADA, it expanded the scope of antidiscrimination based on disability law to reach public as well as private entities, regardless of federal funding.

In addition to the ADA and the Rehabilitation Act (which continues to apply but is subject to most of the same substantive rules as the ADA), there are other federal and state laws that prohibit disability discrimination. Among those are the Air Carrier Access Act and the Vietnam Era Vets Readjustment Assistance Act of 1974.[2]

PURPOSE/INTENT

Congress intended the ADA to have a sweeping effect on the treatment of individuals with disabilities. In many respects, the ADA was designed to overcome limitations imposed on the legal rights of individuals with disabilities by a U.S. Supreme Court decision that individuals with disabilities were not a minority class (like race and sex) and were entitled to heightened constitutional scrutiny of laws that discriminated against them. Congress spoke directly to this issue in the Findings and Purposes section of the ADA:

> [H]istorically, society has tended to isolate and segregate individuals with disabilities, and, despite some improvements, such forms of discrimination against individuals with disabilities continue to be a serious and pervasive social problem. . . . [I]ndividuals with disabilities are a discrete and insular minority who have been faced with restrictions and limitations, subjected to a history of purposeful unequal treatment, and relegated to a position of political powerlessness in our society, based on characteristics that are beyond the control of such individuals and resulting from stereotypic assumptions not truly indicative of the individual ability of such individuals to participate in, and contribute to, society. . . . It is the purpose of [the ADA] to provide a clear and comprehensive national mandate for the elimination of discrimination against individuals with disabilities[.][3]

To accomplish the ADA's goals, Congress adopted a coverage model based on an individualized assessment of "disability." Rather than define disability categorically (i.e., diabetes, mental retardation, loss of a limb, etc.), Congress chose what has been called the "three-pronged approach." An individual must either have a physical or mental impairment that substantially limits a major life activity, have a record of such an impairment, or be regarded as having such an impairment.[4] The specifics of each of these prongs are discussed in the next section. The consequence of adopting this approach is that every case must be analyzed closely to determine whether the individual involved has a disability. No presumptions can be made, even in cases that might otherwise seem obvious.

CLIENT SERVICES

The first step in determining whether a client may need a referral for services related to disability discrimination is to understand the basic coverage of the ADA. As noted above, the threshold issue is whether the individual has a disability as defined by the statute. Once it is determined that the client might have a disability, the next issue is whether the client's situation is one that may potentially be covered by the ADA. If so, the client should be referred either to the appropriate enforcement agency or to an attorney. Each of these steps in the evaluation process is discussed below. The ADA is an extremely detailed statute, and this chapter is at most a broad overview of its provisions.

Disability

Although there are three prongs to the definition of disability, most of the emphasis has been on the first prong, often referred to as the "actual disability" prong. This prong itself has three parts: the individual must (1) have a mental or physical impairment that (2) limits a major life activity, and (3) that limitation must be substantial.

Physical or Mental Impairment. The physical and mental impairments covered by the ADA are defined very broadly. Physical impairments include almost any disorder or condition that affects any of the body's systems. Mental impairments include "any mental or psychological disorder, such as mental retardation, organic brain syndrome, emotional or mental illness, and specific learning disabilities."[5]

Limits on Major Life Activities. The physical or mental impairment must have an effect on a "major life activity." Major life activities are defined functionally to include such things as "caring for oneself, performing manual tasks, walking, seeing, hearing, speaking, breathing, learning, and working."[6] This list is not exhaustive. For example, the U.S. Supreme Court in 1998 added reproduction to the list.[7] There has been much litigation regarding whether other activities—such as sleeping, getting along with others, lifting, and other activities—should be included, with mixed results.[8]

Substantial Limitation. The physical or mental impairment must not only affect a major life activity, it must substantially limit that major life activity. This is often the stumbling block to an ADA claim. The regulations interpreting the ADA provide that an impairment is substantially limiting when it renders the individual unable to perform a major life activity that an average person can perform or significantly restricts the condition, manner, or duration under which an individual can perform a major life activity as compared to the same factors for an average person.[9]

The U.S. Supreme Court has adopted a restrictive view of this requirement. Although in 1998 it held that asymptomatic HIV infection substantially limited a claimant's ability to reproduce, the next year it held that neither corrected severe myopia nor controlled hypertension were substantially limiting.[10] In the latter two cases, the Court held that the individual's condition must be evaluated in its present, mitigated state. In other words, if the individual has access to medications or other assistive devices that in effect reduce the impairment such that the individual can function similarly to an average person who does not have that impairment, the individual does not have a disability under the ADA.

Given the difficulty of proving the substantial limitation of major life activities, individuals need to develop a record of how their physical or mental impairments limit their daily home and work lives. In some cases, the testimony of the individual may be sufficient. In other cases, with disorders or conditions having less readily recognizable effects, expert testimony from doctors, vocational rehabilitation counselors, economists, and others may be required.

Record of and Regarded as Having a Disability. An individual who does not currently have a physical or mental impairment that substantially limits a major life activity may nonetheless still have a "disability" under the ADA in two other ways. The individual may have a "record" of having such a disability. A "record" includes medical or personnel records. This prong covers those individuals who at one time had an actual disability but who may have been cured or be in remission.[11] In addition, the individual may be regarded by others as having a disability. This prong protects against unfounded assumptions and stereotypes about individuals with certain conditions or disorders. However, as with the actual disability prong, the individual must show that whatever the condition or disorder he or she is regarded as having, it would be substantially limiting.

Exclusions. The ADA also contains several exclusions and limitations on what can be considered a disability. For example, the Act specifically excludes certain conditions from the definition of disability, including the following: transvestitism, transsexualism, pedophilia, exhibitionism, voyeurism, gender-identity disorders not resulting from physical impairments, or other sexual disorders, compulsive gambling, kleptomania, pyromania; and psychoactive substance-use disorders resulting from current illegal use of drugs.[12]

The Act also significantly limits the coverage of individuals with substance-abuse problems. Individuals who are "currently engaging in the illegal use of drugs" are not considered qualified individuals with a disability under the Act, if the employer acts on the basis of that drug use. If the individual has a substance-abuse problem that involves drug usage, that individual must qualify for coverage by having completed a supervised drug rehabilitation program, participating in such a program, or being otherwise successfully rehabilitated, and be no longer engaging in illegal use of drugs. A person erroneously regarded as engaging in illegal use of drugs may qualify as an individual with a disability. Employers are not limited under the ADA in their ability to adopt drug-testing programs, although they must use any information they gather in a manner that is consistent with the other provisions of the Act.[13]

Alcoholism is treated somewhat differently from illegal use of drugs. Rather than a blanket exclusion from coverage, alcoholism may be considered a disability. Alcohol testing is considered a medical exam and is subject to limitations under the Act. However, an employer may prohibit the use of alcohol in the workplace, require that employees not be under the influence of alcohol at the workplace, and hold an alcoholic employee to the same job performance and behavior standards as nonalcoholic employees, even if any unsatisfactory performance or behavior by the alcoholic employee is attributable to that person's alcoholism. Employers may also require employees to conform with the standards of the federal Drug-Free Workplace Act of 1988, the Department of Defense, the Nuclear Regulatory Commission, and the Department of Transportation.[14]

Coverage

The ADA contains separate titles addressing employment; goods and services provided by private businesses; construction and alterations of commercial facilities; government services, programs, and activities; and telecommunications. The employer/business's obligations are different under each of these titles.

Employment. Title I of the ADA prohibits discrimination against a "qualified individual with a disability" because of that disability in regard to hiring, firing, promotion, benefits, and other terms and conditions of employment. All employees of private businesses with fifteen or more employed are covered by this part of the Act, as well as state and local government employees. Bona fide private membership clubs are exempt.[15]

In addition to prohibiting traditional forms of discrimination, such as refusing to hire someone solely because that person has a disability, Title I prohibits failing to provide reasonable accommodations to individuals with disabilities that might enable them to perform the job in question.[16] Reasonable accommodations include modifying the job itself (modified work schedules, reassignment to a vacant position, etc.), modifying the workplace (adjusting the height of counters and desks, providing accessible bathrooms, etc.), and providing assistive equipment or devices (TDD phones, computer aides, interpreters, etc.). The employee's right to a reasonable accommodation extends beyond the tasks of the job itself to the benefits that accompany the job (such as use of a lunchroom) as well as to the very act of applying for a job (such as making application materials accessible to individuals with vision impairments upon request).[17]

Only qualified individuals are entitled to reasonable accommodations. "Qualified" means being able to perform the essential functions of the job with or without reasonable accommodation.[18] The employer's judgment as to what is essential is given significant deference. Written job descriptions prepared before the individual is hired are considered evidence of what the job requires, along with any other relevant facts.[19]

If a task is identified as essential, the employer can require the individual to do it, although the employer must allow the individual to perform it in a reasonable alternative manner. For example, a job in a warehouse might require moving boxes from one location to another. The employer can require the employee to move the boxes but cannot require that the employee manually lift and carry those boxes. If the employee has the ability to move the boxes using some other technique that is just as effective, such as with a dolly, the employer must allow the individual to use it as a reasonable accommodation.[20] Determining whether something is a reasonable accommodation is very fact-intensive and requires an interactive process between employer and employee.

Employers have several defenses to accommodation requests. Employers may claim that the accommodation would pose an undue hardship in terms of difficulty or expense.[21] If the employer uses a qualification standard or test (such as an agility test or an educational requirement) that tends to screen out individuals with disabilities, the employer may defend that standard or test as job-related and consistent with business necessity.[22] Finally, the employer may claim that the individual with a disability poses a direct threat to the health and safety of others in the workplace, or even to the employee him- or herself.[23]

A number of special rules apply to medical examinations. Employers are prohibited from requesting a medical exam or making medical inquiries before offering a job. After a job offer, the employer may request a medical exam and may withdraw the offer of employment if the employee fails the exam, but the exam must be used in a manner that is consistent with the rest of the ADA standards. After the employee begins work on the job, he or she can be asked to undergo a medical examination only if it is job related and consistent with business necessity.[24]

Goods and Services. Title III of the ADA prohibits discrimination by "places of public accommodation" in the provision of goods and services.[25] "Places of public accommodation" fall into one of twelve categories: places of lodging; establishments serving food and drink; places of exhibition or entertainment; places of public gathering; sales or rental establishments; service establishments; public transportation terminals, depots, or stations (but not those related to air travel); places of public display or collection; places of amusement or recreation; places of education; social service center establishments; and places of exercise or sports recreation.[26]

Businesses that fall into one of those categories are not only prohibited from discriminating based on disability, they also have an affirmative duty to remove architectural barriers in their facilities, to the extent the removal is "readily achievable."[27] "Readily achievable" means easily accomplishable and able to be carried out with little difficulty or expense. Some things that are readily achievable include rearranging tables, chairs, display racks, and other moveable items; installing ramps; and adding raised markings on elevator control buttons.[28] In addition, places of public accommodation must provide their goods and services to individuals with disabilities in the most integrated setting appropriate, make reasonable modifications in policies and practices necessary to accommodate individuals with disabilities, and provide the auxiliary aids and services (such as TDD phones) necessary to prevent individuals with disabilities from being excluded from access to the goods and services offered.[29]

As with employers, the operator of a place of public accommodation has several defenses. It may defend an accommodation request by asserting that the requested modifications would fundamentally alter the nature of the goods and services. It may defend a request for provision of auxiliary aids and services on the grounds it would pose an undue burden, meaning it would be of significant difficulty or expense. As mentioned above, it also need only remove architectural barriers when their removal is readily achievable. If barrier removal is not readily achievable, the business should provide reasonable alternative means for accessing its goods and services. This might include bringing items to a customer in a store that is otherwise self-serve, for example.[30]

Places of public accommodation are under the obligation to have removed those architectural barriers that are readily achievable in advance of any individual with a disability seeking the business's goods or services. In other words, this is an affirmative obligation under the statute, not one triggered by a customer's request.

Commercial Facilities. If a business does not qualify as a place of public accommodation, it may nonetheless have responsibilities under the ADA to make its place of business accessible to individuals with disabilities if it builds a new facility or alters an existing one. This part of the ADA applies to "commercial facilities," which are nonresidential facilities whose operations affect interstate commerce. Railway transport is exempt, as are facilities covered by or expressly exempted from coverage under the Fair Housing Act of 1968.[31]

Any facilities constructed for first occupancy after January 26, 1993, are required to comply with the ADA Accessibility Guidelines (ADAAG) unless it is structurally impracticable to do so. Cost is not a defense.[32] The guidelines set out requirements for door width, sink height, seating, grab rails, ramps, and so on. This part of the ADA is perhaps the strictest in demanding accessibility to individuals with disabilities. Some parts of the ADAAG are open to interpretation, however, such as a requirement that stadiums and theaters provide "comparable lines of sight" to individuals seated in wheelchairs. At present, there is a split opinion regarding whether this requires seating that allows individuals in wheelchairs to be able to see over spectators standing in front of them.[33]

If a commercial facility is altered or remodeled, the ADAAG also apply. The standard is whether the alteration affects the usability of or access to the space. A change in something as common as flooring may trigger this, although routine maintenance like painting does not. Those portions of the facility being altered must be made compliant with the ADAAG "to the maximum extent feasible." This exception applies only in the rare case where the nature of the facility makes it virtually impossible to comply fully with the ADAAG. The facility, must, however, comply to the maximum extent that it can.[34]

In addition to the actual area being altered, the path of travel to and from that area must be made accessible, if the area being altered is one containing a primary function of the facility. "Path of travel" is the means by which the area is entered or exited and includes both exterior (sidewalks, parking areas) and interior (hallways, lobbies) elements. For example, remodeling the sales floor in a department store affects a primary function of the store. The store must make the path of travel to and from the sales floor accessible. Restrooms, telephones, and drinking fountains serving the altered area are included as part of the path of travel.[35]

Facilities have an obligation to make the path of travel fully accessible unless the cost is disproportionate, which means it would cost more than 20% of the cost of the primary alteration. That 20% figure is on top of the cost of the primary alteration. In other words, if the project cost is $10,000, the business must spend up to another $2,000 to make the path of travel accessible. If it would cost more than that to make the path of travel fully accessible, the business must do what it can for $2,000. The regulations interpreting the ADA set out a priority list in cases in which the cost would be disproportionate, with an accessible entrance being first priority.[36]

Government Services, Programs, and Activities. Title II of the ADA prohibits state and local governments from discriminating in the services, programs, and activities they provide to the public.[37] This title also includes a prohibition on discrimination in public transportation programs.[38]

"Services, programs, and activities" are broadly defined. For the most part, anything that involves interaction with the public will be covered, from legal services to children's recreational programs to zoning. The government's obligations primarily mirror those of private businesses and employers, with one significant exception: Whereas places of public accommodation are required to make their facilities accessible to the extent it is readily achievable, public entities are only required to make their programs accessible as a whole when viewed in the entirety.[39] This gives public entities somewhat more flexibility in how they comply with Title II's antidiscrimination mandate. For example, a courthouse need not make every courtroom accessible to individuals with disabilities as long as it makes one courtroom accessible (assuming that is enough to meet the demand).[40] A place of public accommodation, by contrast, would be required to make the entire portion of its facility which is open to the public accessible to the extent it is readily achievable.

Title II also extends to how individuals may be required to receive services. The regulations interpreting the Act require that public entities administer their services, programs, and activities in the "most integrated setting appropriate to the needs of qualified individuals with disabilities."[41] While this does not require public entities to provide community-based services or programs that they would not otherwise provide, it does require that individuals with disabilities not be unnecessarily institutionalized when they otherwise qualify for community-based services. A state that argues it does not have the funding available to place the individual in the more integrated setting must show that it is making reasonable progress toward reducing its waiting list.[42]

Educational Discrimination. Among the services, programs, and activities of public entities covered under Title II is primary and secondary education, although the scope of coverage varies between the two levels. Private schools are also covered under Title III as places of public accommodation. Exams and courses offered by private companies for such things as application, licensing, and credentialing are covered under a special provision in Title III.[43]

Elementary educational services are generally subject to another statute, the Individuals with Disabilities Education Act (IDEA).[44] Reasonable accommodations, such as wheelchair accessibility, that do not relate to educational needs per se are subject to the ADA.[45] At the secondary level, the ADA may require not only physical accommodations but also modifications in entrance requirements, testing procedures, and academic standards for continuing enrollment, among other things. Private entities that offer exams and courses also must offer those services in a place and manner that is accessible to individuals with disabilities, or offer alternative arrangements that are accessible.[46]

Courts tend to give educational institutions great deference in defining their programs and setting their entrance standards. For example, the U.S. Supreme Court has held that a medical school cannot be required to eliminate the clinical portion of its program in order to accommodate a student with a hearing or vision disability.[47] At the same time, when the requested accommodation is not as broadly programmatic, schools have been required to show that they have evaluated whether the accommodation would fundamentally alter the nature of the education program.[48]

Associational Discrimination. The ADA also protects individuals from discrimination based on their known relationship with someone who has a covered disability. An employer may not deny a qualified employee equal jobs or benefits because of that relationship.[49] A place of public accommodation also may not deny goods or services to such individuals.[50] Although Title II does not include similar associational discrimination language, its language is broad enough that it arguably may be construed to also prohibit associational discrimination in government services, programs, and activities.

Telecommunications. Title IV of the ADA requires that telephone carriers provide telephone relay services in the areas in which they generally provide their services.[51] This includes TDD and other devices that allow for two-way communication between an individual who uses a nonvoice terminal device and one who does not. Other aspects of telecommunication, such as accessible phone equipment, are addressed under separate statues, including the Telecommunications for the Disabled Act and the Telecommunications Act of 1996.[52]

Mass Transportation. The ADA regulates both public and private transportation systems. Title II applies to public systems while Title III applies to private systems.[53] Public school transportation is exempted from the statute but college and university transit systems are not. Vehicle accessibility, station and boarding facilities, routes, and training of individuals working within the system, among other things, are all subject to ADA rules. For example, the Act specifically requires that vehicles purchased by public entities after July 26, 1990, for operation on fixed routes (such as bus routes and rapid rail systems) must be accessible, whether they are new, used, or remanufactured. Until all vehicles in the system are accessible, paratransit services must be provided.[54] Other aspects of mass transit, such as physical accessibility of boarding facilities, are subject to the general rules of Title II and Title III.

Pursuing an ADA Claim

Employment discrimination claims under the ADA must first be pursued through an administrative agency. Claims against places of public accommodation and state and local governments (with the possible exception of employment-related claims) may be brought directly in either federal or state court.

Procedures for Employment Discrimination Claims. An administrative charge first must be filed in order to pursue a claim for employment discrimination under Title I of the ADA. Where and when to file can be a bit complicated. While the EEOC has general authority over Title I cases, the law also provides for deferral initially to a state or local agency that also has authority to hear claims and grant relief. In some states, the EEOC and the state or local agency may have an agreement that designates one or the other as the agency which will pursue the claim, and allows filing with that agency to suffice. In other states, the charge needs to be filed with both the EEOC and the state or local agency within the proscribed time limits. The time limit for filing the charge with the EEOC is either 180 days (in a state without a state or local agency) or 300 days.[55] In any event, the time limits are rather short and a potential claimant should be encouraged to contact the EEOC or legal counsel as soon as possible.

The EEOC has authority to pursue claims on behalf of individuals who have experienced a violation of their rights. As a general rule, however, the EEOC only takes a limited number of cases, usually involving issues of significant public importance or a group or class of affected individuals.

A charge is simply a "clear and concise statement of the facts, including pertinent dates, constituting the alleged unlawful employment practices" verified by the person filing the charge.[56] The charge should contain enough information to put the charged party on notice of the alleged discrimination claim against it. The EEOC or the state or local agency has standard charge forms to complete.

Once a proper charge is filed, the law provides that the EEOC has 180 days to investigate and attempt to resolve the claim.[57] It is not uncommon, however, for the claimant to request what is called a "right-to-sue" letter earlier than that. The right-to-sue letter closes the file with the EEOC and permits the claimant to proceed in either federal or state court with a private cause of action. The private suit must be filed within 90 days of receipt of the right-to-sue letter. If an early right-to-sue letter is not requested, the EEOC either may proceed to find reasonable cause to believe the discrimination occurred and send the case to a hearing before an administrative law judge, or find a lack of reasonable cause, in which case it also issues a right-to-sue letter to the claimant.

Generally speaking, the relief available for employment discrimination claims includes back pay, reinstatement, compensatory relief (such as for emotional distress), and punitive damages, although the latter two are capped depending on the number of employees the employer has.[58] The U.S. Supreme Court has held that suits for money damages under Title I of the ADA against states are barred by principles of sovereign immunity.[59] This does not affect claims against local forms of government, such as cities and counties.

Procedures for Other Claims. Claims against places of public accommodation for failure to remove architectural barriers, failure to make modifications in policies, or other matters covered by Title III of the ADA may be brought directly in either federal or state court. Alternatively, the U.S. attorney general may initiate suit if the Department of Justice has reasonable cause to believe that there has been a pattern or practice of discrimination by a place of public accommodation, or the case involves an issue of general public importance. Private suits under Title III may seek only injunctive relief, not money damages. If the Department of Justice pursues the claim, civil penalties may be assessed, ranging from $50,000 for a first violation to $100,000 for subsequent violations.[60]

There is no requirement that claims against state or local entities under Title II be filed with any administrative agency. A private cause of action has been implied into this part of the Act, although the exact parameters of that claim are still being fleshed out in the courts.

Notes

[1] The Rehabilitation Act of 1974, 29 U.S.C. § 794(a) (2000).

[2] The Air Carrier Access Act, 49 U.S.C. § 41705 (2000); The Vietnam Era Veterans Readjustment Assistance Act of 1974, 38 U.S.C. §§ 4211-4215, (2000).

[3] 42 U.S.C. § 12101(a)(2), (7); (b) (1) (2000).

[4] *Id.* § 12102.

[5] 29 C.F.R. § 1630.2(h)(2) (2003).

[6] 29 C.F.R. 1630.2(h)(2)(i) (2003).

[7] *Bragdon v. Abbott*, 524 U.S. 624 (1998).

[8] See, e.g., *McAlindin v. County of San Diego*, 192 F.3d 1226 (4th Cir. Cal. 1999); *Pack v. Kmart Corp.*, 166 F.3d 1300 (10th Cir. Okla. 1999) (sleeping); *Taylor v. Dover Elevator Sys.*, 917 F.Supp. 455 (N.D. Miss. 1996) (getting along with others); *Mellon v. Federal Express Corp.*, 239 F.3d 954 (8th Cir. Ca. 2001) (lifting).

[9] 29 C.F.R. § 1630.2(j)(1)(i)(ii) (2003).

[10] *Murphy v. United Parcel Serv.*, 527 U.S. 516 (1999) (controlled hypertension was not substantially limiting); *Sutton v. United Air Lines*, 527 U.S. 471 (1999) (severe myopia was not substantially limiting); *Bragdon v. Abbott*, 524 U.S. 624 (1998) (HIV substantially limited plaintiff's ability to reproduce).

[11] 29 C.F.R. § 1630.2(k) (2003); *Id.* app. § 1630.2(k).

[12] 42 U.S.C. § 12211.

[13] *Id.* § 12210.

[14] ADA Title I EEOC Technical Assistance Manual I-8.4, I-8.7-8.10 (1992); Preemployment Disability-Related Questions and Medical Examinations, EEOC Notice No. 915.002 (Oct. 10, 1995).

[15] 42 U.S.C. §§ 12111(2), (5), 12112(a).

[16] *Id.* § 12112(b)(5).

[17] ADA Title I EEOC Technical Assistance Manual Part I-III.

[18] 42 U.S.C. § 12111(8).

[19] ADA Title I EEOC Technical Assistance Manual I-2.3(a).

[20] *Id.* I-2.3(b), I-3.8(4).

[21] 42 U.S.C. § 12111(10); 29 C.F.R. § 1630.2(p).

[22] 42 U.S.C. § 12113(a).

[23] *Id.* § 12113(b).

[24] *Id.* § 12112 (d); *see also* Preemployment Disability-Related Questions and Medical Examinations, EEOC Notice No. 915.002 (Oct. 10, 1995).

[25] *Id.* § 12182(a).

[26] *Id.* § 12181(7). As with Title I, private clubs and religious organizations are exempt. *Id.* § 12187.

[27] *Id.* § 12182(b)(2)(A)(iv).

[28] 28 C.F.R. § 36.304 (2003).

[29] 42 U.S.C. §§ 12182(b)(1)(B); (2)(A)(ii), (iii).

[30] *Id.* §§ 12182(b)(2)(A)(ii)-(v).

[31] *Id.* § 12181(2).

[32] *Id.* § 12183(a)(1); 28 C.F.R. § 36.401(a), (c). The ADAAG can be found in the ADA Title III Technical Assistance Manual III-7.0000 (1993).

[33] Compare *Paralyzed Veterans of America v. D.C. Arena L.P.*, 117 F.3d 579 (D.C. Cir. 1997) (requiring clear lines of sight over standing spectators) *with Caruso v. Blockbuster-Sony Music Entertainment Center*, 193 F.3d 730 (3d Cir. 1999) (not requiring clear lines of sight).

[34] 42 U.S.C. § 12183(a)(2); 28 C.F.R. § 36.402.

[35] 28 C.F.R. § 36.403.

[36] *Id.*

[37] 42 U.S.C. § 12132. In *Bd. of Trustee's of the Univ. of Ala. v. Garrett*, 531 U.S. 356 (2001), the Supreme Court held that Congress unconstitutionally allowed states to be sued by private parties for money damages under Title I of the ADA. A case challenging Title II on similar grounds is pending before the Court. *Tennessee v. Lane*, 315 F. 3d 680 (6th Cir.), *cert. granted*, 123 S.Ct. 2622 (US June 23, 2003). As the Court recognized in *Garrett*, however, states may still be liable for injunctive relief in private lawsuits, and for money damages in suits brought by the federal government. *Garrett*, 531 U.S. at 374 n. 9.

[38] *Id.* §§ 12141-12149.

[39] 28 C.F.R. § 35.150.

[40] ADA Title II EEOC Technical Assistance Manual II-5.1000.

[41] 28 C.F.R. § 35.130(b)(1)(iv).

[42] *Olmstead v. L.C.*, 527 U.S. 581 (1999).

[43] 42 U.S.C. § 12189.

[44] 20 U.S.C. §§ 1411-20 (2000).

[45] *See* Laura F. Rothstein, *Disabilities and the Law* § 2.06 (2d ed. 1997).

[46] 42 U.S.C. § 12189.

[47] *Southeastern Community College v. Davis*, 442 U.S. 397 (1979).

[48] See, e.g., *Wynne v. Tufts Univ. Sch. of Medicine*, 976 F.2d 791 (1992) (finding medical school adequately evaluated alternatives to multiple choice testing of medical student).

[49] 42 U.S.C. § 12112(b)(4).

[50] *Id.* § 12182(b)(1)(E).

[51] 47 U.S.C. § 225.

[52] 47 U.S.C. § 610(b) (amendment to the Communications Act of 1934); *Id.* § 255.

[53] 42 U.S.C. §§ 12141-49 (public mass transport providers); *id.* § 12184 (private mass transport providers).

[54] *Id.* §§ 12142-43.

[55] *Id.* § 2000e-5(e) (2000).

[56] 29 C.F.R. § 1601.12(a) (2002).

[57] 42 U.S.C. § 2000e-5(f)(1).

[58] *Id.* § 1981a(2), (b); *id.* § 2000e-5(g)(1). There is a defense to damages if the employer can prove it would have made the same adverse employment decision even if the unlawful criterion was not considered. In that case, the employee may receive only injunctive relief and attorney's fees. *Id.* § 2000e-5(g)(2)(B).

[59] *Bd. of Trustee's of the Univ. of Ala. v. Garrett*, 531 U.S. 356 (2001).

[60] 42 U.S.C. § 12188.

Advocacy and Guardianship

David P. Moxley & Michael D. Paul

The pervasiveness of advocacy within human services and social welfare as well as the expansion of advocacy services over the past thirty years in the United States are indicative of a society that requires special mechanisms in order to address the needs of those groups whose members are easily victimized, neglected, or abused. This is particularly true for those coping with disabilities, or those who possess social, physical, or biological characteristics or qualities that the greater society, its institutions, and its citizens may devalue, find offensive, or even reject. Advocacy suggests that such groups and their members experience diminished status within the greater society, and within those organizations and institutions whose purpose is to meet human needs (Moxley & Freddolino, 1990).

Advocacy is not to be confused with guardianship, another form of social assistance designed to address the needs of individuals who are impaired and who legally cannot handle their affairs, make decisions that pose critical life consequences, or enter into contractual transactions. Guardianship is an outcome of judicial decision making, requires legal representation, and, while there are different levels of guardianship, can limit the freedom, autonomy, and self-determination of those individuals who are assigned the status of ward. While advocacy advances the status of certain individuals or groups, the purpose of guardianship is clearly to protect or otherwise guard the legal interests of the ward.

This chapter offers a framework for understanding advocacy within American society and elaborates on guardianship of individuals whose impairment severely limits the scope and substance of their decision making. This chapter should help human service professionals understand advocacy and guardianship by illuminating ways they can incorporate advocacy into their practice, and by recognizing that advocacy and guardianship are different. Each of these two issues is addressed in turn.

ADVOCACY IN HUMAN SERVICES

The authors recognize that advocacy is a rich idea with tremendous variation. As formal initiatives, advocacy programs operate at national, state, and local levels; may operate internal to human service systems; or can operate externally (Freddolino & Moxley, 1988). At grassroots levels, groups petitioning the society for respect, dignity, and responsiveness to their social needs may undertake advocacy. Recipients, ex-recipients, family members, and citizens all may participate in advocacy and serve as advocates of one kind or another. For the human service professional involved in the provision of rehabilitative, health, or social services, the complexity of advocacy can be bewildering. Nonetheless, advocacy alternatives can be a vital resource to the helping professions as a way of extending community support, facilitating role change of recipients, and protecting and advancing the rights of recipients who are often easily marginalized.

Purpose and Scope of Advocacy

Within the context of American culture, advocacy often is a voluntary activity in which advocates undertake action to improve the status of those individuals and groups who are disenfranchised or marginalized from the mainstream of community life. This voluntary activity may be national or statewide in scope, or it may involve grassroots action at community levels in which citizens, recipients of services, ex-consumers, or parents and family members organize advocacy activities and programs. Within this realm, the aim of advocacy is to advance or otherwise improve the status of individuals and groups whose status can be—and often is—diminished within society (Freddolino, Moxley, & Hyduk, 2004). Advocacy also is formalized programmatically and organizationally as rights protection and advocacy services designed to ensure that members of protected classes (such as people with disabilities) do not experience rights violation, neglect, or abuse within those programs mandated to meet their needs.

Rationale and History

Many of the reasons for legitimizing advocacy emanate from the cultural configuration of social welfare as a principal social institution in the United States. Within American society there is deep suspicion about the purpose and aims of social welfare. Culturally, there is concern that social welfare should not be a dominant institution, that it should not interfere with the functioning of other social institutions such as the economy, and that social welfare benefits should be limited in scope, time, and amount. The absence of strong social rights within American society limits the social welfare claims people can make and, as a consequence, many people must go without the essentials of daily life, perhaps slipping into poverty permanently or moving in and out of poverty based on the dynamics of the economy.

In a social welfare system in which benefits are organizationally based and professionally mediated, the factors of coverage, access, quality, and adequacy loom large in influencing the need for advocacy. Systems of service cannot accommodate everyone and cannot be responsive to the diverse qualities, characteristics, and cultural attachments of those individuals who seek service. There is always the possibility that systems of care will simply fail to be responsive to certain individuals (Moxley, 1997).

Limited and reactive societal responses to serious social issues weigh heavily in creating a need for advocacy. Particular groups within American society experience considerable social marginalization as a result of diminished status, stigma, and social rejection. People with physical disabilities, people with psychiatric disabilities, and people with certain diseases or illnesses often experience outright neglect or abuse (Barnartt & Scotch, 2001). Co-variation of these various disabilities or conditions with other social circumstances, such as homelessness, compounds the consequences of neglect (Freddolino & Moxley, 1992). Limited housing and weak social provisions such as vocational development, income, and education further compound the violation of human rights and increase the potential of neglect and abuse, particularly for those individuals and groups who have difficulty speaking on their own behalf. Labeling and related negative social reaction amplify the visibility of deviance, leading to social isolation or relegating individuals to specialized programs of resocialization and social control. Encapsulation of individuals within total institutions can place individuals at risk for rights violation and for neglect and abuse.

It is in this context that advocacy emerges as a central element of social welfare in the United States. As social policy has evolved in the United States, so has advocacy. Almost every piece of major social welfare legislation since the 1960s and 1970s incorporated specialized bills of rights, safeguards for rights protection, and programmatic arrangements for responding to rights violations. Most of these policy provisions focused on those populations with greatest risk for abuse and neglect, either because their disabilities were so severe that they could not protect themselves or speak for themselves or because they were confined to total institutions that regimented care, over-medicated and dehumanized recipients, and deprived people—often times the most vulnerable—of essential human rights.

The indictment of the total institution undertaken by social scientists in the 1950s, 1960s, and 1970s offered tangible evidence for the rights violations rampant in state institutions. Exposés of degradation within state mental retardation facilities, psychiatric institutions, and nursing homes further fueled awareness that society's most vulnerable were experiencing systematic neglect and abuse (Rothman & Rothman, 1984). Provisions for rights protection and advocacy took root in the developmental disabilities legislation, and by the mid-to-late 1970s federally mandated rights protection and advocacy programs were well established in almost every state of the union. While many of these programs focused on addressing the rights of people with developmental disabilities, their service capacity grew incrementally as other groups were added through policy change and legislative mandate. Many rights protection and advocacy programs added specialized functions addressing rights violations of specific groups, and assumed added responsibility for facilitating the inclusion of people in housing, education, vocational development, and employment.

Consumer groups and people who directly felt the sting of stigma did not wait passively for the formation and institutionalization of rights protection and advocacy programs. Movements in mental health, physical disabilities, developmental disabilities, homelessness, and welfare rights, to name a few, formulated their own critiques of social policy, programs, and services. These movements forged their own advocacy alternatives, often equating advocacy with consciousness raising, awareness building, networking, and direct social action (Zinman, Howie the Harp, & Budd, n.d.).

Variation in Forms of Advocacy Services and Activities

Advocacy is not a homogeneous idea. Indeed, there is great variation in forms and types of advocacy. Understanding this variation is essential to grasping the role of advocacy in health, rehabilitative, social, and human services.

Voluntary National Organizations. Social action, mutual support, and self-help characterize a considerable amount of advocacy. Individuals or groups who represent the interests of people whose diminished status results in negative social consequences—including rejection and marginalization, discrimination, neglect, and even outright abuse—often undertake this form of advocacy. Nationally, a number of voluntary advocacy organizations address social inequity and foster social justice. Often these organizations are products of social movements and social action that seek to improve or otherwise enhance the status of a particular group or population.

The National Organization of Women, rooted in the historic women's suffrage and rights movement, is a good example of a national voluntary entity whose sole purpose is to advance the status and well-being of women who have sustained considerable discrimination. The Children's Defense Fund, devoted to elevating children out of poverty, and the NAACP, whose mission is to advance the status of black Americans, are two more examples of national voluntary advocacy organizations committed to achieving social justice for large segments of the population.

Within the realm of rehabilitation and human services, disability activists have formed their own umbrella organizations to advocate for status enhancement. For example, members of ADAPT are assertive people with disabilities who use social action tactics to expose discrimination, rights violations, and mistreatment of people with physical disabilities. They agitate for new benefits and resources and engage in social action to improve services, increase the responsiveness of programs, and enhance mobility. In the field of HIV/AIDS, ACT UP (AIDS Coalition to Unleash Power) agitates and demonstrates for the enhancement of medical programs, the availability of pharmacological therapies, and the improvement of social services.

Like ADAPT, ACT UP undertakes direct action, often targeting institutions that fail to meet the needs of those who suffer from AIDS. ACT UP and ADAPT both use adversarial strategies to address the inequities their members face in American society. Both organizations seek status enhancement and fair and compassionate treatment of those individuals coping with the legal, social, psychological, health, and economic consequences of situations that the greater society, its institutions, and its citizens may ignore, neglect, or stigmatize. Similarly, the ex-patient movement in mental health undertakes activities to expose the consequences of society's treatment of people labeled as mentally ill, expose inequitable treatment, and reveal the negative consequences of professional dominance and control over people who are coerced into mental health care.

Assertive members of advocacy organizations who directly and often substantially bear the negative effects of social issues and societal neglect not only are resources for social change, they also often demonstrate new conceptions of identities and roles in which people who are stigmatized stand up for themselves, become vocal about what they want, and assert themselves—behaviors that stand in stark contrast to a passive and obedient conception of a consumer of services.

Alternatively, a national organization like the National Alliance for the Mentally Ill (NAMI) or other entities like mental health consumer organizations, may define advocacy as seeking enhanced mental health benefits, access to mental health care, an improvement in the quality of services, and parity in the financing of mental health and physical health care. This kind of advocacy organization may eschew direct action within local communities and seek the establishment of local groups that offer mutual support, foster relationships with service providers, offer member education, work on projects designed to foster mental health access, and monitor the quality of care.

But while advocacy organizations may possess different cultures, employ different strategies and tactics, and support different aims, taken collectively these national entities represent advocacy efforts that emerge out of and influence social movements. ADAPT, for example, is part of the disability rights movement and is part of the constellation of efforts whose advocacy seeks the affirmation of rights, the creation of new policies and programs that advance the rights and status of people with disabilities, and define new identities and roles for people with disabilities (Charlton, 1998). As parts of social movements, national organizations serve an important role in building awareness, critiquing social arrangements that negatively affect the people they represent, demanding new social arrangements and benefits to meet human needs, and changing or creating service systems.

National advocacy organizations are an important resource for advocates. They provide information and education, offer timely resources (such as policy analyses), identify new models, articulate new visions of what is possible for people who experience social marginalization, provide technical assistance to local advocates and advocacy organizations, and sustain networks among those individuals who commit to social action and advocacy. Most of all, however, the value of national advocacy organizations rests in their grand narratives. They can energize local action by offering rationales and explanations justifying advocacy.

Grassroots Citizen Advocacy. Grassroots efforts sometimes emerge among citizens who are concerned about the marginalization of particular individuals and groups. In the 1970s, Wolfensberger and Zauha (1973) recognized the importance of citizen advocacy, a form of advocacy in which common citizens choose freely to support and represent people with disabilities. These citizens voluntarily and freely choose these roles, since there is no organizational or societal requirement for them to do so. Wolfensberger and Zauha suggest that this is perhaps the purest form of advocacy because there really is no conflict of interest—the citizen advocate does not coerce the person into social action, nor is there a need to meet any state or national mandate that stipulates advocacy as a legal requirement. There is no need for professional credentials, and there is no formalization of the advocacy role. The citizen advocate engages the person with a disability based on a motivation to serve and to help.

The premise of citizen advocacy resides in the reality that some individuals cannot speak for themselves, that human service professionals have a conflict of interest and cannot speak on behalf of persons who are impaired, and that the citizen advocate is best positioned to guard and protect the best interests of the person. The formation of a strong relationship between a citizen and a protégé who is severely disabled infuses this form of advocacy with power. While an advocate may befriend a protégé and participate with the individual in recreation, cultural, or avocational activities, the primary role of citizen advocates is to ensure that the rights of protégés are not compromised, that their needs are met, and that their best interests are protected.

Grassroots Consumer-Run Advocacy. Consumers themselves may join together to create their own support systems incorporating elements of mutual support and self-help, a culture that reinforces an outsider identity, and alternative forms of service (Moxley & Mowbray, 1997). These innovations may stand apart from the formal system of care, create new relationships among consumers, and offer educational, vocational, residential, recreational, and other opportunities. Consumer-run services can be a direct expression of the needs of participants, and they can place participants into new roles involving administration, governance, and leadership. This means that the programs themselves are under recipient and not professional control (Moxley & Mowbray, 1997).

Arguably, these arrangements are an expression of advocacy because recipients or those individuals who bear the negative effects of social issues create their own support systems to fill gaps in existing services that form due to the absence of professional vision, limited benefits, poorly designed programs, or community inaction. This form of advocacy at grassroots levels may demonstrate to professionals what is needed and what can be done, particularly in those areas characterized by therapeutic nihilism. Grassroots action among members of the gay community during the early AIDS crisis resulted in models of home-based social services, crisis intervention, and social support, features that most professionals now consider to be essential aspects of a good system of community-based services. Frequently those who are most in need take action well before professionals, suggesting that professionals themselves may be late adopters of recipient-led innovation.

Mandated Rights Protection and Advocacy Services

External Rights Protection and Advocacy. State and federal statutes have institutionalized organizational entities with a legal mandate for the protection of the rights of people who receive services within various programs, including mental health facilities, nursing homes, prisons, rehabilitation programs, or community-based residential services. These organizational entities operationalize federal rights protection mandates for specific populations (e.g., the elderly, people with psychiatric disabilities, or people coping with HIV/AIDS), are independent of social welfare or human service programs, and operate independently, often under charter, from state government. Within the advocacy field, these programs are considered external since they serve a watchdog function overseeing state human service bureaucracies and those private organizations—whether private for profit, quasi-public, or non-profit—that receive funds from federal or state governments.

Often these organizational entities are designated as rights protection and advocacy services and their mission is to protect the rights of those individuals who are at risk of neglect or abuse. Rights-protection advocates may offer recipients outreach; education about their rights; screening for rights violations; the receipt, screening, and disposition of complaints; provision of information and referral to lawyers or other rights protection specialists; case services to resolve legal complaints; and representation within administrative or legal venues.

Many external programs are socio-legal in character (Freddolino & Moxley, 1988). They combine both social and legal services and, as a consequence, may be multidisciplinary in their staffing complement. External rights protection and advocacy programs may include social service specialists, health care professionals, paralegal personnel, and attorneys. Often their scope of service is quite broad, and they must staff in a manner that enables them to address not only the various types of issues service recipients may report, but also the complex issues that emanate from the characteristics of the recipients (e.g., their level of disability), the substantive nature of the alleged rights violation (e.g., an issue that involves the expression of sexuality), the medical status of the recipient, or the type of setting within which they reside or otherwise receive services.

In addition to the provision of case services, the external rights protection and advocacy organization may engage in class- or systems-change advocacy as well as policy advocacy, seeking outcomes that will improve the well-being, quality of life, or safety of certain groups (e.g., people with severe disabilities who reside in total institutions like mental retardation facilities, nursing homes, or correctional programs). The organization may engage in litigation on behalf of individuals or classes of individuals in circumstances in which there has been a serious violation of basic rights.

Rights-protection and advocacy programs possess serious limitations created largely by the reaction paradigm of advocacy they incorporate to guide their day-to-day work. A requirement that recipients initiate the process of advocacy assumes that they have the capacity or freedom to complain, have access to devices or equipment to communicate their complaints, are free of intimidation or retaliation, and can use the specific key words and language that will trigger an appropriate response from intake personnel, who often are overworked and harried.

Some rights-protection and advocacy programs adopt proactive paradigms in which they invest heavily in education and awareness building among recipients and human service personnel about the scope of recipient rights, how these rights may be violated, and the procedures and practices that programs can put into place in order to prevent rights violation from occurring in the first place. In addition, a proactive paradigm incorporates outreach to recipients who are most at risk of rights violation, the early assessment and determination of needs that programs do not meet, and an assessment of the environment to ensure that the human service program does not jeopardize recipients, can protect their safety, and can meet their requisite needs for a dignified lifestyle. Proactivity demands considerable resources, an investment that can often outstrip the modest funding of most external agencies.

Internal Rights Protection and Advocacy. While external programs serve a watchdog function over human service programs and bureaucracies, some systems maintain their own internal advocates and serve as a frontline and internal capacity for addressing complaints and issues that recipients or their representatives may raise. Although there is considerable variability in internal rights protection and advocacy approaches, typically they follow a traditional service-oriented paradigm in which an office of recipient rights receives complaints, screens and assesses the situation, undertakes an investigation, and makes a disposition. In circumstances in which the internal recipient rights officer identifies a rights violation, the cases may be referred within the service bureaucracy for correction, direct supervisors may become involved, and personnel may be disciplined. In cases in which there is a determination of a criminal violation, the cases may be referred to a prosecutor who may follow through with the filing of a complaint against a staff member or a facility. In some cases, facilities may be found negligent or in violation of state or federal statutes or civil rights laws, thereby necessitating some kind of court action. However, from the authors' experience, in these kinds of cases external rather than internal rights protection and advocacy programs are more likely to pursue remedies.

Administratively, any human service agency that receives state and federal funds must have a staff member whom the program designates as a rights officer. The program itself must display prominently in a public location the rights recipients enjoy. The program must not only have a procedure for informing recipients of their rights but must also employ a procedure for alerting the officer about alleged rights violations, and they must implement a specific procedure for reaching a disposition within a defined period of time. Making recipients aware of their substantive rights, establishing a culture and setting that is receptive to the identification of complaints, and offering specific mechanisms for complaint resolution are not best practices. They are essential practices that all human service organizations receiving state or federal funds must follow.

Not all internal programs are adversarial. Other options include client-assistance programs that offer internal advocacy to resolve barriers to access and utilization, ombudsman programs that facilitate the resolution of recipient-identified problems, alternative dispute resolution, or mediation that bring parties to the table to reconcile differences, and other conflict resolution approaches that try to prevent the escalation of disputes into full-blown complaints.

Whatever approach a system uses, it will be internal to the program—meaning that there is always the possibility that the officer receiving or hearing the complaint and the entire process may place the interests of the system above those of the recipient. In cases in which recipients and their representatives suspect a conflict of interest operating in the resolution of their complaints, they may proceed outside of the program or system, direct their complaint to an external program, or secure counsel of a public interest law firm or private attorney.

GUARDIANSHIP AND HUMAN SERVICES

Guardianship is not advocacy, although the guardian may serve as an advocate ensuring that the person who is impaired does not experience abuse and neglect or oppression because of characteristics or qualities that emanate from their status, disability, or impairment.

Disadvantages of Guardianship

Guardianship represents an intrusive legal procedure in which a court designates someone other than the person himself to be responsible for the decisions, affairs, and responsibilities for an individual who has been determined by a court of law as lacking the necessary competence to be self-directed or otherwise autonomous. From a legal perspective, guardianship is appropriate when a person cannot manage himself, care for himself, or manage or otherwise oversee property.

Courts appoint guardians when it is determined legally that a person requires a substitute decision maker. Such appointment is made when the court determines that the person is legally disabled due to physical incapacitation, mental deterioration, serious and disabling mental illness, or a developmental disability. A guardian does not have to be a person, since a court also may consider the appointment of an institution, an agency, or a specialized guardianship organization. It may seem paradoxical, but in some cases a court system may designate a person as his or her own guardian. This is likely an outcome of a legal process in which there is a need to establish a person's competence.

Guardianship is a restrictive alternative for the management of disability or impairment, and it is a controversial one. In American culture, autonomy, self-direction, and self-sufficiency are cardinal values few institutions are willing to reduce or otherwise erode. Courts are cautious in the appointment of a guardian and, therefore, a formal judicial process is needed in order to establish guardianship, whether of the person or the estate. Guardianship is a legal process and the assignment of the label "ward" is a legal status. Symbolically, guardianship means that a person gives up some or all of the freedom and discretion American culture assigns to adults.

The establishment of guardianship can be a very difficult experience and an emotionally wrenching one for the person who becomes a ward. Since the legal establishment of guardianship requires a court decision, there must be evidence presented establishing the incapacity or impairment of the person in question. People coping with dementia or serious impairments that compromise their ability to care for themselves, or to make decisions about their estates, may be aware of the process and find it distressing. Medical or psychological evidence may be introduced to establish incapacity and the person may resist this diagnosis, fight the appointment of the guardian, or otherwise resist assignment to a new status. The requirement that the person appear in court may be quite distressing, and the public record that ensues may be a source of embarrassment or shame for the individual and his or her family. Thus, not only the guardianship decision is public—the legal establishment of incapacity and disability is also part of the public record.

The establishment of guardianship creates other serious problems for the ward. The court may require the guardian to be a resident of the state in which the guardianship is established, or it may require a bank or trust that oversees the person's financial affairs to be authorized to do business within the state. Such residency requirements may place restrictions on family members who live in other states, disqualifying them from service as guardians.

Another serious problem is that guardianship proceedings make the person's record of assets public. The court typically requires an inventory of assets and establishes procedures for the payment of bills, the resolution of debts, and the sale of certain assets. Guardians can be accountable for all expenditures, and stringent reporting requirements often involve the submission of receipts as well as reports of assets and expenditures of funds. This process of reporting and oversight can cost money, and the guardian may look for reimbursement for time and effort. Guardianship, therefore, can incur considerable cost including attorney time, fees for court appearances, and accounting expenses. In addition, examination fees must be paid to physicians or other qualified health professionals who provide the court with assessments, examinations, or evaluations. Attorneys or other professionals serving as guardians ad litem who review appropriate medical evidence, inform the person of their rights, and make an evaluation of the need for guardianship also may charge fees for such proceedings and counsel. These fees can quickly add up, and the person's estate likely will be responsible for their payment.

An often-overlooked disadvantage of guardianship lies in the restrictions courts may place on the investment of the ward's assets. Some courts will enforce a "prudent person" standard, in which the guardian must invest the ward's assets in conservative instruments that yield a limited return over time. Thus, the ward may be at a financial disadvantage over time, and assets may not grow at a rate to fulfill the ward's future needs.

Media exposés of guardianship that periodically emerge reveal some of the serious disadvantages of guardianship and perhaps even the potential abuse or neglect that is inherent in this kind of role. Typically, there is no formal credentialing of guardians and some courts may not be very mindful of who is appointed to serve as a guardian. Even though a person may nominate a guardian in a durable power of attorney, the courts are under no obligation to make such an appointment. Although the court may consider someone designated by the person with the disability, the judge will likely consider the best interests of wards and will make those appointments they consider most appropriate for the people whose status they adjudicate.

Lawyers, accountants, and investment personnel who may serve in the role may charge large fees for little service and may confine their attention to the management of the ward's affairs, without a strong personal relationship or bond with the ward or the ward's family. Guardians may neglect to respond to the needs of the person, and to ensure that the person is safe and living in dignified circumstances. There really is no requirement for the guardian to serve as an advocate. Some courts may counter the potential of the misuse of the ward's assets by requiring the guardian to post a surety bond that protects the use of assets by another party. Legally, guardians do not have many restrictions, so it is very important for guardians to be trustworthy.

However, guardians may hold significant personal accountability and liability for the management of their wards' assets and their safety and well-being.

There are legal mechanisms people can use to reduce the likelihood of guardianship, or to nominate the people they want to serve as guardians. Instruments like a durable power of attorney or a living will can serve as a means for people to designate the individuals they want to nominate as guardians. Also, an instrument like the durable power of attorney does not normally mandate a court proceeding or residency requirements, and the agent appointed under the power of attorney does not have to account to the court for assets and their management. While guardianship can create enormous fees, the durable power of attorney costs little. A person may avoid guardianship if there are provisions for a surrogate decision maker who is available to help the person make and execute important life decisions.

Given the restrictiveness of guardianship, and an understanding of how supportive services can help people with disabilities make and act on decisions, there is a growing interest in alternatives to guardianship. These alternatives may involve the establishment of personal advocacy relationships, citizen advocacy, and forms of socio-legal support that help people with disabilities to protect their interests, use their assets, and enter into relationships for services. The self-determination movement in developmental disabilities has been at the forefront in establishing and evaluating these alternatives.

The Rationale for Guardianship

With so many disadvantages, why does guardianship persist? At least in theory, guardianship establishes the protection of the person and seeks to ensure the proper management of assets, proper care, and protection against exploitation. However, third parties cannot deal directly with the person whose impairment or disability has been legally established. They must transact business directly with the guardian and seek his or her consent for the use of assets, investments, the provision of services, and involvement in activities like research or experimental treatments.

Thus, human service professionals, for example, who often address critical life circumstances and decisions on behalf of a person with disability, do not have the agency to work independently of a guardian. They must keep guardians informed about the well-being, health, and living circumstances of the person who is disabled, and they must confer with guardians when significant life decisions must be made. Human service professionals will form a relationship with the guardian and communicate regularly with this person or with representatives of the organization that serves as guardian.

But human service professionals may find varying degrees of involvement among guardians. Some may be very interested in the person, seeking information and participating in important events such as the development of an annual plan of service, while others may be somewhat disengaged or detached. Legally, however, human service professionals should follow up with guardians when a major life event occurs which leads to changes in a service program or protocol, if the person is injured or otherwise harmed, if the person becomes ill and requires medical care, or if the person transitions into new living arrangements. While these are only some of the circumstances requiring contact with guardians, good human service practice stipulates regular communication with the guardian as if the person or organization were a family member. Keeping guardians apprised of the status and progress of their wards will facilitate a relationship that will be important to human service professionals at points requiring critical life decisions.

Scope of Guardianship

There is a range of guardianship alternatives that can create a continuum of restrictiveness on the decision autonomy and freedom of persons with disabilities. *Limited guardianship* restricts the scope of decisions people with disabilities can make on their own behalf. The person with a disability can make some decisions about his or her person or estate, and the guardian—that is, the limited guardian—can only make those decisions the ward cannot make, typically involving complex issues pertaining to personal care, health, or finances. *Plenary guardianship* is more restrictive in the sense that the guardian has the authority to make all decisions regarding the person or the estate. This type of guardianship is likely ordered when the person has serious cognitive, mental, or physical limitations.

Alternatively, guardianship may not be so pervasive. Guardianship can be divided into either *guardianship of the person* or *guardianship of the estate*. Under the latter guardianship, wards relinquish decisions about the management of property, finances, and assets. Under the former guardianship, wards relinquish decisions regarding their care, because there has been a legal determination that the person does not understand these decisions, is not fully cognizant of their implications or consequences, or cannot communicate them because of serious physical restrictions or limitations. Often, the need for guardianship may be time limited. Courts may order *temporary guardianship*, a protection that may not exceed a specified time frame, for example, 60 days, when there is an emergency situation in which a person requires immediate protection from some imminent harm, is incapacitated. or is otherwise seriously disabled.

Testamentary guardianship allows parents of people with serious disabilities to designate a guardianship arrangement at their demise or incapacitation. The will or other instrument may designate this person or agency, but the court is under no obligation to follow either the preferences of family members or the designation that is made in a legal instrument, such as a will. Courts will likely take into consideration their interpretation of the best interests of the person with the disability, the evaluation the ad litem provides, and other circumstances in considering the guardianship appointment and the particular person or entity assigned this status.

The Intersection of Advocacy, Guardianship, and Human Services

Some guardianship entities are chartered by state government, but they operate as nonprofit organizations offering a range of guardianship, advocacy, and, in certain circumstances, case management services. These entities may carry the designation of *state guardian*. They offer guardianship services and other human services to individuals who have no other alternative and who must rely on the state for the provision of guardianship. While these nonprofit organizations may receive funding from state government, perhaps through state departments of mental health or developmental disabilities, they operate externally to the state bureaucracy and are similar to external rights protection and advocacy alternatives. Nonprofit guardianship organizations may also seek funds from other sources such as Medicaid and bill for the provision of case management.

The scope of services; the integration of advocacy, guardianship, and case management; and their relative independence of the state human-services bureaucracies make these nonprofit entities unique. Much like external advocacy programs, they may incorporate an interdisciplinary staff of health professionals, socio-legal personnel, attorneys, and specialists in the provision of guardianship and advocacy. State governments contract with these entities to offer guardianship services, address the legal process required to establish a guardian, and provide ongoing oversight of the well-being of wards at state-supported facilities. These guardianship agencies may outpost personnel in a variety of settings, including inpatient psychiatric facilities, community programs, state mental retardation facilities, nursing homes, and community-based social service agencies. They may support satellite offices that locate personnel close to the residences or day programs of their wards.

The personnel of alternative guardianship agencies likely carry caseloads of wards and must monitor the needs, well-being, and status of the people to whom they offer guardianship. They likely visit facilities regularly, interacting with their wards, care providers, and administrators to ensure that the people they serve get what they need to live as good a life as possible. They participate in medical decisions, participate in person-centered planning, and sustain a friendly if not family-like relationship with the people they serve. Nonetheless, large caseloads and the mandate to personalize guardianship make such positions quite demanding.

Yet another challenge to such a model lies in the blending of guardianship, advocacy, and case management. While these helping roles can be quite complex—addressing the decision scope of wards (guardianship), undertaking activities to enhance their status and well-being (advocacy), protecting rights, and facilitating the organization and articulation of an array of services (case management)—their integration creates a distinctive model of helping. Effective alternative guardianship programs that offer such a complex range of services avoid ethical pitfalls by clearly articulating their loyalty to the people they serve. These guardian-advocate case managers are not responsible to the system of services but rather to the person with whom they maintain a legally sanctioned relationship.

Typical Referral Questions and Issues

National Advocacy Organizations. Human service professionals can refer recipients to national advocacy organizations based on the issue they face or the identities recipients are forming in relationship to a social movement.

- What issues do recipients raise about their status? Do they feel a sense of marginalization and do they experience discrimination? Do they identify with the plight of others who carry a similar label? Do they want opportunities to gain information, education, and awareness that pertain to a movement for social justice, equity, and opportunities?
- Is the growing awareness among the people the human service professional serves coalescing into new identities that include a desire for activism and self-advocacy in collaboration with peers? Are there enough participants to form a local membership organization that is affiliated with a national organization?
- Do human service professionals want to collaborate with self-advocates in facilitating the access of recipients to the resources national organizations offer, through seminars, conferences, literature, and Web-based information and education?

Grassroots Citizen Advocacy. Human service professionals can become increasingly aware of the local grassroots advocacy alternatives available to the people they serve, particularly those available through advocacy groups citizens and laypeople offer.

- Are there locally based consumer or recipient advocacy organizations that offer citizen advocacy alternatives? The human service professional may want to assess these within various sectors including physical health, mental retardation and developmental disabilities, mental health, and serious mental illness.
- Do recipients experience marginalization and social stigma? Do recipients experience social isolation and feelings of devaluation? Are recipients too dependent on highly structured and limited human service programs and professionals? Can recipients benefit from a sustained and flexible relationship with other people who can facilitate opportunities, help them access a range of community resources, and protect them from neglect or abuse within the community?

Grassroots Consumer-Run Advocacy. Some communities may offer advocacy alternatives operated by recipients or ex-recipients who may not find much value in human services. These people may organize local support and self-help initiatives.

- Is the recipient discouraged by what human service professionals are willing to offer in terms of practical support?
- Does the recipient gravitate toward self-help and mutual support opportunities?
- Does the recipient want to offer support to peers, that is, to people who experience similar circumstances?
- Do recipients want to take direct action within the community, engage in awareness building, and organize consciousness raising activities about how communities create negative consequences for people coping with marginalization, discrimination, and/or stigma?
- Do recipients want to link their identities to a local social movement that offers them new opportunities and experiences and alternatives to being patients or consumers?
- Is the recipient interested in developing a new organizational entity within a local community that offers support to peers?

External and Internal Rights Protection and Advocacy. In whatever kind of formal human service program recipients participate, recipients have rights that are stipulated in state and federal law. Human service professionals should be aware of these rights and the possibility that services and service providers may abridge or otherwise compromise them.

- Are recipients confined to a total institution in which they have little freedom? Are they dependent on personnel who control their movement and the resources or opportunities they can enjoy?
- Do recipients complain about unfair or arbitrary treatment that limits their mobility, decision making, and opportunities?
- Are recipients subjected to punishment, confinement, or corporal punishment?
- Do recipients experience physical abuse, neglect, or harsh treatment within a program?
- Do recipients display visible signs of emotional distress or physical abuse?

Guardianship. Front-line human service professionals likely interact with the people they serve on a regular basis and become sensitive to changes in behavior, cognition, and mental status indicative of the need for legally sanctioned protection of either recipients' property or their person.

- Is recipients' cognition or decision-making ability so impaired that the human service professional believes they need surrogate decision makers?
- Do recipients engage in risky or harmful behavior that suggests impairment of decision-making ability and self-direction?
- Are there alternative support systems so recipients have adequate decision-making support to preclude guardianship?

- Do recipients have property, assets, or investments that are in jeopardy because of their cognitive limitations, impairment, or inability to make decisions?
- Is it worthwhile to work with recipients immediately in preparing a living will or durable power of attorney that can be used to outline their wishes and identify potential guardianship arrangements or other forms of protection?
- Are family members available to serve as guardians? Are they willing to serve in such a capacity?
- Do recipients who are undergoing legal processes of guardianship have emotional support and sustenance?

SUMMARY

Advocacy and guardianship are complex. Although these forms of social response to people with serious disabilities or impairments are easily divisible, there is nonetheless considerable variation within both advocacy and guardianship. Under some arrangements advocacy and guardianship may actually blend, making it hard to distinguish between the two forms of assistance. The rich variation, however, equips the frontline human service professional with a number of resources for serving recipients in more effective ways. The availability of advocacy alternatives reminds human service professionals that they cannot meet all the needs of the people they serve and that national and grassroots advocacy alternatives as well as formal rights protection and advocacy programs exist to enhance the human rights and status of people coping with a range of disabilities or impairments.

The availability of guardianship means that human service professionals must be mindful of how they interact with people whose status is protected and who have formally relinquished their decision-making authority and autonomy. The blend of guardianship, advocacy, and case management suggests that there are new and emergent ways of orchestrating services for people coping with disabilities and who, as a result of impairment, depend on an array of publicly supported human services.

References

Barnartt, S., & Scotch, R. (2001). *Disability protests: Contentious politics, 1970–1999*. Washington, DC: Gallaudet University Press.

Charlton, J. I. (1998). *Nothing about us without us: Disability, oppression, and empowerment*. Berkeley: University of California Press.

Freddolino, P., & Moxley, D. (1988). The states' role in fine tuning the new federal mandate for rights protection and advocacy for people labeled mentally ill. *New England Journal of Human Services, 8*(2), 27–33.

Freddolino, P., & Moxley, D. (1992). Refining an advocacy model for homeless people coping with psychiatric disabilities. *Community Mental Health Journal, 28*(4), 337–352.

Freddolino, P., Moxley, D., & Hyduk, C. (2004). A differential model of advocacy in social work practice. *Families in Society, 85*(1), 119–128.

Moxley, D. (1997). *Case management by design: Reflections on principles and practices*. Chicago: Nelson-Hall.

Moxley, D. (2002). The emergence and attributes of second-generation community support services for persons with serious mental illness: Implications for case management. *Journal of Social Work in Disability and Rehabilitation, 1*(2), 25–52.

Moxley, D., & Freddolino, P. (1990). A model of advocacy for promoting client self-determination in psychosocial rehabilitation. *Psychosocial Rehabilitation Journal, 14*(2), 69–82.

Moxley, D. P., & Mowbray, C. T. (1997). Consumers as providers: Forces and factors legitimizing role innovation in psychiatric rehabilitation. In C. T. Mowbray, D. P. Moxley, C. A. Jasper, & L. L. Howell (Eds.), *Consumers as providers in psychiatric rehabilitation* (pp. 2–34). Columbia, MD: IAPSRS.

Rothman, D. J., & Rothman, S. M. (1984). *The Willowbrook wars: A decade of struggle for social justice*. New York: Harper & Row.

Wolfensberger, W., & Zauha, H. (Eds.). (1973). *Citizen advocacy and protective services for the impaired and handicapped*. Toronto: National Institute on Mental Retardation.

Zinman, S., & Budd, S. (n. d.). *Reaching across: Mental health clients helping each other*. Riverside: California Network of Mental Health Clients.

Client Assistance Programs and Protection and Advocacy Services

Charlene J. Blankenship

Client Assistance Programs and protection and advocacy systems comprise the nationwide network of congressionally mandated, legally based disability-rights agencies. Both of these programs/systems were mandated as a response to the need for protection of the rights of individuals with disabilities. This chapter will discuss both of these programs, and the services offered.

CLIENT ASSISTANCE PROGRAMS

The impetus for Client Assistance Programs (CAP) in state vocational rehabilitation agencies was dissatisfied individuals with disabilities speaking out about issues they faced when accessing state vocational rehabilitation. These individuals were frustrated with the labyrinth they were sometimes forced to endure when seeking services or answers from state vocational rehabilitation systems. Pilot projects were established by Congress in an effort to find a satisfactory way to ameliorate the problems these individuals faced. The requirements for these pilot projects were (1) the assurance that project staff be able to communicate with top vocational rehabilitation administrators, and (2) that there be no conflict of interest with other vocational rehabilitation duties project personnel may be performing. These pilot projects were the forerunners of the Client Assistance Programs that would become a requirement in each state and territory as a condition for receiving vocational rehabilitation program funds under Title I of the Rehabilitation Act of 1973.

Client Assistance Programs became mandatory for states and territories through the Rehabilitation Act of 1973, P.L. 93-112, Section 112, as amended. In 1984, Section 112 required the implementation of assistance programs to inform and advise clients and client applicants of all available benefits under the Rehabilitation Act, and to help any who request assistance in their relationships with projects, programs, and community rehabilitation projects providing services under the Act. This includes assistance to clients or applicants in pursuing legal, administrative, or other appropriate remedies to ensure the protection of their rights under the Act. A Client Assistance Program can also provide information about itself to the public and information on the available services under the Rehabilitation Act to any person with disabilities in the state. The Client Assistance Program must provide information on available services and benefits under Title I of the Americans with Disabilities Act to individuals with disabilities in each state and territory, especially with regard to individuals who traditionally have been unserved or underserved by vocational rehabilitation programs. The Client Assistance Program may also provide the cost of travel for a client, client applicant, or attendant in connection with the provision of assistance under this program. In providing assistance and advocacy under this subsection with regard to services under this title, a Client Assistance Program may provide assistance and advocacy services that are directly related to facilitating the employment of the individual (Professional Management Associates, Inc., 1986).

In a state's application for a grant for CAP funds under the Rehabilitation Act, the governor designates a public or private agency in the state to conduct the Client Assistance Program. The designated agency must be independent of any agency providing treatment, services, or rehabilitation to individuals under the Rehabilitation Act—unless, prior to February 22, 1984, there was an agency in the state that directly carried out a Client Assistance Program under Section 112 (Professional Management Associates, Inc., 1986).

There are 56 Client Assistance Programs throughout the United States and U.S. Territories. Exactly one-half of the CAPs are housed in protection and advocacy programs. Sixteen are housed in a variety of state and private entities, including governor's office, legal aid, and a private law firm. The remaining 12 are located internally in state vocational rehabilitation agencies, obviously, where they were located prior to February 22, 1984. The internal CAPs are located in the states of Alabama, California, the District of Columbia, Illinois, Kansas, Maine, Maryland, Michigan, Nebraska, Nevada, North Carolina, and North Dakota. While the governor in these states designated state vocational rehabilitation to administer CAP, not all of these states actually run the CAP program. Some of these states have chosen to contract with an outside entity to manage the CAP. For example, some states have contracted with their protection and advocacy services to administer the Client Assistance Program.

The Client Assistance Program is an advocacy program. CAP helps clients and applicants understand the rehabilitation services available under the

Rehabilitation Act, and to provide information to individuals with disabilities. For example, the CAP staff person may explain the status system used in vocational rehabilitation, or the order of selection used in some states. The program assists individuals with disabilities, who qualify under the Rehabilitation Act, to receive the appropriate rehabilitation services from state vocational rehabilitation, community rehabilitation providers, independent living, and Projects With Industry.

Client Assistance Programs offer an array of services both at the individual advocate level and at the system advocacy level. Services offered include:

- Explaining to current and prospective clients how the rehabilitation system works.
- Explaining what an individual with a disability must do to obtain vocational rehabilitation, independent living, or projects with industry services.
- Answering questions about the rehabilitation system, independent living, and projects with industry.
- Making individuals with disabilities aware of their rights under the Rehabilitation Act of 1973 as amended, and under the 1990 Americans with Disabilities Act.
- Teaching individuals how to advocate for themselves.
- Advocating for clients who encounter problems in the rehabilitation system, independent living system, or Projects With Industry System.
- Initiating communication between clients and their counselors or case managers.
- Mediating or negotiating between clients and their counselors or case managers.
- Helping to prepare and, if appropriate, provide for adequate representation in the appeals process or hearing.
- Advocating on systemic issues within state vocational rehabilitation community rehabilitation, independent living, and Projects With Industry.
- Disseminating information about CAP services.
- Providing information about Title I of the Americans with Disabilities Act of 1990 regarding employment.
- Providing the cost of travel for a client, client applicant, or attendant in connection with the provision of assistance under the Client Assistance Program.

Consistent with legislative requirements outlined in the Rehabilitation Act, Client Assistance Programs practice mediation as a means of conflict resolution. Mediation attempts to support the underlying relationship between clients and their counselors or case managers and avoid the development of a win–lose situation. While CAP usually works through mediation, the program is authorized to pursue legal, administrative, and other appropriate remedies. Under no circumstances are Client Assistance Programs allowed to initiate class action lawsuits.

The Office of Special Education and Rehabilitation Services Administration (OSERS) regulate Client Assistance Programs. The Rehabilitation Services Administration (RSA) has developed program monitoring instruments for use by RSA in evaluating performance and activities of the CAP-designated agencies. RSA is concerned with appraising the degree of compliance of the CAP agency with the governor's assurances. In addition, RSA conducts case reviews to determine eligibility of persons receiving services and whether the services provided are authorized under the CAP. One-third of the CAPs are monitored each year.

PROTECTION AND ADVOCACY SERVICES

The second system of programs that comprise the nationwide network of congressionally mandated, legally based disability-rights agencies is the protection and advocacy services (P & A) system. As was previously mentioned, one-half of the CAPs are located in P & As. When located in a P & A, the Client Assistance Program is one of the legislated programs offered by the P & A. Protection and advocacy programs administer congressionally legislated, distinctly specific programs to address the needs of different segments of the population of persons with disabilities.

Protection and advocacy services are federally mandated systems in each state and territory that provide protection of the rights of persons with disabilities through legally based advocacy. P & As were established to address outrage at the abuse, neglect, and lack of appropriate and quality programming in institutions for persons with disabilities (National Association of Protection and Advocacy Systems, 2003). Similar to Client Assistance Programs, protection and advocacy services are designated by the governor in each state and territory. Pursuant to the Rehabilitation Act, each state must provide assurance that the system is and will remain independent of any service provider.

Protection and advocacy systems work for the benefit of individuals with disabilities on a national level through effecting legislative and policy changes. These systems are the principal providers of legally based advocacy services to persons with disabilities in the United States. Together, P & As across the country devote substantial resources to ensuring full access to inclusive educational programs, financial entitlement programs, health care, accessible housing, and productive employment opportunities (Gross, 2001). According to the National Association of Protection and Advocacy Systems Web site (2003), activities of protection and advocacy services fall into four major areas: investigations and mediating, information dissemination and technical assistance, legal and litigation services, and education and training. Specifically, these areas include the following:

1. Investigating, negotiating, or mediating resolutions to problems reported by service-eligible individuals.

2. Disseminating information and providing technical assistance to individuals, attorneys, governmental agencies, service providers, and other advocacy organizations.

3. Providing legal and litigation services to eligible individuals and groups.

4. Providing education and training for interested individuals or groups.

The National Association of Protection and Advocacy Systems (2003) identifies the following main beliefs as guiding principles for legally based advocacy for persons with disabilities:

- *Equality, equity and fairness.* People with disabilities are full and equal citizens under the law. They are entitled to equal access to the same opportunities afforded all members of society. People with disabilities are entitled to be free from abuse, neglect, exploitation, discrimination, and isolation, and to be treated with respect and dignity.

- *Meaningful choice and empowerment.* People, regardless of age, type, and level of disability, have the right to make choices with respect to both daily routines and major life events.

- *Support and participation.* Services and supports are shaped by the unique needs and preferences of each individual, and assure and enhance opportunities for integration in all aspects of life. Services are age appropriate and premised on the fact that people with disabilities continue to learn, change, and develop throughout their lives. For children such growth is best accomplished within families, and for adults, within integrated communities rather than institutions.

- *Independence.* Advocacy services are based on a philosophy of equal access, peer support, and self-determination, to be achieved through individual, professional, and system advocacy. Services are delivered in a manner that maximizes leadership, independence, productivity, and integration of individuals with disabilities.

- *Cultural competency.* Advocacy services reflect, and are responsive to, the diverse cultural, ethnic, and racial composition of society (National Association of Protection and Advocacy Systems, 2003).

Protection and advocacy services are comprised of six—and in some cases, seven—programs that form a comprehensive system of advocacy and protection for persons with disabilities. Following are descriptions of programs housed in the protection and advocacy system. Each of these programs is funded by different components of the federal government, and is designed to provide services to different segments of individuals with disabilities, thus forming a comprehensive system of services.

The Protection and Advocacy for Persons with Developmental Disabilities (PADD) Program was created by the Developmental Disabilities Assistance and Bill of Rights (DD) Act of 1975. Protection and advocacy programs are required by the DD Act to set up a system to pursue legal, administrative, and other appropriate measures to protect and advocate for the rights and interests of individuals with developmental disabilities. The 1994 amendments to the DD Act expanded the system to include a program serving Native Americans. Oversight of the Persons with Developmental Disabilities Programs is provided by the Administration for Children Youth and Families, Administration on Developmental Disabilities (ADD).

In 1986 Congress established the Protection and Advocacy for Individuals with Mental Illness (PAIMI) Program. The state agency designated by the governor of each state and territory to administer the PADD Program will also be the designated agency to administer the PAIMI Program. PAIMI does for individuals with mental illness what PADD does for individuals with developmental disabilities. That is, PAIMI provides protection and advocacy for the rights of people with mental illness, as well as investigation of reports of abuse and/or neglect in facilities that treat individuals with mental illness. Centers for Mental Health Services are the administrators of the PAIMI Program.

The Protection and Advocacy for Individual Rights (PAIR) Program was established by Congress as a national program under the Rehabilitation Act in 1993. Programs were established to protect and advocate for the legal and human rights of persons with disabilities. The PAIR Programs was established to serve individuals with disabilities that were not eligible to be served by other advocacy programs. Thus, with the establishment of the PAIR Program, an all-inclusive system was put in place to advocate for the rights of all individuals with disabilities. The protection and advocacy system designated to serve as the PADD Program in each state and territory received funding to operate the PAIR Program. Rehabilitation Services Administration (RSA) is the government entity overseeing the PAIR Program.

The Protection & Advocacy for Assistive Technology (PAAT) Program was created in 1994 when Congress expanded the Technology-Related Assistance for Individuals with Disabilities Act (Tech Act) to include funding for P & As to give assistance to individuals and those in their support system in accessing technology devises and services. The National Institute on Disability and Rehabilitation Research (NIDRR) administers the PAAT Program.

The Protection and Advocacy for Beneficiaries of Social Security (PABSS) Program was established in 1999 for individuals with disabilities who receive Supplemental Security Income (SSI) or Social Security Disability Insurance (SSDI) and want to work or return to work. The PABSS Program was a response to the Ticket to Work and Work Incentive Improvement Act (TW-WIIA). The intent of TW-WIIA was the removal of barriers to employment, therefore reducing the individual's dependency on cash benefit programs. The Social Security Administration funds the protection and advocacy system in each state and territory for the purpose of providing information and advocacy services to beneficiaries with disabilities who want to work. The PABSS Program provides advocacy or other services that beneficiaries with disability may require while gaining employment.

In 1996, Congress authorized the establishment of state grants to improve access to health care and other services for individuals with traumatic brain injuries. Competitive grants were awarded in 2002 to P & A systems in 28 states, four U.S. territories, and one tribal agency. The grant program is administered by the Health Resources and Services Administration through its Maternal and Child Health Bureau.

SUMMARY

Client Assistance Programs and the protection and advocacy systems comprise the nationwide network of congressionally mandated, legally based, comprehensive disability-rights agencies. With the addition of programs targeting individuals with developmental disabilities, mental illness, and persons with disabilities that are not covered elsewhere, a far-reaching nationwide system is in place to assure individuals with disabilities are served by an advocacy agency.

Advocacy does not mean adversarial, however. CAPs and P & As use mediation as a means of resolving conflicts without destroying the underlying relationships between clients and counselors or case managers. CAPs throughout the country and territories work to resolve issues and problems that occur between clients and vocational rehabilitation, independent living, or projects with industry. Every attempt is made to resolve issues without legal action.

Protection and advocacy services are legal services. The CAP for the state where the P & A is located may be housed in the P & A. Services in the P & A fall into areas of investigations and mediation, information dissemination and technical assistance, legal and litigation services, and education and training.

References

Gross, G. P. (2001). The protection and advocacy system and collaboration with legal services programs. *Management Information Exchange Journal*, Summer 2001. Retrieved August 5, 2003, from http://www.napas.org/MIEarticleFinal301.htm.

National Association of Protection and Advocacy Systems. (2003). Retrieved August 5, 2003, from http://www.protectionandadvocacy.com/other/origins.

Professional Management Associates, Inc. (1986). Evaluation of the Client Assistance Program. Rockville, MD: Author.

Children and Family Services

Ruth Anne Rehfeldt

The purpose of children and family services is to support, supplement, or substitute for the parental care of children. Services are typically necessary because of some dysfunction in the parenting role, be it the death, unemployment, substance abuse, or incarceration of a parent. Services may also be necessary due to parents' tendencies toward abusing or neglecting their children. The range of services delivered to such families and the conditions under which services are mandated has varied historically. Today, public policy favors services that will prevent a child's out-of-home placement and thus preserve the natural family. When family preservation is not possible, children are to be placed in the least restrictive community setting possible.

History/Legislation

Child welfare services have undergone many changes over the past several centuries. These changes have been accompanied by changes in children's role in society. During the 1600s and 1700s, legislation required that parents exercise rigid discipline over their children's behavior. Parents were required by law to severely punish children who did not act in accordance with their religious upbringing. This legislation encouraged suspicious, hostile views toward delinquent or neglected children (Pawson & Russell, 1985). Child labor was common, as the discipline of work was believed to be valuable for a child. Children could only be removed from their homes by court order, but hard labor or abuse were seldom conditions under which a child was removed. Rather, fatherless or destitute children were often removed

225

from their birth homes so that they could learn a trade or skill (Cohen, 1992). The first public orphanages and almshouses were established during this time period; these facilities had the responsibility of educating and providing for orphans and destitute children.

By the 1800s, hundreds of children resided in the almshouses of larger American cities. Specialized institutional care became a common placement for children with psychiatric or developmental disorders. Concerned about the unsavory conditions of these service settings, middle-class women began advocating for improved services for children, and, along with legislators, triggered the establishment of juvenile courts, child labor laws, birth legislation, universal education, mandatory school attendance, standards for children's institutions, and schools of social work (Pawson & Russell, 1985). Other key developments during this time period included the establishment of the Charity Organization Society (COS), which provided aid to the poor, and the New York Children's Aid Society, which was responsible for launching the concept of foster care by placing thousands of homeless children into rural family homes. This era is noteworthy for the new emphasis on healthy family life.

Services for children and families evolved extraordinarily during the first half of the twentieth century. The first White House Conference on Child Welfare resulted in the creation of programs to enable delinquent and dependent children to remain living in their birth homes. Foster care became more common and congregate institutional care became less common. Adoption became a formal option for children who were unable to remain with their natural parents. The Child Welfare League of America was created and remains the most organized political body in child welfare today. When the Social Security Act was passed in 1935, a number of new programs were established that affected child welfare, including the National School Lunch Program (1954), federal funding for Aid to Dependent Children (1956), and the extension of child welfare services to rural areas (Cohen, 1992). During the 1940s through the 1960s, the use of institutional care continued to decline, and foster care and adoption became more widely utilized. Institutions existed primarily to meet the needs of children with psychiatric or developmental disorders, who were believed to be unsuitable for adopted or foster families. Head Start, an early childhood education program for impoverished children, was established by the federal government in the 1960s.

Several key pieces of legislation were passed during the 1970s through the present that profoundly influence child welfare services today. First, the Child Abuse Prevention and Treatment Act, Public Law 93-247, was passed in 1974. This law secured the provision of financial resources to states for the identification and treatment of child abuse and neglect. Second, the Indian Child Welfare Act was passed in 1978, mandating that Native American children who are placed out of the home must maintain a connection either to their own tribe or to their Native American heritage more generally. In the event that a Native American child must be placed with an adopted or foster family, the possibility of placing the child with relatives, tribal members, or members of another tribe must be explored first.

Third, the Adoption Assistance and Child Welfare Act of 1980, Public Law 96-272 (AACWA), was passed to facilitate the long-term durability of relationships between children and their natural parents. The act calls for the provision of services that will prevent a child from being placed out of the home; adoptive or foster care must only be explored when restoration of the natural family is impossible. The AACWA additionally requires state agencies to implement a case system with case reviews occurring at least every six months (Stein, 1991). Under AACWA, courts must rule that the states did in fact make all reasonable efforts to maintain or restore the family in order for the state agency to receive funding for services. Should a child be removed from the home, he or she must be placed in the least restrictive community setting and efforts must be made to restore the natural family as soon as possible. Services to maintain or restore the family can include 24-hour emergency caretaker services, day care, crisis intervention, individual or family counseling, emergency financial assistance, and substance-abuse counseling (Stein, 1991).

Fourth, the Omnibus Reconciliation Act was passed in 1981, allowing for the consolidation of funding for some programs into block grants. This resulted in less funding for certain services. Fifth, Transitional Independent Living Program for Older Foster Children, Public Law 99-272, was passed in 1985. This law requires states to provide transitional-living services, including vocational and daily living-skills training, for children ages 16 and older who are living in foster care so that they can function independently as adults.

During the past 30 years, the appropriateness of institutions as a service setting for children with and without disabilities has been further questioned, and the belief that such placements restrict children's rights is now widely recognized. It is also recognized that the family has the power to protect its cultural, religious, and social integrity from outside interference, but the state has the power to intervene in family matters in exceptional circumstances (Pawson & Russell, 1985). Today, child welfare services typically include adoption, day-care services, foster family service, and protective services.

Funding

The Social Services Block Grant (Title XX) is the primary source of federal funds for social services. Most states spend approximately half their Title XX allocation on child welfare services (Stein, 1991). These funds are used to support a wide array of preventive services, including the investigation and treatment of child abuse and neglect. Several types of financial assistance programs are available to families. These include cash grants available for low-income families under the Aid to Families with Dependent Children (AFDC) Program, in-kind benefits that can be used toward the purchase of food under The Food Stamp Act, medical services covered by Medicaid, and housing assistance (Stein, 1991). A family's income and monthly expenses are taken into consideration in order to determine their eligibility for AFDC and Medicaid. The availability of child protective services does not depend on income. Child welfare services are provided mainly through public and not-for-profit community agencies. Some private for-profit agencies, such as group homes or day-care centers, also provide services in many communities.

Personnel

Professional and paraprofessional workers in child and family welfare come from a variety of educational backgrounds and experiences. Workers usually have a bachelor's or master's degree from a human services discipline such as psychology, rehabilitation, education, or social work. The bachelor's-level caseworker is likely to perform intakes, conduct family assessments to identify abuse or neglect, refer family members for supplemental services, seek substitute services for children who require temporary out-of-home placement, and coordinate and monitor all services in which a family is par-ticipating. A master's-level caseworker is likely to perform these same func-tions, in addition to training and supervising subordinates. Some individuals with master's degrees may also provide counseling. Studies have shown that families are most likely to participate in services if their caseworker has an advanced degree (i.e., master's degree or higher) (see Mueller & Pekarik, 2000). However, Corcoran (2000) found that bachelor's-level caseworkers were equally effective in preventing out-of-home placements.

Some states require that child protective services be delivered by teams. A team might include, for example, a child and family welfare worker, a law enforcement officer, an educator, a school counselor, an attorney, and a phy-sician. Clients report that case workers are most helpful when they spend time with the family, are supportive and nonpunitive, listen to and encourage family members, and provide concrete services such as buying groceries or making house repairs (Benvenisti & Yekei, 1986). Indeed, service outcomes appear to be positively correlated with the degree of empathy and rapport established between caseworkers and clients (cf. Lazaratou, Vlassopoulos, & Dellatolas, 2000).

PURPOSE/INTENT

The executive summary of the third national incidence study of child abuse and neglect reported substantial increases in the incidence of abuse and neglect since 1986 (Sedlak & Broadhurst, 1996). The incidence of physical abuse has nearly doubled, sexual abuse has more than doubled, and the rate of emotional abuse along with physical and emotional neglect has multiplied by more than two and a half times (Sedlak & Broadhurst, 1996). In addition, many children are living in impoverished conditions. A decade ago, 25% of all children were considered poor, and 7,300,000 children were receiving public welfare (Cohen, 1992). Forty percent of all homeless people included families with children (Cohen). It is likely that these statistics are even higher today. Thus, the current need for services for impoverished, dependent, neglected, and abused children cannot be underscored enough.

The purpose of child and family services is to arrange for and provide supportive, supplemental, or substitute care for a child whose physical and psychological needs are not being met by his or her parents. Whereas in previous years the focus of services was on meeting the needs of the child, services today are oriented toward empowering the entire family. In addition, children were more frequently removed from their homes in previous years. The harmful effects of disrupting children's relationships with their caregivers are widely recognized today. For this reason, child and family welfare workers seek to provide parents with the resources, training, and support necessary to enable them to continue caring for their children in their own homes. Examples of preventive services include referring family members for other medical or psychological services; teaching parents appropriate communication and discipline techniques; arranging for emergency services such as crisis counseling, shelter care, and financial assistance; providing homemaker services; and arranging for child day-care and transportation to needed appointments. Should conditions be such that a child can no longer remain living with his or her parents, services focus on what problems need to be resolved so that the family can be reunified. When reunification is impossible, efforts are made to find a suitable home for the child.

Special Case-Management Needs

Clients typically come from diverse cultural backgrounds and experiences. There are usually more differences than similarities between the families. For this reason, it is important that caseworkers be culturally competent and able to communicate empathy, warmth, and genuineness to people from a variety of different backgrounds. Although the number of minority families in the service delivery system is disproportionately high, no service delivery model exists for Asian/Pacific, African-American, or Hispanic families. Family members may have been the target of racial prejudice or discrimination at some point during their lives and as a result may be resistant to and hostile toward caseworkers for fear of encountering prejudice again (cf. Cohen, 1992). However, certain minority groups often have a strong commitment to the family. A caseworker who can tailor services toward the family's cultural beliefs and practices will have a more productive relationship with the family than a caseworker who fails to do so. Many caseworkers today are Caucasian. Efforts are needed to attract ethnically diverse workers to the field so that caseworkers with firsthand insight into minority clients' cultural backgrounds can be assigned cases accordingly. Cultural competence is also critical with rural families, who often come from impoverished and uneducated backgrounds.

Children receiving welfare services frequently have more sophisticated medical needs than other children. This may be particularly the case for children living in foster care, whose health care is no longer the responsibility of the natural parent. Physical conditions resulting from malnourishment, neglect, or injury are to be expected, as are emotional disturbances. Thus, such children have a need for thorough and well-coordinated medical attention. It is important for case managers to ensure that children receive regular physical examinations and check-ups. Moreover, in 1999 only 60% of the states included foster children in managed health-care plans (cf. Leslie, Kelleher, Burns, Landsverk, & Rolls, 2003). Some children may continue to be covered under their parents' Medicaid while in foster care, but the time period involved is often questionable. Confusion may exist between foster parents, natural parents, case managers, and school personnel as to who is responsible for arranging for and securing payment for the child's medical services.

CLIENT SERVICES

Open communication between health-care providers, Medicaid representatives, and case managers about the scope and coverage of services for children is imperative (Leslie et al., 2003). These services are discussed in the following section.

Child Protective Services

Protective services are provided for neglected, abused, dependent, and impoverished children. Services are initiated following a report of abuse or neglect to a social service agency or an abuse hotline. Professionals working in social service, medical, psychological, educational, and law enforcement settings are mandated by law to report instances of suspected child abuse or neglect. In most states the law covers physical and sexual abuse, where physical abuse is defined as purposeful physical injury that imposes the risk of death, impaired health, or loss of function; and sexual abuse is defined as any type of sexual act or pornographic photography (Stein, 1991). The law also covers physical and emotional neglect in most states, where neglect is defined as failure to deliver proper care to a child, and emotional neglect is defined as any act that results in a child's decreased emotional functioning (Stein).

The number of calls made to child-abuse hotlines has increased so dramatically in recent years that not all reports can be followed up with an investigation. For this reason, those reports that involve victims over the age of 18, lack specific detail about the incident, or fail to identify the person inflicting the abuse or neglect upon the child are often screened out and not pursued. If there is sufficient information to initiate an investigation, the investigation will begin within 24 to 48 hours following the filing of the report. The person conducting the investigation must determine whether the child should be removed immediately from the home and placed in protective custody, whether there is evidence to sustain the allegation, and whether the case should be referred to court. This decision is based on observations of the interactions between family members in the home as well as information obtained from others who may have witnessed signs of abuse or neglect, such as teachers, day-care providers, and physicians.

If the investigation reveals that abuse or neglect did in fact occur, services must be instated that will prevent its recurrence. Services typically include case management, counseling, and referrals for other emergency and non-emergency services. Services today generally focus on the entire family, but with 72% of abused and neglected children shown to suffer from emotional disturbances (Trupin, Tarico, Low, Jemelka, & McClellan, 1993), child-centered services are also critical.

A family's cooperation and involvement at the beginning of services is a strong predictor of service outcome. Families who keep appointments with caseworkers and follow through on assigned tasks are more likely to eventually have their cases closed than families who are uncooperative and noncompliant (Dawson & Berry, 2002). Child and family welfare workers' caseloads have been increasing in recent years. In order for a caseworker to maintain a manageable caseload, the number of case closures in a given period must approximately equal the number of new cases assigned. Thus, there is considerable pressure on caseworkers to close cases. In addition to client cooperation and compliance, caseworkers can also better guarantee case closures by providing services directly in the family's home that teach practical, everyday skills, deliver concrete services, encourage and motivate clients, and teach constructive communication and conflict resolution skills. Case management must be broadly focused, and families should be empowered to share in the establishment of goals and objectives.

Foster Care

In past decades children who were placed in foster care often remained there for indefinite periods, and a child's natural parents seldom received training or support that would help them regain custody of their child. Today, children are placed in substitute care while the natural parents participate in services intended to reunify the family unit as quickly as possible. Reasons for foster care include evidence that abuse or neglect is occurring repeatedly, is life threatening, or is occurring following services. Foster care may also be necessary due to the incarceration, death, or legal incompetence of a parent. Efforts to resolve whatever issues resulted in the removal of the child are to begin immediately following placement, as dictated by a written case plan. Case plans specify services underway, tasks assigned to parents with time frames for completion, parent and child visiting schedules, and consequences for parents' compliance with or failures to comply with the written plan (Stein, 1991). In cases where it is not possible to reunify the family, or where attempts to do so have failed, the assignment of a legal guardian or adoption is pursued. Most children who are reunited with their natural parents return home within the first 12 to 18 months following placement (Stein, 1991).

Many children presently in foster care are adolescents, while few are toddlers or infants. Many African American and Native American children are currently in foster care. Native American children have been shown to remain in foster care for relatively longer periods of time than other children (Cohen, 1992). Although the Indian Child Welfare Act (1978) mandates that efforts should be made to place Indian children in the foster care of a relative or tribal member, many Native American children are placed into the homes of Caucasian families. Caucasian children are by no means underrepresented in foster care.

Individuals interested in serving as foster parents must complete a rigorous criminal background check and physical examination prior to being approved for foster parenting. Foster parents are financially compensated for each child placed into their care and receive initial and ongoing training. Often those who serve as foster parents come from large families and had the responsibility of caring for other siblings. They are commonly from lower middle-class backgrounds. Finding suitable foster parents is not always an easy task, as older children requiring foster care are likely to have delinquency issues. In addition, the role may be difficult: Foster parents are to include the child's natural parents in the child's life as much as possible, yet compensate for the nurture and protection that those same parents failed to provide. Foster homes must be stable, consistent environments that are not overly strict.

Adoption

Adoption is pursued when a child for whatever reason cannot be reunited with his or her natural parents. In order to be eligible for adoption, a child's parents must have freely given up their rights as parents or those rights must have been terminated by a judge. States' laws mandate different reasons for the termination of parental rights. Common reasons include the parent's abandonment of the child or a judge's ruling that a parent is unfit. A parent may be judged to be unfit if the child continues to be at risk for abuse or neglect following previous services. A parent with a serious substance-abuse problem or a chronic mental illness may also be judged to be unfit. Adoption may not be possible under certain conditions, however, such as when professional judgment holds that it is in the child's best interest not to be adopted. This may be the case for children who are close to the age of 18 or for children who have spent a number of years in foster care.

Regular adoption is arranged by public and licensed private adoption agencies. Such agencies help expecting parents make plans for terminating their parental rights following the birth of their baby. They also help arrange for the adoption of babies by willing individuals who are judged to be appropriate for the parenting role. The adoption agency may also provide post-adoption services to assist adoptive parents and children in their adjustment to their new family life. Independent adoption consists of a natural parent placing a child into the home of adoptive parents without the involvement of a social service agency. The arrangement is sometimes made by the physician or attorney for one of the families. With independent adoption there is no way to ensure that the adopted family's lifestyle is appropriate for the child, and there are no services available to the family following the adoption.

Black market adoption, which is illegal, refers to the arrangement by a third party for a pregnant woman to give up her baby to another individual following its birth. The third party, often an attorney or physician, is paid to make the arrangements. Unlicensed adoption agencies also occasionally serve as the third party. Black market adoption is analogous to baby-selling, as the third party makes a profit from the exchange of the baby. Given the length of time that many couples spend trying to conceive and the length of time that many couples spend waiting to adopt a baby through regular adoption, black market adoptions, particularly of foreign babies, are rather common today.

Requirements as to who could adopt via regular adoption have changed in the past several decades. At one time the criteria were quite rigid: Adoption was generally permitted only for younger, childless couples who could provide medical documentation proving their inability to conceive. The requirements today are more flexible: Single parents and older parents are permitted to adopt, as well as parents who may already have one or more child of their own. The past three decades have seen such a huge increase in the number of adoptions that the wait for an available child can last several years. In 1984, for example, 2 million couples competed for 58,000 children placed for adoption—a ratio of 35 couples to one child (Wilson, 1985). Despite this, it can be difficult to find homes for non-Caucasian children. Adopting a child is also a costly endeavor. Since 1999, adopting a child through a public agency could cost up to $2,500, while adopting a child domestically through a private agency could cost anywhere from $4,000 to $30,000 (Carangelo, 2000).

SUMMARY

Several centuries ago children were valued for their labor. If a parent was unable to provide for a child, the child was sent away to learn some skill or trade that would benefit society. Children and family services today recognize the necessity of a stable, healthy family life for a child's physical and psychological development. If a child is at risk for or is experiencing abuse or neglect, legislation mandates that services be delivered to prevent the abuse or neglect from recurring and to sustain the family unit. Caseworkers in child and family welfare typically have a bachelor's or master's degree from a human services discipline. Preventive services are most effective when concrete, practical services are provided directly in the family's home and when caseworkers establish empathy and rapport with their clients. Should it be necessary to remove a child from the home temporarily, placement in the least restrictive setting—most frequently a foster home—is pursued. During this time, the child's natural parents are required to participate in services that will lead to the family's reunification. Adoption is an option for children whose parents have given up their parental rights or for whom those rights have been terminated by a judge.

References

Benvenisti, R., & Yekei, H. (1986). Family intervention: A description and evaluation. *Society and Welfare, 7,* 142–155.

Carangelo, L. (2000). *Statistics of adoption: 2000 edition.* Palm Desert, CA: Access Press.

Cohen, N. (1992). *Child welfare.* Boston: Allyn & Bacon.

Corcoran, J. (2000). Family interventions with child physical abuse and neglect: A critical review. *Children and Youth Services Review, 22,* 563–591.

Dawson, K., & Berry, M. (2002). Engaging families in child welfare services: An evidence-based approach to best practice. *Child Welfare, 81,* 293–318.

Lazaratou, H., Vlassopoulos, M., & Dellatolas, G. (2000). Factors affecting compliance with treatment in an outpatient child psychiatric practice: A retrospective study in a community mental health center in Athens. *Psychotherapy and Psychosomatics, 69,* 755–780.

Leslie, L. K., Kelleher, K. J., Burns, B. J., Landsverk, J., & Rolls, J. A. (2003). Foster care and Medicaid managed care. *Child Welfare, 82,* 367–393.

Mueller, M., & Pekarik, G. (2000). Treatment duration prediction: Client accuracy and its relationship to dropout outcome, and satisfaction. *Psychotherapy, 37,* 117–123.

Pawson, G. L., & Russell, T. (1985). The practice of community work in child welfare. In S. H. Taylor & R. W. Roberts (Eds.), *Theory and practice of community social work* (pp. 353–387). New York: Columbia University.

Sedlak, A. J., & Broadhurst, D. D. (1996). Executive summary of the third national incidence study of child abuse and neglect. Washington, DC: U.S. Department of Health & Human Services, national clearinghouse on child abuse and neglect information.

Stein, T. J. (1991). *Child welfare and the law.* New York: Longman.

Trupin, E. W., Tarico, V. S., Low, B. P., Jemelka, R., & McClellan, J. (1993). Children on protective service caseloads: Prevalence and nature of serious emotional disturbance. *Child Abuse & Neglect, 17,* 345–355.

Wilson, A. B. (1985, July 8). Adoption: It's not impossible. *Business Week,* 112.

Women's Centers

Laura Dreuth Zeman

Women's centers provide a range of services to victims of domestic violence that address increasing safety as well as improving the well-being of women and their children. Through a variety of assistance programs, including crisis support, legal advocacy, counseling, community education, and temporary housing, these centers seek to improve individuals' ability to function independent of abusive relationships and to decrease the degree of impairment to their functioning following violent and traumatic events.

HISTORY/LEGISLATION

Grassroots movements in the United States associated with the women's movement began to develop sexual assault and domestic violence programs during the 1970s. Many of these programs began as consciousness-raising groups designed to support women by providing them with a forum to share their intimate feelings and experiences (Piercy & Freeman, 1972). These groups supported the feminist principle, called "Personal is Political," which assumed that what happened to women as individuals also happened to women as a group, and further, that one aspect of resolving problems was through political action against the social constraints that oppressed women (Chicago Women's Liberation Union, 1971).

Women's groups founded on the principles of the feminist movement grew and maintained services in communities for 20 years before there was formal international and national legislation which mandated and funded protection and services for battered and abused women. Despite efforts to promote social change through grassroots actions, without legislation and formal institutional support violence against women continued to be a widespread problem in the United States. Data indicated that, in the 1990s, their husbands or boyfriends killed 28% of female murder victims (Federal Bureau of Investigations, 1995) and that approximately 1 in 5 adult women experienced a complete rape (Koss & Harvey, 1991).

In 1994, the United Nation's General Assembly adopted the Declaration on the Elimination of Violence against Women (United Nations, 1994), which represented the first international and formal resolution that violence against women constituted a violation of women's fundamental rights. Specifically, it defined the term "violence against women" to include any gender-based violence that is either physical, sexual, or psychological, including threats and coercion, and broadly extended violence to acts that could occur in either public or private settings. Thus, the resolution expanded the definition of violence against women to include violence in the home as well as broader political acts (United Nations, 1994). It further recognized that such violence "is a manifestation of historically unequal power relationships between men and women" that includes discrimination against women and is a "crucial social mechanism by which women are forced into a subordinate position compared with men" (United Nations, 1994).

That same year, the United States enacted the Violence against Women Act (VAWA) as Title IV of the Violent Crime Control and Law Enforcement Act of 1994 (P. L. 103-322). This was considered a turning point in the efforts to draw serious attention and recognition to the extent of violence against women. This groundbreaking legislation required states to establish sexual assault and domestic violence coalitions charged with organizing victim service activities, and collaborating and coordinating with federal and local entities engaged in activities that address support for female victims of violence. It also required training for law enforcement officers and courts involved in protecting victims and holding perpetrators of assault accountable for their actions. This action was supported in 2000 in the Violence against Women Act of 2000 (Public Law 106-386), which authorized the attorney general to award grants to state coalitions for assistance to support service activities and coordinate efforts on behalf of victims.

Funding

Through the Violence against Women Act of 2000, Congress appropriated over $11 million a year for fiscal years 2001 through 2005 to fund grants to state sexual assault and domestic violence coalitions. The ground rules for these grants were expanded in 2003 under the Family Violence Prevention and Services Act (Dept. of Health and Human Services, 2003) to extend grants to coalitions that fund domestic violence service-delivery systems that include intervention, prevention, and public education for victims and their dependents.

The criteria for receiving the 2003 federal grant indicate that state coalitions support community-based programs that demonstrate inclusiveness in delivery of services to minorities, disabled, and persons from ethnic and rural communities. These programs must also provide a basic range of services that include crisis intervention, assessment, intervention, and prevention services for families experiencing sexual assault and domestic violence. In addition to these basic services, federal guidelines encourage states to fund community-based programs that provide support services for families, including transitional housing, child care, job training, and counseling for mental health and substance abuse issues, and that demonstrate coordination with state child protection services. The 2003 guidelines for funding also include the first suggestion that states consider extending eligibility for grants to programs that address date rape and violent dating relationships (Dept. of Health and Human Services, 2003).

The community-based programs are considered members of state coalitions and are expected to participate in activities organized by the coalitions, including training and political action, as well as to serve as local referral sources. While local programs are not accredited by state coalitions, they are expected to be nonprofit, private agencies that receive funding from a variety of sources. Examples of funding sources include local and private foundation grants, program-specific fund raising, and insurance reimbursement for specific services, such as individual and group psychotherapy.

In order to quality for insurance reimbursement, staff that provide those services must meet professional credential criteria specified by the insurance including, but not limited to, licensure in the state as a professional counselor, social worker, or psychologist. Other than therapy staff, most employees of women's centers have either master's degrees or bachelor's degrees in social services. Positions such as shelter director or agency coordinator are often filled by masters-level professionals with training and experience in working with women who experience some form of domestic violence and sexual assault. Professionals with bachelor's degrees in human service fields frequently fill positions such as crisis counselors, prevention staff, and court advocates.

PURPOSE/INTENT

Rationale

Women's centers exist in the United States because of years of activism on behalf of women's groups to transform domestic violence from a private issue to a public one. One feminist and author noted that the public tends to maintain a minimal perception of battered women and further minimizes the risk of harm they face in their own homes (Schneider, 2000). In particular, Schneider noted that the same year the U.S. Congress passed the Violence against Women Act (1994), O.J. Simpson was charged with murdering his ex-wife, Nicole, and her friend, Ron Goldman. Subsequently there was a trial with national media coverage. Feminists and activists were outraged (Meyer, 2001), not only at the outcome of the trial, where Simpson was acquitted, but that the allegations of a history of domestic assault in the Simpson family, as well as many other families, were not at the forefront of the media attention.

According to feminists, the lack of focus on battering and its prevalence in cases of homicide where women are victims reflected cultural attitudes that informally sanction domestic battering and sexual assault (Martin, 1999; Meyer, 2001). It is these assumptions of cultural sanctioning of gender aggression that draw skepticism about the potential effectiveness of efforts directed exclusively at social policy to influence change (Martin, 1999). Feminists and women's activists prefer a combined approach emphasizing the growth of community-based services that support women where the abuse occurs, along with social policy, because a combined approach is considered more effective than social policy alone.

Utilization

National statistics on service use among persons who experienced domestic violence are difficult to develop due to the multifaceted nature of the problems and, therefore, the many avenues victims use to enter care. Women may present at police stations, to private and public attorneys, to state welfare departments, or to health or mental health providers. For the purposes of this chapter, estimates of national use were developed using available estimates from the state of Illinois. It was assumed that these might be typical usage rates. These rates were then projected to national population figures using U.S. Bureau of Census data (2003) to create estimated rates of use for domestic violence services in the nation.

In fiscal year 2002, the Illinois Coalition against Domestic Violence (2003) reported that it funded domestic violence shelters/walk-in counseling programs that provided the following:

- Over 553,000 hours of direct client services.
- 47,384 adult clients of domestic violence (96% of whom were women) with services.
- 11,019 children of victims of domestic violence with services.
- 252,300 days of shelter provided to adult victims and their children.
- 302,619 persons provided with public education that included community-based programs, professional development, and school-based prevention programs.

If national norms were estimated using U.S. Bureau of the Census population data (2003) and based on the Illinois utilization statistics, it could be expected that national utilization of federally supported domestic violence programs might resemble the following annual profile:

- Over 12.7 million hours of direct client services.
- 1.1 million adult clients of domestic violence.
- 253,400 children of victims of domestic violence with services.
- 5.8 million days of shelter provided to adult victims and their children.
- 7 million persons provided with public education that included community-based programs, professional development, and school-based prevention programs.

CLIENT SERVICES

Crisis Intervention

Crisis intervention usually consists of providing around-the-clock immediate response services to victims of domestic violence and their families. Most crisis intervention services incorporate 24-hour hotlines with trained staff and volunteers who answer phones to provide information, support, and referrals. Some programs also include immediate support in the form of staff and volunteers who are available to accompany victims as they access health and community services such as emergency-room health care and law enforcement agencies, or to escort them to temporary shelters. Victims can directly contact crisis hotlines. In some communities, local hospitals and police have arrangements to contact hotline workers when they believe a victim requires additional support.

Shelters

Shelters are safe havens for victims and are often located in secret locations to assure residents' safety. The goals of most shelter programs are twofold: to provide a temporary safe place for victims of domestic violence, and to support women who have long-term goals of living violence-free and independent. To meet these goals, shelters offer a variety of services that include liaison with courts to establish restraining orders, brief counseling, assistance in locating jobs, enrolling in public assistance, arranging child care, and arranging permanent housing. Shelter staffs also provide a protective barrier between the victim and abuser and provide emotional support.

The availability of space usually limits how long victims can stay in shelters, but the range in length of stay can be from one or two nights to eight weeks. Some shelters have a "no turn away" policy, which means that if the shelter beds are full, they work with each woman in crisis to access another shelter program or utilize hotel/motel partnerships that provide temporary rooms at either discounted rates or no at cost to the shelter. Many shelters limit their occupants to women, and some require that residents be drug and alcohol free during their stay.

Counseling

Counseling of domestic violence victims typically takes the form of problem-solving approaches that seek to define the problem, select goals, identify
solutions, and provide support while the client implements the solution
(Compton & Galaway, 1999). This form of counseling is brief, structured,
focuses on the immediate problems, and is provided by trained professionals.
Resolving problems that are immediate can help victims change their abusive
situations and also functions to prepare victims for longer-term counseling by
mental health professionals that addresses underlying issues leading to abusive relationships. When victims are ready for longer-term counseling, referrals are usually made to local mental health professionals.

Adolescent Services on Dating Relationships

Adolescent services generally include education on the rates and impact
of violence in dating relationships and date rape. Many programs include
public outreach in schools or community groups. Some programs provide
family and individual counseling to address relationship issues for teens. Programs may also include assistance in obtaining and enforcing restraining
orders against batterers of teen victims.

Community Education

Women's centers incorporate public education to serve two primary
goals. One goal is to reduce the occurrence and severity of domestic violence
and sexual assault in the community through increasing awareness of its
prevalence and solutions. It also intends to educate and train professionals
about domestic violence and sexual assault. To accomplish these goals, many
women's centers offer a speaker's bureau and provide community awareness
workshops, newsletters, and education series on pertinent topics.

Referral Questions

Human service workers typically ask two types of questions that, when
combined, might help determine whether a person or family is appropriate
for referral for domestic violence services. These types of questions include
the batterer's condition and the extent to which the victim experiences typical
barriers to leaving the situation. Answers to these questions combine to
develop a profile of the situation and determine the level and intensity of the
problem. Both are considerations in the determination of the service needs of
the victim.

The batterer's history of family violence and personal violence record are
considered important factors in determining the severity of the problem
(National Coalition against Domestic Violence, 2003). In particular, if a batterer grew up in a violent family it is more likely that he will resort to violence
to solve problems. Likewise, similar questions about the batterer's behavior

are indicators of whether violence will be chosen as a way of dealing with feelings. The National Coalition against Domestic Violence (2003) recommends that human service workers ask these questions in their assessment of service need: Does the batterer tend to use force or violence to "solve" problems; have a quick temper; overreact to little problems and frustration? Is the batterer cruel to animals?

Other important behaviors in assessing the severity of the problem include whether one or more partners in the relationship abuse alcohol or other drugs. Batterers often include persons with fixed ideas of women and men's roles in the family, to the extent that they believe they are superior and their partner is expected to submit to their orders. In the batterer's mind, this justifies the use of force to exert power. Other questions to examine include whether the batter exhibits a tendency toward jealousy, and if the batterer has access to weapons.

Another determination of the severity of the problem is identifying the factors that influence the victim to stay in an abusive relationship. Reasons why women stay generally fall into three major categories: lack of resources, institutional responses, and traditional ideology (National Coalition against Domestic Violence, 2003). In terms of immediate resources, victims may have any combination of the following that limit their mobility: dependent children, no access to bank accounts or credit cards, or no out-of-home employment. Institutional barriers often include clergy or religious community members who are committed to preserving the relationship, and police or court resistance to legitimate the problem or provide support. Finally, many women hold traditional beliefs that prevent them from seeking relief or leaving abusive relationships. For example, they may believe that divorce is wrong, that they are responsible for making their marriage work, that the abuser is only responding to outside pressures that will go away with the victim's support, or that they need to maintain the relationship with the abuser to validate their self-worth.

CONCLUSIONS AND IMPLICATIONS FOR HUMAN SERVICE WORKERS

A significant concern that underscores the complexity of caring for domestic violence victims is the reality that many abused women return to the abuser after seeking help and perhaps after temporarily leaving the home or relationship. This return to the abuser complicates the healing process by placing the victim in a highly volatile situation and causes the victim to be alienated from a supportive treatment community. There are many reasons behind this dynamic, including economic and social dependency on the batterer, which may prohibit the victim's ability to be self-sufficient.

Another reason that increases the likelihood the victim will return is a common theme in violence cycles that includes a period of seemingly loving behavior by the batterer extended to the victim following aggressive incidents. During this phase, the abuser tries to make up for the battering incident. This behavior often instills in victims a belief and hope that their abuse will stop.

When the victim reunites with her partner, she is likely to leave the care system that is dedicated to reducing domestic violence. On their own in a potentially violent intimate relationship, victims are not only isolated from support services but may also find themselves alienated from the domestic violence treatment community. Staffs in women's centers tend to consider the victim's return to their abuser as a treatment failure attributed greatly to the victim's refusal to follow treatment recommendations.

Thus, alienation from treatment specialists confounded by living in a potentially violent relationship places the victim at greater risk and places a greater responsibility on the general medical and human service workers to identify and support domestic violence victims. Case managers and medical professionals are often the only people women will turn to for help and are often the only ones with whom women feel comfortable talking about their concerns and safety issues.

Even if a request for help is not explicit, the opportunity to help may be lost if domestic violence is not addressed. There are important issues to consider with each patient when domestic violence is identified. First is that her situation is taken seriously and that she is treated with compassion by care professionals. Second, case managers and medical professionals should have a working knowledge of community resources that can provide treatment, safety, advocacy, and support. Referral to these resources is crucial to address whatever physical, substance abuse, and psychological problems are present. The immediate concern is for the safety of the woman and her children.

There are many efforts aimed at educating medical professionals and human service workers to identify signs of domestic violence as well as training them on treatment and crisis intervention strategies. The goal of these programs is training a wider base of treatment professionals to identify and support victims, who may be alienated or isolated from shelters and domestic violence professionals, in order to assure their immediate safety, as well as reconnecting victims with a community of support. Training programs also include preparing case managers to create accurate documentation of the evidence of potential violence that can support legal investigations into battery crimes. This documentation record includes details on complaints of injuries of conditions that may be related to the abuse, including quotes from victims, names of alleged perpetrators, and whenever possible photographs of bruises and wounds.

Future policy revisions may include requiring medical professionals and human service workers to report cases of domestic violence much as they are required to report abuse against children or the elderly and disabled. Many professionals in the field believe mandated reporting would drive away the patients it is intended to help. However, others believe that mandated reporting of suspected cases of domestic violence could increase the vigilance regarding treatment and care of potential violence victims and could lead to saving lives of women and their children.

References

Chicago Women's Liberation Union. (1971). *Consciousness raising*. Chicago: Author.

Compton, B., & Galaway, B. (1999). *Social work processes* (6th ed.). Pacific Grove, CA: Brooks and Cole.

Department of Health and Human Services. (2003). Administration for children and families. Program Announcement No. OCS 03-01. *Federal Register, 68* (72).

Illinois Coalition against Domestic Violence. (2003). *ICDAV mission statement*. Retrieved September 23, 2003, from http://www.ilcadv.org/

Federal Bureau of Investigation. (1995). *Uniform crime reports, November 1995*. Clarksburg, WV: Author.

Koss, M., & Harvey, M. (1991). *The rape victim: Clinical and community interventions* (2nd ed.). Newbury Park, CA: Sage.

Martin, M. (1999). From criminal justice to transformative justice: The challenges of social control for battered. *Contemporary Justice Review, 2*(4), 415–436.

Meyer, N. (2001). Now you see it, now you don't: The state of the battered women's movement. *Off Our Backs, 31*(10), 22–24.

National Coalition against Domestic Violence. (2003). *Intimate partner violence: A special report from the Bureau of Justice Statistics*. Retrieved September 23, 2003, from http://www.ncadv.org/publicpolicy/intimate.htm

Piercy, M., & Freeman, J. (1972). *Getting together: How to start a consciousness raising group*. Cape Cod, MA: Cape Cod Women's Liberation Organization.

Schneider, E. (2000). *Battered women and feminist lawmaking*. New Haven, CT: Yale University.

United Nations. (1994). *Declaration on the elimination of violence against women*. General Assembly Resolution 48/104. New York: Author.

U.S. Census Bureau. (2003, 2002). *Data profiles*. Retrieved September 23, 2003, from http://eire.census.gov/popest/data/states/ST-EST2002-ASRO-01.php

Family Planning

Ilana Lehmann

Family planning, reproductive rights, and population control have been viewed traditionally as women's issues—central to all three is the ability to prevent unintended births. In 1997 the Office of Population Affairs mandated that by 2002 all Title X service grantees were to be required to have at least one project providing family-planning services to men (Male Involvement Projects, 2000). This federal mandate provides political recognition of a man's role in the prevention of unintended births.

Addressing the needs of men and women to limit family size combines three sensitive issues, any one of which is controversial in and of itself: sex, gender, and personal rights. The connection between reproduction and sexual activity may seem simple and obvious, but it is in fact complex and obscure. This complexity is due, in part, to the shared difference of morals, religion, and culture. The issue of personal rights is less difficult to discuss because the concept of individual rights has long been a basic principle of American politics and the law.

The history of contraceptive practices can be traced back beyond biblical times (McFarlane & Meier, 2001). The locus of control for contraception was initially within the man's purview. The advent of modern medicine moved contraception increasingly into the control of women. As our culture has now come to view contraception as a shared male-female responsibility, the American polity has reflected this shift.

The legal history of contraception is relatively short. Politicians have traditionally been reluctant to take a position in this area. Rather, it has been the medical community that has prompted much of the legislation that has become the basis of American family planning policy. While the majority of

Americans have come to regard birth control as an important individual right, opinion on abortion remains sharply divided (Baer, 2002).

HISTORY/LEGISLATION

The passage of the first law relating to contraception occurred nearly a century after the founding of the nation. The 1873 legislation—the Act for the Suppression of Trade in and Circulation of Obscene Literature and Articles of Immoral Use (commonly referred to as the Comstock Law)—was an attempt to limit access to written materials relating to contraception. Instead, the law hampered physicians' ability to respond to couples' requests for more reliable methods of contraception. The medical community had responded with an increase in the availability of condoms and written material on contraception during the mid-1850s. Prior to the passage of the Comstock Law, there had been no federal involvement in contraception. This statutory linkage of contraception and obscenity remained in place for nearly 100 years (Back, 1989).

U.S. v. One Package, 86 F 2d 737 (1937) was the landmark case that invalidated the federal Comstock Law. In the same year, North Carolina was the first of seven southern states to establish state-supported family-planning programs. Not until the 1960s did any state outside the South adopt an affirmative policy on family planning. To the contrary, many states had "little Comstock" laws "regulating" the use of contraceptive devices.

The Federal Drug Administration approved "the pill" as a method of contraception in 1960, and within two years of this approval approximately 1.2 million women had utilized it. This number is especially remarkable in light of the fact that it was not until 1965 that the U.S. Supreme Court ruled in *Griswold v. Connecticut*, 381 U.S. 479 (1965) that states could not prohibit the use of contraceptives by married couples.

The right of married couples to use contraceptive devices (*Griswold*, supra) was extended by the U.S. Supreme Court to single people in *Eisenstadt v. Baird*, 405 U.S. 438 (1972) and to adolescents in *Carey v. Population Services*, 432 U.S. 678 (1977). The extension of reproductive and contraceptive rights culminated in *Roe v. Wade*, 410 U.S. 113 (1973), which found a right to abortion in the right to privacy that the U.S. Supreme Court decided was contained within the Ninth Amendment to the Constitution (McFarlane & Meier, 2001).

Funding

Federal funding of family-planning practices has closely followed decisions in the courts. Following the *Griswold* decision by the U.S. Supreme Court, the Office of Economic Opportunity (OEO) awarded the first direct federal grant for family-planning services. In the next two years, 1965–1967, OEO spent an estimated $5.6 million for family planning services.

Six statutes have authorized all federal support for family planning services: Title IV-A, Title V, OEO, Title X, Title XIX, and Title XX. Except for Title X, the other statutes are not categorically specific, and the status of family planning services in these statutes is "just one of several programs" funded.

Title XIX of the Social Security Act, the Medicaid program, was enacted in 1965. While family-planning services were not included in this statute, the regulations under Title XIX do specifically mention family-planning services. The purpose behind Title XIX was to encourage states to develop a unified system for providing medical care for persons who were indigent or otherwise unable to pay for services. The Act "permitted" family-planning services.

In 1967 Congress specifically mandated the provision of family-planning services under the auspices of two other federal programs, Titles IV-A (the Social Services Program for Mothers and Children) and Title V (the Maternal and Child Health and Crippled Children Act) of the Social Security Act. Under Title IV-A, the federal government covered 75% of the costs of the program and the states were responsible for the balance. Unlike Title XIX, family planning was required under Title IV-A. Even so, many states did not make these services available to persons covered under this act.

Title X of the Public Health Service Act, the Family Planning Service and Population Research Act (PL 572), is the only federal Title that provides specific categorical funding for family-planning services for low-income women. Passed in December 1970, Title X also provided grants for population research.

In 1994 nearly two-thirds of the 6.6 million women who received contraception services did so at one of the 4,200 clinics receiving Title X funds. In the 1980s Medicaid had surpassed Title X funds as the largest source of public funding for family-planning services (Frost, 1996).

Title XX of the Social Security Act, Block Grants to the States for Social Services, was passed in 1975. In 1976 Congress amended the Act, giving states the option to provide family-planning services on a universal basis without regard to income. Family planning and day care were the only programs to receive such preferential treatment. In the 1980s the state match requirement for Title XX funds was eliminated.

Personnel

Title X funds provide for the training of family planning clinic personnel through general training programs. Between 1972 and 2000, Title X funds were used to provide training for more than 5,000 nurse practitioners. As a result, nurse practitioners have become the primary providers of Title X services, accounting for an estimated 80% of the services rendered each year.

Health departments represent nearly half of the agencies providing publicly funded family-planning services. Hospitals and community health centers account for another one-sixth of public agencies providing these services.

Nonmedical family-planning clinic staff typically includes outreach workers or community health personnel. Their primary responsibilities are to contact individuals in need of family-planning services, initiate family-planning counseling, and assist in appropriate referrals to auxiliary support services. Currently there is no national certification for family-planning professionals. These workers are typically at a master's degree level and are often licensed social workers or counselors that have met the standards for licensure in the state where they are employed.

Medical staff at family-planning clinics may include physicians, who often serve in a dual capacity as clinic directors. Nurse practitioners, registered nurses, and medical assistants may also be part of these staffs.

Turnover at family-planning clinics is reportedly high. Between 1994 and 1997, one clinic out of seven closed or discontinued family-planning services. These closures resulted from a variety of factors: clinics were merged with other agencies, consolidated with other health related centers, or experienced very high turnover. However, the overall number of clinics providing family-planning services has remained stable, with new clinics opening in areas where such closures have occurred (Frost, 1996).

PURPOSE/INTENT

Family-planning services are provided in one of two fashions: (1) through a private physician, or (2) through one of several publicly funded programs. As unintended pregnancy is highest among teenagers and low-income women, these two groups are also the most significant in terms of number of clients for the approximately 7,000 federally funded family-planning centers (Frost, 1996).

Private Medical Services

Approximately 70% of American women in their childbearing years have private insurance coverage, which often provides for enrollment in a Health Maintenance Organization (HMO). The Freedom of Choice for Family Planning Services Act requires that enrollment in an HMO does not restrict the person's choice of a provider for family-planning services. HMOs are allowed various options in the manner of providing payments to providers outside their networks, including capitation of payments, but they cannot restrict an individual's choice of provider (Family Planning Services, 2003).

Insured women tend to be older, more educated, and of higher income levels than women served by the publicly funded family-planning centers. They are also less likely to be a member of a minority and more likely to be married. Fewer than half of insured women sought family-planning services for contraception (Frost, 2001).

Half of the counties in Arkansas, Georgia, Idaho, Kansas, Kentucky, Mississippi, Missouri, Nevada, Oklahoma, Tennessee, and Wyoming lack a private obstetrician-gynecologist. However, these same counties have one or more publicly funded family-planning clinics (Frost, Ranjit, Manzella, Darroch, & Audam, 2001).

Private Family Planning Nonprofit Organizations

Title X funds are provided to health departments, hospitals, community or migrant health centers, and "other" agencies. In 1997, one in 20 of the "other" agencies was a Planned Parenthood affiliate. Planned Parenthood still claims to be not only the world's oldest but also the largest not-for-profit reproductive health organization (Fact Sheet, 2000). However, between 1994 and 1997 the number of family-planning agencies that were Planned Parenthood affiliates fell by 12–14%. Moreover, according to the same report, all Planned Parenthood sites that had terminated contraceptive services had closed during this period (Frost, 2001). The new clinics that provide family-planning services are mostly community or migrant health centers, not Planned Parenthood affiliates.

State/Federal Publicly Funded Agencies

State and local funding comprise approximately 30% of the operating costs of family-planning centers. A patchwork of other funding sources constitutes the balance of these costs.

Title XIX of the Social Security Act is the Medicaid program. Medicaid policies for eligibility, services, and payment are complex and vary from state to state. A person who is eligible for Medicaid in one state may not be eligible in another state. Also, states have a lot of latitude in determining the family-planning services they will offer. According to federal Medicaid guidelines, states may choose to include in their definition of family-planning services "only those services which either prevent or delay pregnancy," or they "may more broadly define the term to also include services for the treatment of fertility." There is only one specific restriction regarding family-planning service: "abortions may not be claimed as a family planning service" (McFarlane & Meier, 2001, p.73).

Utilization Criteria

According to the Centers for Disease Control and Prevention (CDC), nearly five million women received health care services at family-planning clinics in 2002. They were predominantly young, poor, and had never had a child. While the majority of these women are white, a disproportionate number of black clients based on demographics are served at these clinics (Frost, 1996).

Adolescents made up between one-fourth and one-third of the contraceptive clients at publicly funded clinics in 1997. This population generally seeks care from these centers for both economic and confidentiality reasons. Few of these clients are covered by private insurance unless through a parent's policy. Obtaining care through private insurance generally requires notification of the parent policyholder of such medical care.

All states allow minors to receive contraceptive care without parental consent or notification. Title X stipulates services must be provided without regard to age. In addition, Title XIX (Medicaid) has a supremacy clause that states that federal confidentiality allowances supercede any restrictive state statutes. As in the case of all federal family-planning statutes, these laws do not apply to abortion services (McFarlane & Meier, 2001).

Special Case-Management Needs

Publicly funded family-planning services are not provided by any one entity. Knowledge of community resources is essential to assist individuals in obtaining appropriate services. If the individual is already receiving Medicaid assistance, the options for services are greater than those who do not qualify for this program. Many health departments are the primary source of Title X family-planning funds. It is important to consider an individual's cultural and religious characteristics when making the appropriate referral.

CLIENT SERVICES

The focus of family-planning services generally has an emphasis on contraception. However, most family-planning agencies offer other services. These include preventive and specialized reproductive health care such as Pap tests, testing and treatment for sexually transmitted diseases, prenatal and postnatal care, infertility testing, counseling, and treatment.

Education

Education and counseling are viewed as important components of family-planning services. However, Titles V, X, XIX, and XX of the federal acts, as well as most state laws, seldom fund any educational services beyond individual contraception counseling.

The 1978 Adolescent Health Service and Pregnancy Prevention Act (PL 626) had funded comprehensive pregnancy-prevention services for adolescents, including family life and sex education. This legislation was replaced with the Adolescent Family Life Act (PL 25, 1981), which some liberals called the "Chastity Act" as it focused on the prevention of adolescent sexual relations. The act did in fact provide for funding "necessary services to prevent adolescent sexual relations" (McFarlane & Meier, 2001, p. 49).

The "new welfare" legislation of the 1990s did allot $50 million a year for the purpose of funding abstinence education programs in states. According to McFarlane and Meier (2001), numerous studies in the 1995 report by the Institute of Medicine have demonstrated that abstinence cannot be counted as a major means of reducing rates of unintended pregnancies.

Education programs that include information about contraception and sexually transmitted diseases are provided by most schools but not with any uniform content or delivery. Most of the education programs enacted by the various government, nonprofit, and for-profit agencies have focused on providing written materials regarding contraception choices. This includes the paid advertisements about Norplant and Depo-Provera that are seen in magazines directed to a teenage audience.

Teen pregnancy continues to be a problem that is inadequately addressed by the programs currently in place. The proportion of adolescent women who are unmarried at the time of giving birth increased dramatically since the 1960s, from 15% to 75% in 1998 (McFarlane & Meier, 2001)

Medical Screening and Counseling

The counseling at most Title X clinics focuses on the prevention of pregnancy. Counselors are encouraged to spend more time with teenage clients. And while Title X clinics cannot limit access to family-planning services to individuals based on age, the clinics are required by law to encourage minors to involve their parents in their decision making regarding family planning (McFarlane & Meier, 2001).

In addition to contraceptive counseling and screening, most clinics offer a wide range of services that are critical to sexual and reproductive health. These services include cervical cancer screenings and counseling; breast health information and instruction in self-examination; testing for high blood pressure, anemia, and diabetes; screening and counseling for sexually transmitted diseases; safe-sex counseling; and basic infertility screening.

Medical Assistance and Referral

The range of services available to women at Title X-funded clinics has become comparable to those offered to women whose primary source of care is a private provider. Even so, women obtaining services at non-Title X clinics are significantly less likely to have obtained preventive gynecological care (Frost et al., 2001).

Oral contraceptives continue to be the most frequently chosen method of contraception, especially among women under age 20. The next most frequent method is condoms. The increase in condom use has been attributed to growing concern about human immunodeficiency virus infection (HIV) and other sexually transmitted diseases expressed by the Centers for Disease Control and Prevention ("Achievements," 1999). Some clinics have begun restricting oral contraceptives to women over the age of 35 due to some increased health risks. Private physicians are less likely to make the same restriction.

The slight decline in adolescent pregnancy can be attributed to the increased use of long-acting hormonal contraception such as Depo-Provera and Norplant, largely because these methods do not require as vigilant a degree of adherence as other methods ("Achievements," 1999).

Typical Referral Questions

Family-planning services are available from private practitioners and publicly funded facilities. Questions that human services practitioners may be asked are listed below, with some direction on providing answers.

Where can I get family-planning services?

The first step in finding family-planning services is to call the local health department. If they are not the provider of Title X-funded services, they are most often able to direct you and your client to a program that will fit with their needs. Most clinics operate on an appointment basis. Hours of operation vary. The first phone call is a good opportunity for the client to inquire about what to expect on the first visit.

How much will it cost?

The answer to this question is usually nothing. Once at a clinic, the individual may need to provide income verification. If the individual is already receiving Medicaid assistance, there will be no charge to that individual. Even individuals with modest incomes may have little or no fee for family-planning services since Title X clinics generally operate on a sliding-scale fee basis.

Will my parents be notified?

At a Title X clinic or a Medicaid provider the answer is no, not unless individuals want to inform their parents. Minors who are sexually active cannot be denied services due to their age.

What should I expect at the first visit?

It is helpful to assure a client before sending them to a clinic that the staff members are caring professionals who will try to make them feel comfortable. The health care they will receive is confidential and individualized. Specific information about what kind of medical examination will be performed can be obtained when the call for an appointment is made.

References

Back, K. (1989). *Family planning and population control: The challenges of a successful movement.* Boston: G. K. Hall.

Baer, J. A. (2002) *Historical and multicultural encyclopedia of women's reproductive rights in the United States.* Westport, CT: Greenwood Press.

Centers for Disease Control and Prevention. (1999). *Achievements in public health, 1900–1999 family planning.* Retrieved September 30, 2003, from http://www.cdc.gov/epo/mmwr/preview/mmwrhtml/mm4847a1.htm

Centers for Medicare and Medicaid Services. (2003). *Family planning services: State Medicaid manual, chapter 09-88, section 4270.* Retrieved October 3, 2003, from http://www.cms.hhs.gov/manuals/pub45pdf/sm4270.pdf

Frost, J. (1996). Family planning clinic services in the United States, 1994. *Family Planning Perspectives, 28*(2). Retrieved September 19, 2003, from http://www.agi-usa.org/pubs/journals/2809296.html

Frost, J. (2001) Public or private providers? U.S. women's use of reproductive health services. *Family Planning Perspectives, 33*(1), 4–12.

Frost, J., Ranjit, N., Manzella, K., Darroch, J., & Audam, S. (2001). Family planning clinic services in the United States: Patterns and trends in the late 1990s. *Family Planning Perspectives, 33*(2), 113–122.

McFarlane, D. R., & Meier, K. J. (2001). *The politics of fertility control: Family planning and abortion policies in the American states.* New York: Chatham House.

Office of Population Affairs, Office of Family Planning, U.S. Department of Health and Human Services. (2000). *Male involvement projects.* Retrieved October 3, 2003, from http://opa.osophs.dhhs.gov/titlex/opa_male_projects_review_july2000.pdf

Planned Parenthood Federation of America. (2000). *Fact sheet: Planned Parenthood services, 2001.* Retrieved October 1, 2003, from http://www.plannedparenthood.org/library/BIRTHCONTROL/Services.html

Public Aid/Assistance Programs

Saliwe M. Kawewe & Otrude N. Moyo

The social welfare delivery system of any society reflects its dominant values—hence, the existence of social welfare programs delivered through cash and in-kind social insurance and public assistance benefits. In the United States, the financial and public aid system has been fragmentary and at times confusing—a reflection of a mixture of compassion and a persistent resentment manifest in the American public's reluctance to provide assistance to the poor, particularly those considered able bodied (with the exception of temporary assistance during times of catastrophe and the "deserving poor"). It is, therefore, not surprising that social insurance programs compatible with the work ethic entrenched in American society receive much support and are considered politically viable as opposed to public assistance programs.

Although most of the present-day social insurance programs originated with the New Deal of the 1930s, the public assistance system has a long history dating as far back as the colonial period, in the form of the Elizabethan Poor Laws (Day, 2003). Over the years several assumptions and ideologies have contributed to various changes regarding what to do about social welfare. The issue of social expenditure and the role of government have continued to dominate the political debate, with the input of various social scientists being sought to devise efficient and effective ways to administer resources, particularly for the poor.

Social welfare benefits generally fall along a continuum ranging from in-kind to cash benefits (DiNitto, 2001, 2002) within two types of service delivery systems. The first type of program is income maintenance through social insurance [Social Security (OASDI), Unemployment Compensation (UC), Workers Compensation (WC), and Medicare], for which services are delivered ungrudgingly. Considered entitlements, social insurance programs provide income and services to the qualifying workforce, past and present. However, the second type of program, the focus of this chapter, is public assistance/aid benefits (PA) [Supplemental Security Income, Temporary Assistance for Needy Families, Food Stamps, Child Nutrition, Medicaid, Public Housing, and General Assistance]. PAs are generally categorical, delivered grudgingly, means-tested, and flawed with stigma, myths, and controversy in contrast with social insurance programs. The following section presents a general overview of the history/legislation, structure and funding, purposes, and client services of public assistance programs in the United States.

The general reluctance and confusion regarding the provision of public assistance to the poor, particularly those presumed able-bodied poor, has a history based on mixed expressions of compassion, public anger, and frustration reflected in a series of changes often manifested in stringent public aid eligibility standards. An ongoing controversy has been whether the poor ought to be provided a monthly income or commodities to cover their basic necessities. This issue has spurred years of debate and remains unresolved. Nevertheless, an array of federal and state public assistance efforts combining both in-kind and cash benefits have emerged.

History/Legislation

Prior to the Great Depression of the 1930s, the federal government played a minor role in social welfare. At the state level, there were specialized utilities to serve the needy such as hospitals, schools, asylums, and prisons that had evolved in the 1700s. By the nineteenth century, these initiatives had been expanded by separating the "deserving poor" (those with physical and mental disabilities, including offenders who remained in almshouses and prisons) from the "nondeserving" (able-bodied) poor, who where placed in workhouses. At the same time the federal government assumed responsibility for certain programs affecting Native Americans, veterans, immigrants, and federal offenders.

At the turn of the twentieth century, widows' and mothers' pensions surfaced in some states. A far cry from the type of government responsibility that followed the stock market crash of 1929 and the ensuing Great Depression, these programs served as important precedents to the Social Security Act and the New Deal of the 1930s and beyond (Frielander & Apte, 1980; Johnson, 1995). They were later incorporated into the framework of the nation's Social Security as Aid to Dependent Children (ADC) and insurance survivor benefits.

According to the social welfare historian Trattner (1999), the system of public aid as we know it has not moved far from the earliest legislation of the Elizabethan Poor Laws passed in 1601 in England.[1] These laws dealt stringently with the able-bodied poor through the enforcement of residency requirement policies of "passing on" and "warning out" (DiNitto, 2002). American colonists utilized four ways of assistance to the needy: (1) auctioning them to the lowest bidder; (2) placing them, including the sick, in a foster family willing to care for them at the lowest cost; (3) granting them indoor relief (assistance delivered within institutions such as workhouses/poorhouses); and (4) subsidizing the underpaid able-bodied poor required to work outside with outdoor relief (assistance in their own homes). This fourth alternative was given only after the first three strategies had failed (DiNitto, 2002; Dolgoff &Feldstein, 2003; Friedlander & Apte, 1980; Johnson, 1995). This form of relief was funded from the local poor tax. As social Darwinism, the work ethic, and Calvinistic philosophies prevailed, charity workers, doctors, politicians, and welfare administrators emphasized "scientific charity" during the eighteenth and nineteenth centuries. The poorhouses became institutions for the aged and infirm who were considered "deserving," while the able bodied were termed "nondeserving" poor.

The Great Depression and the New Deal

Until the 1920s, most aid was provided through private charity. Rapid immigration, urbanization, and industrialization of the period between 1870 and 1920 precipitated mounting social problems—poverty, overcrowding, and unemployment—forcing state and local governments to assume more responsibility in social welfare by establishing laws governing mothers' aid, as well as pension laws for widows, the aged poor, the disabled, and the blind. The Great Depression following the stock market crash of 1929 resulted in a dramatic decrease in prices, increased unemployment, poverty, and a high demand for welfare. Contrary to the "rugged individualism" of the previous era, which placed the main responsibility for social welfare under multiple philanthropic institutions, families, churches, local governments and communities, the Great Depression transformed American philosophy regarding public responsibility and human need by forcing the federal government to assume a major responsibility for social welfare through the introduction of the "New Deal." Subsequent improvisations to this government program included social provisions for relief, recovery, and reform.

Thus, the 1935 Social Security Act, the watershed of current welfare legislation, included social insurance and grants-in-aid to states for public assistance to the elderly, the disabled, and dependent children. Job Opportunities and Basic Skills (JOBS) programs, employment services, unemployment compensation, child welfare, urban aid, public housing, vocational rehabilitation, and education also enabled many Americans to "get by." To date, variations of these programs still exist. It is important to note that the New Deal was supportive of and sympathetic with the organized labor movement, which has historically played a role in improving living standards and better working conditions for the labor force.

1960—2000

The 1960s and 1970s were a time of great ferment in which a human rights revolution in the form of powerful social movements swept the nation. The civil rights movement sought equal rights for racial minorities, and the war on poverty pushed for the social inclusion of disenfranchised Americans into the economic mainstream. The Vietnam antiwar movement achieved its goal, while the women's rights movement gained momentum, intensifying its focus on the rights of prisoners, children, mental and other patients, veterans, the aged, disabled, nursing-home residents, abortion, sexual orientation, and so forth (Brieland, Costin, & Atherton, 1985).

The 1980s represented the era of the "New Federalism" in the form of Reaganomics, which increased defense spending and decentralized social programs from federal government to states, and in particular cutting the budget for categorical or means-tested programs. Mired in a recession deeper than the Great Depression as witnessed by the increase of poverty rate from 11.7 to 15.3% (35.3 million reflecting the highest rate since the mid-1960s), 12 million unemployed, a record-breaking economic deficit, and the feminization of poverty, the federal government passed a law according a $9.6 billion relief package in which $4.6 billion was earmarked for public job creation and $5 billion for distressed states as subsidy to extend their unemployment compensation programs.

In public debates, the language of labeling public assistance recipients as cheats, lazy, freeloaders, and so forth continued to be heard. It influenced the enactment of the 1996 Personal Responsibility and Work Opportunity Reconciliation Act. This was a controversial and dramatic reversal of six decades of federal social policy that had guaranteed some type of safety net to the nation's dependent citizens, particularly children and the destitute, through a minimum level of financial assistance.

The Twenty-first Century

During the early twenty-first century we continue to see conflicting empirical findings and legislative debates regarding definitions and causes of poverty with no viable solution. The United States has embarked on a massive public decentralization, privatization, and moralization of poverty reduction programs under the presumption that the work ethic, regardless of the amount of income earned and unavailability of work for everyone, will eliminate impoverishment. Up until three decades ago there was a general consensus about public interventions; poverty was attributed to worker exploitation and the dominance of business interests in the 1920s, to macro-economic depression in the 1930s, and to absence of opportunity due to racial and sexual discrimination in the 1960s. The respective solutions entailed fair labor standards and minimum wage; work programs, economic recovery, and a safety net of public assistance and social insurance programs; and expansion of opportunity through gender and civil rights legislation, accessibility to job training, early education programs, nutrition, and health care.

However, with the overall economic growth between the 1970s and 2000, one of the most conservative stances evolved, accompanied by increasing schisms regarding causes of poverty. Consequently, contemporary political style dictates that public assistance programs promote poverty. Clearly, the United States has developed its public social welfare programs around the principles of the work ethic, means-testing, private philanthropic efforts, and corporate welfare. Hence, mandatory work for the poor has become the centerpiece of U.S. legislation aimed at eliminating all caseloads except for the unavoidable vestiges of poverty (DiNitto, 2002). Unfortunately, however, the twenty-first century's adverse forces of economic globalization such as outsourcing, militarism, unemployment, underemployment, and various forms of racial and gender discrimination erode the viability of the work ethic as the main solution to poverty reduction.

TEMPORARY ASSISTANCE FOR NEEDY FAMILIES

The largest, most popular, and myth-filled public assistance program, initially termed Aid to Dependent Children (ADC) under the 1935 Social Security Act, was renamed Aid to Families with Dependent Children (AFDC) in 1962. It was further amended to its current name, Temporary Assistance for Needy Families (TANF), under the Personal Responsibility and Work Opportunity Reconciliation Act (PRWORA) of 1996, designed to reduce federal AFDC spending by $55 billion within a six-year period.

With the inclusion of Aid to Dependent Children in the original Social Security Act of 1935, the federal government assumed a shared responsibility for dependent children, intending to be involved only on a short-term basis (Lynn, 1977; Rein, 1970). It was anticipated that the program would eventually be phased out, once families became consumers of social insurance programs—that is, all parents would be employed and work-based income maintenance programs would cover their families. Single mothers were getting aid on behalf of their children. After several minor changes in the law, mothers in an ADC family became eligible for assistance, including medical coverage, but fathers were ineligible (man-in-the-house rule). In 1958, a cost-of-living formula was developed that gave more to states with lower per-capita income than to wealthier states. In 1961 an anti-recession initiative added an "Unemployed Parent" component to ADC named ADC-UP (Aid to Dependent Children with Unemployed Parents). This provision allowed aid to children when an able-bodied father was unemployed and ineligible for the social insurance program of Workers Compensation (DiNitto, 2002; U.S. Government, 1993).

To emphasize its family orientation, ADC's name was changed in 1962 from Aid to Dependent Children to Aid to Families with Dependent Children (AFDC), also covering a second parent in those states with AFDC-UP when one of the parents was incapacitated. AFDC-UP was changed in 1967 to Aid to Families with Dependent Children with Unemployed Father (AFDC-UF). The Supreme Court ruled this program unconstitutional as it discriminated against unemployed mothers. Thus, the AFDC-UP status was reinstated, but only half the states opted for it. Very few fathers made benefit claims in the adopting states. Significant changes were made to AFDC-UP through the passage of the Family Support Act of 1988. Although it became mandatory for states to have the program, no dramatic increase in the clientele rolls occurred (DiNitto, 2002; U.S. Government, 1993).

As in any federal-state public assistance program, eligibility criteria were diverse among states, with many states disqualifying the long-term unemployed. The sizeable number of able-bodied parents receiving public aid has historically fueled public debates about the morality of public assistance recipients. Despite the absence of evidence that public assistance increases female-headed families with children, freeloading charges were made against AFDC policy, alleging that the program increases the number of illegitimate children. In the past, so-called "midnight raids"—humiliating and unannounced home visits to welfare recipients' homes intended to prevent able-bodied men in the house from accessing ADFC benefits—were a frequent practice. Today the practice of monitoring welfare recipients to see if they comply with the rules is accomplished through more sophisticated, high-tech means, such as electronic checks issued by states and the federal government.

Financial assistance to children has had fierce opponents who have argued that public assistance is too costly. Contrary to what is often stated by social welfare system opponents, cash programs to the poor represent only a small portion of the federal budget—cash outlays of less than 5% of the annual budget. The Supreme Court ruled in 1968 that denying children services because there was a man in the house was unconstitutional.

In 1975 Congress turned to the Office of Child Support Enforcement, enforcing child-support collections from absent parents though the Social Security Act, Part D of Title IV, originally initiated in the 1950s. The rising divorce rate escalated AFDC rolls, leading to the more stringent Child Support Enforcement (CSE) Amendment of 1984. Methods to collect child-support arrears were toughened and expanded to include non-AFDC children. Despite all this effort, only 8% of the $21 billion owed (DiNitto, 2002) was recovered. In 1991, 44% (decreasing to 40% in 1993) of eligible families did not even have an order of support. States were required to award the first $50 to the AFDC family, but now under TANF states have revoked the practice. The federal government pays 66% of the operating state costs, 90% of the paternity determination test fees, and between 80 to 90% of automated tracking costs. While the states have to share the collections they make with the federal government, states also get incentives encouraging them to collect more. A state's noncompliance with federal guideline enforcement results in reduced TANF grants as a penalty.

Structure and Funding

Prior to the enactment of the PRWOR, the federal government offered matching grants to states for their participation/offering of AFDC Program: for each federal dollar received, states were required to spend some predetermined amount on the program. Thus, states were to match federal spending. Although the program was optional, every state chose to qualify for matching funds and operated an AFDC program under federal guidelines. These guidelines included provisions guaranteeing that (1) anyone who wished to apply could do so; (2) all eligible persons received assistance for as long as they qualified; (3) the plan would operate throughout the entire state; and (4) the state government was responsible for administering the program, although localities could participate. The cost of AFDC was shared by federal, state, and local government. The federal funds came out of general revenues and were available for all eligible recipients. The 1996 legislation altered the 61-year-old structure of AFDC.

Whereas the former AFDC program operated under entitlement to assistance, PRWORA, one of the most important pieces of legislation since the Social Security Act of 1935, introduced radical features through the disentitlement principle, rescinding 60 years of federal entitlements to support poor children and families. Families receiving five years of cumulative assistance would no longer be eligible to receive cash assistance. Federal funding was capped at a set amount and provided through a TANF block grant; and states required families to work after two years on assistance (DiNitto, 2002; Karger & Stoez, 2003; Stapleton, Wittenburg, Fishman, & Livermore, 2001).

Block grants differ from matching grants in that states get a set amount of money through a block grant. The amount provided to a state each year is determined in advance by the federal government and cannot be increased. Eligibility, needs, and benefit levels continue to be set at the state level. Like AFDC, TANF varies from state to state. Each state determines the minimum standard of need, the level of annual income below which a family must fall, to qualify for aid. The standard of need is based on the minimum cost of living in that state, as determined by state officials and approved by the federal government through DHHS. The federal government expenditure reflects 1% of AFDC/TANF (Karger & Stoez, 2003).

Purpose

The rationale for public assistance is grounded in the concept of a safety net in which government insures that its citizens receive a minimum level of resources necessary for subsistence without falling below a certain poverty level (Karger & Stoez, 2003). Thus, there are 51 safety nets, one for each state in the United States. The program was designed to provide cash assistance to needy families with dependent children. Need was recognized as falling below a poverty line and due to incapacity, death, or continued absence of a parent, or in some cases the unemployment of both parents. However, according to Segal and Brzuzy (1998), the primary underlying goal of programs designed to aid the poor—particularly when women with children are involved—has been to support the American economic and social system rather than to redistribute resources or change the value structure (Abramovitz, 1996; DiNitto, 2002; Karger & Stoez, 2003; Piven & Cloward, 1993). Public assistance programs were meant to cushion people during times of downturn, not to redistribute wealth from the rich to the poor.

Services

The number of poor people on public assistance has declined since the early 1970s. Between 1973 and 1989, the number of poor families with children rose by 50%, but that of AFDC families only grew by 20%. By 2000, TANF cases had decreased 47%. In 1991 two-thirds of the poor (21.2 of 33.6 million) did not receive financial assistance from AFDC and more than one-third received neither food stamps nor Medicaid. The average nation's TANF participation rate was 38%.

Under TANF, which replaced the AFDC, JOBS, and the Emergency Assistance Program, there would no longer be a guarantee that all eligible individuals would receive assistance. Adult recipients of TANF are required to participate in work and/or school activities. Individuals are required to participate for at least 20 hours per week in unsubsidized or subsidized employment, on-the-job training, or to provide child-care services to individuals who are participating in community services. Penalties for failure to work are set by each state.

SUPPLEMENTAL SECURITY INCOME

History/Legislation

In 1972, Supplemental Security Income (SSI) replaced the previous categorical federal/state programs of Old-Age Assistance and Aid to the Blind that had originally been provided through the 1935 Social Security Act, and the Aid to the Disabled program that had been added in 1956. These three programs, originally state operated with a multiplicity of eligibility requirements and benefit-payment systems, were federalized and unified to create one public assistance operation. Although the federal government funds SSI and administers the program through the Social Security Administration, it is a means-tested, residual, antipoverty public-assistance program. Responding to the rising number of those disabled by drug and alcohol addiction (DAA), the federal government passed the Social Security Independence and Program Improvements Act in 1994, placing new restrictions that required participants to enter a substance-abuse program and only receive benefits for 36 months. There was an exception only for those who had no access to treatment. These individuals would continue to receive Medicaid and Medicare coverage, unless there was noncompliance, for 12 months. This act also spawned a Commission on Childhood Disability charged with the responsibility of reevaluating the definition of childhood disability.

Structure and Funding

Whereas OASDI is funded through FICA payroll taxes, SSI is funded through general tax revenues. The payments are adjusted according to any other income received, such as wages or other program benefits (Segal & Brzuzy, 1998; Social Security Administration, 1993a, b). SSI expenditures increased from $5 billion in 1974 to over $29 million in 2000. Because of the low level of benefits and requirements for eligibility, 28 states supplement SSI with a grant, which they sometimes let the federal government administer as well. The Supreme Court decision in the *Sullivan v. Zebley* case made children eligible for SSI if they had a disability comparable to that of an eligible adult.

Purpose

Disability at any age and illness in old age can cause severe financial stress. SSI provides cash assistance to senior citizens aged 65 or older, including disabled adults and children whose income falls below the poverty level. Additionally, the program covers individuals disabled by DAA. In practice, many people on SSI rolls live below the poverty line unless also receiving Social Security and food stamps.

Services

As in other public assistance programs, Medicare and Medicaid provide health coverage for SSI recipients. Complex red tape and stringent eligibility typical of means-tested programs keep many eligible people off SSI rolls. PRWORA tightened the definition of disability for children by excluding maladaptive behavior (such as attention deficit disorder) as a medical criterion for disability. Consequently, many poor children who previously qualified for cash assistance under SSI have been recategorized and their participation terminated. To qualify for SSI the applicant has to have limited resources valued at less than $2,000 for an individual and $3,000 for a couple. In 1974 there were 3.25 million on SSI rolls; that number had doubled to 6.9 million by 1999.

Though they can be higher than TANF benefits, SSI benefits are not generous. In 1999 the average monthly payment was $369, and in 2000 an individual and a couple received $512 and $769, respectively. The number of people with disabilities applying for services increased from 2.4 in 1984 to 3.4 million in 1999, with 20 and 79% of them being seniors and those with disabilities, respectively (Social Security Administration, 2000). In 1999, 31% on

SSI rolls were aged 65 or older, 50% aged between 18 and 64, while 13% (1 million) consisted of children under the age of 18, the fastest-growing recipient category. Over 60 and 50% of these children and adults respectively had either a mental/emotional disorder or mental retardation. Between 1980 and 1994 DAA recipients rose from 23,000 to 86,000, costing the federal government $1.4 billion.

GENERAL ASSISTANCE/GENERAL RELIEF

There is no federal program that provides cash assistance to single able-bodied men or women under the age of 65 who are poor. This responsibility is left to the states and the locality or county in which they live. The typical effort to provide economic assistance to this population is usually referred to as General Assistance (GA).

History/Legislation

In 1992, 9 states had no GA programs at all and 10 other states had only partial programs (Center on Budget and Policy Priorities, 1996). Over the past few years, GA programs have come under attack from those who are opposed to providing any economic assistance to people who do not fit into the centuries-old categories of worthy poor. The result has been severe cutbacks and cancellation of GA programs. For example, in 1991, Ohio decreased the program from year round assistance to six months coverage in a calendar year. For the other six months, even if eligible persons still had economic need, they were on their own. In Maine the state has not adjusted allotments since the late 1980s.

Structure and Funding

Not all states have the GA program and eligibility requirements, and benefits vary according to locality. Including the District of Columbia, 35 states have GA programs, 24 of them having statewide uniform eligibility rules and schedules. Of these 35 states, 9 lack uniform state programs while requiring all counties to have some variation of GA. Although Virginia and Wisconsin do not have statewide GA, they provide funding and supervision for counties that elect to have the program. PRWORA enabled many states to shift GA to their TANF program.

Purpose

GA programs were designed as a stopgap measure to ongoing or short-term needs of low-income people waiting for or ineligible for federally funded cash assistance such as TANF or SSI.

Client Services

Generally, able-bodied adults without children are least likely to be eligible for GA. Between 1996 and 1998 the number of states catering to this population decreased from 15 to 13. Additionally, many states delivering services to this population provide in-kind benefits or limit the duration of cash assistance. Most states limit GA to the severely poor whose incomes are below the poverty line. Regardless of family size, most states set the income limits at between $1,000 and $2,000, while they also tend to ignore some assets, such as a car or home. Because most states require GA recipients to work, those who fail to comply lose benefits for some time. GA programs are more likely to serve families with children, the disabled, or elderly people. Thirty-four states provide such assistance for people awaiting SSI, while 24 states provide GA to children or families with children not eligible for TANF due to living with an unrelated adult. GA caseloads are small. Nineteen of the 35 statewide GA programs tightened restrictions on immigrants, similar to PRWORA.

IN KIND-ASSISTANCE: FOOD STAMPS AND OTHER PUBLIC SUBSIDIES

History/Legislation

Even though the PRWORA of 1996 saved the Food Stamp Program from being converted into a block grant, substantial changes were made through more stringent eligibility rules. Many who previously qualified can no longer do so. Only certain categories of legal immigrants, such as seekers of political asylum and refugees, can qualify for benefits. The act contains stiffer work requirements and makes it easier for states to operate food stamp employment and training programs. Evolving from the moral categorization of poor as deserving and nondeserving, the issue of whether public aid should be in-kind or monetary has continued to prevail. Advocates of the commodity approach contend that provisioning of in-kind benefits, including food products (those available from agricultural surpluses), food stamps based on the 1964 Food Stamp Act, free school lunches through the 1965 Child Nutrition Act, supplemental food for pregnant women and children (WIC), low-income housing, and rent and day-care subsidies land squarely on their targets—protecting people who are in desperate need. These advocates believe that the cash approach is flawed because it does not ensure that recipients will purchase the basic commodities and services they need. They argue that money can be diverted to meet other (frivolous) needs of recipients. In this regard, they fault cash assistance as misplaced, since money subsidies cannot be controlled at the point of consumption. They argue that only through in-kind assistance is society able to exercise a measure of control over the final utilization of the tax dollar (Gilbert & Terrell, 2002).

Structure and Funding

The Food Stamp Program, accounting for 2% of federal government expenditure, operates in all 50 states and the District of Columbia, U.S. Virgin Islands, and Guam. State and federal government share most administrative costs equally, with the latter carrying all cost of the value of the food stamps, distributing, printing and redeeming the stamps through the nation's Federal Reserve System. In 1997 appropriations were $26.1 billion, declining to $25.1 billion in 1998. Advocates of cash benefits argue that commodities rob people of their dignity because they do not allow them the food choices that other citizens have. They believe that most responsible people use cash benefits wisely and that stamps or even the new electronic benefit cards unnecessarily embarrass or stigmatize participants in grocery stores. Moreover, they argue that neither stamps nor electronic benefit cards can be used to purchase cleaning supplies, paper goods, and other necessities that account for approximately 25¢ of every dollar spent in grocery stores by other shoppers.

Since many food stamp recipients also receive TANF, SSI, or both, advocates of cash benefits point to the administrative savings that would accrue from simply adding the value of food stamps to the public assistance checks already being sent. The argument is that cash provisions are optimal because cash gives its users maximum choice, therefore "maximizing their utility" by fulfilling their necessities in the "normal" way. Gilbert and Terrell (2002) argued further that, theoretically at least, it can be demonstrated that, given $50 to spend freely, an individual on welfare will invariably achieve a higher level of satisfaction than one given $50 worth of goods and services specified by someone else. This position, of course, assumes a consumer who is rational and capable of judging precisely what is in his or her best interest. It further assumes that maximizing the preferences of individuals also serves the good of the broader community—that the choices made by consumers for their own welfare aggregate together to advance the common welfare.

The appeal of the argument for cash benefits lies in its reliance on consumer sovereignty. There is a compelling quality to the argument for an individual's freedom of choice. In essence, it posits the right to self-determination, the right to use one's resources for whatever the psychological or material benefits derived, and, conversely, the right to command one's resources toward whatever future is desired. It is the right of individuals to exercise self-indulgence as well as self-denial (Gilbert & Terrell, 2002).

Purpose

The Food Stamp Act of 1964 provides for in-kind benefits in the form of food subsidies initially distributed as food stamps/coupons, checks, and now electronic cards for purchasing designated food products. Ideally, food stamps fall in the middle of the continuum representing a compromise between those who prefer to deliver nutrition benefits using cash and those who prefer to do so using commodities. It continues by far to be available to the broadest spectrum of the population compared to any other public assistance program. Though recipients must be poor to qualify, it is considered the nation's non-categorical PA program.

Client Services

Once certified, recipients collect their monthly food stamps, coupons, or electronic cards by mail or at a designated post office or bank, with many now receiving them through electronic transfer. The number of participants fluctuates, depending on various factors such as unemployment, economic recession, and loosening or tightening of eligibility criteria. While there were approximately 28 million recipients (11% of the population) in 1994, the number had decreased to 19 million by 1998. Most participants also receive other public assistance such as TANF and SSI, with 91% of the program's recipient households having poverty-level incomes.

CONCLUSION

All these programs have their potential uses in an attempt to minimize poverty. In the discussion we have shown how a combination of compassion and resentment of the poor shape the U.S. social welfare services. PRWORA through TANF converted over 60 years of financial assistance and public aid based on the entitlement philosophy of the Social Security Act of 1935 into labor policy and privatization of social services, and changed public policy into tax policy (Karger & Stoez, 2003). Debates on techniques by which poverty could be overcome most effectively or efficiently are value driven. Specifically, to what extent do Americans want to redistribute income in order to eradicate poverty? As it stands, most public-aid policies are designed to tide people over in times of downturn, not to redistribute wealth from the rich to the poor. Clearly, a policy to redistribute wealth, although possible, is not practical because of its incompatibility with contemporary American values.

Note

[1] U.S. laws were amended several times—for example, the Act of Settlement of 1662, which empowered the authorities to remove and return to his former residence any person occupying a property renting for less than ten pounds a year, who, in the opinion of the authorities, might become poverty-stricken at some future time. It was expected by the various parishes that they would in this way be protected from the poor who "belonged elsewhere." It was three centuries later, in *Shaprio v. Thompson* (U.S. Supreme Court, April 1969) that laws using eligibility for public assistance to determine residency were declared unconstitutional. See Dolgoff & Feldstein (2003).

References

Abramovitz, M. (1996). *Regulating the lives of women: Social welfare policy from colonial times to present*. Boston: South End Press.

Brieland, D., Costin, L. B., & Atherton, C. R. (1985). *Contemporary social work: An introduction to social work and social welfare* (3rd ed.). New York: McGraw-Hill.

Cavanaugh, D. A., Lippitt, J., & Moyo, N. O. (2000). Resource guide to selected federal policies affecting children's social and emotional development and their readiness for school. In Robin Peth-Pierce (Ed.), *Off to a good start: Research on the risk factors for early school problems and selected federal policies affecting children's social and emotional development and their readiness for school.* (pp. 96–188). Chapel Hill: University of North Carolina, FPG Child Development Center.

Center on Budget and Policy Priorities. (1996). *The new welfare law.* Washington, DC: Author.

Day, P. J. (2003). *A new history of social welfare.* Boston: Allyn & Bacon.

DiNitto, D. M. (2001). *Social welfare: Politics and public policy* (5th ed.). Boston: Allyn & Bacon.

DiNitto, D. M. (2002). *Social welfare: Politics and public policy* (Study Edition). Boston: Allyn & Bacon.

Dolgoff, R., & Feldstein, D. (2003). *Understanding social welfare* (6th ed.). Boston: Allyn & Bacon.

Friedlander, W. A., & Apte, R. Z. (1980). *Introduction to social welfare* (5th ed.). Englewood Cliffs, NJ: Prentice Hall.

Gilbert, N., & Terrell, P. (2002). *Dimensions of social welfare policy* (5th ed.). Boston: Allyn & Bacon.

Jansson, B. S. (2001). *The reluctant welfare state* (4th ed.). Pacific Grove, CA: Brooks/Cole.

Johnson, W. H. (1995). *The social services: An introduction.* Itasca, IL: F. E. Peacock.

Karger, H. J., & Stoez, D. (2003). *American social welfare policy: A pluralist approach* (4th ed.). Boston: Allyn & Bacon.

Lynn, L., Jr. (1977). A decade of policy development in the income-maintenance system. In R. R. Haveman (Ed.), *A decade of federal antipoverty programs: Achievements, failures and lessons.* New York: Academic Press.

Piven, F. F., & Cloward, R. A. (1993). *Regulating the poor: The functions of public welfare.* New York: Vintage Books.

Prigmore, C. H., & Atherton, C. R. (1994). *Social welfare policy: An analysis and formulation.* Lexington, MA: D.C. Heath.

Rein, M. (1970). *Social policy issues: Issues and change.* New York: Random House.

Segal, E. A., & Brzuzy, S. (1998). *Social welfare policy, programs, and practice.* Itasca, IL: F.E. Peacock.

Social Security Administration. (1993a). *Social Security handbook* (11th ed.). SSA No. 65-008. Washington, DC: U.S. Department of Health and Human Services.

Social Security Administration. (1993b). *Social Security programs in the United States.* SSA publication 13-11758. Washington, DC: U.S. Department of Health and Human Services.

Social Security Administration. (1998). *OASDI trustees report.* Retrieved December 15, 1998, from http://ww.ssa.gov/OACT/TR/TR98/trtoc.html.

Social Security Administration. (2000). *Facts: SSI.* Retrieved August 10, 2000, from http://www.ssa.gov:80/statistics/fastfacts/pageii.html

Stapleton, D. C., Wittenburg, D. C., Fishman, M. E., & Livermore, G. A. (2001). Transitions from AFDC to SSI prior to welfare reform. *Social Security Bulletin, 64*(1), 84–114.

Trattner, W. I. (1999). *From poor law to welfare state: A history of social welfare in America* (5th ed.). New York: The Free Press.

U.S. Government, Committee on Ways and Means, U.S. House of Representatives. (1993). *Overview of entitlement programs, 1993 Green Book.* Washington, DC: U.S. Government Printing House.

SECTION V

Education and Human Services

Career and Technical Education

Clora Mae Baker & John S. Washburn

The career and technical education program, formerly known as the vocational education program, is one of the most complex and misunderstood aspects of American education. It is distinguished from other educational programs in that it includes participation by students of all ages—elementary through adult. Career and technical education is sometimes defined as a *process* of career development that prepares youth and adults for employment in occupations with education requirements of less than a baccalaureate degree. It may also be defined as a *program* (e.g., agriculture, consumer and family sciences, trades and industries, health, business/office occupations).

This chapter is intended to define and describe the career and technical education program and clarify its role in preparing youth and adults for work for both educators and counselors alike. A summary will define changes anticipated in the future as a result of new federal legislative initiatives.

PURPOSE/INTENT

Career and technical education is one of several major systems in the United States that prepare people for work. The military, programs supported through the Workforce Investment Act (WIA), business and industry, apprenticeship, public school career and technical education, and private vocational schools primarily emphasize preparation of individuals for work (National Council on Employment Policy, 1982). Universities are the primary source of training for professions requiring advanced degrees. There are substantial student transfers among the various employment and training systems (e.g., WIA funds may be used to purchase training from the career and technical education system).

Career and technical education has two broad purposes—preparation of youth and adults for work, or for further education to prepare for work. Most career and technical education programs occur in high school, technical institute, and community college settings. They are often focused on preparing new entrants into the workforce but also serve incumbent workers.

Career and technical education programs can be distinguished only by the nature and level of preparation students receive for work, not by the age of the student. Students enrolled in career and technical education courses in the public school have markedly different expectations. Many of the students will have repeated contact as adults with institutions that offer job-training experiences. Some students may enroll in one or two courses (e.g., keyboarding), while other students will concentrate on a sequence of courses to master job entry-level skills (e.g., dental assistant, welding). There are career and technical education programs designed to prepare students for a particular occupation (e.g., office assistant) or for a cluster of occupations (e.g., building trades). Other programs prepare students for job-specific programs (e.g., nurse assistant). Yet other programs are designed to prepare students for a particular job for a specific employer.

Generally, high school and adult-age students have the opportunity to participate in coursework in one of several clusters in agriculture, health, business, family and consumer science, and the industrial areas. In those clusters, agricultural production (farming), general merchandising, nursing, child care, accounting, secretarial, electronics, auto mechanics, and drafting enroll the largest number of students.

Approximately two-fifths of the students who enroll in career and technical education in the high schools are in courses that are not designed for particular jobs or occupations. These are courses designed to orient students to work (e.g., introduction to business). Most of the students enrolled in career and technical education programs in community colleges are preparing for a particular job or occupation. Therefore, a career and technical education program may be very general in nature (e.g., general business), or very specific (e.g., dental assistant training).

The career and technical education program continues to serve a sizeable number of students. After a period of decline in the 1980s, in 2000 more than 700,000 high school seniors nationally pursued an occupational program of study. According to the National Assessment of Vocational Education (Silverberg, Warner, Fong, & Goodwin, 2004), between 42.0 and 46.2% of all high school graduates take more than 3.0 occupational credits while in high school.

History/Legislation

During the decades immediately after 1900, there was a major impetus for vocational education (now called career and technical education), with strong support from the business community. Industrialists focused on the need for highly skilled labor and alleged that the factory system had made the apprenticeship system obsolete. It had become difficult and economically inefficient to allow informal, on-the-job learning in modern factories.

Business leaders argued that better trained workers would be more satisfied with their jobs because of increased understanding and appreciation of their role in an industrial economy; that industrial accidents, absenteeism, and labor turnover would decrease; and that increased productivity would be the result of a satisfied, more stable work force. The political influence of the business community and the impact of its arguments were evidenced by the establishment of numerous study committees and advocacy groups. Ultimately, a report from the Commission on National Aid to Vocational Education led to the passage of the Smith-Hughes Act, which provided the first federal aid for career and technical education (Barlow, 1967).

The Smith-Hughes Act of 1917 initiated the first program of federal grants-in-aid to promote career and technical education below the collegiate level. Money was made available for teachers of agriculture, trade, home economics, and industrial subjects. Subsequent legislation added provisions for funding for health, business, and office occupations.

A major shift in the nature of career and technical education legislation occurred in 1963. The Vocational Education Act of 1963 and subsequent legislation focused on service to students in contrast to prior legislation that provided for training personnel in a few selected occupational categories. The intent of Congress was to provide career and technical education for all people and all occupations, except those which were identified as professional occupations requiring a baccalaureate or higher degree. Recently, the Congress passed new legislation for career and technical education.

The Carl D. Perkins Vocational and Applied Technology Education Act of 1990 and its successors continued the focus on services to students; however, its purpose has been expanded. Resources are allocated to more fully integrate academic and occupational skills provided for students. Also, Congress intends an economic development focus for new federal career and technical education legislation. Career and technical education is seen as a program to prepare America's workforce in a more competitive, global economy (American Vocational Association, 1990b).

The Perkins Acts continued to focus on the special needs of single parents, displaced homemakers, single pregnant women, criminal offenders, the disadvantaged, the handicapped, and limited-English-proficient youth and adults. There are special programs for community-based organizations, consumer and homemaking education, career guidance and counseling, and business/labor/education partnerships, among others.

Administrative Structure

In all 50 states, there is one state agency responsible for the administration of career and technical education. The locus of responsibility may lie in one of four entities: The agency responsible for elementary and secondary education, the agency for higher education, a separate board of career and technical education, or some other entity. However, each state must have a sole state agency to distribute federal funds for career and technical education available through the Perkins Act.

Career and technical education programs are financed largely by local funds with relatively small amounts of federal funding, given the high cost of delivering courses/programs. Some states also allocate funds for career and technical education programs. Federal and state funds available for career and technical education are intended to pay for the excess costs of offering career and technical education programs beyond those costs associated with offering a regular program (e.g., English, mathematics).

Career and Technical Education Programs. In the United States, Bottoms and Copa (1983) identified various types of institutions that offer career and technical education programs. *High schools* will typically offer programs in family and consumer sciences, business education, agriculture, industrial arts/technology education, or health occupations. Academic and vocational subjects are offered in the comprehensive high school.

Some school districts support *career and technical education high schools.* These are usually specialized schools where a majority of students are enrolled in career and technical education subjects. Students in these schools will often receive academic coursework in the school.

The National Research Center for Career and Technical Education (Mitchell & Russel, 1990) noted several career and technical education high schools that have received national attention. For example, the Chicago High School for Agricultural Sciences is a magnet school offering agricultural subjects not common in an urban environment. The Murry Bergtraum High School for Business Careers in New York City is recognized for networking with the business community and serves 2,500 students from New York City's five boroughs. The minority population constitutes 80% of the 2,400-student body at the John H. Francis Polytechnic High School in Sun Valley, California. This school serves students throughout the Los Angeles Unified School District.

In the 1960s, many states supported the development of *area vocational centers.* Some area centers are designed to serve high-school-age youth. Other area centers are designed to serve post-secondary-age youth. Most centers are shared-time facilities, providing career and technical education to students from a number of high schools in a region. These students will normally receive their academic coursework in the regular high school and travel to the center two or three hours a day for vocational training. Similarly, post-secondary area career and technical education schools often provide instruction only for career and technical education programs, not academic coursework.

Many states have *community colleges*, which are two-year, degree-granting institutions. Most of the community colleges provide general and career and technical education programs; many of the community colleges' associate degree programs will be designed so that students can transfer to colleges or universities. Other programs will be designed for students who wish to receive an associate of applied science or certificate in an occupational area.

Some states have *technical institutes*, which are degree-granting institutions offering (primarily) career and technical education programs. Technical institutes normally focus on training to provide immediate job placement.

Some *four-year institutions* across the United States offer two-year programs. For example, Southern Illinois University at Carbondale offers associate degree programs in the College of Applied Sciences and Arts in a number of career and technical education program areas.

Finally, some states support *skill centers*, which are somewhat different than other institutions described earlier. These are usually very specialized institutions that provide career and technical education to economically disadvantaged students.

Types of Course Sequences

Each career and technical education program offers a series of courses, designed in a logical learning sequence, for job entry or further education. Ideally, the school modifies course sequences based on community and student interest, labor market information, and the availability of resources. A program at the secondary level for a general office clerk occupation might include a course sequence as follows:

Ninth Grade—Orientation
Orientation to General Business—one semester
Keyboarding I—one semester

Tenth Grade—Orientation
Keyboarding II—one semester
Computers in Business—one semester

Eleventh Grade—Skill Preparation
Accounting I—one semester
Office Equipment Applications or Word Processing—one semester *or*
Machine Transcription—one semester

Twelfth Grade—Skill Preparation
Office Procedures and/or Model Office—one year *or*
Cooperative Office Occupations—one year

It is important to note there are several patterns of participation for students enrolled in high school career and technical education courses. While some students may enroll in a complete sequence of courses designed to prepare them for a career, other students may only take one or two courses in a sequence. In high school, some youth are ready to take courses that will help them achieve well-defined career goals; others are not. Students completing a sequence of courses in a career and technical education area may choose to enter employment upon graduation from high school. Other students will continue their education at a post-secondary institution.

For example, at a local community college the student, or returning adult, may choose to pursue an associate degree in banking and finance. In addition to general education coursework, a typical banking and finance program might include the following occupational courses:

First Year—Fall Semester	*Second Year—Fall Semester*
Accounting I	Economics
Business Mathematics	Bank Accounting
Principles of Banking	Database Management
Business Seminar	Basic Programming
Introduction to Business	
First Year--Spring Semester	*Second Year—Spring Semester*
Accounting II	Business Correspondence
Principles of Management	Business Electives
Money and Banking	Marketing and Management

Students enrolled in post-secondary banking and finance programs might also be working part-time in a financial institution. It is not unusual for a graduate to enter a full-time position for a few years and then decide to continue his or her education at a university level. However, baccalaureate degree programs at the university level do not receive career and technical education funding.

Ideally, programs are articulated from one educational level to the next. However, there is some unnecessary duplication of effort between career and technical education providers. Students may not necessarily be guaranteed that all of their vocational training at one level will be considered at they progress to the next. A federal legislative initiative funded through the Perkins legislation and titled *Tech-Prep* is addressing this problem by funding programs that link occupational preparation in grades 11–14. Tech-Prep initiatives require the collaboration of secondary and post-secondary institutions.

Course Delivery

Career and technical education courses are provided in a number of different ways. Many agencies share instructional responsibilities with other public and private agencies in the surrounding area. Sometimes, the school will provide experiences in cooperation with business, industry, or government. Listed below are examples of the different strategies schools use to provide career and technical education:

- *In-school vocational instruction:* classroom and laboratory experiences conducted within the school's existing facilities.

- *Cooperative agreements:* instructional responsibilities for a course(s) within a particular career and technical education program shared by schools of the same type. The area career and technical education center described previously is an example of this type of arrangement.

- *Contractual arrangements:* instructional responsibilities for contractual ventures shared by schools of different types. For example, a private cosmetology school might provide instruction for high school students.

- *Extended classroom:* community facilities utilized as extensions of specific programs. For example, a nursing home might be used as a site to provide instruction for certified nurse assistants.

- *Cooperative education:* paid work experiences where students alternate study in school with on-the-job training.

- *Apprenticeship training:* career and technical education programs offered for apprentices who are employed to learn skill trades (e.g., carpentry, plumbing).

- *Supervised occupational experience:* a cooperative effort on the part of the school and students' parents or guardians wherein vocational experiences are provided at home, school, or another suitable location under the supervision of an instructor. For example, an agriculture student might have a special summer project on the family farm.

ISSUES FOR THE FUTURE

Certainly, the career and technical education program will change in the future. The definition of career and technical education in the Carl D. Perkins Vocational and Applied Technology Education Act and its successors noted that such programs should focus on competency-based applied learning that contributes to an individual's academic knowledge, higher-order reasoning and problem-solving skills, work attitudes, and general employability skills, as well as the occupational skills necessary for economic independence.

The continued success of the career and technical education program will require new curriculum, teacher retraining, outlays for new equipment, and expanded partnerships with the private sector. Continued student participation in traditional career and technical education offerings will have dilatory consequences on students' futures—unless they have access to the content of new technologies such areas as fiber optics, information processing, bio-technology, and electronics.

Changes in skill requirements for jobs must also be viewed in the context of significant demographic shifts in the workforce. The Hudson Institute's (Judy & D'Amico, 1997) *Workforce 2020* report noted that "the workforce would continue to grow slowly, become older and more female and including more minorities . . . and that new jobs in the service industry would require a higher skill level" (p. xiii).

The career and technical education program of the future must be sensitive to changes in workforce patterns and characteristics among workers such as age, ethnicity, and gender. Programs for adults needing training or retraining and for special populations should grow in number. Also, career and technical education programs must continue to be sensitive to the intensive investment in new technology by U.S. business and industry. Many believe that the United States cannot be competitive in the global economy with large numbers of job/skill mismatches. Partnerships between the schools that offer career and technical education and business, industry, and government will likely expand.

The career and technical education program is only one of several major systems that prepare people for work. However, it is likely it will continue to serve as the primary system in the educational arena assisting youth and adults to prepare for work or further education in preparation for later employment.

References

American Vocational Association. (1990a). *Fact sheet: Career and technical education today.* Arlington, VA: Author.

American Vocational Association. (1990b). *The AVA guide to the Carl D. Perkins Vocational Applied Technology Education Act of 1990.* Arlington, VA: Author.

Barlow, M. L. (1967). *History of industrial education in the United States.* Peoria, IL: Bennett.

Bottoms, G. L., & Copa, P. (1983, January). A perspective on career and technical education today. *Phi Delta Kappan,* 348–354.

Judy, R., & D'Amico, C. (1997). *Workforce 2020.* Indianapolis: Hudson Institute.

Mitchell, V., & Russel, E. (1990). *Exemplary urban career-oriented secondary school programs.* Berkeley, CA: National Center for Research in Career and Technical Education.

National Council on Employment Policy. (1982). *A career and technical education policy for the 1980's.* Washington, DC: National Council on Employment Policy.

Silverberg, M., Warner, E., Fong, M. & Goodwin, D. (2004) *National assessment of vocational education.* Washington, DC: U.S. Department of Education.

Adult Education

Bridget A. Hollis

Adult education does not have one concrete meaning. It appears to be a field of study and an educational practice whose scope and significance is poorly understood. To most people, the words adult education evoke an image of night classes at a local high school or perhaps another such prominently labeled activity (Akin, 1992). Adult education can mean different things to different people. Darkenwald and Merriam (1982) gave a process definition that allows self-teaching and self-directed learning: "Adult education is a process whereby persons whose major social roles are characteristic of adults' status undertake systematic and sustained learning activities for the purpose of bringing about changes in knowledge, attitudes, values, or skills" (p. 9).

Darkenwald and Merriam (1982) state the most common way of demarcating adult education from other forms of education:

> Adult education is concerned not with preparing people for life, but rather with helping people to live more successfully. Thus if there is to be an overarching function of the adult education enterprise, it is to assist adults to increase competence, or negotiate transitions, in their social roles (worker, parent, retiree etc.), to help them gain greater fulfillment in their personal lives, and to assist them in solving personal and community problems. (p. 9)

One of the most inclusive and comprehensive definitions of adult education was established in 1976 by the General Conference of the United Nations Educational, Scientific and Cultural Organization (UNESCO):

> The term adult education denotes the entire body of organized educational processes, whatever the content, level, and method, whether for-

mal or otherwise, whether they prolong or replace initial education in schools, colleges, and universities as well as apprenticeships whereby persons regarded as adult by the society to which they belong develop their abilities, enrich their knowledge, improve their technical or professional qualifications, or turn them in a new direction and bring about changes in their attitudes or behavior in the two-fold perspective of full personal development and participation in balanced and independent social, economic, and cultural development. (p. 2)

A more current definition, established by The Adult Education and National Literacy Act of 1991, states that adult education is a service to help out-of-school adults 16 years of age and older to: (a) acquire the literacy and language skills needed to function effectively in society; (b) benefit from job training and retraining in order to obtain and retain employment; and (c) continue their education to at least the level of high school completion. According to Kapel (1991):

Although there is confusion concerning what constitutes adult education, there appear to be some common characteristics: (1) the programs serve adults; (2) they may be offered by a variety of instructions, such as public schools, colleges, churches, technical intuitions, cooperative extension services, governments, industry, or professional associations; (3) they be may offered in a variety of settings and environments; (4) academic credit may or may not be given; (5) diplomats or certificates may be earned; (6) programs have unique goals and thrusts; (7) participants maybe males or females; (8) programs are found in almost every country of the world; and (9) most individuals pursuing adult education do not meet their own educational, emotional, or psychological needs. (p. 12)

HISTORY/LEGISLATION

History

No full understanding of the current educational situation in a nation is possible without knowledge of practices and theories that contributed to its growth. Only in the past two centuries has the field of adult education acquired a definite form of organization. In the last decade of the twentieth century nearly 40 million people enrolled in the programs of the U.S. Adult Education and Literacy System (AELS) (Sticht, 1998). It grew from several trends, such as the spread of public education, the stimulating effects of urbanization, and an increased interest in educational activities on the part of many older men and women (Sticht). Of the more than 31 million enrollees in the AELS from 1992 through 1999, 7.9 million were the working poor, more than 3.3 million were welfare recipients, 9.3 million were unemployed, and 2.2 million were incarcerated (U.S. Dept. of Education, 2000). More than two-thirds of the 15 million enrollees during 1992–1996 had not completed 12 years of education or received a high school diploma, and more than 3.4 million were immigrants (U.S. Dept. of Education, 1998).

It is likely that adult education in the United States started during the colonial period. Lyceum groups, which were an American association for popular instruction of adults featuring lectures, concerts, and other methods, were concerned with the dissemination of information on the arts, sciences, history, and public affairs. The earliest American forms of adult education were the public lectures given in the lyceum and at the Lowell Institute of Boston, endowed by John Lowell in 1836. In 1873 in Chautauqua, New York, John Heyl Vincent and Lewis Miller proposed to a Methodist Episcopal camp meeting that secular as well as religious instruction be included in the summer Sunday-school institute. Established on that basis in 1874, the Chautauqua institute evolved into an eight-week summer program offering adult courses in the arts, sciences, and humanities, somewhat resembling the lyceum movement.

In 1926 the Carnegie Corporation organized the American Association for Adult Education (AAAE), which later became the Adult Education Association of the U.S.A. From 1926 to 1941, the Carnegie Corporation provided administrative support for the AAAE, and funding mainly relied on membership dues. In 1951, the AAAE approached the Department of Adult Education of the National Education Association (NEA) to discuss the formation of a new association. This new association, now called the Adult Education Association of the United States of America (AEA/USA), is a major vehicle for promoting the professionalization of adult education.

In 1952, the National Association of Public School Adult Educators (NAPSAE) was formed as an affiliate of the AEA/USA. In 1953, NAPSAE also affiliated with the NEA, and in 1955 it dropped its affiliation with the AEA/USA and became a department of the NEA, with full strength of the NEA's strong lobbying experience behind it (Knowles, 1977). While the National Commission on Adult Literacy was lobbying for a federal adult literacy program in the late 1950s, the NAPSAE/USA was lobbying for an Adult Education Act that would help professionalize the adult education field.

Federally subsidized adult education, as we think of it today, was a mandate for the education of adults as part of the Economic Opportunity Act of 1964. In 1966 it became known as the Adult Education Act, which was extended several times since, most recently in 1991. The act had three purposes: (1) to enable all adults to acquire basic skills; (2) to enable adults who so desire to continue their education to at least the level of completion of secondary school; and (3) to make available to adults the means to secure training that will enable them to become more employable, productive, and responsible citizens. In addition to funds for ABE programs, the Adult Education Act currently includes programs for the unemployed, immigrants, minority groups and women with special needs, institutionalized adults, older adults, and individuals with disabilities.

Four amendments to the Adult Education Act of 1966 contributed to the growth of the AELS over the last third of the twentieth century. In 1970, amendments to the Adult Education Act of 1966 lowered the age of those who could participate from eighteen to sixteen years. Also in 1970, amendments expanded educational services to go beyond ABE for those students with fewer than nine years of education, those who spoke English as a second language, or those who wanted citizenship classes. New provisions were included for adult students desiring to complete high school or pass the GED. In 1978, amendments expanded services beyond the school-based definitions of basic skills—such as "ninth grade" or "high school"—to include a functional, competency-based definition for adults who might have high school diplomas but whose basic skills were considered too low to permit them to function well in society. In 1988, amendments further expanded services to permit partnerships with business, labor unions, and educators to provide workplace literacy programs for employees with limited basic skills (Rose, 1991; U.S. Dept. of Education, 1991).

Another factor contributing to the growth of the AELS during this period was a large influx of immigrants that created heavy demand for English-language education, especially from 1981 to 1990, when some 7.3 million immigrants came to the United States (Sticht, 1998). In addition to the amendments that expanded the number of adults entitled to services under the Adult Education Act of 1966, several amendments expanded the number of education service providers eligible for funding through the act. The major changes are described by Rose (quoted in Moore & Stavrianos, 1995, p. 5):

- Amendments in 1968 permitted state grants to private nonprofit agencies in addition to the public schools and public nonprofit agencies already eligible to receive state grants.

- Amendments in 1978 required state plans to describe how the delivery of educational services could be expanded beyond schools, particularly by public or private nonprofit organizations, and to reach out to those least educated and most in need.

- Amendments in 1984 allowed grants to for-profit agencies.

- Amendments in 1988 permitted special grants to workplace literacy programs, English literacy programs, and programs for commercial drivers, migrant farm workers, and immigrants.

- The National Literacy Act of 1991 (Public Law 102-73) replaced the Adult Education Act of 1966 and further encouraged the expansion of the number of nonprofit education providers eligible for federal funds by including a requirement that every provider in a state have "direct and equitable access" to federal basic grant funds.

The changes in the Adult Education Act, influencing the eligibility of adult populations and of service providers from 1966 to the end of the century, reflect the relative influence of three major groups. The first group consisted of professional associations of adult educators who advocated for the broad, liberal education of adults for self-improvement, which eventually became the contemporary call for "lifelong learning." This group followed the lead of the American Association of Adult Education (1926 to 1951) as it transformed first into the American Association of Adult Education in the United States of America (1951–1982) and then into the American Association of Adult and Continuing Education (1985–present).

Another influential group was made up of the associations for public school teachers and administrators, who were in favor of diverse educational programs for adults that would ultimately have equal footing with the K–12 system as part of a public adult education system. This group of mostly public school-based educators formed several professional associations of the National Education Association, Department of Adult Education (1924–1951), then the affiliate of the AEA/USA known as the National Association of Public School Adult Educators (1952). This group eventually became a part of the NEA and then became a separate organization known as the National Association for Public and Continuing Adult Education (NAPCAE). Continuing education was added to include the many community college educators who were engaging in noncredit adult education through divisions of continuing education. Other influential organizations include the Council of State Directors of Adult Education and the National Adult Education Professional Development Consortium (NAEPDC) (1990–present), established to provide state adult education staff a presence in Washington, DC.

In addition, many community-based adult educators followed in the footsteps of Cora Wilson Stewart and advocated for basic literacy education for adults. Among the groups exerting particularly strong influence over the last third of the century have been Laubach Literacy (1955–present; Laubach Literacy, 1999) and Literacy Volunteers of America, Inc. (1962–present; Colvin, 1992). The Commission on Adult Basic Education (COABE) (1971–present), which started as a part of the AAACE and is now a separate organization, has also been a strong advocate for adult basic literacy education (Campbell, 2000). In 1981, the National Coalition for Literacy was formed by 11 associations concerned with adult literacy education (Newman & Beverstock, 1990). By the end of the century it included more than 30 organizations and was firmly established as the primary advocacy organization for adult literacy education in the United States.

LEGISLATION/AUTHORITY

Funding

Federal funding and support for adult education have been provided through many legislative acts, including the Vocational Education Act (1963), the Economic Opportunity Act (19640, the Manpower Act (1965), the Adult Education Act (1966, amended 1970), the Comprehensive Training Act (1973), the Life Long Learning Act (1976), and, for a broader spectrum of learners, the Carl D. Perkins and Applied Technology Act of 1984. The office of Vocational and Adult Education, under the U.S. Department of Education, administers grants, contracts, and technical assistance programs for adult education, literacy, and occupational training. Most federal funding for these programs is administered through the states and individual communities. Other major federal providers of adult education include the Department of Agriculture and Department of Defense.

In 1965, the federal adult education program received federal funds of some $18.6 million for some 38,000 enrollments. By 1999, federal funds had increased to more than $365 million and enrollments to more than 3.6 million (Sticht, 1998). While the funding rate grew sporadically, enrollments appear to have grown at a fairly constant rate up to 1997. Over the years, the federal funding share of adult education has declined and the share of matching funds by states and local education agencies has increased. In 1966, federal funding for adult education was around $20 million for some 377,660 enrollees ($53 per enrollee), while state and local funding was around $10 million ($26 per enrollee). By 1998, federal funds for adult education had risen to more than $345 million for some 4 million enrollees ($89 per enrollee), while around $958 million ($240 per enrollee) was available for adult education from state and local matching funds (Sticht, 1998; U.S. Dept. of Education, 2000).

Federal funds allocated for adult education are determined by a formula based on the number of persons over age 16 who have not completed high school in each state. States distribute funds to local providers through a competitive process based on state-established funding criteria. Eligible providers include these local educational agencies; community-based organizations; correctional educational agencies; postsecondary educational institutions; public or private nonprofit agencies; institutions or organizations that are part of a consortium, including a public or private nonprofit agency; and organizations or institutions.

Personnel

The role of adult educator has been defined broadly. Among the adult educator role descriptions found in the literature are: teacher, instructor, helper, facilitator, consultant, broker, change agent, and mentor (Boud & Miller, 1998; Johnson, 1998). Adult educators have also been described as teachers and administrators in vocational programs and community colleges, human resource managers, corporate trainers, continuing educators, technical instructors, and computer trainers. Their job titles indicate the variety of adult education and training opportunities in both the private and public sectors.

Because of the variety of adult needs, adult education is very diverse in nature. There are many settings in which it is taught, and contemporary adult education can take many different forms. Colleges and universities have instituted evening programs, extension work, courses without credit, and correspondence courses. In addition, community colleges have been especially active in the area of distance learning programs (with courses transmitted by satellite to numerous locations). Organizations designed to relieve illiteracy are instrumental in adult education, as are the schools established to teach the English language and American customs to the foreign-born. Adult education is also sponsored by corporations, labor unions, and private institutes. The field now embraces such diverse areas as vocational education, high-school equivalency, parent education, adult basic education (including literacy training), physical and emotional development, practical arts, applied science, and recreation as well as the traditional academic, business, and professional subjects. Each year millions of Americans participate in these programs. At the local level, public schools have been active in furnishing facilities and assistance to private adult education groups in many communities. Community centers, political and economic action associations; and dramatic, musical, and artistic groups are regarded by many as adult education activities.

Training

By the first quarter of 2000, dozens of states were initiating and implementing standards and accountability systems to better monitor the effectiveness of adult basic education (ABE) programs. Training for adult education teachers varies from state to state. The U.S. Department of Education's development of a National Reporting System (NRS) and the accountability requirements contained in Title II (the Adult and Family Literacy Act) of the Workforce Investment Act of 1998 have reinforced a system of standards and accountability. The context of ABE content standards is changing, and the changes have implications for teacher standards and certification. A range of possibilities is open to states as they consider how best to certify or credential ADE educators, from accepting any level of K–12 certification to creating a unique and separate certification for adult teachers. Currently, 17 states require that anyone hired to teach ABE full- or part-time be a certified K–12 teacher. At least four states provide waivers for special circumstances; nine others require some form of adult certification. In three states teacher certification and an adult certification or other requirements are requisite.

Many factors have converged over the past decade to steadily accelerate the drive for professionalization in the field of adult literacy. In a number of states, professional development support and infrastructures have become well established, and efforts to codify these efforts in systems of certification are underway (Belzer, Drennon, & Smith, 2001; National Institute for Literacy, 2000).

PURPOSE/INTENT

Rationale

Life in the twenty-first century seems more complex than ever, as adults cope with the demands of multiple roles, the stresses of a fluid workplace, and the pressures of child and elder care. Individuals feel compelled to update their work-related knowledge and skills and to keep up with the proliferation of information. Family resource management is increasingly complex, with expanded choices and decisions that must be made about utilities, banking, investments, retirement planning, and so on. A long list of causes for these increased demands is easily found (Daly 2000; Niles, Herr, & Hartung, 2001): technological advances; the changing nature of work, workplaces, and working relationships; international economic competition; the changing demographics of workers, families, and communities; and longer life spans. The Internet has made it easier to access information yet more complicated to apply critical judgment to what one finds there. Furthermore, the trend of increasing numbers of older adults as a proportion of the total population is expected to continue: by 2030, a total of 20 percent of the United States' population will be age 65 or over (Digest of Education Statistics, 2001).

The stated goal of adult education for many practitioners in the field is bringing about social change and balancing all of the demands in our ever-changing society. Some believe it is a combination of these two goals that is the true objective of adult education. Researchers in the field state that social change is brought about through the education of the adult. Other goals include the self-actualization of the individual, or learning for learning's sake. Knowles (1977) states, "the mission of adult education is satisfying the needs of the individual institutions, and society" (p.15).

Utilization Criteria

To better understand the adult learner, one must look at the demographic makeup of adult participants, their reasons for participating in adult education programs, the different types of learners, and the environments that best suit these adult learners.

A recent publication by the National Adult Literacy Database (NALD) documents the demographics of those enrolled and participating in adult basic education (ABE), adult secondary education (ASE), and English-as-a-second language (ESL). In 1999, 44.5% of adults 17 years and older participated in some type of adult education program: 1.1% participated in ABE programs and .9% in ESL programs, 9.3% in part-time postsecondary education, and 22.2% in career- or job-related courses (Digest of Education Statistics, 2001). Also in 1999, 14.7% of adults 17 years old and older with an eighth-grade education or less participated in some education between ninth and twelfth grades (without a diploma); and 34.8% of those with a diploma participated in an adult education program (Digest of Education Statistics).

The NALD also offers the following information, which gives us a better idea of who today's adult learners are. The general trend in adult education participants' ethnicity has seen a decline in White (non-Hispanic) and Black adults from 1979 to 1993, and an increase in Hispanic and Asian participants. White participants dropped from 47% in 1979 to 36% in 1993, while

Black enrollments dropped from 23% in 1979 to 18% in 1993. During this same time period, Hispanic enrollments rose from 21 to 31%, an increase of 10%, and Asian enrollments jumped from 7% in 1979 to 14% in 1993. These changes paralleled the changes in enrollments in ABE, ASE, and ESL (Digest of Education Statistics, 2001).

To define the goal of adult education, experts in the field have compiled typologies that describe the stated goals (Dwyer, 2004). This compilation reveals a common thread of goals that can be summarized in five categories:

1. *Liberal*—the studies of the humanities and of social and natural science. Knowledge valued for its own sake, the goal is to be an educated person;

2. *Work-related*—occupational or vocational career development;

3. *Relational*—programs in which personal growth is a priority. The aim is to develop effective relationships, provide leadership training, and improve self-esteem, or foster self-actualization efforts and offer learning related to home, family, and leisure;

4. *Compensatory*—literacy and adult basic education; and

5. *Political*—adult education activities related to citizenship responsibilities in a democracy. Teach civil and social responsibility, and support and maintain good social order. This is also used for cultural criticism, social action, and social transformation (adult education) (Dwyer, 2004).

The educational threshold of American society is on the rise, and a high school education has become the minimum educational standard. For those who do not attain this level of education, adult basic and secondary education is likely to be the only way out of this educational underclass. The idea of "getting ahead" in America is still based on education, and those who aspire to get a better job or advance their current economic status are encouraged to raise their level of education to at least the minimum standard, and often higher.

Adult education is increasingly becoming a work-related phenomenon. Given advancements in technology and heightened education requirements to get a job or to "move up the corporate ladder," continuous improvement in knowledge and skills is necessary. In addition, many jobs require obtaining or renewing a license or certificate, which makes it understandable that the workplace is quickly becoming the fuel that is changing the nature of adult education.

In the workplace, much of adult education is mandated by the employer or by the profession itself, such as with continuing education programs. The challenge with this type of required education is in making it a true learning experience for the participant and not a waste of time and resources for both the employer and employee. Adults participate in learning for their social welfare and other cognitive interests, partially as a result of society's becoming more egalitarian, the increasing need for a second income, the passage of affirmative action legislation, the feminist movement, and, generally, the growing recognition that gender is rarely a predictor of effectiveness on the vast majority of jobs.

Also, the idea of improving oneself through education is a growing trend. This is especially true for older, retired Americans who want to keep themselves "sharp" and perhaps fulfill a long held desire for higher education. Adults of all ages have diverse interests and need or want to attend an adult education program to pursue them—for example, community courses in history or technology, cooking, or parenting classes, health and wellness, foreign language, home improvement, or pet obedience.

Special Case-Management Needs

Collaboration has become the byword of the 1990s as a strategy for systemic change in human services, education, government, and community agencies. Increasingly, both public and private funding require collaborative efforts. The advent of block grants is creating an urgent need for integrated, locally controlled services. Shrinking resources are causing many organizations to consider the potential benefits of working together. States are looking at ways to integrate their economic, workforce, and technology development efforts (Bergman, 1995). Perhaps most important is the realization that the complex problems and needs of families, workers, and communities are not being met effectively by existing services that are "fragmented, crisis oriented, discontinuous, and episodic" (Kadel, 1991, p. vi). Collaboration involves more intense, long-term efforts than do cooperation or coordination. Collaborating agencies make a formal, sustained commitment to accomplishing a shared, clearly defined mission. Collaborative efforts can overcome such problems as fragmentation of client needs into distinct categories that ignore interrelated causes and solutions. They can make more services available or improve their accessibility and acceptability to clients (Melaville & Blank, 1993).

Technological developments have also affected adult learning research and theory building. In adult education, technology is emerging as both a delivery system and a content area. Although technology is used in adult literacy education for many purposes—information management, e-mail and electronic list communication, curriculum development, assessment, evaluation, and research, among others—one of its most important uses is to enable and strengthen teaching and learning.

CLIENT SERVICES

One-stop career centers are collaborative efforts among agencies that have traditionally provided employment and training services such as information, counseling, referral, and placement. U.S. Department of Labor funding has supported their development in several states. Before the federal initiative, a prototype arose in Waukesha, Wisconsin (Anderson, 1996), where the Workforce Development Center provides an integrated, seamless system of employment services through the joint efforts of nine public and private agencies, including the state job service, a technical college, child care center, labor organization, and county health and human services department. A foundation owns the building in which the combined agencies' staffs are located; a local area network, client-tracking software, and access to the state JobNet enables information sharing. The center has shortened the time and cost of dependency on public funds and given employers access to a worker pool.

The Learning Community (Bendle/Carman-Ainsworth City Schools, 1996) in Flint, Michigan, is an example of the trend toward integrated family service centers. From a collection of independent programs that began networking, it has grown into a formal collaboration that shares administrative resources and core services. Participants include the public school system, adult basic education, Head Start, Even Start, employment services, and community education programs. Adults have opportunities to improve academic, job, and parenting skills; find employment; and help their children learn. Children participate in educational and enrichment activities, and families are supported with child and health care, transportation, food, and clothing. Beyond its core service agencies, the Learning Community works with a variety of public and private human service agencies and businesses.

Ultimately, successful collaborations focus on changing the system, whether it be integrated family service delivery such as the Learning Community, one-stop career/employment services such as the Workforce Development Center (Anderson, 1996), or a learning consortium for small-business worker training such as the National Workforce Assistance Collaborative (Bergman, 1995). The key is the quality of personal and professional relationships among the people in the agencies and communities involved. People must recognize that collaborations require patience and trust, take time to build, and accommodate organizational and community cultures, and they must remain focused on the "big picture" of a better future for their constituencies.

The evolutionary nature of careers and the diverse and ongoing learning paths individuals take to realize their career goals is evident in the debate about the value of vocational certificates, associate degrees, and baccalaureate degrees. The need for education to have personal value is evident in the choices one makes. Requiring economic investment, as well as investments of personal time and effort, continuing education after high school must be seen as critical to one's career progression.

According to the National Alliance of Business (1998), new jobs in the twenty-first century will require higher levels of education. Marchese (1999) recommends that educational institutions look to their corporate and for-profit competitors to see how they incorporate career-based quality improvement and assessment as a means of ensuring industry-relevant competency. In this regard, four-year colleges, community colleges, corporate universities, professional societies, and private enterprises are all major competitors in the challenge to provide meaningful education and training to the current and future workforce.

References

Akin, M. (1992). Adult basic education. In *Encyclopedia of educational research* (Vol. 1, pp. 30–34). Farmington Hills, MI: Thomas Gale.

Anderson, R. T. (1996). *Beyond "one-stop shopping": An integrated service delivery system for job seekers and employers.* Pewaukee, WI: Waukesha County Workforce Development Center.

Belzer, A., Drennon, C., & Smith, C. (2001). Building professional development systems in adult basic education. In J. Comings, B. Garner, & C. Smith (Eds.), *Annual review of adult learning and literacy* (Vol. 2). San Francisco: Jossey-Bass.

Bendle/Carman-Ainsworth Community Schools. (1996). *The learning community: A pro-family system of education and community services.* Flint, MI: Author.

Bergman, T. (1995). *Approaches to forming a learning consortium.* Washington, DC: National Alliance of Business.

Boud, D., & Miller, N. (1998). Animating learning: New conceptions of the role of the person who works with learners. In J. C. Kimmel (Ed.), *39th annual adult education research conference proceedings.* San Antonio, TX: University of the Incarnate Word.

Campbell, A. (2000). *A brief history of the National Commission on Adult Basic Education.* Bryan, TX: Querida Enterprises.

Colvin, R. J. (1992). *A way with words: The story of Literacy Volunteers of America, Inc.* Syracuse, NY: Literacy Volunteers of America.

Daly, K. (2000). *It keeps getting faster: Changing patterns of time in families.* Ottawa, Ontario: Vanier Institute of the Family.

Darkenwald, G. G., & Merriam, S. B. (1982). *Adult education: Foundations of practice.* New York: Harper and Row.

Digest of Education Statistics. (2001). *Postsecondary education.* Retrieved February 20, 2004, from http://www.ed.gov/index.jhtml

Dwyer, R. J. (2004) Employee development using adult education principles. *Industrial and Commercial Training 36*(2), 79–85.

General Conference of the United Nations Educational, Scientific and Cultural Organization. (1976). *Recommendations on the development of adult education.* Retrieved March 1, 2004, from http://www.niace.org.uk/Information/Lifelong_Learning/Adult_education.htm

Johnson, R. (1998, July). Adult learning in a civil society—Exploring roles for adult educators? In *Papers from the 28th Annual SCUTREA Conference. Research, Teaching and Learning: Making Connections in the Education of Adults.* Exeter, England: University of Exeter.

Kadel, S. (1991). *Interagency collaboration: Improving the delivery of services to children and families.* Tallahassee, FL: Southeastern Regional Vision for Education.

Kapel, D. (1991). Adult education. In *American educator's encyclopedia* (Vol. 1, p. 12). Westport, CT: Greenwood.

Knowles, M. S. (1977). *A history of the adult education movement in the United States.* Melbourne, FL: Krieger.

Laubach Literacy. (1999). *Only the educated are free—Epictetus.* Syracuse, NY: Author.

Marchese, T. (1999, March–April). The certificates phenomenon. *Change, 31,* 4

Melaville, A. I., & Blank, M. J. (1993). *Together we can: A guide for crafting a profamily system of education and human services.* Washington, DC: U.S. Department of Education and U.S. Department of Health and Human Services.

Moore, M., & Stavrianos, M. (1995, June). *Review of adult education programs and their effectiveness: A background paper for re-authorization of the Adult Education Act.* Submitted to U.S. Department of Education. Washington, DC: National Institute for Literacy.

National Alliance of Business. (1998, Summer). The multifaceted returns to education. *Workforce economic trends*. Washington, DC: Author. (ERIC Document Reproduction Service No. ED419983.)

National Institute for Literacy. (2000). *The professionalization of adult education: Can state certification of adult educators contribute to a more professional workforce?* Washington, DC: Author.

Newman, A., & Beverstock, C. (1990). *Adult literacy: Contexts and challenges*. Newark, DE: International Reading Association.

Niles, S. G., Herr, E. L., & Hartung, P. J. (2001). *Achieving life balance*. Columbus: ERIC Clearinghouse on Adult, Career, and Vocational Education, Center on Education and Training for Employment, The Ohio State University.

Sticht, T. (1998, September). *Beyond 2000: Future directions for adult education*. Washington, DC: Division of Adult Education and Literacy, U.S. Department of Education.

Sticht, T., & Armstrong, W. (1994). *Adult literacy in the United States: A compendium of quantitative data and interpretive comments*. Washington, DC: National Institute for Literacy.

U.S. Department of Education. (1991). *History of the Adult Education Act: An overview*. Washington, DC: Office of Vocational and Adult Education, Division of Adult Education and Literacy.

U.S. Department of Education. (1998). *Adult education: Human investment impact 1992–1996*. Washington, DC: Office of Vocational and Adult Education, Division of Adult Education and Literacy.

U.S. Department of Education. (2000). *State-administered adult education program: Program year 1992–1999*. Washington, DC: Office of Vocational and Adult Education, Division of Adult Education and Literacy.

Special Education

Debra A. Harley & Kristine Jolivette

Special education is a discipline that encompasses various specialties (e.g., behavior disorders, learning disabilities, mental retardation, developmental disabilities). The meaning and significance of special education often is unclear to persons who have not formally studied or been actively involved in the area for some reason (e.g., consumer, parent, advocate). Frequently, special education is marked by semantic and philosophical differences surrounded by a plethora of terminology used to communicate in the field. In addition to the perplexing nomenclature, constant change occurring in labels, technology, delivery systems, policy, funding, and legislation causes continuous ambiguity and confusion. The interaction of and resistance to these potent factors work against development of an understanding of special education as a discipline or practice.

The purpose of the chapter is to decode and clarify the dimensions and intent of special education as a discipline and a practice. First, information is provided on the meaning and scope of special education. Second, national legislation and subsequent amendments, including funding sources, are discussed. Next, a review of the expansion of populations served in special education is highlighted, with examples of typical questions as part of the referral process. Fourth, the service delivery system for students with disabilities is presented. Finally, the interface between special education and rehabilitation is discussed. The chapter concludes with implications for the future and next direction in special education.

THE MEANING AND SCOPE OF SPECIAL EDUCATION

A functional understanding of the meaning and scope of special education can be achieved through assimilation of concepts related to key terminology. The integration of important concepts provides the basis for a theoretical, as well as practical, understanding of what can be a complex and puzzling education enigma. The phrase *special education* once referred to an area of specialization in the education profession. Most frequently it was used to connote the existence of an activity or a specific program option within the broad spectrum of the overall educational system. Meyen and Skrtic (1988) extended the meaning by including functionality in their definition. They define special education as follows:

> a broad term covering programs and services for children who deviate physically, mentally, or emotionally from the normal to an extent that they require unique learning experiences, techniques, or materials in order to be maintained in the regular classroom, or specialized classes and programs if the problems are more severe. (p. 592–593)

Another definition frequently referenced in the literature is credited to the United States Office of Education (USOE, 1977). That definition indicates that special education is

> specially designed instruction, at no cost to the parent, to meet the unique needs of a handicapped child, including classroom instruction, instruction in physical education, home instruction, and instruction in hospitals and institutions. (p. 42478)

The USOE definition accentuates the breadth of the delivery system for special instruction and indicates that it is "free" to parents. Both definitions above provide a rather perfunctory understanding of special education. A clear, functional understanding of the meaning of special education is hardly possible without integration of the meaning of other key terms. Related terminology used today includes "special needs" and "children, youth, and persons with disabilities." These terms provide additional substance for understanding special education as a discipline, and they append a utilitarian perspective to the profession. Both are common terms that allude to a wide range of individuals who do not meet expectancy in terms of "typical" or "normal" growth and development. Not meeting expectancy should be viewed along both sides of a behavioral and intellectual continuum, with gifted students at the upper limits and retardation at the lower limits.

Increased human rights advocacy (e.g., civil suits) and political forces (e.g., formation of professional-parent organizations; International Council for Exceptional Children [CEC]), elevated respect for the dignity of persons with disabilities. Carefully considered language, incorporated in federal and state legislation, repudiates use of the terms synonymously. Now, first-person language is used to describe the individual first and a characteristic, such as a disability, second. An illustration of first-person language specific to special education is "Jessi, who has a speech and language impairment" instead of "language-impaired Jessi." In addition, federal law has replaced the phrase "handicapped children" with "children with disabilities" to further promote societal respect for persons with disabilities. The sanctioned terminology used by the federal government also has reflected societal shifts, as illustrated in the landmark legislation Education for All Handicapped Children Act of 1975 (EHA) and its subsequent renaming in October 1990 as the Individuals with Disabilities Education Act (IDEA). This positive humanistic force has encouraged society to discontinue or deemphasize terminology that perpetuates negative connotations and promotes a disposition known as *handicappism*. Handicappism is manifested as a set of ideas, assumptions, and practices that promote different and unequal treatment of people due to visible or presumed physical, mental, and/or behavioral differences (Meyen & Skrtic, 1988).

HISTORY/LEGISLATION

The field of special education and our knowledge of disabilities have led to the evolution of multiple national initiatives that mandate the provision of appropriate services to those with disabilities within and across learning environments. Forces within and outside the field of special education have guided this evolution. Federal and state legislation has exerted tremendous influences on how, when, and what type of delivery is received by those who are eligible for special education services. The earliest legislation to provide services for individuals with disabilities, dating back more than a century and a half, aimed at providing institutional care or rehabilitative services to specific disability types.

Specific state and federal laws that mandate services for individuals with disabilities drive current practices in special education. In essence, it is no longer permissible to exclude students with disabilities from school, provide them with unequal educational opportunities, and treat them negatively, differentially. In November of 1975, the U.S. Congress passed the Education of All Handicapped Children Act (EHA; P.L. 94-142). This piece of legislation capitalized on prior outcomes of court cases and state and federal legislation to generate a national law with broad reaching effect—reaching every school-age child in the nation who has a disability. The law was a blueprint for educational reform for students with disabilities. Major provisions in the law targeted past educational practices that were blatantly unfair, discriminatory, and resulted in undue, lasting, harmful effects on the nation's population. Students with disabilities could no loner be erroneously labeled, "silently" barred from public school programs, or segregated in isolated classrooms apart from their peers without disabilities without appropriate reason or justification. The following section includes a discussion of the present IDEA (1997) and the protections afforded to students with disabilities.

Individuals with Disabilities Education Act (IDEA)

First, all rights and protections were extended to preschoolers with disabilities by mandating a free and appropriate education for all children ages three to five, and a new early intervention program for infants and toddlers, birth through two years of age, was established. Through amendments, Congress also established new state grant programs for infants and toddlers with disabilities. This provision does not mandate that states must provide services to all infants and toddlers who are developmentally delayed, but it does establish strong financial incentives for state participation.

Second, the disability categories under which students with disabilities can be identified have been expanded. Thirteen categories have been defined for identification and eligibility purposes. These categories now include these:

- specific learning disability (SLD, commonly referred to as a communication disorder or CD in the literature);
- speech and language impairments (S/L);
- mental retardation (MR, range of mild to profound);
- emotional disturbance (ED, commonly referred to as emotional and behavioral disorder or EBD in the literature);
- other health impairments (OHI);
- multiple disabilities;
- autism;
- orthopedic impairments (OI);
- hearing impairments (HI, range of mild to profound);
- developmental delay (DD, for children ages three to nine years);
- visual impairments (VI, range of low vision to blindness);
- traumatic brain injury (TBI); and
- deaf-blindness (a combination).

Third, the description of allowable disciplinary actions and procedures has been clarified. However, this text is frequently discussed and debated whenever reauthorization occurs and is currently underway. When students with disabilities engage in inappropriate behaviors that defy school rules, the school begins the manifestation determination process to assess whether the inappropriate behavior was due to the student's disability or not. The result of the manifestation determination provides the school with two appropriate actions. One, if the inappropriate behavior was due to the student's disability, the school continues to deliver services as written in the IFSP or IEP. Second, if the behavior was not due to the student's disability, the school may impose disciplinary actions such as those that would have been taken if the student did not have a disability. If the latter is the case, the student may be suspended and/or their placement changed, but the school is still legally obliged to continue delivering the services outlined in the student's IFSP or IEP, no matter where the student is being educated (e.g., home). When a student with a disability has a history of or the potential to engage in inappropriate behaviors, the behavior intervention plan (BIP) needs to be written and implemented based on behavioral assessments. A BIP should include evidence-based strategies and interventions that teach the student appropriate replacement behaviors within a positive behavioral support environment.

Fourth, the provisions outlined in current legislation have been expanded and clarified for purposes of identifying and implementing an appropriate education for the student with disabilities. There are six major provisions outlined in the 1997 Amendments to IDEA and each is listed and briefly described below.

Zero Reject. This provision states unequivocally that students with disabilities be educated. In particular, the severity or complexity of an individual's disability is not cause for denying him/her an education. In addition, students with disabilities aged six to seventeen will be provided with an education; if outside that age range, if the state provides educational services to students without disabilities then the students with disabilities are to be afforded with an education too. Under zero reject, states also engage in Child Find activities in which they canvas the state for individuals who may have disabilities but have not already been identified as such.

Nondiscriminatory Identification and Evaluation. This provision provides guidelines on the procedures states may follow when identifying students potentially eligible for special education, and for the continuous evaluation of students already identified as having a disability. The premise of nondiscriminatory identification and evaluation center on assessment (a) that is conducted by a multidisciplinary team using multiple tools, (b) the tools used are provided in the individual's native language, and (c) the tools are free of cultural and racial biases.

Free, Appropriate Public Education (FAPE). This provision is complex and encapsulates many of the key components of current legislation. FAPE in its name requires that states provide students with disabilities with an education appropriate to meet their needs, confer educational benefits, and that is free of charge. In addition, each student identified will have either an *individual family service plan (IFSP)* if the student is three years or younger or an *individual education plan (IEP)* if the student is between the ages of 3 and 21, with each of these plans outlining the individually designed instruction the child/student will receive. The IFSP focuses on the needs of the child and family and provides assistance with coordinating all services identified between agencies and the family. The IEP focuses on the needs of the student in relation to services provided in school. Under the auspices of the IFSP and IEP, a *behavior intervention plan (BIP)* also is written if social deficits and/or excesses are identified, and an *individual transition plan (ITP)* also may be written if transitions from grades (e.g., preschool to kindergarten) or from adolescence to adulthood (e.g., age fourteen or older) are occurring. Guidelines for the necessary components for an appropriate IFSP, IEP, BIP, and ITP are provided in detail in IDEA. Both the IFSP and IEP, and any subsequent plans, are written by a multidisciplinary team that includes family members and, when appropriate, the student. Under FAPE and embedded within a student's IFSP or IEP are related services required to meet the needs of the student. Services defined and allowable under IDEA include audiology, counseling, medical services, physical therapy, occupational therapy, orientation and mobility, parent counseling/training, rehabilitation counseling, recreation, transportation, assistive technology and devices, psychological therapy, and social work (IDEA 34, C.F.R. § 300.13).

Least Restrictive Environment (LRE). This provision outlines a continuum of educational placements in which students with disabilities may be educated, with a focus on educating students with disabilities alongside their peers without disabilities. One end of this continuum (least) is the general education classroom, and the other end (most) is a hospital or institutional setting. The unique needs of the student are what assist the multidisciplinary team in making placement issues. In recent years, the specific placements offered on the continuum have changed, primarily in combining general education classrooms with consultation and/or collaboration with a special education teacher. In the past, students with disabilities were excluded from the general education classroom and curriculum; however, present law states that a justification be written by the team if the student is to be excluded from either.

Due Process and Procedural Safeguards. This provision is the outgrowth of disagreements between schools and families and the unfair, unilateral decision-making processes of the past. A set of safeguards is now outlined that focuses on parental notification, consent, evaluation and assessment decisions, and access to student records. These safeguards also describe the process in which schools and families may engage when disagreements arise. In addition, monetary compensation for attorney's fees if the disagreement goes to court and for private schooling and services has been clarified.

Parental and Student Participation. This provision clarifies the roles of families and students, when appropriate, in the decision-making process for all aspects of a student's education. Families and students, when appropriate, are to be active participating members of IFSP and IEP teams. This means that they are notified of and are invited to team meetings in which their opinions, concerns, and questions can be heard and addressed, and that schools engage both parents and students in the decision-making process.

No Child Left Behind

Recently, a new federal law called *No Child Left Behind* (U.S. Dept. of Education, 2002) was passed by Congress that clarifies the roles of the federal government and the provisions of the Elementary and Secondary Education Act (ESES, 1965). This law redefines academic and social achievement goals for all children and youth with disabilities through specific provisions outlined for K–12 schools. The major provisions of NCLB have implications not only for the educational services provided to all children and youth but also for how and what services schools will provide. One provision under NCLB is that schools are expected to provide reading instruction so that every child will be able to read by the end of third grade (U.S. Dept. of Education, 2002). Another provision is that all children and youth will be taught by a "highly-qualified teacher" by the year 2005. Other major provisions include assessment of student reading and math abilities to demonstrate achievement, and families' options to move their children from failing and/or unsafe schools to higher-performing, safer schools. Meeting the provisions set forth in NCLB will be challenging to schools. More specifically, meeting the unique needs of students with disabilities (e.g., those with reading or behavioral problems) as outlined in both IDEA (1997) and NCLB remains a concern for advocates for those with disabilities, such as the Council for Exceptional Children.

In addition to the legislation discussed above, other federal laws affect special education and students with disabilities and exceptional learning needs. These include two types of laws: (a) those that create an entitlement or authorize services (i.e., Rehabilitation Act and Tech Act), and (b) those that prohibit discrimination against, and because of, disabilities (i.e., Section 504 and the Americans with Disabilities Act [ADA]) (Turnbull, Turnbull, Shank, & Smith, 2004). "Basically, IDEA and the Rehabilitation Act deal respectively with education and training for employment, while Section 504 and ADA make sure that the students can put their education and training to use through the IEP and its transition provisions" (Turnbull et al., 2004, p. 36).

SPECIAL EDUCATION POPULATIONS

The number of children and youth with disabilities being served under IDEA continues to steadily increase. Increases may be due to a variety of factors such as the addition of a disability category (e.g., developmental disability), better identification tools and increased success of child-find practices (i.e., the identification of young children with disabilities in need of services), and federal incentives to educate all students. The *Twenty-third Annual Report to Congress on the Implementation of the Individuals with Disabilities Education Act* (U.S. Dept. of Education, 2001) indicates that during the 1999–2000 school year, 588,300 preschoolers with disabilities and 5,683,707 students with disabilities aged 6 to 21 years received special education services under Part B of IDEA. In addition, 205,769 preschoolers with disabilities received special education services under Part C of IDEA. The number of students in all three age groups has steadily increased each year, with a 2.6% increase from the previous school year for students with disabilities aged 6 to 21.

According to the *Twenty-third Annual Report to Congress,* four disability categories continue to compromise the bulk of those students served. During the 1999–2000 school year, 50.5% of those with disabilities were served under the category of specific learning disability, 19.2% under speech and language impairment, 10.8% under mental retardation, and 8.3% under emotional disturbance (U.S. Dept. of Education, 2001). These four disability categories are typically referred to as high-incidence given the number of students served under them. One disability category, developmental delay, has had the highest increase in the number of students served. This increase may be due to more states using that category to provide services to children three to nine years of age. Race and gender differences consistently interface with the data on disability categories and the age identified for services (U.S. Dept. of Education, 2001). For example, more African American males are identified for emotional disturbance than their White male and female and African American female counterparts. Another example is that 20% fewer African American students with disabilities graduate as compared with their white counterparts. In addition, the identification of white preschoolers with disabilities decreased in the 1999–2000 school year as an increase in the number of Hispanic preschoolers occurred. Overall, two times more males are served under IDEA than females (Heward, 2003).

Given the wide range of exceptional learning needs of students served, understanding the referral process of special education is critical. The process is sequential and includes prerequisites for each phase. Following is an example of typical questions related to the referral process asked by parents and professionals. Although not an exhaustive list, these questions serve to guide educators and human service professionals in the process. Parents frequently ask the following questions: Is my child eligible for special education services and what does that mean? For what type of related services does my child qualify? Who will pay for special education and related services? Professionals may ask the following questions: For which disability category is the child eligible? How old does the child have to be for rehabilitation counselors to get involved with the special education process? How can community-based agencies be involved in the special education process to make sure that each agency and service is a part of the referral process? Who will serve as the point of coordination of services?

SERVICE DELIVERY SYSTEM

Students with disabilities are educated in a variety of settings under IDEA (1997) with emphasis on the delivery of instruction in the *least restrictive environment* (LRE). In selecting placements for students with disabilities, it is necessary to follow the principles of LRE. The initial emphasis of service delivery was on a continuum of services (e.g., cascade) within the LRE for students with disabilities. There are at least seven levels of a continuum of services from least restrictive to most restrictive. These levels range from the general education classroom, general education classroom with consultative services, general education classroom with instruction and services, general education classroom with resource room services, full-time special education classroom, special school, and special-facilities nonpublic school (day or residential) (Lewis & Doorlag, 2003). Most students with disabilities are served in public schools with their peers without disabilities in the first four levels. That is, the majority of students with mild disabilities, including those with learning disabilities, mild mental retardation, speech and language disorders, and emotional disturbance spend some, if not all, of their school day in the general education classroom along with students without disabilities (Mastropieri & Scruggs, 2004). This delivery-system option is commonly referred to as a *stay-put* option.

Consultative services (levels 2 and 3) refer to a triadic process in which the consultant (special instructor or therapist) provides services (e.g., expert or professional advice) to the individual through a third party (e.g., teacher, parent, caregiver). In a *resource room* model (level 4), students with disabilities are *pulled out* of the general education class for a designated time period to receive specialized instruction (e.g., language, math, reading) in a resource room. Conversely, a *self-contained* model of instruction is one in which students receive all or most of their classroom instruction from special education teachers (level 5). Yet, these students still have opportunities to interact with peers without disabilities during recreational activities, such as music, lunch, and school events (Mastropieri & Scruggs, 2004). In some cases, the need for specialized instruction is such that a special school or other facility (levels 6 or 7) is required. At either of these levels, students with disabilities are able to receive more specialized and individualized services that increase the probability of maximizing their functional capabilities.

The *team* approach is another service delivery option, involving collaboration. This team typically consists of the special educator, general educator, related school personnel who will provide services to the student, an administrator or school representative, the parents or guardians of the student, school and/or student advocates, and the student (when appropriate). The special educator typically serves as the coordinator and point of contact for other team members regarding the provision of services for students with disabilities.

Collaboration is recognized as an approach that is beneficial across most areas of education and human service delivery (Harley, Tice, & Kaplan, 2000). "Collaboration is defined as a coordinated or united effort among individuals to solve a problem rather than as a vague, poorly defined process in which the primary outcome is improved affiliations and perceptions between individuals" (Sugai & Tindal, 1993, p. 19). Sugai and Tindal stress that the incorporation of collaboration into the service delivery approach of special education and human service programs is valuable for several reasons. First, it is characterized as a cooperative set of behaviors specifically directed at solving a problem. Second, collaboration is viewed as the outcome of an effective problem-solving activity and interaction. Overall, collaboration serves as the nexus for special education, vocational rehabilitations, and other human service agencies in the unified and holistic approach to service delivery.

More recently, the full-inclusive model has dominated discussion of service delivery models. *Full inclusion* refers to placing and serving students with disabilities, regardless of severity or type, entirely within the general education classroom for the entire school day (Crockett & Kauffman, 1998). However, full inclusion is not without controversy and is viewed as counterproductive to the philosophy of a continuum of services (Howard, Williams, Port, & Lepper, 2001). Proponents and opponents of both full inclusion and a continuum of services offer ample justification for and against both of these service delivery models.

The utilization of full inclusion has been variously justified by identifying social, philosophical, ethical, legal, and empirical arguments (Howard et al., 2001). Arguments of proponents of full inclusion indicate that inclusion is a civil right (e.g., children with disabilities have the right to be educated alongside peers without disabilities), reduces stigma (e.g., segregated classes and pull-out are stigmatizing), is more efficient (e.g., students lose valuable time from general education instruction and activities during pull-out times), and promotes equality (e.g., it is the fair, ethical, and equitable thing to do) (Mastropieri & Scruggs, 2004).

Opponents of full inclusion present arguments that sociological barriers exist, prohibiting ample justification for full inclusion with concomitant implementation (Howard et al., 2001). Gerrard (1994) describes six major objections to inclusion. One, there is a lack of input by general educators. Two, there is a lack of empirical evidence to support effectiveness of full inclusion for all students. Three, there is practitioner resistance. Four, contradiction exists in educational reform in which educators are being pressed to improve educational achievement, while simultaneously schools are being pressured to be leaders in promoting equity. Five, separate schooling is necessary to protect students with disabilities from rejection by their peers without disabilities. Finally, any attempt to meet the needs of students with disabilities in the general education classroom is impractical. That is, specialized instruction and education cannot be conducted effectively in a general education setting.

A *continuum of services* "offers specialized, differentiated, individualized and intensive instruction, all of which are continuously evaluated for effectiveness" (Fuchs & Fuchs, 1998, p. 3). In fact, Fuchs and Fuchs defined inclusion as a continuum of services that depend on general classroom and various options in terms of special education placements and related services. Recent data show that placement of specifically designed instruction and where it is delivered to students with disabilities continue to occur in less restrictive environments, such as general education classrooms (U.S. Dept. of Education, 2001). According to the *Twenty-third Annual Report to Congress*, in the last decade there has been an increase from all age groupings between 6 and 21 years of students served under IDEA who receive services for less than 21% of the day outside a typical general education classroom. Interestingly, the data also suggest that African American students with disabilities are more likely to receive special education services in more restrictive placements (e.g., separate schools) than any other ethnicity of students with disabilities. In addition, students with emotional disturbance, mental retardation, and multiple disabilities are more likely to receive services in more restrictive settings for a larger percent of the school day as compared to students eligible for services in other categories (U.S. Dept. of Education, 2001).

SPECIAL EDUCATION AND REHABILITATION COUNSELING

Given their provision of services to persons with disabilities, the disciplines of special education and rehabilitation are indisputably interrelated. In fact, one can presume that special education and transition services for school-age children are a prelude to rehabilitation services for adults with disabilities. A distinction between education and rehabilitation has been sustained through definitions that refer to separate roles without pointing out their similarity or compatibility. The distinction routinely conveyed is that special education implies "a learning process" and rehabilitation implies "a readaptation process" (Bitter, 1979). Viewing the two service areas as separate limits the potential scope and magnitude of service provisions to persons with disabilities and impedes service and research advancement in both fields. However, past evidence (e.g., deBettencourt, Vallecorsa, & Flint, 1995; Fossey, Hosie, Soniat, & Zirkel, 1995) and a more recent focus (e.g., Edmondson & Cain, 2002; Harley et al., 2001) have stressed the need for interface and cooperation between special education and rehabilitation.

Legislatively (e.g., ADA, IDEA, Section 504) and practically (e.g., transition services, supported employment), special education and rehabilitation are connected and have interrelated responsibilities (Edmondson & Cain, 2002). The growing significance of Section 504 has made it important that general educators have a "working knowledge" of this and other special education laws (Fossey et al., 1995). In addition, the importance of transition services for students with disabilities in relation to positive adult outcomes has been espoused in the literature (Hanley-Maxwell & Szymanski, 1992). In fact, the mandate to provide transition services requires special educators to reach beyond traditionally defined parameters of school-based activities to provide services that relate to much broader, long-term goals (e.g., transition, community-based services). According to Edmondson and Cain, special education not only is responsible for assuring that transition services are provided to students with disabilities, they also are expected to collaborate with other agencies for the provision of these services. Clearly, by definition and intent, transition services are to be a coordination of services between special education and vocational rehabilitation (Edmondson & Cain, 2002; McMahan & Baer, 2001).

The two fields share linkages in several other ways. The most obvious link is the provision of services to persons with disabilities in order to maximize their functioning in the least restrictive/most inclusive environment. Special education works with persons from birth to age 21, while rehabilitation works with those who are at least 16 years of age because of its emphasis on employment. Although the age of the target group and service outcome differ, this difference is somewhat artificial at the upper age limits for special education and the lower age limits for rehabilitation.

Special education and rehabilitation share a formal approach to service planning and documentation. Both require a written plan of services. For special education, an IFSP is required for early childhood services, an IEP for school-aged children, an ITP for high school students, and an individual plan of employment (IPE) for rehabilitation consumers. Rehabilitation counselors typically serve as members of the transition team for students with disabilities. In many ways, the logical progression of services (e.g., IFSP, IEP, ITP, IPE) for persons with disabilities promotes *wrap-around planning* in which integrated services are provided through school and community-based agencies, validating the long-term benefits possible.

Vocational rehabilitation counseling also shares the utilization of consultation with special education as part of professional practice. Within special education, rehabilitation consultation can be an indirect service, and it is frequently interdisciplinary. The rehabilitation professional can provide either *expert consultation* (e.g., design and implementation of an intervention, with ultimate success of the intervention) or *process consultation* (e.g., partnership between the consultant and consultee to design and implement changes in which success is the responsibility of both parties) (Lynch, Habeck, & Sebastian, 1997).

Special education and vocational rehabilitation also are connected through the School-to-Work Opportunities Act (STWOA) of 1994. The U.S. Congress passed the STWOA to help states and local communities develop school-to-work transition programs to prepare *all* students for work and further education, and to increase their opportunities to enter high-skill careers. The STWOA includes a variety of school-based and work-based learning opportunities that elicit post-program planning and coordination of services among special education and vocational rehabilitation (Benz, Yovanoff, & Doren, 1997).

CONCLUSION

This chapter has provided background information and a framework for a functional understanding of special education as a service provider of students with disabilities, and its interrelationship with vocational rehabilitation. The future has certain implications for special education as a profession, practice, and field of research. Clearly, implications exist for the development of integrated curricula and across training of special educators, general educators, and vocational rehabilitation personnel (Edmondson & Cain, 2002). States must adjust their teacher preparation programs to respond to students as they matriculate in school and transition into the community. Similarly, placement issues of students with disabilities need to reinforce the various components of service delivery to support life changes across their life span. Concomitantly, wrap-around services in school and vocational rehabilitation must be linked effectively to outcomes. Finally, the provisions in IDEA should more precisely define what is meant by highly qualified personnel and clarify how the law is connected with qualifications of related service personnel. Administrative, artificial, and procedural barriers to effective service delivery must be removed in order to facilitate the process of true collaboration. As educators and service providers, we must realize that tomorrow's outcomes for individuals with disabilities are only as good as today's services.

References

Benz, M. R., Yovanoff, P., & Doren, B. (1997). School-to-work components that predict postschool success for students with and without disabilities. *Exceptional Children, 63*, 151–165.

Bitter, J. A. (1979). *Introduction to rehabilitation.* St. Louis: C.V. Mosby.

Crockett, J. B., & Kauffman, J. M. (1998). Taking inclusion back to its roots. *Educational Leadership, 56*, 74–77.

deBettencourt, L. U., Vallecorsa, A. L., & Flint, R. (1995). Counselor preparation: Training in providing transitional services to students with disabilities. *The Learning Consultant Journal, 14*, 10–18.

Edmondson, C. A., & Cain, H. M. (2002). The spirit of the Individuals with Disabilities Education Act: Collaboration between special education and vocational rehabilitation for the transition of students with disabilities. *Journal of Applied Rehabilitation Counseling, 33*, 10–14.

Education of All Handicapped Children Act, 20 U.S.C. § 1471 et seg. (1975).

Fossey, R., Hosie, T., Soniat, K., & Zirkel, P. (1995). Section 504 and "front line" educators: An expanded obligation to serve children with disabilities. *Preventing School Failure, 39*, 10–14.

Fuchs, D., & Fuchs, L. S. (1998). Competing visions for educating students with disabilities: Inclusion versus full inclusion. *Childhood Education, 74*, 309–316.

Gerrard, L. C. (1994). Inclusive education: An issue of social justice. *Equity and Excellence in Education, 27*, 58–67.

Hanley-Maxwell, C., & Szymanski, E. M. (1992). School-to-work transition and supported employment. In R. M. Parker & E. M. Szymanski (Eds.), *Rehabilitation counseling: Basics and beyond* (2nd ed., pp. 135–163). Austin, TX: Pro-Ed.

Harley, D. A., Tice, K., & Kaplan, L. (2000). Professional border crossing: Implications of collaboration between vocational rehabilitation counselors and social workers in public schools to assist students with disabilities and families. *Journal of Rehabilitation Administration, 25*, 137–143.

Heward, W. L. (2003). *Exceptional children: An introduction to special education* (7th ed.). Upper Saddle River, NJ: Merrill.

Howard, V. F., Williams, B. F., Port, P. D., & Lepper, C. (2001). *Very young children with special needs: A formative approach for the 21st century.* Upper Saddle River, NJ: Merrill.

Lewis, R. B., & Doorlag, D. H. (2003). *Teaching special students in general education classrooms.* Upper Saddle River, NJ: Merrill.

Lynch, R. T., Habeck, R., & Sebastian, M. (1997). Professional practice: Consultation. In D. R. Maki & T. F. Riggar (Eds.), *Rehabilitation counseling: Profession and practice* (pp. 183–196). New York: Springer.

Mastropieri, M. A., & Scruggs, T. E. (2004). *The inclusive classroom: Strategies for effective instruction.* Upper Saddle River, NJ: Pearson.

McMahan, R., & Baer, R. (2001). IDEA transition policy compliance and best practice: Perceptions of transition stakeholders. *Career Development for Exceptional Individuals, 24*, 169–186.

Meyen, E., & Skrtic, T. (1988). *Exceptional children and youth* (3rd ed). Colorado: Love.

No Child Left Behind Act (NCLB). (2002). P.L. 107-110.

Sugai, G. M., & Tindal, G. A. (1993). *Effective school consultation: An interactive approach.* Pacific Grove, CA: Brooks/Cole.

Turnbull, R., Turnbull, A., Shank, M., & Smith, S. J. (2004). *Exceptional lives: Special education in today's schools* (4th ed.). Upper Saddle River, NJ: Merrill Prentice-Hall.

United States Department of Education. (2001). *Twenty-third annual report to Congress on the implementation of the Individuals with Disabilities Education Act.* Washington, DC: Author.

United States Department of Education. (2002). *No Child Left Behind Act of 2001.* Retrieved December 8, 2004, from http://www.ed.gove/offices/OSESE/esea

United States Office of Education (USOE). (1977, August 23). Implementation of part B of the Education of the Handicapped Act. *Federal Register, 42*, 42474–42518.

Centers for Independent Living

Robert F. Kilbury, Barbara J. Stotlar, & John M. Eckert

HISTORY

According to Lachat (1988), "Independent Living (IL) emerged as a concept in the 1960s with the creation of self-help networks among individuals with severe disabilities who were attempting to live in the community" (p. 1). Most agree the IL or disability rights movement began in Berkeley, California, when the administration at the University of California tried to prevent the late Ed Roberts from going to college there because he was "too disabled" (Levy, 1988). Roberts's vocational rehabilitation counselor had allegedly refused to pay for him to attend college because he was deemed to have "no vocational potential." Other historians point to the story of Judy Heumann, who despite passing the oral and written portions of the licensure examination for school teachers, was prohibited from applying her trade by the New York Board of Education because she could not pass the physical exam due to her disability (Levy).

Either way, it can be asserted with little fear of contradiction that the IL movement was begun more than thirty years ago by a segment of the disabled community—specifically, those with significant physical disabilities. Persons with polio, spinal cord injuries, multiple sclerosis, and cerebral palsy were among the early disability groups most widely represented (DeJong, 1979). These individuals were hindered by a world which was largely inaccessible to them, and they began to fight to change that world. Roberts eventually attended UC–Berkeley, initiated the Disabled Students' Program there, founded the first Center for Independent Living (CIL) within the community, was appointed director of the state vocational rehabilitation agency in California in 1976, and co-founded the World Institute on Disability (WID) prior to his death in 1995. Heumann won her lawsuit and worked as a teacher at her former elementary school in New York City prior to joining Roberts at the CIL in Berkeley in 1973. Heumann co-founded WID with Roberts and for a number of years served as assistant secretary of the Office of Special Education and Rehabilitative Services within the U.S. Department of Education for the Clinton Administration.

Such social movements as civil rights, women's rights, deinstitutionalization, demedicalization, consumerism, and self-help had profound influences on the IL movement (DeJong, 1979). In the past decade, the National Council on Independent Living (NCIL) recognized ten principles of independent living: advocacy, barrier-removal, civil rights, consumerism, consumer control, cross-disability, deinstitutionalization, demedicalization, peer role models, and self-help (NCIL, 1997). Independent living was both a reaction against and an alternative to the traditional vocational rehabilitation (VR) model, which had not always effectively served persons with significant disabilities. It can be thought of as both a social movement and a unique service delivery model.

While there are many definitions for IL programs, Frieden (1983) describes them as follows:

> a community-based program with substantial consumer involvement that provides directly or coordinates indirectly, through referral, services severely disabled individuals need to increase their self-determination and to minimize their dependence on others. (p. 62)

Several authors describe three types of IL programs: Centers for Independent Living (CILs), IL residential programs, and IL transitional programs (Frieden, 1983; Rubin & Roessler, 1987). While residential components are generally viewed as being inconsistent with the intent of the IL movement due to their segregatory nature, transitional and residential programs have nevertheless proven their worth throughout the history of rehabilitation. For the sake of clarity, however, this chapter will focus exclusively on CIL programs.

CILs are cross-disability, nonresidential, community-based, not-for-profit organizations run by a board of directors, 51% of whom must be persons with disabilities. CILs are mandated by the Rehabilitation Services Administration to provide the four core services of *advocacy, independent living skills training, information and referral* (I & R), and *peer counseling*. After the first true CIL was established by Roberts and Heumann in 1972 in Berkeley, California (Levy 1988; Rubin & Roessler, 1987), CILs emerged in Boston, Chicago, Houston, New York, and other major metropolitan areas. Today there are more than 430 nationwide (Independent Living Research Utilization Project, 2003).

LEGISLATION

The groundwork for federally funded CILs was laid by the passage of such legislation as the Architectural Barriers Act of 1968, the Urban Mass Transit Act Amendments of 1970, the historic Rehabilitation Act of 1973, and the Education of All Handicapped Children Act of 1975 (Goldman, 1985). Importantly, with its emphasis on civil rights, active participation of the consumer, and serving persons with the most significant disabilities, the Rehabilitation Act of 1973 paved the way for consumerism and empowerment in the field of rehabilitation. Section 504, patterned after the 1964 Civil Rights Act (Rubin & Roessler, 1987), reinforced the notion that people with disabilities had rights that should be protected by law. Specifically, it stated:

> No otherwise qualified handicapped [sic] individual in the United States
> . . . shall, solely by reason of his handicap [sic], be excluded from participation in, be denied the benefits of, or be subjected to discrimination under any program or activity receiving federal financial assistance. (Sherman & Zirkel, 1980, p. 331)

Widely described as the Bill of Rights for persons with disabilities, Section 504 took several years to be written and has never been adequately implemented or enforced (Rubin & Roessler, 1987). In fact, it was only after nationwide demonstrations by individuals with disabilities that Joseph Califano, then secretary of Health, Education, and Welfare, finally signed the federal regulations pursuant to the Section on April 28, 1977 (Levy, 1988). Through that empowering effort, people with disabilities discovered that they had a potent voice. They also learned that in order to attain their rights, coordinated advocacy would be required.

A continuation and expansion of this empowerment led to the passage of the landmark Americans with Disabilities Act of 1990, signed by President George Herbert Walker Bush on July 26, 1990. Americans with disabilities also were integrally involved in the health-care reform debates of the early 1990s and had considerable influence on the creation of the Workforce Investment Act of 1998, the Ticket to Work and Work Incentives Improvement Act of 1999, and the Help America Vote Act of 2002.

Funding

While Section 130 of the Rehabilitation Act of 1973 provided for several demonstration grants for CILs, it was not until the passage of the Rehabilitation, Comprehensive Services, and Developmental Disability Amendments of 1978 that CILs were legislatively legitimized by the appropriation of federal funds (Rubin & Roessler, 1987; Valera, 1983). Valera (1983) describes this legislation as "the single most far-reaching piece of legislation ever offered to the disability community" (p. 45). The law mandated that citizens with disabilities be involved in the management, direction, and provision of services in these centers (Laurie, 1979).

Title VII of the 1978 amendments provided federal funding which enabled CILs to proliferate in the late 1970s and early 1980s. Part A of Title VII provided monies for state rehabilitation agencies to develop IL programs. Part B monies allowed these agencies and other entities to start CILs. Part C, not funded until 1986, was designed to provide IL services to older, blind individuals (Rubin & Roessler, 1987). It is important to note that the total of all three portions of this funding amounted to only $40 million in 1986, a tiny initiative compared to the Vocational Rehabilitation (VR) program. The 1992 amendments brought the creation of statewide independent living councils charged with developing in conjunction with the state's VR agency the State Plan for Independent Living, which maps the expansion of CILs and the provision of IL services in the state. In 1998, the Workforce Investment Act of 1998 was passed, including the amendments to the Rehabilitation Act in Title IV.

Personnel

All CILs are directed by a board of directors, which is responsible for setting policy for the organization as a service provider. As indicated, CIL boards are mandated to be comprised of a majority of persons with disabilities who reflect the community through their policy-making role. Some states go beyond this requirement by mandating that centers be membership organizations. In these instances, the board of directors is required to solicit involvement from consumers in the community (members), who in turn select the board.

Direct service and administrative staff are responsible for policy implementation and daily service provision. The backbone of all CILs is the direct service providers who implement the array of services described below. Service providers, while usually either full- or part-time paid employees of the CIL, may also be volunteers whose background or experience is particularly effective in dealing with a particular consumer's issue(s). Whether paid staff or volunteers, direct service providers are generally persons with disabilities who have encountered discrimination and barriers to independent living themselves.

Depending on the needs of their particular community and their level of funding, many CILs hire individuals who serve as independent living specialists, advocacy coordinators, housing or transportation specialists, personal assistant coordinators, deaf or blind services specialists, and other roles. With the passage of the ADA and Ticket to Work legislation, some CILs have also hired ADA accessibility specialists and even benefits planners.

PURPOSE/INTENT

The rationale for CILs is that individuals with disabilities are often the best resources in facilitating the consumer's (never to be referred to as *client* in

IL) choice of options. All too often, the VR system has been perceived by the disability community as being too narrow in its definition of "rehabilitation." With VR's primary focus on "vocational closure," other aspects of daily living are sometimes overlooked. Independent living has a more holistic view of rehabilitation and provides services that reflect this broader perspective.

Independent living focuses on serving individuals with significant disabilities, regardless of considerations of vocational rehabilitation potential. Such services promote empowerment, self-help, consumerism, and "changing the environment" rather than the individual. This orientation provides an alternative paradigm to VR.

Gerben DeJong (1983) provided a conceptualization of how IL and VR differ. While in VR the focus is on changing the individual "client" or "patient" by professional intervention (VR counselor, physical therapist, or physician); in IL the focus is on removing barriers to full participation and integration, reducing dependence on professionals, and facilitating the empowerment of the "consumer." In the VR model, the focus is on the individual with a disability; in the IL model, the focus is on the "disabling environment." In the former paradigm, the professional is in control; in the latter, the consumer of services assumes control over these services. Finally, the desired outcomes of VR include employment, maximizing activities of daily living, and improved motivation; in IL the goals include self-direction, placement into the most integrated setting appropriate to their needs, increased self-esteem, and social productivity.

CILs attempt, through both individualized and community-wide programs, to create a world that is more accessible for everyone. This might entail training an individual who is deaf to use a text telephone (TTY) so that they can call the police, fire department, hospital, or—through a communication assistant at an interstate relay center—the local pizza delivery restaurant. It might involve referring personal assistants to consumers so that they can hire a worker to provide the care they need to live in an apartment rather than in a nursing home or other institution. It could include assisting a consumer in finding a wheelchair-accessible apartment, or in filling out applications for employment or housing assistance, or in completing Medicaid or Social Security forms. Disability awareness presentations, which create a more accessible attitudinal environment, also epitomize this process.

Utilization Criteria

Should the human service provider have a consumer with a disability who might benefit from peer counseling or IL skills training (whether such training involves the use of adaptive equipment, computer technology, or attainment of entitlement programs), referral to a CIL would be appropriate. If the provider knows of a situation where an individual might benefit from housing or transportation assistance, the referral of a personal assistant, or TTY or braille training, a referral to a CIL would be appropriate. Additionally, CILs are equipped to deal with situations where the parent of a child with a disability receiving services under the Individuals with Disabilities Education Act would benefit from advocacy with the school system. If there is a need to determine whether your facility is fully accessible to and useable by individuals with a variety of disabilities, you should call a CIL for technical assistance. If you ever have a question about disability issues or policies and wonder: "What would a person with a disability think about this?", contact your local CIL.

Special Case-Management Needs

As all CIL services are consumer directed, active participation on the part of the individual with a disability in goal development and service delivery is critical for positive outcomes. While federal funding sources may require proof of disability for services to individuals (exceptions being services provided to family members, community outreach, and requests for I & R), most CILs also receive foundation, state, or local funding that is more discretionary in nature.

INDEPENDENT LIVING SERVICES

With the exception of the four core services required by federal law (advocacy, IL skills training, information and referral, and peer counseling), CILs pursue their mission through a variety of programs and services defined by the needs of individuals within the communities in a particular catchment area. For example, variables that may affect the menu of services provided include whether the catchment area is urban or rural, the type and scope of existing resources within the area, the sources of funding the CIL receives, and the priorities given to identified service needs by the consumers of such services. This diversity makes describing CIL service delivery from state to state, or even county to county, difficult. However, it is this flexibility to respond to the individual needs of the consumers residing in these communities that makes CIL services both effective and unique.

Persons considering referral to a CIL should contact the organization in their area for a listing of services provided. These services often can be ascertained through the Internet as well. The following sections are meant to encourage the reader to do so, as well as to acquaint the professional with common CIL services. This portion of the chapter begins with the four core services mandated by federal law and concludes with other services many CILs provide.

Advocacy

Ed Roberts was fond of saying, "The three most important things are advocacy, advocacy, and advocacy, not necessarily in that order." The provision of advocacy by CILs is therefore central to their mission and takes two distinct tacks. *Consumer* or *individual advocacy* includes an array of services that either train or support individual consumers or consumer groups in presenting their issues or needs to others in order to "achieve, maintain, or improve their independent living goals" (Budde, Lachat, Lattimore, Jones, & Stolzman, 1987, p. 11). The gist of such services is to assist individuals in attaining their rights, entitlements, or access to activities denied them on the basis of disability. Under some circumstances, and only on consumer request, CIL staff may act (temporarily) on an individual's behalf while at the same time providing whatever adjunct services are necessary to empower the individual to advocate on his or her own in the future.

Community or *systemic advocacy* includes services that articulate the position of the disabled community at the local, state, or federal level. This advocacy is provided to affect the removal of barriers and disincentives to integration and choice for persons with disabilities, the development of community options, or changes in policy that are disabling to the populations served by the CIL (Budde et al., 1987). An excellent example of systemic advocacy has been the recent participation of CIL staff in the development of state Olmstead Plans, consistent with the U.S. Supreme Court *Olmstead v. LC* (1999) case. This important decision required states to provide services "in the most integrated setting appropriate to the needs of qualified individuals with disabilities" (*Olmstead v. LC*, 1999, 6).

IL Skills Training

CILs assist consumers, either individually or in groups, in developing the skills they identify as needing to achieve their goals for independence and choice. Areas of training are varied but typically include the management of personal assistants, the use of assistive technology, money-management, assertiveness or self-advocacy skill development, and activities of daily living. Many CILs have orientation and mobility training to assist individuals who are blind or visually impaired. Others have training in order to facilitate the ability of consumers to independently utilize mass transit.

Information and Referral (I & R)

I & R is a response to requests from individuals or community stakeholders for practical information relating to disability issues or concerns. Such information is provided with the intent of "increasing public knowledge about the needs, issues, resources, services, and advancement of persons with disabilities and independent living" (Budde et al., 1987, p. 16). CILs therefore can be thought of as a clearinghouse of information needed by consumers, their families, other service providers, communities at large, or anyone else interested in increasing options for persons with disabilities or removing architectural, attitudinal, or communication barriers from society. Typically, the type of information request ranges from situation specific (e.g., local options for transportation, housing, community resources and benefits, assistive technology, and daily living techniques) to more general inquiries concerning the ADA, disability law, statistical trends, and the like.

Persons requesting I & R from a CIL need not have a disability, nor must they reside within the agency's catchment area. Referring parties may expect to receive a listing of additional resources or direct referral to another agency designed to better address the issue or inquiry in question. If CILs don't immediately know the answer to your specific inquiry, they are often able to provide direction to someone who does.

Peer Counseling

Peer counseling programs and services vary widely. However, peer support at a CIL is usually provided by an individual who has made the successful transition into community living and has disability-related experiences, knowledge, and coping skills. These individuals provide information, a common experiential base, support, and direction to others who desire to make a similar transition (Schlatzlein, 1978). This orientation is the cornerstone of all service provision at CILs.

Depending on the CIL's funding and method of service delivery, peer counseling may be provided by either a staff person or by a peer volunteer (often a former consumer of services), either in the CIL itself or in the field. Some CILs utilize an instructional approach wherein peer counselors are viewed as educators providing training in independent living skills, thus deemphasizing the traditional therapeutic expectations associated with the "role of counselor." Others use an I & R approach in which peer counseling is conducted by phone, by mail, or even via the Internet. Regardless of the process utilized, consumers will receive this service from a role model and a link to resources within the community, and one who is willing to share personal experiences to facilitate the consumer's ability to assume control of and choice over life options.

SPECIALIZED SERVICES

Many CILs respond to the needs of their communities and populations by creating new services or by adapting core services to better accommodate special needs or underserved groups. These specialized services include interpreter or reader referral, mobility training, TTY distribution and training, brailling services, support groups, and ADA technical assistance, to name a few.

Personal Assistance Management and Referral

For many individuals with physical disabilities, the difference between living in the community and institutionalization is the availability of qualified personal assistants (PAs). A PA is hired, managed, and fired (when necessary) by the individual with the disability and are often paid for by state agencies. Services are defined by the consumer to meet his or her specific needs. Such services can include housekeeping, laundry, and meal preparation, as well as personal care. Many CILs provide a variety of services to facilitate this unique relationship. For consumers with disabilities they provide training to develop the necessary skills to recruit, interview, hire, train, supervise, and terminate PAs.

Persons interested in seeking jobs as PAs are provided training that covers the philosophy which guides the program—that of the consumer being the employer, even though the state might pay the PA. Such training might also include an introduction to various disabilities and basic skills training. Some CILs also maintain referral lists of PAs who have completed their training and provide them to consumers seeking PAs. It is then the consumer's responsibility to interview the potential PA, specify the tasks that will be involved in the job, and provide the training the PA will need to meet the consumer's specific needs.

The value of a good PA program is easily measured by the observable effect it has on the consumer's quality of life, level of independence, and increased ability to participate in community life. The additional value is the savings a state realizes by providing in-home services as opposed to supporting the individual in a costly institution.

Community Reintegration

For a number of years, CILs have worked sporadically to help individuals with disabilities who find themselves in a nursing home to transition back into the community. With the impetus of the *Olmstead* decision and some federal grant money from the Center for Medicare and Medicaid Services, several states have begun to set up an infrastructure to help individuals with disabilities in this transition process. In Illinois, where there are more than 12,000 individuals with disabilities between the ages of 18 and 59 living in skilled nursing facilities (Illinois Center for Health Statistics, 2003), more than 500 individuals previously living in nursing homes have transitioned back into the community during the past five years through the Community Reintegration Program funded by the state. Not only is the quality of life for these individuals enhanced, but such reintegration services are extremely cost-effective, since nursing home care is more than twice as expensive as personal assistance provided in the community.

Outreach and Technical Assistance

Through their commitment to the creation of a barrier-free environment, CILs provide services within their communities that promote this mission. *Community education and outreach* includes public presentations, workshops, and in-service training designed to increase the public awareness of the needs and rights of persons with disabilities, as well as the dissemination of the IL philosophy. CILs generally have written materials, videotapes, and other media available that promote the empowerment of persons with disabilities to strive for self-imposed IL goals, both as individuals and as a minority group. *Technical assistance* is provided by most CILs and includes consultation with city planners, building contractors, and businesses concerning architectural, programmatic, and communication accessibility. Community initiatives to increase the opportunities for equal participation in classrooms, work sites, polling places, and recreational settings are also provided. With the advent of the ADA in 1990, some CILs have also begun to provide technical assistance to employers on their responsibilities under the law, tax incentives for businesses to make their programs and services accessible to persons with disabilities, and the reasonable accommodation process.

Typical Referral Questions

The consumers of CIL services are typically either self-referred or referred from other agencies. By far, the most important question the consumer or referring agency should explore is: "Does the consumer wish to increase independent functioning in one or more areas of life?" Other possible referral questions include, "What barriers to independence has the consumer identified?" and "Are they willing to take responsibility for change in their own lives?"

THE FUTURE OF CILS AND DISABILITY RIGHTS

While CILs operate in order to make themselves obsolete, the slow progress toward equal social participation for Americans with disabilities will apparently be needed well into the twenty-first century. The National Organization on Disability (1998) unveiled the results of their latest comprehensive telephone survey of Americans with disabilities who are older than the age of 16. Some of the key findings included that only 29% of Americans with disabilities of working age reported being employed either full- or part-time (this compares to 79% of the general population). People with disabilities are still roughly three times as likely than their nondisabled neighbors to report household incomes below $15,000 in 1997. Citizens with disabilities are also much more likely to report that inadequate transportation poses a problem for them, that they socialize less, and—importantly—are significantly less likely to be registered to vote (National Organization on Disability). Given these pervasive, sobering statistics, it seems safe to assert that in spite of concerted efforts of the IL movement for the past three decades, advocates with disabilities have a lot more work to do before the aspirations of citizens with disabilities to achieve the American Dream are fully realized.

References

Budde, J. F., Lachat, M. A., Lattimore, J., Jones, M., & Stolzman, L. (1987). *Standards for independent living centers.* Lawrence, KS: Research and Training/Center on Independent Living.

DeJong, G. (1979). Independent living: From social movement to analytic paradigm. *Archives of Physical Medicine and Rehabilitation, 60,* 435–446.

DeJong, G. (1983). Defining and implementing the independent living concept. In N. M. Crewe & I. K. Zola (Eds.), *Independent living for physically disabled people* (pp. 4–27). San Francisco: Jossey-Bass.

Frieden, L. (1983). Understanding alternative program models. In N. M. Crewe & I. K. Zola (Eds.), *Independent living for physically disabled people* (pp. 62–72). San Francisco: Jossey-Bass.

Goldman, C. D. (1985). Disability rights: A perspective on advocacy. *Journal of Intergroup Relations, 13*(2), 34–40.

Illinois Center for Health Statistics. (2003). *Long-term care facility profiles (October, 2002).* Springfield, IL: Author.

Independent Living Research Utilization Project. (2003). Houston, TX: Author.

Lachat, M. A. (1988). *Independent living service model: Historical roots, core elements, and current practice.* Hampton, NH: Center for Research Management.

Laurie, G. (1979). Independent living programs. *Rehabilitation Gazette, 22,* 1.

Levy, C. W. (1988). *A people's history of the independent living movement.* Lawrence, KS: Research and Training Center on Independent Living.

National Council on Independent Living. (1997). Arlington, VA: Author.

National Organization on Disability. (1998). *Lou Harris 1998 survey of Americans with disabilities.* Washington, DC.: Author

Olmstead v. L.C. Ex. Rel. Zimring, 119 S. Ct. 2176 (1999). Washington, DC.

Rubin, S. E., & Roessler, R. T. (1987). *Foundations of the vocational rehabilitation process* (3rd ed.). Austin, TX: Pro-Ed.

Schlatzlein, J. E. (1978). *Spinal cord injury and peer counseling/peer education.* Unpublished manuscript. Minneapolis: University of Minnesota.

Sherman, M., & Zirkel, P. (1980). Student discrimination in higher education: A review of the law. *Journal of Law and Education, 9*(3), 301–341.

Valera, R. A. (1983). Changing societal attitudes and legislation regarding disability. In N. M. Crewe & I. K. Zola (Eds.), *Independent living for physically disabled people* (pp. 28–48). San Francisco: Jossey-Bass.

Public/Specialized Transportation

Nancy K. Zemaitis

Transportation is the movement of people and goods from one location to another. Throughout history, the economic wealth and military power of a people or a nation have been closely tied to efficient methods of transportation. Transportation provides access to natural resources and promotes trade, allowing a nation to accumulate wealth and power.

History/Legislation

Transportation systems and the routes they use have greatly influenced both how and where people live. Reliable transportation allows a population to expand throughout a country's terrain and to live comfortably in remote areas far from factories and farms. The growth and expansion of the United States were directly related to the means of transportation available at the time. The more compact cities of the U.S. eastern seaboard are the result of early human- and animal-based transportation systems that allowed only short trips. The more rambling cities of the western United States are the result of an automobile-based transportation system that permits much longer travel distances.

Americans have utilized every type of transportation in existence. Human-powered transportation, such as walking or bicycling—and in the case of some people with disabilities, operating manual wheelchairs—relies entirely on human muscle power for movement. Americans have ridden horses and in covered wagons, they currently ride in or drive cars, and they use buses, subways, cable cars, trains, airplanes, and ferries to get from one place to another.

History

According to Foner and Garraty (1991), prior to 1825, no city in the world possessed a public transportation system. In the United States, horse-drawn carriages for hire (called hackneys) carried the public on short trips, and stagecoaches served a similar function for more distant journeys.

The omnibus, which originated in France and was common in the bigger cities in the United States in 1829, was the next form of public transportation (Foner & Garraty, 1991). The omnibus was a combination of the hackney and the stagecoach. It carried more people on shorter trips. Placing the omnibus on iron rails was the next major innovation. In 1832 the horse-drawn streetcar, popularly known as the horsecar, combined the low cost, flexibility, and safety of animal power with the efficiency, smoothness, and all-weather capability of a rail right-of-way. The next innovation was the cable car. Passenger vehicles ran along tracks, but the power came from giant steam engines that moved the cable. The first American railroads were designed for long-distance rather than local travel. But they sought ridership wherever they could find it and very early on built stations whenever their lines passed through rural villages on the outskirts of the larger cities.

The typical trolley in 1885 resembled a nineteenth-century railroad car. It had metal wheels, open platforms, and large windows all around. About half the size of a modern bus, it rode on the small railroad tracks that were especially designed for its use.

Because the streetcar, whether powered by an animal or an electric wire, could not eliminate congestion on the streets, transit experts soon turned to the notion of a public right-of-way for their busiest lines. Two methods were possible: elevated trains and subways. The elevated was the older mode, the first line in New York having opened in 1870. Faster and more capital-intensive than the horsecars with which it initially competed, the "els" were noisy, unsightly, and dirty, even after electrification began to replace the small steam engines after 1900. A better solution was underground transit, which became necessary when the elevated structures themselves became an impediment to the smooth flow of traffic.

Meanwhile, according to Foner and Garraty (1991), the private automobile became the primary form of transportation in the United States. Led by Henry Ford and his moving assembly line, American automobile registrations climbed from 1 million in 1913 to 10 million in 1923, when Kansas alone had more cars than France or Germany, and Michigan counted more than Great Britain and Ireland combined. By 1927, when the American total had risen to 26 million, the United States was building about 85 percent of the world's automobiles, and there was one motor vehicle for every five people in the country.

As the country's transportation system grew, and networks of highways, train tracks, and jet streams crisscrossed from north, south, east, and west, people with disabilities were finding that they were having problems accessing the very transportation systems that were such an integral part of the nation's growth.

Legislation

The Intermodal Surface Transportation Efficiency Act (ISTEA), the Transportation Equity Act for the 21st Century (TEA-21), and the Wendell H. Ford Aviation Investment and Reform Act for the 21st Century (AIR-21) are three of the laws that govern transportation. By passing these bills, Congress provided rural America with many tools to address its transportation system in a holistic manner (National Transportation Library, 1998).

Many government agencies play important roles in regulating the safety and environmental aspects of motor vehicles. The U.S. Environmental Protection Agency (EPA) regulates the permissible levels of pollutants that may be emitted from motor vehicles. Other agencies regulate safety and fuel efficiency requirements. The federal and state governments provide traffic control rules and regulations that dictate how motor vehicles are to be operated, and the federal government issues manuals and guidance that assure uniformity in the use of traffic control devices from one state to another. Various other agencies regulate rail, air, and maritime transportation.

Transportation and Persons with Disabilities. The U.S. Census Bureau (2002) reports that nearly 50 million people have a disability. The employment rate for people with disabilities is 57%, compared to 63.9% for people without disabilities. Among those with severe disabilities, the employment rate is about 30%. The mean earnings in 2000 for those with work disabilities was $33,109, about $10,000 less than earnings for people without disabilities of the same age distribution.

As stated earlier, transportation is the movement of people and goods from one location to another. For people with disabilities transportation may not be so easily defined. On March 13, 2002, Secretary of Transportation Norman Y. Mineta stated that "accessibility to transportation is a civil right" (2002, para. 10). He went on to say, "To be inclusive, transportation must be accessible to all Americans, including persons with a physical or mental disability" (para. 17) and "We must work, not only to fulfill the promises of the ADA, but also to move beyond those promises" (para. 21).

The 1990 Americans with Disabilities Act (ADA), Title II, prohibits discrimination in transportation provided by state and local governmental entities such as bus, railway, subway, and other forms of ground transportation. Title III of the ADA prohibits discrimination in privately operated transportation services such as limousines and hotel shuttle services. An important focus of the legislation was to provide employment opportunities for, and prevent discrimination against, people with disabilities. In effect, the ADA strives to eliminate disability as a factor in the rates of employment, education, and income. Transportation difficulties may contribute to lower employment rates among people with disabilities.

The Department of Transportation has oversight responsibility for ensuring the implementation of paratransit services as required by the ADA. The ADA requires that communities with fixed route transit services provide comparable complementary paratransit services for those individuals who are unable to access the fixed route service because of a disability.

Section 504 of the Rehabilitation Act prohibits discrimination in transportation services that receive federal funding. Finally, the Air Carrier Access Act prohibits discrimination on the basis of disability in air travel. It applies only to air carriers that provide regularly scheduled services for hire to the public. Requirements address a wide range of issues, including boarding assistance and certain accessibility features in newly built aircraft and airport facilities.

STRUCTURE AND FUNDING

The U.S. government is responsible for supervising transportation systems. This includes the management of planning, construction, funding, and regulation of these systems. The transportation needs of the American people are studied by the government, and resources are allocated to address these needs.

The federal government regulates many important aspects of transportation, including transportation system planning, market competition, and vehicle design and safety. The U.S. Department of Transportation is responsible for the nation's transportation system. Every state also has a department of transportation (DOT), and every county and city also has some organization with responsibility for local transportation ("Transportation," 2003).

The Access Board is an independent federal agency devoted to accessibility for people with disabilities. It operates with about 30 staff and a governing board of representatives from federal departments and public members appointed by the president. Key responsibilities of the board include these:

- developing and maintaining accessibility requirements for the built environment, transit vehicles, telecommunications equipment, and for electronic and information technology;
- providing technical assistance and training on these guidelines and standards; and
- enforcing accessibility standards for federally funded facilities.

Over 70 federal programs have been identified that might provide funding for community transportation. In order for coordinated transportation services to obtain the benefits of broad-based funding, it is necessary to understand which funds are available and what are the requirements of the agencies that make the funds available. While not addressing all federal funding available for transportation services, this section provides an overview of various programs funded through the Departments of Transportation, Health and Human Services, and Education.

Planning Guidelines for Coordinated State and Local Specialized Transportation Services (2000) contains helpful information about the oversight of transportation in the United States. For example, the U.S. Department of Transportation programs that have the most effect on services for persons with special transportation needs are administered by DOT's Federal Transit Administration (FTA). FTA is the principal source of federal financial assistance to America's urban, suburban, and rural communities for the planning, development, and improvement of public transit systems. Public agencies that have been approved by an individual state to coordinate services for older persons and persons with disabilities may receive funds from FTA to implement service delivery programs.

Transit planning efforts are required to be integrated with highway planning activities, which are funded through the Federal Highway Administration (FHWA). These funds, in addition to funds from FTA, are considered flexible; that is, if states and localities so desire, some funds from FHWA-administered programs may be used for transit rather than highway purposes. This ability to flexibly apply DOT funds for local needs can be a major resource for localities responding to specific mobility needs.

FTA has a formal process for planning, program development, review, and approval of projects. There are distinct federal, regional, state, and local components and responsibilities in the grant process; the intent is to facilitate a collaborative process of achieving a consensus on transportation investment priorities. As experience and research have indicated, communities that include their ADA paratransit services in a coordinated transportation effort achieve lower per-trip costs and higher-quality service for ADA paratransit users (U.S. Dept. of Health and Human Services, 2000). When ADA paratransit resources are included in coordination efforts, they increase the availability of vehicles, personnel, and expertise to the larger effort of the provision of transportation in a community.

U.S. Department of Health and Human Services funds a wide variety of research and service provision programs. HHS programs funding the provision of health or human services permit expenditures of funds for transportation services, with a few exceptions. The most notable exception is Medicare, which provides funds for medical services and equipment for persons 65 years or older and persons with disabilities. Medicare does not pay for non-emergency transportation but does pay for appropriate emergency ambulance service.

The Older Americans Act directs Area Agencies on Aging (AAA) to consider transportation as a priority service as the AAA is developing its service plan. The Head Start Program encourages but does not require grantees to provide for the transportation of children participating in the program. Medicaid requires that states include in their state Medicaid plan an assurance that program recipients will have access to medical services. The states have significant discretion on how they fulfill the assurance-of-access commitment. In the Temporary Assistance for Needy Families Program (TANF), transportation is an allowable expenditure of TANF funds. However, the states have significant discretion in the specific use of the funds, from purchase of vehicles and payment of insurance costs to payments to transit providers to assist in extending routes or service hours.

Many of the recipients of HHS funding are multi-service organizations. Transportation is seen as an ancillary service enabling them to accomplish their key missions, and transportation is only one of many services offered to their clients.

The U.S. Department of Education has funding available for transportation services. Public school pupils are transported at public expense. Transportation is provided as an ancillary service through the Rehabilitation Act for those people with disabilities who request assistance in obtaining employment. States and local communities also may have funding to support transportation initiatives—for example, human service agencies may announce grant opportunities to support state initiatives.

PURPOSE/INTENT

In his *New Freedom Initiative* in February of 2001, President George W. Bush said:

> Every American should have the opportunity to participate fully in society and engage in productive work. Unfortunately, millions of Americans with disabilities are locked out of the workplace because they are denied the tools and access necessary for success.
>
> Transportation can be a particularly difficult barrier to work for Americans with disabilities. In 1997, the Director of Project Action stated that "access to transportation is often the critical factor in obtaining employment for the nation's 25 million transit dependent people with disabilities." Today, the lack of adequate transportation remains a primary barrier to work for people with disabilities: one-third of people with disabilities report that inadequate transportation is a significant problem.
>
> The Federal Government should support the development of innovative transportation initiatives and partner with local organizations to promote access to alternate methods of transportation.

According to the Department of Transportation's Bureau of Transportation Statistics, transportation difficulties keep over half a million people with disabilities at home. Transportation plays such an important role in daily living that, without it, persons with disabilities might never be able to leave their homes. Through a nationwide survey, the Bureau of Transportation Statistics (2003) found the following:

- Nationally, almost 15 million people in this country have difficulties getting the transportation they need. Of these, about 6 million (40 percent) are people with disabilities.

- More than 3.5 million people in this country never leave their home. Of these, 1.9 million (54 percent) are people with disabilities.
- About 560,000 people with disabilities indicate they never leave homes because of transportation difficulties.

Survey respondents with disabilities were asked to categorize the kinds of difficulties that made travel outside the home impossible. The one difficulty cited most frequently was the lack of a personal vehicle. Other difficulties cited by respondents included public transportation availability or cost, physical problems that made using transportation too difficult, and personal preferences, such as not wanting to ask others for help or having to depend on someone else for transportation.

CLIENT SERVICES

Transportation for people with disabilities is an accommodation issue. Americans use various means of transportation and systems to move around in their neighborhoods, communities, the nation, and worldwide. Accommodations may be necessary to "level the playing field" for people with disabilities to live, learn, work, and play as they desire. One of the main factors as accommodations are made is to utilize a universal design—that is, the accommodations should benefit more than one category of people. For instance, a person using a wheelchair accesses sidewalks using ramps that are built as part of the construction. These ramps are also used by delivery personnel pulling a dolly of supplies and by a young child riding a tricycle while on an outing with the babysitter. Another example of accommodation is an audible pedestrian signal: Technologies now exist that enable audible signals to be incorporated into standard pedestrian signal systems.

Modified Vehicles for an Individual's Use

Many persons with disabilities need specific types of modifications or adaptive equipment added to their motor vehicles to meet their transportation needs. According to the Bureau of Transportation Statistics, *Safety Issues for Vehicles Adapted for Use by Persons with Disabilities* (2002), the number of persons using adapted vehicles has increased. The 1990 National Health Interview Survey (NHIS-D) estimated 299,000 adaptive equipment users, while the 1994 and 1995 NHIS-D estimated 510,000—an increase of 211,000 users over a five-year period.

Modifications to vehicles result in the ability of persons with disabilities to drive the vehicles themselves, or permits them to access a vehicle while someone else does the driving. The introduction of new technology continues to broaden opportunities for people with disabilities to drive vehicles with adaptive devices. The types of vehicles that are modified include passenger cars, vans, minivans, pickups, sport utility vehicles, tractors, and heavy trucks or motor homes. Common types of modifications include: hand controls, drivability from a wheelchair, lift, wheelchair securement, automatic door opener, steering control device, dropped floor, modified safety belts, power seat base, ramp, modified switch/touch pads, wheelchair/scooter hoists, raised roof, low-effort steering, low-effort braking, remote ignition, zero-effort steering, electronic gas/brake, and left foot accelerator (Bureau of Transportation Statistics, 2002).

Modifications are usually categorized by their complexity. Four common categories that state vocational rehabilitation offices may identify are these:

- Modifications with high-level driving systems, including remote steering packages.

- Modifications required for driving from a wheelchair. Includes, but is not limited to, lowered floor conversions, foot steering, low-effort conversions, horizontal steering, braking and throttle servo controls (a device or combination of devices that automatically control a mechanism) ("Servomechanism," 2003).

- Modifications requiring driver transfer into the driver's seat or dependent transport. Including but not limited to raised tops and/or doors, mechanical hand controls and steering devices, and six-way power transfer seats.

- Modifications including but not limited to car-top carriers, wheelchair lifters/loaders, and mechanical hand controls and steering devices (spinner knobs, etc.).

The process to modify a vehicle is very specific and is based on the experience of driver rehabilitation specialists and other professionals who work with individuals requiring adaptive devices for their motor vehicles. It is centered around a proven process, which is defined in the brochure *Adapting Motor Vehicles for People with Disabilities* (NHTSA, 2002–2003). The process includes evaluating the individual's needs, selecting the right vehicle, choosing a qualified dealer to modify the vehicle, training the operator, and maintaining the vehicle. Some manufacturers of vehicles offer rebates or reimbursements on new vehicle modifications.

In some cases, it is necessary to alter or even remove federally required safety equipment to make those special modifications. In those cases, it may not be possible to enable individuals with disabilities both to enjoy the opportunity to drive or ride in a motor vehicle and to receive the benefits from the full array of federally required safety features. The National Highway Traffic Safety Administration and the DOT published a final rule allowing for an exemption to facilitate making needed vehicle modifications by providing guidance to modifiers on the types of modifications that can be made without unduly decreasing the level of safety provided to the vehicle occupants and to others. The exemption is limited, in that it allows repair businesses to modify only certain types of federally required safety equipment and features under specified circumstances.

Public Transportation

The Access Board (2003), described in a previous section, developed the *Accessibility Guidelines for Transportation Vehicles.* The publication provides minimum guidelines and requirements for accessibility standards to be issued by the DOT for transportation vehicles required to be accessible by the ADA. Following is a listing of the types of transportation vehicles with some examples of the accessibility guidelines.

Buses, Vans, and Systems. A bus is defined as any of several types of self-propelled vehicle, other than an over-the-road bus, intended for use on city streets, highways, and busways. The term includes minibuses, transit buses, articulated buses, double-deck buses, and electric-powered trolley buses. Self-propelled, rubber-tired vehicles designed to look like antique or vintage trolleys or streetcars are considered buses.

Access to a bus occurs either through a "fixed route" or through a "paratransit service." A fixed-route bus service conveniently carries commuters throughout the community using a set schedule and routing. A paratransit service could be either a prearranged curb-to-curb service for persons with disabilities or a "dial-a-ride" service. Sometimes a person must be determined eligible for curb-to-curb service, depending on local policy. There is usually a guideline that sets a minimum distance for curb-to-curb services to occur (for example, three-fourths of a mile of the total distance traveled must be on the regular route). "Dial-a-ride" paratransit service is a non-fixed route service utilizing vans and small buses to provide prearranged trips to and from specific locations within the service area.

Guidelines for buses, vans, or systems include mobility aid accessibility. For example, all vehicles need to have a boarding device, such as a lift or a ramp, and there must be sufficient clearance for someone in a wheelchair to access the vehicle. The guidelines specify the slope of the ramp. New buses ordered on or after August 26 of 1990 must be accessible.

Privately operated bus and van companies that have purchased new over-the-road buses on or after July 26, 1996, must be accessible. Other private transportation operations, including station facilities, must meet the requirements for public accommodations.

Rapid Rail Vehicles, Light Rail Vehicles, Commuter Rail Cars, and Systems. A rapid rail vehicle is a subway-type vehicle railway, or one that operates on elevated or at grade-level track, separated from other traffic. A light rail vehicle is a streetcar type of vehicle operated on city streets, and on semi-private or private right of ways. Commuter rail transportation means short-haul rail passenger service operating in metropolitan and suburban areas.

Compliance dates were specified in the law. For example, after July 26, 1995, existing rail systems must have one accessible car per train. Existing stations were to be accessible by July 26, 1993 (extensions were possible), and intercity rail stations (Amtrak) must be made accessible by July 26, 2010.

Accessibility guidelines include such things as auditory and visual warning signals that alert passengers of closing doors, priority seating signs for persons with disabilities, and the desired measurements—that is, a route through the rows of seats shall be at least 32 inches wide to accommodate wheelchairs. There must be coordination with the boarding platform; for example, the horizontal gap between the vehicle and the platform shall be no greater than three inches. Step treads and ramps, when the door is open, should have lighting.

Intercity Rail Cars and Systems. This is transportation provided by Amtrak, which is the National Railroad Passenger Corporation. It is intended for paying passengers using intercity rail transportation. Guidelines for the Amtrak cars or systems address the accessibility of dining (single and bi-level), lounge, and sleeper cars as well as passenger coaches. Specifications address doorway width, movement within the car, and boarding direction—that is, the lift permits both inboard and outboard facing of wheelchairs and mobility aids.

Over-the-Road Buses and Systems. An over-the-road bus is a vehicle characterized by an elevated passenger deck located over a baggage compartment. Guidelines for these vehicles include specifications for knuckle clearance from the handrails and moveable aisle armrests to permit easy entry or exit.

There are also accessibility guidelines defined for other vehicles and systems that do not fit into the above categories. These include automated guideway transit vehicles or "people movers"; trams (vehicles that provide a shuttle service) and high-speed rail cars; monorails; and systems. The guidelines also mention ferries, excursion boats, and other vessels; however, the section was "reserved" as of September 2003, pending public hearings by the Access Board.

Anyone believing that the public transportation vehicle or system in their locality is not in compliance with the Americans with Disabilities Act may file complaints with either the Department of Transportation or the Attorney General (privately operated bus and van companies), or may file private lawsuits.

EXPANDING TRANSPORTATION OPTIONS

"Transportation is the tie that binds communities as well as nations, liking us to home, daycare, school, the workplace, medical care, retail stores, and entertainment" (Slater, 2000, para. 45). Agencies with transportation as their primary mission (such as public transit agencies) and agencies with other primary missions (such as human service agencies) are now both involved in offering specialized transportation services. Generally, the agencies that were dealing with human service transportation needs were doing so in a "silo" or "stovepipe" fashion. The funds and policies that regulated this type of transportation were very narrow and constrained. The transportation needs of one agency's clients could be served without coordination, but often at considerable expense and with some service quality problems. Many agencies had similar client travel needs, but fiercely guarded the rights and interests of their own clients against competing interests, and guarded the prerogatives of their own turf from outsiders. Few of these agencies were working with public transit agencies to secure transportation services for their clients and few public transit agencies were attempting to serve human service clients (U.S. Dept. of Health and Human Services, 2000).

In 1986 the Coordinating Council for Access and Mobility was formed to encourage and support the coordination of community transportation resources. The Coordinating Council has worked with states and localities to identify successful coordination practices and the technical assistance that is needed to support the development of these activities.

The result of transportation coordination at the local level can include more people accessing services, increased mobility for all consumers, better quality of service for riders, cost savings, upgraded maintenance programs, better reporting and record keeping, more equitable cost sharing between participating agencies and individuals, more professional delivery of transportation services, and safer transportation services.

In communities a variety of public and private agencies provide transportation services to persons who are disadvantaged in their ability to obtain transportation. These agencies and organizations often include the following:

- departments of social services, which arrange Medicaid transportation as well as transportation for persons with low incomes;
- departments of health and mental health, which provide medical trips;
- Area Agencies on Aging, which transport clients to senior centers and other service destinations;
- vocational and/or developmental disabilities departments, which transport clients to employment and training;
- departments of employment, which are responsible for implementing U.S. Department of Labor funded programs, such as those serving individuals who are moving from welfare to work;
- departments of education, which transport many students and provide specialized transportation for vocational rehabilitation students;
- public transportation agencies, which provide general public transportation services as well as complementary paratransit services to transport persons with certified disabilities wherever the public transit agency provides fixed-route transportation (public transit agencies sometimes also offer special services for the elderly); and
- many different private non-profit organizations, such as the Red Cross and faith-based organizations, which provide transportation to a variety of persons for different purposes. (U.S. Dept. of Health and Human Services, 2000).

There are resources available that assist local communities to coordinate services. The DOT may solicit proposals from localities for the express purpose of coordination. On the whole, eligible project planning activities that could be funded include (a) the preparation of implementation plans and designs incorporating safe, livable elements; (b) the assessment of environmental, social, economic, land-use, and design impacts of projects; (c) feasibility studies; (d) technical assistance; (e) participation by community organizations and the business community, including small and minority-owned businesses and persons with disabilities; (f) the evaluation of best practices; and (g) the development of innovative design, land-use, and zoning practices (National Transportation Library, 1998).

The solicitation may ask the localities to create a network of alternate transportation through community-based and other providers. Proposals may establish a competitive matching grant program to promote access to alternative methods of transportation. One example of a matching grant program is a dollar-for-dollar match, which will go toward the purchase and operation of specialty vans, assisting people with down payments or costs associated with accessible vehicles, and extending the use of existing transportation resources. Many times these projects are selected on the basis of the use of innovative approaches to developing transportation plans that serve people with disabilities.

There are also organizations available to assist local communities in coordinating their transportation systems. For example, The Rural Passenger Transportation Technical Assistance Program helps small communities enhance economic growth and development by improving community transportation services. Technical assistance is limited to planning and may support transit service improvements and expansion, system start-up, facility development, development of marketing plans and materials, transportation coordination, training, and other public transit problem-solving activities.

The Rural Transit Assistance Program is a program of the Federal Transit Administration. Every state is funded to set up its own RTAP program and develop services tailored to its mobility needs. In addition, states work in partnership with RTAP's national program, tapping into and benefiting from a variety of services.

Transportation cuts across all strata of American life. Access to transportation is needed by all people, whether disabled or not. It is imperative that when a community is making plans to enhance or build a transportation system that all "end-riders" be part of all aspects of the development, including planning, implementing, and evaluating the final product.

References

Access Board. (n.d.) *Accessibility guidelines for transportation vehicles.* 36 CFR Part 1192. Retrieved July 10, 2003, from http://www.access-board.gov/transit/html/vguide.htm

Access Board. (2003, August). *Board to hold public meeting in Seattle on vessel access* [Notice].

Americans with Disabilities Act (ADA) of 1990, 42 U.S.C. 12101 et seq.

Bureau of Transportation Statistics. (2002, June). *Safety issues for vehicles adapted for use by persons with disabilities.* (Research Note).

Bureau of Transportation Statistics. (2003, April). Transportation difficulties keep over half a million disabled at home. (Issue Brief Number 3).

Bush, G. W. (2001). *New freedom initiative.* Retrieved July 10, 2003, from http://www.whitehouse.gov/news/freedominitiative/freedominitiative.html

Community Transportation Association of America. (n.d.) *Rural Passenger Transportation Technical Assistance Program.* Retrieved September 27, 2003, from http://www.ctaa.org

Community Transportation Association of America. (n.d.) *Rural Transit Assistance Program.* Retrieved September 27, 2003, from http://www.ctaa.org

Exemption from the Make Inoperative Prohibition. 49 CFR Part 595. Final Rule, *Federal Register* (2001, February).

Federal Transit Administration, U.S. Department of Transportation. (n.d.) *Transportation coordination toolkit.* Retrieved December 8, 2004, from http://www.fta.dot.gov/library/policy/guide/chl.html

Foner, E., & Garraty, J. A. (Eds.). (1991) *Readers companion to American history.* Boston: Houghton Mifflin.

Indiana Vocational Rehabilitation Policy and Procedure Manual, effective 10/01/2003.

Mineta, N. Y. (2002, March 13). *Federal Transit Administration's accessible transportation 2002: A national dialogue reception.* Washington, DC: U.S. Dept. of Transportation. Retrieved October 8, 2004, from http://www.dot.gov/affairs/031302spa.htm

National Highway Traffic Safety Administration (NHTSA). (2002–2003). Adapting motor vehicles for people with disabilities [Brochure]. Retrieved July 10, 2003, from http://www.nhtsa.dot.gov/cars/rules/adaptive/brochure/brochure.html

National Transportation Library, Bureau of Transportation Statistics, Dept. of Transportation. (1998). *Transportation toolbox for rural areas and small communities* [Electronic version]. Retrieved July 13, 2003, from http://ntl.bts.gov/ruraltransport/toolbox/index.cfm

"Servomechanism." (2003). *Microsoft® Encarta® online encyclopedia.* Retrieved July 13, 2003, from http://encarta.msn.com. © 1997–2003 Microsoft Corporation, all rights reserved.

Slater, R. (2000, October 10). A new transportation policy architecture for a new century. *International Transportation Symposium.* Washington, DC. Retrieved October 18, 2004, from http://www.useu.be/ISSUES/slater1010.html

"Transportation." (2003). *Microsoft® Encarta® online encyclopedia.* Retrieved July 13, 2003, from http://encarta.msn.com. © 1997–2003 Microsoft Corporation, all rights reserved.

U.S. Architectural and Transportation Barriers Compliance Board (Access Board). *About the board.* Retrieved August 15, 2003, from http://www.access-board.gov

U.S. Census Bureau, Facts for Features, CB02-FF.11, July 12, 2002.

U.S. Department of Health and Human Services and The Federal Transition Administration. (2000). *Planning guidelines for coordinated state and local specialized transportation services.* Retrieved August 4, 2003 from www.fta.dot.gov/library/policy/guide.pdf

U.S. Department of Housing and Urban Development

Celia Williamson

Like any other cabinet-level federal agency, the U.S. Department of Housing and Urban Development (HUD) is a complex and dynamic organization, addressing its primary mission through a multitude of programs that have changed considerably over time. All of these activities, however, are grounded in HUD's primary mission: "helping to create decent homes and a suitable living environment for all Americans" (Mayer, 1995, p. 1). That mission helps to frame the discussion that follows. HUD's view is that stable homes and communities provide the framework for stable families and, beyond that, a stable and productive society.

HISTORY/LEGISLATION

Federal support of housing began in earnest in the 1930s in response to the Great Depression. Unemployment rates had risen to nearly 25% (Stegman, 1995). Families were losing their homes and farms and finding themselves on the street. In an effort to stem the tide of this growing problem, the federal government stepped in with programs to support mortgages and refinancing of homes. A small program for public housing was also created at that time, as much as an effort to provide jobs for the construction industry as to provide affordable housing (Bratt, 1997).

These initial efforts were supplemented in the 1940s, as a federal housing loan program for war veterans became the first of several housing finance programs. The goal was to increase home ownership across America, building a solid foundation for families and communities. In 1947 these separate programs were brought together to form the Housing and Home Finance Agency (HHFA), the precursor to HUD. In 1949, an urban renewal program was established in the HHFA to allow cities to eradicate dilapidated housing in slum areas and to replace it with habitable units. This early effort helped to broaden the federal focus from individual home ownership to interventions at a neighborhood level. The "slum clearance" program was not without critics, however, who complained the program was cumbersome and intrusive, resulting in the removal of more housing than it replaced and contributing to the displacement of poor and minority families (Thompson, 2003).

In the 1950s the Housing Act experienced only modest increases in funding and scope. Mortgage supports and urban renewal projects continued, and the HHFA began to provide low-cost loans to nonprofit organizations to build rental housing for the elderly (Scruggs, 1995; Stegman, 1995).

Throughout this early pre-HUD period, the primary federal emphasis in housing was on providing financial tools to support home ownership and the construction of low-cost housing. Early efforts in urban renewal did establish a direct link between HUD and local communities, however, and a precedent was set for federal support of building projects carried out by non-governmental agencies (Thompson, 2003).

The Creation of HUD

The tumult of the 1960s played a key role in broadening the scope of federal involvement in housing and community development. Social unrest highlighted the condition of America's inner cities. Riots, demonstrations, and boycotts made it clear to America that there were significant injustices that must be corrected if the nation was to survive. The impact of discrimination on access to schools, workplaces, and housing was increasingly clear (Downs, 1995; Thompson, 2003).

In response to these issues, Congress enacted the Department of Housing and Urban Development Act of 1965. It replaced the HHFA with HUD and positioned it as a Cabinet-level federal agency, raising its visibility and its scope of responsibility. Robert Weaver was appointed as the first Secretary of HUD and the first African American member of a presidential cabinet (Foote, 1995). Almost immediately a "Model Cities" program was initiated, targeting neighborhoods for urban planning and renewal and involving citizens in the planning process. HUD was expected to facilitate work across governmental programs and with citizen groups, working within targeted neighborhoods so that multifaceted problems could be addressed in multifaceted ways. Though short-lived, this program set the stage for greater community involvement in decision making.

Other changes were equally important. One week after the assassination of Dr. Martin Luther King, Congress enacted the Civil Rights Act of 1968 (also referred to as the Fair Housing Act), which made discrimination in housing illegal—not just in government-funded housing but throughout the public and private sectors (Stegman, 1995).

Thus, the 1960s were a decade of significant expansion in the scope of HUD's programs and mission. The early focus on financial tools for home ownership was expanded to include fair housing and enhanced community renewal responsibilities that emphasized service programs and community input as well as construction of housing. From 1962 to 1972 the federal budgetary investment in housing-related programs quadrupled, growing from just over $800 million to over $3.6 billion (Thompson, 2003).

In 1973, then President Nixon issued a moratorium on any new monies for HUD, calling for an extensive review and restructuring of its program. His plan was to fold HUD into a larger agency devoted to community development—a move that might have helped to coordinate urban policy initiatives but also would have diluted the federal focus on housing. In the end, HUD remained intact but was given increased community development authority through the 1974 Housing and Community Development Act, which was signed into law by President Ford just two weeks after Nixon's resignation. Under this act, seven different urban assistance programs were combined into the current Community Development Block Grant (CDBG) funds, which are awarded on a formula basis to qualifying cities. Under this plan, cities have a relatively stable base of funding that is targeted at the local level to support housing, infrastructure, and other urban development needs. Section 8 of the 1974 act also combined several separate rental assistance programs, allowing for project-based construction and renovation and, even more importantly, for a voucher-based system of rent support that allows more flexibility and portability of housing assistance to families (Thompson, 2003).

During the late 1970s, while President Carter struggled to draft a comprehensive urban policy, Congress was targeting HUD as a potential source of funds for antipoverty programs, talking again of combining HUD with other agencies. These struggles and the quick return of the presidency to Republican hands resulted in little lasting change for HUD in the waning years of that decade (Scruggs, 1995). The HUD budget grew steadily during this period, however, as the different programs continued to expand their activities. At its peak in 1978, HUD's budget reached over $32 billion (Bratt, 1997).

In 1981, President Reagan took office with the goal of reducing federal spending and federal regulation. In response to this initiative, HUD focused its energies on reducing fraud and mismanagement in public housing, reducing paperwork in CDBG programs, increasing the investment portfolio that supports the federal mortgage insurance programs, and reducing expenditures in public housing. For the eight years of Reagan's presidency, HUD's expenditures were reduced by over $26 billion (Foote, 1995). From 1981 through 1989, the number of new households to receive federal rental assistance dropped from over 300,000 to just over 80,000 per year. The budget for federal rental assistance dropped precipitously (Bratt, 1997). This left public housing as the most severely damaged of HUD's programs. During this same period, two new programs came under HUD's jurisdiction, however. The Indian Housing Act gave HUD new responsibilities for Native American housing needs, and the Stewart McKinney Act focused on providing services for the growing number of homeless in American cities. Both acts were placed under HUD's jurisdiction (Stegman, 1995).

The administration of the elder George Bush essentially extended Reagan's initiatives through the early 1990s, with one significant addition. HUD Secretary Jack Kemp personally championed the establishment of Enterprise Zones, which were placed in several large metropolitan areas in an effort to stimulate reinvestment in city centers that were being abandoned by residents and businesses alike. The Bush administration also initiated several small grants that focused on HUD's collaboration with other federal programs. These have primarily been directed at crime control, youth employment, and welfare reform (Foote, 1995; Scruggs, 1995).

Throughout the Reagan and Bush administrations, the size of HUD's budget made it a target for cuts. In addition, the agency suffered from a series of high-profile difficulties that left the agency vulnerable to attack. In 1989 a scandal involving influence peddling and favoritism rocked the agency. Prominent political figures had pocketed millions of dollars for helping developers win politically rigged contracts. This scandal revealed an agency with poor fiscal and management control, and programs and branches that did not communicate well. This presented a significant potential for fraud, waste, and abuse. Indeed, in 1994 the agency was cited as "high risk" by the Government Accounting Office (GAO). HUD was the first federal agency to receive such a designation (U.S. Dept. of Housing and Urban Development [HUD], 1997).

In addition, several high-rise public housing complexes were slated for demolition, giving the public a graphic image of the failures of past efforts in creating public housing. While the move from concentrated public housing in "the projects" or "vertical slums" (Kreyling, 1999) to rent subsidies that families could take with them into the private market was actually a significant advance in housing policy, the image of imploding buildings left the general public with a negative view of the federal role in affordable housing. Most HUD housing was in good condition, but media reports left the impression that the government had become the worst kind of slum landlord, causing rather than correcting urban blight (Thompson, 2003).

In the mid-1990s, when President Clinton took office, HUD found itself in difficult straits. With a severely reduced budget and a workforce that had experienced significant cuts, the agency was now under threat of being entirely dismantled by Congress. HUD's response, first under Secretary Henry Cisneros and then under Secretary Andrew Cuomo, was to undertake a comprehensive agency restructuring (Cuomo, 1997). By the end of the restructuring process, the agency was operating with less than half of its previous staffing levels. Many of its services were contracted out to private providers. New technologies were introduced to help the different branches of the agency communicate more quickly and efficiently with each other. Programs to address dilapidated housing under HUD's jurisdiction were expanded. By 1998, the agency was garnering praise for its efforts from private groups and the Conference of Mayors and it received an increase in appropriations in the 1999 budget (Cuomo, 2000).

During the latter part of the Clinton administration, the agency began to focus on the program that had suffered most under the previous administrations: rental assistance for low-income families. A pair of departmental reports issued in early 1999 made it clear that the nation was in a crisis in regard to providing affordable housing to low- and moderate-income families, and the situation was about to get worse (HUD, 1999a, b). Many of the nation's affordable housing units had been developed under contracts that were now expiring, leaving the apartment owners with the option to no longer accept HUD rental subsidies for their tenants. To make matters worse, the federal government had stopped appropriating new funds for housing subsidies for a five-year period, beginning in 1995. As a result, there were fewer housing units available and fewer vouchers to help low-income families pay the rent. Families in need, however, were growing in number, reaching 5.3 million families by 1997 as housing costs were rising faster than family incomes (HUD, 1999c). This represents 12.5 million people who were experiencing a housing crisis, either living in substandard housing or paying over half of their income for rent. The waiting lists for rental assistance grew sharply, with an average waiting period of almost one year. In the worst cases, waiting lists for housing vouchers were as much as 8 to 10 years long. In response to these reports and the positive changes within the organization, the 2001 Congress awarded HUD a $32.4 billion budget—the best the agency had seen in some 20 years (HUD, 2000).

When the younger Bush took office in 2001, the efforts at expansion of affordable housing opportunities were deemphasized. The focus of the agency returned to home ownership, the use of tax incentives to encourage both the construction of affordable housing and community development, efforts to decrease discriminatory practices in housing, and efforts to fight homelessness. The proposed budget for 2004 dropped slightly to just over $31 billion (Martinez, 2003).

The Complexity of the Task

Clearly, the direction and goals of any presidential cabinet-level agency are highly influenced by the political ideology of the president and of the Congress that allocates the funds for the agency's programs. In a program that is as resource intensive as housing and community development, it is difficult to plan and carry out an initiative before the next administration comes in with its own ideas and plans. For example, the Model Cities program was first conceived in 1965 and realized in legislation in 1966 under President Johnson. The idea was to focus resources on a limited number of inner-city communities, to encourage long-lasting change through citizen participation, and to provide for the coordination of services across governmental agencies at all levels. It was designed to provide a comprehensive array of strategies and a significant infusion of funds in a focused and intensive manner. Lessons learned from the selected communities would then be applied to other communities around the country. Shortly after his election in 1969, however, President Nixon declared that the program had not met its goals and dismantled it. Three years was certainly not enough time for such a multifaceted program to prove itself, yet a change in administration resulted in a change in priority and funding (Foote, 1995; Scruggs, 1995).

It is the long-term civil servants within these agencies who are left with the challenge of finding a way to move forward with the agency's basic mission despite significant swings in the political agenda. Personnel within HUD are trained in a variety of professional areas, including law, urban policy and planning, architecture, real estate, finance, business, public administration, and human services. Most of the direct services that HUD provides are actually delivered in local communities by contract agencies, such as the public housing authorities, or by agencies that receive grants directly from HUD or through CDBG for construction, homeless services, or other supports.

PURPOSE/INTENT

Despite perennial difficulties, HUD continues as a key federal agency for the support of the social infrastructure of America. Homes and communities are, indeed, fundamental ingredients for a stable society. Thus, HUD's basic mission, "helping to create decent homes and a suitable living environment for all Americans" (Mayer, 1995, p.1), has helped to secure its place in the federal structure, despite ongoing talk about its demise. Even if its structure and name undergo changes, the fundamental issue of "a place to live" will stay at the forefront of American policy.

HUD has a fourfold strategy to address its basic mission. It seeks to expand home ownership, increase access to affordable housing, strengthen and empower communities, and assure that all Americans have equal access to housing opportunities, free from discrimination (Martinez, 2003). Each of these areas is the responsibility of a separate assistant secretary, a presidential appointee whose job it is to coordinate various programs and partnerships to achieve the goals of that particular program.

Home Ownership

The Assistant Secretary for Housing is responsible for the goal of expanding home ownership. This is accomplished primarily through the Federal Housing Administration (FHA), which provides mortgage insurance for homes. Unique among HUD programs, FHA is supported through fees and interest rather than tax dollars. When FHA was first created in 1934, only about 10% of Americans owned their own homes. In 2001, that rate was just over 68% (HUD, n.d., c). A key focus of this branch of HUD is to facilitate the purchase of homes by first-time home buyers through education programs, down-payment assistance, and mortgage insurance that encourages banks to "take the risk" on first-time buyers. Almost 80% of FHA loans go to first-time home buyers. If a homeowner defaults on a HUD insured loan, the property is sold through a bid process, allowing the agency to recoup much of the cost and adding to the inventory of moderately priced homes on the market (HUD, n.d., c).

FHA also provides financial tools to assist in the construction and rehabilitation of multi-family housing projects, some specifically targeted to support housing projects that include on-site supportive services for the elderly and people with disabilities.

HUD works through approved local lenders to provide FHA loans to qualified buyers. Those lending agencies can walk applicants through the options available through HUD, including reduced down-payment options, loans for housing renovations, loans for disaster victims, and reverse mortgages for elderly homeowners. The HUD programs that support construction of housing for the elderly and people with disabilities (Sections 811 and 202, respectively) are handled through an annual grant application process. The Notification of Funding Availability (NOFA) usually occurs in the spring of each year and follows a competitive proposal process.

Affordable Housing

The Assistant Secretary for Public and Indian Housing is responsible for providing decent, safe, and affordable rental housing to eligible low-income households within the general U.S. population and in collaboration with Native American tribes. This branch of HUD has developed a number of mechanisms for accomplishing this goal, as the program has grown and learned from its own experience. Early public housing projects were usually owned by HUD or its partners, the local housing authorities. Housing authorities are nonprofit, local agencies that contract with HUD to administer housing projects and programs. Over time, some of these housing developments fell into disrepair and developed reputations as havens for drug use and rodent infestation. The HOPE VI project was initiated to tear down or revitalize public housing projects across the country. The negative image of public housing projects is slowly changing as a result of the investment of over $5 billion in HOPE VI funds and other capital improvement funds provided to local agencies. Today, some 1.3 million families live in public housing projects managed by local housing authorities (HUD, n.d., f).

Other rental assistance programs include a variety of housing choice voucher programs (formerly called section 8 vouchers), which are targeted to particular groups, such as individuals with disabilities. Other voucher programs are tied to particular incentives, such as employment or home owner-ship. In both the project and voucher programs, families pay approximately 30% of their household income for rent. These programs are also adminis-tered through the local housing authorities.

The section 8 voucher program began in 1974 and has received high praise as a vehicle for allowing greater choice and access to opportunity among the working poor (Sard, 2001). Because families that hold vouchers are able to use their vouchers wherever they can find a landlord willing to accept them, the families are more likely to become a part of mixed-income neighborhoods that do not carry the stigma associated with "the projects." Its current incarnation continues to provide these benefits, although they are divided among a series of targeted programs (HUD, n.d., e).

Affordable housing programs comprise 60% of HUD's overall budget. The level of resources and the fact that they provide a form of public assis-tance make them the most susceptible to the changes in the political climate. For 4.5 million families, however, the housing subsidy provided through these programs makes a real difference (Martinez, 2003).

Community Development

As the name implies, the Office of Community Planning and Develop-ment is charged with the community aspects of HUD's primary mission. This branch of HUD "seeks to develop viable communities by promoting integrated approaches that provide decent housing, a suitable living environ-ment and expanded economic opportunities for low and moderate income persons" (HUD, n.d., a, paragraph1). A key tool for reaching this goal is the Community Development Block Grant (CDBG), which allocates funds to over 800 cities and 150 counties. These funds may be directed toward infra-structure, housing, recreation, or other needs. Funds can be used for brick and mortar projects or, in some cases, for the provision of services. Often CDBG funds may help to facilitate partnerships between city, state, federal, and private entities targeted to neighborhood development. The program has distributed over $95 billion since its inception in 1974 (HUD, n.d., a).

The block grant mechanism allows more community input and flexibility than categorical grants and gives these communities a predictable line of funding for long-term planning and investment. In order for communities to receive these funds they must submit a plan that is built on citizen input and is targeted toward HUD's primary mission. They must allocate at least 70% of their CDBG funds to benefit individuals with low to moderate incomes. CDBG funds can also be used as collateral for section 108 loans for long-term infrastructure development and construction (HUD, n.d., a).

The Renewal Communities/Empowerment Zones/Enterprise Commu-nities (RC/EZ/EC) programs also support the community development mis-sion of HUD. These programs focus on the most distressed or economically disadvantaged communities in America. They provide tax advantages and grants to leverage business investment, job creation, and redevelopment initiatives. Other community development tools include grants to address environmental contamination, grants for youth employment projects, and grants that help cities reclaim property that has been abandoned to create new homes and neighborhoods (HUD, n.d., d).

Services to address the problem of homelessness also fall within the mission of the Office of Community Planning and Development. The McKinney-Vento Homeless Assistance Act is a primary vehicle for communities to fund homeless shelters, supportive services, and projects and is designed to facilitate the creation of a continuum of care that moves individuals and families from homelessness to self-sufficiency. HUD works in collaboration with other federal programs in addressing the needs of America's homeless population.

Non-Discrimination

The Assistant Secretary for Fair Housing and Equal Opportunity is charged with assuring that Americans do not experience discrimination in housing. Federal law makes it illegal to discriminate against individuals based upon race, color, national origin, religion, sex, familial status, or handicap when they want to buy, rent, or obtain financing for housing. It is clear, however, that discrimination still occurs. Using its own investigators and working hand-in-hand with state programs, HUD actively fights this discrimination by promoting voluntary compliance with the law, by screening departmental policies to assure that they are not discriminatory, and by active prosecution of those who violate the law (HUD, n.d., b).

HUD as Contractor, Facilitator, and Partner

HUD's programs are delivered through grants to specific nonprofit or for-profit agencies that compete for limited funds under several different program titles. In 2003, over $2 billion was made available in over 40 different grant categories targeted to a range of activities from construction of rental housing for the elderly or people with disabilities and programs for homeless individuals to youth employment programs. Each of these grants has specific criteria designating what agencies or entities may apply. Each year HUD announces the funding availability for each of these programs in a process called the "Super NOFA," where the Notification of Funding Availability for all grant programs is released together. This allows entities to coordinate applications across proposals if appropriate. Grantees become the local agents who deliver HUD-funded services to individuals and families (HUD, n.d., g).

CDBG funds are awarded to most cities with a population of 50,000 or more, based on a formula that considers population, poverty levels, overcrowding, and other factors. In order to receive CDBG funds the city must develop, with citizen input, a plan that outlines the priorities of that locality and commit at least 70% of the funds to projects that benefit low- to moderate-income persons (HUD, n.d., a).

HUD operates an extensive Web site at www.hud.gov that provides a wealth of information about HUD programs, priorities, grants, services, personnel, and contacts for grantees and local housing authorities. The site provides links to legislation, partner programs operated with other federal agencies, and a mortgage calculation tool, as well as helpful advice about home ownership, tenants' rights, and other housing related information.

The criteria to utilize HUD's locally delivered services are set by those local entities within the guidelines of the particular program that funds the initiative. Housing authorities, for example, have some discretion in setting local priorities and procedures for access to rental assistance based on local needs. Income requirements also vary widely from location to location, so it is important for applicants to contact the local agencies regarding eligibility criteria and application procedures. Some HUD programs, especially those for the elderly, people with disabilities, and the homeless, include supportive services as well as housing. Again, local agencies are the best point of contact to determine the range of services, eligibility criteria, and application procedures.

CLIENT SERVICES

Home Ownership

HUD's basic set of services fall within the four primary program offices described above. Mortgage insurance, down-payment assistance and education for first-time home buyers are primarily services of the "housing" office. Increasing home ownership, especially among minority families, is its primary goal. Clients can contact local HUD-approved lenders for information on these services. An updated list of HUD-approved mortgage companies and banks is available on the HUD Web site, searchable by location or company name. HUD contracts with local housing/counseling agencies to provide home-buyer education, helping individuals understand the complexities of the home-buying process, the responsibilities of home ownership, and the details of financial management and qualifying for a loan.

When a homeowner is unable to maintain payment on a HUD-insured home, the lender forecloses on the home, HUD pays the lender what is owed, and then it offers that home for sale. These "HUD homes" are sold at market value and are usually in the low to moderate price range. Individuals interested in buying a HUD home may search the Web site for specific information about homes but must work through a real estate agent to place a bid on a HUD home.

Rental Assistance

Rental assistance for certain low-income individuals and families is provided through over 3,000 local housing authorities nationwide. Eligibility is determined by family income and size, whether the applicant is elderly or has a disability as well as other factors, such as citizenship status or whether the individual has a criminal record. Income limits for eligibility vary significantly from one area to another. These local housing authorities often own and manage multifamily apartment complexes as well as administer voucher programs. The voucher services are targeted to specific needs, and there is some local discretion in setting priorities within a waiting list, so qualifications and the length of time before assistance is actually received will vary from program to program and agency to agency. Clients should be encouraged to make application as soon as possible. The HUD Web site provides a searchable list of housing authorities with local contact information. It is important to call the local office for specifics about application times, procedures, documentation needs, and waiting lists for the various programs. Unfortunately, the current level of federal funding and shortages in affordable housing stock mean that nearly every local agency will have a waiting list. Larger cities are likely to have waiting lists for services that may be several years long. A local agency may even stop taking applications if the waiting list becomes too long. Once a family is accepted into HUD housing, however, they may stay in the program indefinitely, so long as eligibility is maintained and they abide by the lease and contract agreements (Martinez, 2003).

Community Services through CDBG

Some cities use their CDBG funds to offer services to individuals and families. This might include services through homeless shelters, rental assistance, employment programs, assistance for home repair, or a variety of other services. HUD is an almost invisible partner in these services, providing funds but, within broad guidelines, leaving the programs to the discretion of the local community. Requirements for receiving HUD funds include the development of a community plan that has input from local citizens. An active group of citizens can have a real impact on the way these funds are directed if they stay involved over a period of years. Individuals should contact the local city government for a list of services and application guidelines.

Fair Housing

Individuals who feel that they have been discriminated against in any housing-related transaction can file a complaint online at the HUD Web site, or print the form and mail it to one of the regional offices listed on the Web site. They may also write a letter describing the incident and providing contact information. HUD works closely with city and state governmental agencies to facilitate investigations of housing complaints. Those filing complaints should be encouraged to give as much specific relevant information as possible.

Facilitating Access to Services

The HUD Web site (www.hud.gov) is an excellent place to begin an exploration of HUD services and programs. Full descriptions of the programs, general guidelines, and local contact information are available there. It is also helpful for social service providers to maintain professional contacts with local housing authorities and city planning and development offices. As with any social service activity, high caseloads and minimal funding make it difficult to find the time to maintain these ties with the range of providers in a community. The synergistic use of resources across several agencies, however, is often the best way to support clients in tight financial times.

Food, clothing, and shelter are often the "short list" of basic needs. Clearly, housing is a central part of establishing a foothold for client support and empowerment. From the foundation of stable housing people are better able to maintain employment, access education, nurture their children, and build a future for themselves. HUD plays a central role in providing the fiscal tools and programs to help ensure decent housing and a suitable place to live for those most in need in our society.

References

Bratt, R. G. (1997, July/August) A withering commitment. *Shelterforce Online* [A publication of the National Housing Institute]. Retrieved September 29, 2003, from http://www.nhi.org/online/issues/94/bratt.html

Cuomo, A. (1997). *Statement before the Senate hearing on the HUD 20202 reform plan.* Retrieved September 15, 2003, from http://www.hud.gov/library/bookshelf18/testimony/test98/exsum2.html

Cuomo, A. (2000, March 30). Testimony before the Subcommittee on VA, HUD and Independent Agencies Committee on Appropriations, United States Senate. Retrieved September 30, 2003, from http://www.hud.gov/library/bookshelf18/testimony/test00/test33000.html

Downs, A. (1995). HUD's basic missions and some of their key implications. *Cityscape: A Journal of Policy Development and Research, 1*(3), 125–141.

Foote, J. (1995). As they saw it: HUD's secretaries reminisce about carrying out the mission. *Cityscape: A Journal of Policy Development and Research, 1*(3), 71–92.

Kreyling, C. (1999, September 30). Nashville tries different kind of public housing. *The Weekly Wire.* Retrieved September 30, 2003, from http://weeklywire.com/ww/09-20-99/nash_cl-closer_look.html

Martinez, M. (2003, March 6) Testimony of the Honorable Mel Martinez before the U.S. Senate Committee on Appropriations, Subcommittee on Veterans Affairs, Housing and Urban Development, and Independent Agencies. Retrieved September 15, 2003, from http://www.hud.gov/offices/cir/test30603.cfm

Mayer, N. S. (1995). HUD's first 30 years: Big steps down a longer road. *Cityscape: A Journal of Policy Development and Research, 1*(3), 1–29.

Sard, B. (2001). Housing vouchers should be a major component of future housing policy for the lowest income families. *Cityscape: A Journal of Policy Development and Research, 5*(2) 89–111. [Also available from http://www.huduser.org/periodicals/cityscpe/vol5num2/sard.pdf]

Scruggs, Y. (1995). HUD's stewardship of national urban policy: A retrospective view. *Cityscape: A Journal of Policy Development and Research, 1*(3), 33–68.

Stegman, M. A. (1995). 63 years of federal action in housing and urban development. *Cityscape: A Journal of Policy Development and Research, 1*(3), vi–ix.

Thompson, L. (2003, April) *The history of HUD.* Presentation for the HUD Training Academy's *Operation Braintrust* Program at HUD Headquarters, Washington, DC. Retrieved September 10, 2003, from http://www.hud.gov/webcasts/archives/misc.cfm

U.S. Department of Housing and Urban Development (HUD). (1997). HUD 2020: Management reform plan. *Federal Register, 62*(155), 43204–43234.

U.S. Department of Housing and Urban Development. (1999a). *Rental housing assistance—The worsening crisis: A report to Congress on worst case housing needs.* Washington, DC: Author. Retrieved September 15, 2003, from http://www.huduser.org/publications/affhsg/worstcase00/toc.html

U.S. Department of Housing and Urban Development. (1999b, March). *Waiting in vain: An update on America's rental housing crisis* (ACCN-HUD8693). Washington, DC: Author.

U.S. Department of Housing and Urban Development. (1999c, April). *Opting in: Renewing American's commitment to affordable housing* (ACCN-HUD8719). Washington, DC: Author.

U.S. Department of Housing and Urban Development. (2000). *Cuomo hails best HUD budget in 20 years.* [Press Release, HUD # 00-288] Washington, DC: Author. Retrieved September 15, 2003, from http://www.hud.gov/library/bookshelf18/pressrel/pr00-288.html

U.S. Department of Housing and Urban Development. (n.d., a). *About CPD.* Retrieved September 10, 2003, from http://www.hud.gov/offices/cpd/about/index.cfm

U.S. Department of Housing and Urban Development. (n.d., b). *About FHEO.* Retrieved September 10, 2003, from http://www.hud.gov/offices/fheo/aboutfheo/aboutfheo.cfm

U.S. Department of Housing and Urban Development. (n.d., c). *About housing.* Retrieved September 10, 2003, from http://www.hud.gov/offices/hsg/hsgabout.cfm

U.S. Department of Housing and Urban Development. (n.d., d). *Economic development programs.* Retrieved September 10, 2003, from http://www.hud.gov/offices/cpd/economicdevelopment/programs/index.cfm

U.S. Department of Housing and Urban Development. (n.d., e). *Housing choice vouchers.* Retrieved September 10, 2003, from http://www.hud.gov/offices/pih/programs/hcv/index.cfm

U.S. Department of Housing and Urban Development. *Public housing.* (n.d., f). Retrieved September 10, 2003, from http://www.hud.gov/offices/pih/programs/ph/index.cfm

U.S. Department of Housing and Urban Development. *Grants.* (n.d., g). Retrieved September 10, 2003, from http://www.hud.gov/grants/index.cfm

Community Service Organizations

M. J. Schmidt

In recent years, the number of persons with special needs has grown immensely. Political activism and overall awareness of civil rights for individuals with disabilities have expanded. The array of human services available has improved, and the amount of information and technology specific to special populations has increased dramatically. Funding for human services, however, has become less available. As a result, the job of human service personnel has become increasingly complex. No longer do human service counselors and practitioners rely solely on traditional sources of information and individual knowledge of available services. Instead, human service providers have learned to be more creative in their search for potential client resources. Counselors often must rely on alternative service providers, seek supplemental sources of information, and better access their clients' communities.

Traditionally-oriented and formally trained counselors frequently overlook community service organizations as viable resources. Community service organizations are agencies which typically provide services—both directly and indirectly—to special groups of people or to the community at large (Lewis & Lewis, 1989). Some community service agencies exist primarily to serve a specific population or disability group. Others are interested more globally in serving persons with special needs or in addressing related political, economic, and financial concerns. Finally, some community service organizations are simply local groups (e.g., religious or fraternal organizations) who are willing to help those in need in their community. The American Cancer Society, the American Red Cross, and the Lions Club are all examples of community service organizations.

Community service agencies recognize the need for direct, individualized services and often provide them. They also frequently facilitate self-help groups or mutual support networks. As important as direct services are, however, their primary impact is in supplementing or supporting extant community efforts for the people they serve. Advocacy, information dissemination and research, referral, fund raising, and political action are among their most common activities.

Community service organizations tend to fall into three general categories: specialized agencies—those organized to address specific needs of a group or a specific cause, multiple service agencies—organizations concerned with a variety of special groups and concerns, and fraternal, religious, and other local community service agencies—agencies primarily concerned with providing service to those in need within a given community.

Specialized and multiple-service agencies are generally organized at the national, state, and local levels. Frequently, national offices exist in large metropolitan areas, and state and local affiliates develop as needed. While national offices most often have access to information regarding global issues—including facts about the disability or area of concern, the organization itself, federal law, and the like—state and local offices are commonly the source of direct services and community education efforts.

Specialized and multiple service organizations often consist of small paid staffs and large numbers of volunteer members. Membership is rarely limited to professionals, consumers, or family members. Instead, members tend to represent all of these parties and interested others. Typically, membership dues are requested of those who can pay. Many times, dues are waived or smaller donations are accepted from those who cannot afford the requested amount. Generally, membership entitles one to a regular newsletter or publication, as well as occasional discounts for upcoming seminars and events. Although fraternal, religious, and other local agencies may also be organized nationally, services are primarily rendered on a local level. Membership for these organizations also consists of volunteers.

History/Legislation

Community service organizations have existed for over a century in the United States. As early as 1880, for example, the National Association for the Deaf and the Salvation Army were in operation. However, the number of community service organizations in this country has increased dramatically within the past 60 years. This increase can be attributed to a number of factors, including continually improving survival rates of persons with disabilities, the prevalence of persons with special needs in our society, the civil rights and disability rights movements, and the corresponding increase in human services provided.

The history of community service organizations is quite diverse. Many community services originated in response to legislation; the Disability

Rights Center, for one, was founded in 1976 to protect and enforce the rights of citizens with disabilities. The agency has been concerned with and continues to focus on the enforcement of section 501 of the Rehabilitation Act of 1973. Other organizations have developed to advocate for or against political action or legislation. The National Association of Developmental Disabilities Councils, for example, was created in part to work with legislators to ensure adequate representation of the special concerns of persons with developmental disabilities.

Community service organizations have also been established by professionals, consumers, and family members. The American Criminal Justice Association and the National Rehabilitation Counseling Association were established by professionals in order to create better information sharing and professional networking. Similarly, the National Amputation Association was founded by veterans with service-related amputations. The Alzheimer's Association was established by families of persons with Alzheimer's disease in response to the general lack of available support and information. Many of the existing community service organizations today have been founded by members of specific disability groups or consumers. However, most community service organizations were founded by a mix of interested parties including consumers, professionals, family members, and other advocates.

Although no specific legislation establishes or regulates community service organizations, there are laws that impact their operation. As mentioned, community service organizations have been inspired by legislation such as the Rehabilitation Act and the Americans with Disabilities Act, with their missions encompassing the enforcement of such legislation. Currently, under Executive Orders 13198 and 13199 (2001), faith-based organizations are authorized to receive federal funds to deliver traditional human services, further expanding the depth of community services available.

Funding

Community service organizations can be funded in any number of ways. Often, they rely on multiple methods of financing. The great majority of community service organizations are funded at least in part by private donations. The American Heart Association, for example, is financed entirely in this manner. Many receive monies from federal and state government in the form of grants for special projects. The Retired Senior Volunteer Program, which manages Meals on Wheels programs, is funded by ACTION, the federal domestic volunteer agency. Membership dues also serve to support operations. In fact, most professional and special-interest service agencies request annual dues from their members. Fund raising efforts are also not uncommon. The Muscular Dystrophy Association's annual telethon and more recently concerts for disaster relief (American Red Cross) and funding research (Cure Autism Now) are popular examples. Additionally, some community service organizations charge for printed materials in order to minimize cost. Others, such as Goodwill Industries and the Salvation Army, rely on the resale of goods in thrift shops to generate funds. Some are completely government supported and operated. The National AIDS Information Clearinghouse, for instance, is operated by the Centers for Disease Control.

Regardless of the primary source of funding for community service agencies, information and referral services are typically available at no cost. Support services, such as the National Amputation Association's Amp to Amp Program, the National Burn Victim Association's 24-hour crisis counseling program, and nearly all available online services are provided without cost to the consumer. Often, allowances for those unable to pay can be arranged through the direct service providers in this genre, such as Goodwill Industries and the United Way.

Staffing

Community service organizations are staffed by both paid personnel and volunteers. Many organizations (e.g., United Way, Association for Retarded Citizens, Volunteers of America) operate with relatively small paid staffs and large numbers of volunteers. Fraternal and religious organizations such as the Kiwanis Club and B'nai B'rith Women, consist solely of volunteers differing in education level, experience, and profession. Many special-interest agencies rely on donations of time from affiliated professionals, consumers, and family members. Others, like the Salvation Army, are staffed almost entirely by persons specifically dedicated to that agency.

Qualifications of agency personnel vary greatly. At the national level, some of the best known doctors, advocates, and professionals may be on the staff of a specialized community service organization. Consumers, family members, and volunteers with less formal education may also be present. Despite the difference in area of expertise, staff members of specialized agencies are typically quite familiar with the population or interest of concern. When they lack knowledge directly, they often have the resources to gain information. Hence, they make invaluable resources in terms of networking and referral.

PURPOSE/INTENT

Community service organizations exist to serve individuals in the community. Specialized agencies work primarily with specific disability groups or populations or to address related concerns. Fraternal, religious, and locally based service organizations work primarily to serve the local community and to facilitate projects of interest. Nonetheless, each community service organization develops in order to meet certain goals. Although some agencies are quite focused in their mission, most organizations offer a combination of services to achieve two or three objectives. Often, the mission of specialized agencies is centralization or unification of consumers, family members, and professionals interested in a specific disability. Through unification there is increased networking and information sharing. There is also strength in numbers in terms of political advocacy and fund raising. The objectives of unified disability-specific organizations often include increasing community awareness, advocacy for the rights of the group, improvement in the status of treatment or quality of life, and the provision of support for consumers and their families.

Conversely, some community service organizations develop that are not specifically interested in a particular group, but rather in all persons with special needs. Objectives of these organizations range from service provision, to increased community awareness, to political advocacy. The American Red Cross, United Way, and Goodwill Industries are examples of organizations primarily concerned with service provision to those in need. Other community service organizations develop to advocate specifically for, and protect the rights of, all persons with disabilities. Their objectives primarily reflect education of policy makers, enforcement of current legislation, and the continued advocacy for legislation that will protect the rights of persons with disabilities. Finally, many local community service organizations develop primarily as social groups that are also dedicated to furthering efforts of goodwill in local communities.

Regardless of the specific purpose of these agencies, community service is generally part of the mission. Although direct services may not be available to all who request them, information and referral are typically available. Specialized organizations are often excellent starting places in terms of learning more about a specific population, piece of legislation, or related concern. Local service agencies are also an excellent yet frequently overlooked resource for counselors in terms of volunteer services and money.

SERVICES

In order to achieve their objectives, community service organizations offer a wide range of services—both directly and indirectly—to consumers and the community. These services are offered in varying degrees by different divisions of community service organizations.

Direct Consumer Services

Many state and local offices of community service organizations offer direct services to consumers. The type and quality of these services vary greatly. Individualized services are occasionally available. Agencies like Goodwill Industries offer a wide range of direct consumer services including evaluation, training, counseling, and placement for vocationally disabled persons. Similarly, the National Easter Seal Society offers physical, occupational, and speech and language therapies; vocational evaluation and training; recreational opportunities; and even equipment loans to persons with disabilities. The United Cerebral Palsy Association's direct services include similar therapies, as well as supported and supervised housing. The National Burn Victim Association operates a Medical Disaster Response System that provides emergency services to large numbers of burn victims, as well as free blood to those in need of transfusion.

Individual counseling is also frequently offered directly to individual consumers and their families. Special counseling is also commonly available. For instance, the American Heart Association sponsors Heart to Heart, a one-to-one visitation program for persons with coronary problems. Similarly, the National Amputation Association and Spinal Cord Injury Association offer individualized peer counseling.

Other direct individualized services include meal provision and companionship programs, primarily available through local organizations and most frequently offered to senior citizens and the homebound. Community service organizations like the Children's Defense Fund and the National Coalition for the Homeless also provide legal counseling and assistance. Medical services are provided by various agencies, especially those concerned with prevention, disaster relief, or specific medical conditions, Shriners Hospitals provide free care to children with burns and disabilities. Financial counseling and assistance is also commonly available. The American Kidney Fund provides financial assistance to those suffering fiscal problems as a result of their condition. Special education, outreach programs for those with special needs, and prosthesis/equipment maintenance and repair services are additional services commonly available through many of these organizations.

Specialized community service organizations frequently offer group services as well as individual care. Self-help and support groups are commonly offered by state and local affiliates of community service organizations. Persons with disabilities and their families often experience gaps in their natural support networks. They may benefit from developing mutually supportive relationships with others in similar situations. Self-help and support groups often provide this opportunity. There is any number of such groups sponsored by community service agencies. They include, but certainly are not limited to:

- Alcoholics Anonymous
- American Schizophrenic Association
- Association for Children with Learning Disabilities
- Burns Recovered
- Epilepsy Foundation
- Gay Men's Health Crisis
- Juvenile Diabetes Foundation
- Muscular Dystrophy Association
- National Alliance for the Mentally Ill

- National Association for Retarded Citizens
- National Federation for the Blind
- National Spinal Cord Injury Foundation
- United Cerebral Palsy Association

Community service agencies also sponsor camps, especially for children with special needs. A great many of these camps are free or of minimal cost. They are almost always staffed by professionals and can prove to be a great resource to those counselors working with children. The Brain Injury Association of America, the Muscular Dystrophy Association, the American Diabetes Association, and many other community service organizations are involved in these efforts. Similarly, the Children's Wish Foundation International provides terminally ill children with opportunities to engage in desired activities.

Indirect Consumer Services

Perhaps the greatest component of community service organization work involves indirect services to consumers, including information and referral, research, political action and advocacy, research and training, and fund raising. By and large, the vast majority of community service organizations develop and distribute some form of information specific to their population or area of interest. Pamphlets, articles written for laypersons, scholarly publications, and even audio- and videotapes are widely available from community service organizations. Many publish newsletters or similar publications routinely. Many even maintain libraries of all types of information specific to their interest. For the most part, written information is available for free or for a minimal fee to cover reprint and postage costs.

Information regarding available services—or referral—is also normally available. Quite often, community service organizations are excellent sources of information regarding locally available services for a particular population. In fact, some organizations specialize in information and referral. The Information Center for Individuals with Disabilities, for example, gathers and stores information in 16 subject categories including accessibility, employment, housing, transportation, and personal care. The National Homelessness Information Exchange is designed specifically to supply local service providers with information relevant to the needs of those without homes. Agencies may also be able to refer counselors and consumers to practitioners with experience in a particular disability or condition, identify related support or self-help groups, or provide similar linkages to other agencies or service providers. Organizations such as the National Multiple Sclerosis Society maintain large databases of information to facilitate research and referral. Community service agencies may also provide information regarding potential funding for services.

Another important function of many community service organizations involves political action and advocacy. Occasionally, these agencies advocate for consumers on an individual basis. However, for the most part, advocacy efforts pertain to the group as a whole or to persons with disabilities collectively. The Disability Rights Center and the Disabled Rights Education and Defense Fund are primarily concerned with the protection of the rights of persons with disabilities. They work to educate policy makers as to the needs of these persons, as well as to ensure compliance with existing legislation. The Disabled Rights Education and Defense Fund also trains judges on disability rights compliance standards and maintains the Disability Law National Support Center to identify key disability issues.

Disability-specific community service agencies are also quite active in political advocacy. The National Association for the Deaf promotes legislation and programs to benefit persons with hearing impairments. The American Council for the Blind provides information and advisory services on federal legislation, administrative action, and rule making on both national and state levels. Similarly, the National Alliance for the Mentally Ill and the National Association for Developmental Disabilities Councils work to improve the lives of their populations by informing legislators of their special needs.

Additionally, the National Multiple Sclerosis Society, the Arthritis Foundation, the American Diabetes Foundation, and many other community service agencies sponsor tremendous amounts of research regarding the cure and prevention of disabling conditions, Similarly, many organizations offer funding to researchers, as well its specialized training in state-of-the-art diagnostic and treatment techniques. The Arthritis Foundation, for instance, provides training to doctors in the diagnosis and care of rheumatoid arthritis.

Advocacy efforts regarding accessibility issues or other discriminatory policies affecting target population are yet another illustration of services provided by these agencies with both direct and indirect consumer benefits. The National Council on Disability, the National Coalition for the Homeless, and the National Rehabilitation Association are among the many groups involved in comparable endeavors. Some community service agencies are instrumental in identifying other aspects of the environment that affect the prevalence or severity of the disability or condition, after which efforts to ameliorate or prevent the problem are made. The National Brain Injury Foundation, in this manner, has campaigned heavily for seat-belt and car-seat legislation, as well as for motorcycle and bicycle helmet use.

Finally, community service organizations are commonly involved in fund raising. The Muscular Dystrophy Association, the American Lung Association, the National Multiple Sclerosis Society and the National Easter Seal Society, for example, raise millions of dollars each year. These efforts often involve community participation. Donations, telethons, walk- or bike-a-thons, raffles and lotteries, and simple solicitation of donations are not uncommon. Occasionally, large businesses become involved such as the National Football League's involvement with the United Way.

Community Education Services

Community service organizations are also involved in providing direct education and prevention services to the community at large. These services often take the form of courses or workshops that provide knowledge or skills that the particular populations they serve have identified as important. Women's centers often provide courses on assertiveness, career development, or women's health concerns. The American Cancer Society and the American Heart Association operate national education and awareness campaigns. Agencies concerned with the elderly may provide education related to retirement planning or social security benefits.

Prevention is a common theme of community education. Many community service organizations provide public workshops on healthy lifestyles and even offer screening for certain conditions. The National AIDS Network, for example, provides community workshops and seminars on AIDS prevention issues, and even financially assists other organizations sponsoring AIDS education. Community service agencies also frequently bestow awards to deserving care providers, researchers, consumers, advocates, and educators. Finally, many organizations work directly with allied health professionals to ensure that practitioners are offering state-of-the-art services to the community.

The most recent development in services available through community services organizations has been the widespread use of the Internet. Many, many online services are now available through the Web sites of community service organizations. Such services allow individuals to network without regard to geographical boundaries, expedite the release of new developments and information, and provide new and interesting services including:

- e-mail support groups for individuals with special needs, their families and caregivers;
- links to local resources, listed by zip code;
- discussion groups and forums through which questions can be posed to experts;
- updates on research; and
- educational services.

HOW TO ACCESS

Community service organizations are not difficult to access. They generally can be found in the Yellow Pages of local telephone books under such headings as Community Service Organizations, Social Service Organizations, Fraternal Organizations, and are even listed under churches, synagogues, and other religious affiliations. The Encyclopedia of Associations (Ballard, 2003; Burek, 1991) is also an excellent source for basic information and addresses and phone numbers of national organizations. Similarly,

United Way regularly publishes a resource book that lists basic information, addresses, and phone numbers of community service agencies. Finally, Web sites can easily be accessed directly (e.g., www.cancer.org for the American Cancer Society) or searched online by population or area of concern.

As in any other referral or request for information or services, it is recommended that counselors check with fellow professionals regarding their contacts and resources. It is also recommended that, when possible, counselors refer directly to known individuals in an agency rather than to the agency itself. This process, of course, involves the continual development of professional contacts. In order to facilitate this process, counselors should consider the following:

- Human service professionals should become aware of those agencies in their community involved with service efforts. This includes, but is not limited to, fraternal organizations, local chapters of specialized agencies, religious service organizations, senior citizen organizations, women's centers, university-affiliated services and groups, and government-supported programs and services. Counselors should identify and develop personal contacts at those agencies likely to be used.

- Counselors and practitioners involved with a specific disability group should become aware of the associated specialized organizations and become a member of at least one such association. This is an excellent way of making contacts, keeping up-to-date with pertinent information, finding out about relevant conferences and seminars, and building a professional network.

References

Ballard, P. T. (Ed.). (2003). Encyclopedia of associations (37th ed.). New York: Gale Research, Inc.

Burek, D. M. (Ed.). (1991). Encyclopedia of associations (25th ed.). New York: Gale Research, Inc.

Executive Order 13198. (2001). Agency responsibilities with respect to faith-based and community initiatives. Retrieved October 7, 2004, from http://www.whitehouse.gov/news/releases/2001/01/20010129-3.html

Executive Order 13199. (2001). White House Office of Faith-Based and Community Initiatives. Retrieved October 7, 2004, from http://www.whitehouse.gov/government/fbci/executive-orders.html

Lewis, J. A., & Lewis, M. D. (1989). Community counseling. Pacific Grove, CA: Brooks/Cole.

Rucker, B. (2001, February 15). Faith organizations get funding. *The Daily Beacon, 86*, 26. Retrieved October 7, 2004, from http://dailybeacon.utk.edu/article.php/1793

Contributors

Cheryl L. Anderson is an associate professor of law at Southern Illinois University School of Law, where she specializes in employment and labor law. She has published a number of articles on disability discrimination and sexual harassment law. She has a J.D and B.A. from the University of North Dakota and an LL.M from the Temple University James E. Beasley School of Law.

Jill Anderson, M.S., CCC-A, is a certified audiologist who has held an appointment as instructor and clinical supervisor in the Communication Disorders and Sciences Program of the Rehabilitation Institute at Southern Illinois University Carbondale.

Clora Mae Baker, Ph.D., is an associate professor in Workforce Education and Development at Southern Illinois University Carbondale.

Karen Barrett, Rh.D., is an associate professor of Rehabilitation Services at the University of Maine at Farmington. Originally from Maine, Dr. Barrett completed her graduate work at Southern Illinois University. She returned to Maine to teach in undergraduate rehabilitation education and specializes in civil rights, diversity, and rehabilitation administration.

John J. Benshoff, Ph.D., is professor and coordinator of the Rehabilitation Counselor Training Program, Rehabilitation Institute, Southern Illinois University Carbondale. He received his doctorate from the University of Northern Colorado in 1985. He is a charter fellow of the American College of Addiction Treatment Administrators.

Dr. Charlene J. Blankenship is an assistant professor in the Rehabilitation Services Program at The University of Texas–Pan American. She received both her masters and doctorate of rehabilitation at Southern Illinois University Carbondale.

H. L. Brostrand, MA, CRC, is a doctoral candidate in the Rehabilitation Institute at SIUC. She has been a rehabilitation counselor for more than 10 years in California and has worked in private, public, and substance-abuse settings.

William Crimando, Ph.D., is professor and coordinator of Rehabilitation Administration and Services, Rehabilitation Institute, Southern Illinois University Carbondale. He has numerous research interests and has published in such diverse areas as training and development of rehabilitation counselors and administrators, job placement, and computers in rehabilitation. This is his sixth book.

John M. Eckert, MA, is a public service administrator in the Division of Rehabilitation Services, Home Services Program. He was previously the executive director of the Statewide Independent Living Council of Illinois.

Carl R. Flowers, Rh.D., is an associate professor in the Rehabilitation Administration and Services program, Rehabilitation Institute, at Southern Illinois University Carbondale. Dr. Flowers is a past president of the National Association of Multicultural Rehabilitation Concerns and a former Mary E. Switzer Scholar in Rehabilitation. Research interests include multiculturalism in service delivery, development of rehabilitation professionals, and employment of persons with HIV/AIDS.

Mark Godley, Ph.D., is director of the Research and Training Institute at Chestnut Health Systems, Inc., in Illinois. His research is focused on continuing care management of recovery from substance-use disorders.

Susan H. Godley, Rh.D., is a senior research scientist at Chestnut Health Systems, Inc., in Bloomington, IL. She studies ways to improve treatment approaches for adolescents with substance-use disorders.

Russell J. Hagen, MA, Mdiv., is the CEO of Chestnut Health Systems, Inc., a private, not-for-profit behavioral health service organization. Mr. Hagen has over 30 years of experience in the addiction treatment field.

Debra A. Harley, Ph.D., CRC, is a professor in the Department of Special Education and Rehabilitation Counseling and the Women's Studies Program at the University of Kentucky. Dr. Harley is editor of the *Journal of Rehabilitation* and past editor of the *Journal of Applied Rehabilitation Counseling*. She is a former Mary E. Switzer Scholar in Rehabilitation.

Bridget A. Hollis, Rh.D, CRC, is an assistant professor in Rehabilitation Counseling at South Carolina State University, Orangeburg. She received her doctorate from Southern Illinois University Carbondale. Her research interests include minority issues in counseling and employment outcomes of persons with disabilities.

Rodney Isom, Ph.D., CRC, is an associate professor and the coordinator of the Graduate Rehabilitation Counselor Training Program at the University of North Texas. Dr. Isom has been in private practice since 1977.

Kristine Jolivette, Ph.D., is an assistant professor in the Department of Educational Psychology and Special Education at Georgia State University. Her area of research is emotional and behavior disorders, and she has published in the areas of choice making, functional assessment, behavioral intervention planning, positive behavioral supports, and school safety.

Jewel Jones, Rh.D., CRC, is assistant professor of Rehabilitation Services at University of Maine–Farmington and specializes is aquatic therapy, psychosocial rehabilitation, and therapeutic recreation. She received her degree from the Rehabilitation Institute, Southern Illinois University Carbondale.

Saliwe M. Kawewe, MSW, Ph.D., is professor of Social Work in the School of Social Work, Southern Illinois University Carbondale. A native of Zimbabwe, Kawewe has published 40 scholarly articles, including book chapters, and attended over 30 conferences, making more than 40 professional presentations worldwide. Her research focuses on sustainable socioeconomic development, social welfare, women's and children's human rights, and HIV/AIDS in Zimbabwe.

Robert F. Kilbury, Rh.D., is the director of the Division of Rehabilitation Services, Illinois Department of Human Services. He was formerly the executive director of both the Coalition of Citizens with Disabilities and the Southern Illinois Center for Independent Living.

D. Shane Koch, Rh.D., CRC, LCDC, AAC, is assistant professor and coordinator of Rehabilitation Studies in the Department of Rehabilitation, Social Work, and Addictions at the University of North Texas.

Ilana Lehmann, M.S., is pursuing a doctoral degree in Rehabilitation from Southern Illinois University. She is a psychotherapist, a service coordinator in mental retardation/developmental disabilities, and a placement specialist for Omaha VR.

Irmo Marini, Ph.D., CRC, CLCP, FVE, is currently professor and graduate coordinator of the Rehabilitation Counseling Program at the University of Texas–Pan American. He is certified in rehabilitation counseling and life care planning as well as a registered forensic vocational expert. Dr. Marini maintains an active forensic rehabilitation practice in life care planning and vocational damage assessments. He has also been a vocational expert with the Office of Hearings and Appeals with the Social Security Administration since 1995.

V. Robert May III, Rh.D., is CEO of the Commission on Healthcare Certification, and partner with May Physical Therapy Services LLC in Richmond, VA. He maintains a research affiliation with Southern Illinois University Carbondale, where he provides financial support for doctoral candidates in rehabilitation who are writing their dissertations.

David Moxley, Ph.D., is professor in the Wayne State University School of Social Work, where he co-chairs the Concentration in Community Practice and Social Action.

Otrude N. Moyo, MA, MSW, Ph.D., is assistant professor in the Department of Social Work, University of Maine. Her dissertation is titled *Dealing with Work in Its Context: Household Work Strategies in Bulawayo, Zimbabwe*. She did her undergraduate work at the University of Zimbabwe. She has work experience in southern Africa and the United States, and her research interests include families, work, inequality, and social change.

Michael D. Paul, MSW, CSW, is a doctoral candidate from the Union Institute, where he is completing his studies in Disability Studies and Community and Organizational Development.

Frank D. Puckett, Rh.D., CRC, ATP, is coordinator of distance education for the Department of Rehabilitation and Disability Studies, Southern University, Baton Rouge, LA. He earned his doctorate from Southern Illinois University Carbondale.

Ruth Anne Rehfeldt, Ph.D., is an assistant professor in the Rehabilitation Institute at Southern Illinois University. Her areas of expertise include assessment and intervention for children and adults with developmental disabilities. She has authored over 50 chapters and articles in that domain.

T. F. Riggar, Ed.D., is a professor a the Rehabilitation Institute, Southern Illinois University Carbondale. He is the author of over 70 articles in professional journals and has authored or co-authored 15 books.

Blanca Robles, M.S., CRC, obtained her master's degree in Rehabilitation Counseling at the University of Texas–Pan American in Edinburg, TX. Ms. Robles is a Certified Rehabilitation Counselor and certified Social Security Benefits Counselor with the Valley Association of Independent Living. She also conducts vocational damage evaluations and life care plans for Marini & Associates forensic rehabilitation consultants in the Rio Grande Valley.

M. J. Schmidt, M.A., received her master's degree in Rehabilitation Administration and Services from Southern Illinois University. She worked as the director of operations for ReMed, a community-based provider of neurologic rehabilitation services. She is currently a homemaker and mother.

Kenneth O. Simpson, Ph.D., CCC-SLP, is an associate professor in the Rehabilitation Institute at Southern Illinois University Carbondale and coordinator of the Communication Disorders and Sciences Program. His areas of expertise include augmentative and alternative communication, human interaction, and acquired communication disorders.

Barbara J. Stotlar, ME, has been the program director at the Southern Illinois Center for Independent Living in Carbondale for nearly two decades.

Thomas D. Upton, Ph.D., CRC, is an assistant professor in the Rehabilitation Institute at Southern Illinois University Carbondale. Research interests include functioning post-brain injury, disability attitudes, and forensic rehabilitation.

John S. Washburn, Ed.D., is professor and director of the Center for Workforce Development in the Department of Workforce Education and Development at Southern Illinois University Carbondale.

Celia Williamson, Ph.D., CRC, LCSW, is an associate professor in the Department of Rehabilitation, Social Work and Addictions at the University of North Texas. She spent an academic year working with the U.S. Department of Housing and Urban Development as a Community Builder Fellow in a program created to bring seasoned professionals to promote an understanding of HUD's role, and to increase its responsiveness to the communities it serves.

Nancy Zemaitis, M.S., is an assistant director with Indiana Department of Education, Division of Exceptional Learners, with a concentration on school-to-work transition. She worked for 17 years for Indiana Vocational Rehabilitation Services in various capacities, including oversight of the agency's automation of the case management system, contract development, school-to-work transition, vehicle modifications, and the provision of training and technical assistance.

Laura Dreuth Zeman, Ph.D., is an associate professor in the School of Social Work, Southern Illinois University Carbondale. Her teaching and research specialties include families' and consumers' experiences with social systems, school safety, bullying, and victimization, as well as mental health and health-care policy.

Index